THE KREMLIN'S NOOSE

A volume in the NIU Series in

Slavic, East European, and Eurasian Studies

Edited by Christine D. Worobec

For a list of books in the series, visit our website at cornellpress.cornell.edu.

THE KREMLIN'S NOOSE

PUTIN'S BITTER FEUD WITH THE OLIGARCH WHO MADE HIM RULER OF RUSSIA

AMY KNIGHT

NORTHERN ILLINOIS UNIVERSITY PRESS

an imprint of

CORNELL UNIVERSITY PRESS

Ithaca

First published 2024 by Cornell University Press
Printed in the United States of America

Library of Congress Cataloging-in-Publication Data

Names: Knight, Amy W., 1946- author.
Title: The Kremlin's noose : Putin's bitter feud with the oligarch who made him ruler of Russia / Amy Knight.
Other titles: Putin's bitter feud with the oligarch who made him ruler of Russia
Description: Ithaca : Northern Illinois University Press, an imprint of Cornell University Press, 2024. | Series: NIU series in Slavic, East European, and Eurasian studies | Includes bibliographical references and index.
Identifiers: LCCN 2023035824 (print) | LCCN 2023035825 (ebook) | ISBN 9781501775086 (hardcover) | ISBN 9781501775093 (epub) | ISBN 9781501775109 (pdf)
Subjects: LCSH: Berezovskiĭ, B. A. (Boris Abramovich), 1946-2013. | Berezovskiĭ, B. A. (Boris Abramovich), 1946-2013—Political and social views. | Putin, Vladimir Vladimirovich, 1952—Adversaries. | Oligarchy—Russia (Federation) | Businessmen—Russia (Federation)—Biography. | Russia (Federation)—Politics and government—1991- | Russia (Federation)—Economic conditions—1991-
Classification: LCC DK510.763 .K594 2024 (print) | LCC DK510.763 (ebook) | DDC 321/.5—dc23/eng/20230909
LC record available at https://lccn.loc.gov/2023035824
LC ebook record available at https://lccn.loc.gov/2023035825

This book is dedicated to Vladimir Putin's many victims

Berezovsky was the architect of post-Soviet Russia not once but twice. His first invention was the devilish Yeltsin-era equation where the rich carved out great chunks of state property, then turned their money into power over and over again . . . But it's Berezovsky's second legacy that we live with today: Vladimir Putin. Putin was Berezovsky's creation.

—Owen Matthews, *The Daily Beast*, March 24, 2013

Life in Russia is dangerous for every businessman, not just for billionaires. But I made my choice: I could have sat in the quiet corner, and focused on my science, which I love—but that would never have suited me.

—Berezovsky interview with the BBC, March 2003

CONTENTS

List of Illustrations ix
List of Abbreviations xi
Note on Transliteration xii

Introduction   1
1. Offspring of the Soviet System   5
2. A Meeting in St. Petersburg   23
3. Elections and Beyond   41
4. Behind Kremlin Walls   59
5. Turmoil   78
6. An Heir to the Throne   97
7. Putin's Path to Victory   115
8. A Clash of Titans   132
9. The Outcast versus the Tyrant   150
10. The Kremlin on the Offensive   169
11. A Life Falling Apart   188
12. Berezovsky's End   207

Acknowledgments 227
Notes 229
Index 271

ILLUSTRATIONS

1. Vladimir Putin and Boris Berezovsky.   xiv
2. Berezovsky with his wife Nina and their daughters, Ekaterina (left) and Elizaveta (right), 1977.   8
3. Berezovsky and Petr Aven, 1998.   11
4. The Putins with their two daughters, 1991.   17
5. Anatoly Sobchak and Putin, early 1990s.   26
6. Berezovsky meets with Yeltsin, 1994.   37
7. Berezovsky and Vladimir Gusinsky, January 1998.   43
8. Pavel Borodin, September 1998.   52
9. Berezovsky and Roman Abramovich, June 2000.   56
10. Putin awarded honorary membership in the Faculty of Law, St. Petersburg State University, January 2000.   63
11. Boris Nemtsov and Anatoly Chubais, 1999.   68
12. Galina Starovoitova, August 1998.   82
13. Iurii Skuratov, March 1999.   89
14. Chechen president Aslan Maskhadov.   102
15. Evgeny Primakov and Iurii Luzhkov, August 1999.   112
16. Sergei Dorenko on his nightly news program.   126
17. Yeltsin and Putin, December 31, 1999.   128
18. The Putins in Chechnya, January 1, 2000.   133
19. Berezovsky at the Federation Council, June 28, 2000.   140
20. George Bush and Vladimir Putin with their wives, Crawford, Texas, November 2001.   155
21. Alexander Litvinenko with his daughter Sonia, son Anatoly, and Berezovsky at Berezovsky's mansion outside London.   158
22. Ukrainian president Viktor Yushchenko and Prime Minister Yulia Tymoshenko.   171
23. Andrei Lugovoi, March 2009.   179

24. Badri Patarkatsishvili, right, with Berezovsky, 2005.   189
25. Berezovsky, with Alex Goldfarb (left), after London
    verdict was announced, August 31, 2012.   202
26. *Direct Line* with Vladimir Putin, April 25, 2013.   217
27. Nikolai Glushkov after being arrested in Moscow,
    December 2000.   221

ABBREVIATIONS

CIS   Commonwealth of Independent States (Sodruzhestvo nezavisimykh gosudarstv)

FSB   Federal Security Service (Federal'naia sluzhba bezopasnosti)

FSO   Federal Guard Service (Federal'naia sluzhba okhrany)

GKU   Main Control Directorate (Glavnoe kontrol'noe upravlenie)

GRU   Main Intelligence Directorate (Glavnoe razvedyvatel'noe upravlenie)

MVD   Ministry of Internal Affairs (Ministerstvo vnutrennikh del)

NTV   Russian Nationwide Television Channel

ORT   Public Russian Television (Obshchestvennoe rossiiskoe televidenie)

PA   Presidential Administration

SBP   Presidential Security Service (Sluzhba bezopasnosti prezidenta)

SPS   Union of Right Forces party (Soiuz pravykh sil)

URPO   Organized Crime Directorate of the FSB (Upravlenie po razrabotke prestupnykh organizatsii)

Note on Transliteration

Throughout this book, I use the Library of Congress transliteration system from Cyrillic to Latin script, except in cases where names are well known and there is a familiar spelling, such as Yeltsin (rather than El'tsin) and Berezovsky (rather than Berezovskii) and where names or words are cited in quotations or reference notes with a different transliteration.

THE KREMLIN'S NOOSE

FIGURE 1A. Vladimir Putin. Photo by Mikhail Klimentyev/Russian PPIO.

FIGURE 1B. Boris Berezovsky. Photo by Bertrand Langlois/AFP/Getty Images.

Introduction

> Bad history, like cancer, tends to recur, and there is one radical treatment: timely therapy to destroy the deadly cells. We have not done this. We dragged ourselves out of the USSR and into the "New Russia" still infested with our Soviet bedbugs.
>
> —Anna Politkovskaya, *Putin's Russia*

This book is the story of two Russians who forged a relationship in the early years of the Yeltsin era that would ultimately become a bitter feud, played out against the backdrop of billion-dollar financial deals, Kremlin infighting, and international politics. One, the oligarch Boris Berezovsky, has been dead for over a decade. The other, Russian president Vladimir Putin, is very much alive and in February 2022 began a devastating military campaign in Ukraine that has destroyed large parts of that country, killed thousands of Ukrainians, and displaced millions of others. Putin has also turned his own country into a closed fortress, where democratic freedoms and the rule of law, which began to develop during the Boris Yeltsin presidency, have ceased to exist.

Dubbed the "godfather of the Kremlin" by slain American journalist Paul Klebnikov, Berezovsky, a trained mathematician turned successful businessman and media mogul, played an outsized role in Russia after 1991. Worth a reported $3 billion by 1997, he was a winner in the notorious grab for the spoils of the former Soviet state by those who became oligarchs; he engineered the re-election of Yeltsin as president in 1996 and successfully negotiated an end to the 1995–96 Chechen war. Most importantly, he was crucial in Putin's rise to be elected Russia's president in March 2000.

By the time Berezovsky said his final good-bye to Putin at a private meeting in the Kremlin in August 2000, he had come to regret his support for the Russian leader. Putin had already begun to dismantle the reforms that Yeltsin had introduced and had instigated criminal investigations against some of Russia's top businessmen, Berezovsky among them. Facing possible prosecution and imprisonment, Berezovsky fled Russia in October 2000 and later gained asylum in Britain, where he devoted himself—and his fortune—to a highly publicized campaign against the Putin regime.

Just after Berezovsky left his country for good, Russian political commentator Andrei Piontkovsky observed: "The relationship between Putin and Berezovsky is beginning to resemble that of Stalin and Trotsky. This affair risks ending with Berezovsky getting a bullet in the head."[1] Exiled in Mexico, Leon Trotsky, a former Bolshevik leader who fell out with Stalin, was murdered on the Kremlin's orders in 1940 after years of exposing Stalin's crimes. His murder was a stark reminder of the fate that awaited those who opposed the Soviet dictator, no matter where they sought refuge.

More than seven decades later, in March 2013, Berezovsky was found dead, a scarf tied around his neck, on the bathroom floor of his ex-wife's mansion outside London. Whether Berezovsky's death was a suicide by hanging, as some—including the Kremlin—claim, or murder, as his family and close friends insist, remains a mystery. The British coroner left the cause of death undetermined. But one thing is certain: In Putin's eyes, Berezovsky was a traitor. He had accused Putin of despicable crimes. The fact that Putin was indebted to Berezovsky for helping him gain the Russian presidency made Berezovsky even more treacherous to the Kremlin leader. And Putin has long made it clear that he believes traitors deserve death.[2]

Putin is similar to Stalin in his capacity for revenge. Although his public image is one of a leader who keeps his emotions tightly in check, it is well known that Putin carries deep grudges against those who have challenged him in any way. Maybe this trait, as some have suggested, resulted from Putin's childhood experience as a boy of small physical stature who had to defend himself against bullies on the back streets of Leningrad's impoverished neighborhoods. Or perhaps it relates to his career in the KGB, where even the smallest expression of opposition to Communist dogma was considered a threat. Whatever the reasons, Putin has consistently and clearly revealed his vengefulness in comments like the one he made about Chechens in the autumn of 1999, when he vowed to "rub out the bandits in the crapper." Putin kept his word, launching a brutal military war in Chechnya, which destroyed the capital, Grozny, and caused hundreds of thousands of innocent Chechens to lose their lives.

Numerous killings, or attempted killings, of Putin's political opponents have been widely attributed to the Kremlin. Following my account of several of these cases in my 2017 book *Orders to Kill: The Putin Regime and Political Murder*, more targets and victims were added to the list: the GRU (military intelligence) defector Sergei Skripal and his daughter Iulia were poisoned in Britain with a nerve agent, Novichok, in March 2018; Nikolai Glushkov, Berezovsky's former business associate, was strangled to death at his London home just days after the Skripal attack; and in August 2020, Russia's most prominent opposition politician, Aleksei Navalny, was poisoned with Novichok during a visit to the Siberian city of Tomsk, an attack that he barely survived.

Berezovsky himself had received numerous death threats during his almost twelve years in British exile. In one case, British police arrested a would-be Russian assailant with a gun in Berezovsky's London office building. Apparently to avoid a diplomatic row with Moscow, British authorities simply sent the man back to Russia. The continual barrage of Kremlin demands to have Berezovsky extradited from Britain on bogus criminal charges, although refused by British authorities, added to the sense that Berezovsky was under siege. In 2012, after losing a highly publicized legal case in the London High Court against Roman Abramovich, an oligarch close to Putin, it seemed as though Berezovsky was all but vanquished. He allegedly even wrote to Putin apologizing and saying he wanted to return to Russia. Was that enough to quell the Russian president's thirst for revenge? Or, like Stalin with Trotsky, did Putin need a more final solution to the problem of Berezovsky?

Marina Litvinenko, the wife of ex-FSB officer Alexander Litvinenko—murdered by a dose of radioactive poison—once told me that "with Putin, everything is personal."[3] This goes a long way toward explaining why Putin continued his vendetta against Berezovsky and other political opponents well after he was securely in power in the Kremlin. Berezovsky, arrogant and reckless, was also driven by personal motives in his self-destructive campaign from London to orchestrate Putin's downfall. But the story of their feud goes beyond a clash of personalities. It is part of the larger story of how Russia descended from a fledgling democracy after the Soviet collapse into what today is the one-man dictatorship of Vladimir Putin. Neither Berezovsky nor others who used their vast wealth to promote Putin's leadership and later became his victims were heroes. They not only made the crucial mistake of misjudging Putin; they set the stage for the inevitable demise of Russia's democracy. The "operation successor" carried out by Yeltsin's inner circle to elevate then FSB chief Putin to the presidency was in large part a cynical Faustian bargain, made to protect Yeltsin's family and close associates from corruption investigations. The group, including Berezovsky, thought that they would be able to control Putin after he replaced Yeltsin and keep Russia on a democratic path. They were sorely wrong.

Unlike the many Russian oligarchs who chose to ignore Putin's transformation into a lawless autocrat and gave him their unquestioned support, Berezovsky made determined attempts in exile to reveal the dangers of the Putin regime both to his countrymen and to the West. His warnings were largely ignored. Putin maintained a loyal population by reversing Russia's economic decline and enlisting the state-controlled media to promote his leadership cult. As for the West, its leaders were incredibly slow to acknowledge that Putin was far from being the democrat he purported to be. In a review of a recent London play about Berezovsky and Putin, *Patriots*, his longtime aide Alex Goldfarb made this point clearly: "Those of us who, like Boris, watched from the relative safety of London how Putin transformed the freewheeling Weimar Russia of Yeltsin into a police state still cannot fathom how an army of western policymakers could miss those early signals."[4]

Much of the material for this book comes from the extensive accounts in the Russian media during the period in question, accessed through online archives. I have also relied on Western reporting, biographies of Putin, Berezovsky, and others, Berezovsky's own writings, and personal interviews with family members and close associates of Berezovsky. Documents from the numerous cases involving Berezovsky and adjudicated in British courts and those from the inquiry into the death of Litvinenko have been additional invaluable sources. I have drawn on my own long experience of research and writing about the Soviet Union and Russia—along with numerous visits there—to interpret these materials and create a narrative that I hope will offer readers new insights into Russia's recent history. Kremlin politics has always been an enigma, but that is what makes it so fascinating.

CHAPTER 1

Offspring of the Soviet System

> After I die, they will place my actions on a scale—
> on one side evil, on the other side good. I hope the
> good will outweigh the bad.
>
> —Nikita Khrushchev, as cited in William
> Taubman, *Khrushchev: The Man and His Era*

Although they were both part of the early postwar Soviet generation, Boris Abramovich Berezovsky and Vladimir Vladimirovich Putin could not have been more different. Berezovsky was an exuberant, charismatic Jew and a big spender, who could not hide his passions, especially for women. A former academic colleague of Berezovsky noted: "Boris was like the center of the universe, the focal point to which everyone was drawn . . . A generator of energy."[1] In the words of Berezovsky's close friend, the writer Iulii Dubov: "Everything about him was extravagant, mainly because he did not understand what the golden mean was—adherence to moderation in life . . . He recognized only the extreme positions of the pendulum; in the middle he was bored."[2]

The steely eyed Putin, by contrast, has been described as focused, wary, secretive, a "cold fish," and always in control. Hungarian Prime Minister Viktor Orban observed in 2015: "Is there anybody who has seen the personality of Putin? He is not a man who has a known personality, so don't imagine him as you like to imagine Western leaders."[3] Author Masha Gessen appropriately dubbed Putin "the man without a face."[4] What comes to mind with Putin is Hannah Arendt's observation about the banality of evil.

Growing Up Jewish in the Post-Stalin Era

Berezovsky had just turned six when Stalin died in March 1953, so he had scant experience of life under the Soviet dictator. Putin was not even a year old at the time of Stalin's death. But Stalin's legacy cast a dark shadow on the lives of Soviet citizens for years to come, despite the much-vaunted reforms that came with the so-called thaw under his successor, Nikita Khrushchev. Stalin had more than a million of his citizens executed during his 1936–39 purges and sent a further fourteen million citizens to the notorious Gulag. Just before he died, Stalin had begun a new purge of Jewish doctors, which threatened the broader community of Jewish scientific and cultural figures.

For Berezovsky's parents and other members of Moscow's Jewish intelligentsia, Stalin's sudden death came as a relief. Although antisemitism continued to prevail in all aspects of Soviet life, the danger of indiscriminate arrest and possible execution for Jews ended when Stalin's henchmen, in particular his notorious police chief Lavrenty Beria, put an abrupt halt to the so-called Doctors' Plot.[5] Berezovsky's father, Abraham, was thus able to continue his successful career as a civil engineer for the region of Moscow, even winning an award for his work from the USSR Council of Ministers.

Abraham met his wife, Anna Gelman, when she was studying medicine in Moscow, and the two married in 1943. Twelve years younger than her husband, Anna relinquished her promising medical career when she gave birth to Boris in early 1946, although she later worked as a laboratory assistant at the Pediatrics Institute of the Academy of Sciences. According to a former colleague, Anna was slavishly devoted to Boris, her only child: "She idolized her son, lived her life for him completely . . . She didn't even want a second child because she could not imagine sharing her love for him with someone else."[6] In an interview on the occasion of her son's sixtieth birthday, Anna recalled that when she was once compelled to discipline little Boris by giving him a spanking, she cried afterwards.[7]

In the Soviet Union, nationality was determined by ethnicity. There was no such thing as "Soviet" nationality in passports. Berezovsky's father was Jewish, but Anna, although mainly Jewish, claimed Russian nationality from her mother's side. This meant that Berezovsky could also be legally Russian. According to Berezovsky's daughter Elizaveta, Anna and her husband intended to register Berezovsky as Jewish in his birth certificate. But the woman at the registry told Anna: "Please don't ruin the boy's life. Register him as Russian." And so Berezovsky was officially Russian and when he was sixteen received a Russian passport.[8]

By the grim Soviet standards at the time, the Berezovsky family lived reasonably well. Abraham earned enough so that Anna did not have to work in her son's early years—a rare privilege for Soviet women, especially given that many families were fatherless because of war deaths. And they owned a television, considered a luxury. But in comparison to the children of Moscow's elite—scientists, artists, and military officials—who attended English Special School No. 4 with Berezovsky, the family's lifestyle was quite modest. The Soviet system was highly stratified, and these children did not live in communal apartments, as the Berezovskys did; some of them were even driven to school in family cars. Berezovsky yearned for something better. Anna recalled: "When he was five or six years old, we were walking along Stoleshnikov Lane, and he saw a coat in a store window. He said to me: 'Mother, when I grow up, I will buy you such a coat.'"[9]

Berezovsky began attending the English Special School, on the outskirts of Moscow, in the sixth grade and continued there for the next six years. His overall academic performance was not exceptional, but he did shine in mathematics and represented his school in numerous competitions.[10] In 1962, following his graduation, Berezovsky applied for entrance to the physics department of Moscow State University. He was refused admittance because it was clear that he was Jewish, despite his Russian passport. Former Alfa Bank director Mikhail Fridman, a fellow Jew who came to know Berezovsky well—only to later fall out with him—observed: "He was an absolute Jew both in appearance, by his manner of speaking and intonations, and by his last name, first name, patronymic, and so on. Without any doubt, as a Soviet person who lived a long and productive life in the Soviet system, he fully experienced, I am sure, all sorts of discriminatory antisemitism that was then ubiquitous."[11] Indeed, in his autobiography, Berezovsky describes instances of discrimination against him, but he did not become embittered or try to retaliate: "I prefer not to fight windmills, and I nevertheless consider myself as belonging to the Russian culture."[12]

Berezovsky also recalled that he was far from being a dissident in his youth. On the contrary, he was an enthusiastic and active member of the Komsomol (Communist Youth League) and later, in 1978, joined the Communist Party. When he disagreed with those on his party committee, he did not give up his membership. "I was an example of a classic Soviet careerist," Berezovsky wrote.[13] As Soviet-born British journalist

Peter Pomerantsev observed of Berezovsky, he was representative of a state of mind prevalent among the elite who grew up in the late Soviet Union:

> You ask them if they believed in Communism, and they say: "Don't be silly." "But you sang the songs? Were good members of the Komsomol?" "Of course we did, and we felt good when we sang them. And then right afterwards we would listen to Deep Purple and 'the voices'—Radio Liberty, the BBC." "So you were dissidents? You believed in the end of the USSR?" "No. It's not like that. You just speak several languages at the same time, all the time. There are several 'yous.'"[14]

A Family Man

Rejected at Moscow State University, Berezovsky entered the Faculty of Electronics and Computer Engineering at the Moscow Forestry Institute, where he met Nina Korotkova, who was two years behind him in her studies. The couple married in 1970, and within a year Elizaveta was born. Ekaterina followed two years later. According to Ekaterina: "Mama was incredibly beautiful, and Papa always loved

FIGURE 2. Berezovsky with his wife Nina and their daughters, Ekaterina (left) and Elizaveta (right), 1977. Photo courtesy of Elizaveta Berezovskaya, personal archive.

pretty women."[15] They lived with Berezovsky's parents, who by this time had an apartment on Leninskii Prospekt, near the Forestry Institute, which was spacious by Soviet standards—four rooms. They also had a dacha outside the city. Nonetheless, Berezovsky recalled that, once their two daughters arrived, they had trouble making ends meet on his stipend of a hundred rubles a month, and he had to get a part-time job.[16]

After achieving top marks at the Forestry Institute, Berezovsky was able to pursue graduate studies in the early 1970s at the Faculty of Mechanics and Mathematics of Moscow State University, earning a master's degree in applied mathematics. He then became a researcher at the prestigious Institute of Control Sciences of the USSR Academy of Sciences and was awarded a doctorate there in 1983, as well as becoming the head of a laboratory. The institute attracted the top Jewish scientists in the country. According to one former student: "In the sphere of Soviet life, these were the brightest people who had come together. It was, to a meaningful degree, a Jewish Institute."[17] In December 1991, Berezovsky, with numerous scholarly articles and monographs to his credit, would be elected a corresponding member of the Russian Academy of Sciences in the Section of Mathematics, Mechanics, and Computer Science.

Berezovsky later described this period of his life: "I enjoyed life as a scientist in the Soviet Union. An unregimented working day. I didn't need to be up by eight a.m. and wade through crowds on the subway. I could sleep in, and at the same time could sit up until four in the morning and mull over interesting problems. I led the life of a Soviet artist, not the life of a Soviet worker—at a machine from the starting bell. But from dawn to dusk alone with my thoughts and the company I chose."[18]

But, always restless, Berezovsky could not resist new opportunities. In the late 1980s, the Institute of Control Sciences began collaborating with the largest Soviet automobile manufacturer—AvtoVAZ, located seven hundred miles east of Moscow in the town of Togliatti—introducing computer-aided design and software systems. The collaboration, in which Berezovsky played a key role, enabled him to establish himself with AvtoVAZ management, which proved valuable for his subsequent entry into the automobile market. He later told American journalist David Hoffman: "We simply used the knowledge that I gained professionally, from the institute, and the work we had done at the institute, and started to sell that work."[19]

The connection with AvtoVAZ enabled Berezovsky to become part owner of an automobile while he was still a researcher at the institute. A younger colleague, Leonid Boguslavskii, mentioned to him that his mother had a very old car that was rusty and falling apart. Berezovsky proposed that he would drive the long distance to Togliatti to have it repaired at AvtoVAZ, and then he and Boguslavskii would share ownership of the vehicle. Boguslavskii insisted on first giving Berezovsky a driving test, which Berezovsky failed outright. As Boguslavskii recalled: "Here I experienced Boria's absolutely fantastic powers of persuasion—how he could convince someone by alternating warmth and charm with compelling arguments. He pressured me to give in and drove off to Togliatti."[20] Boguslavskii later learned that on the way Berezovsky flew into a ditch and rolled the car but somehow accomplished his mission.

By all accounts, Berezovsky was an incorrigible womanizer. As the 1980s grew on, he apparently tired of Nina—he was also losing interest in mathematics—and took up with a woman who was twelve years younger than he was—Galina Besharova. Besharova came from a working-class family and was employed at the Blagonravov Institute of Machine Building in Moscow. She observed after Berezovsky's death in 2013: "Boris had a very rare quality among men—he could charm everyone . . . His charisma was irresistible. It was very hard to say 'no' to him."[21] For a while Berezovsky was able to lead two separate personal lives, but at one point, much to his chagrin, he arrived at Sheremetevo Airport from a trip to the United States to find that both his wife and his girlfriend had showed up to meet him.[22]

Although Besharova gave birth to his son, Artem, in 1989, Berezovsky did not divorce his wife and marry Besharova until 1991. By the time the couple had a daughter, Anastasia, in 1992, Berezovsky was already involved with a Russian beauty named Elena Gorbunova, a former student at Moscow State University, who was almost twenty years his junior. In 1993, after Berezovsky moved in with Gorbunova, Besharova left Russia to take up residence in London. In 2011, she won from Berezovsky the largest divorce settlement ever awarded in Britain, $150 million.[23]

One person whose close friendship with Berezovsky spanned his relationships with the three women was Petr Aven, the billionaire former director of Russia's Alfa Bank, who testified in the Robert Mueller probe about Putin and the 2016 Trump campaign. Aven's father, Oleg, was a director of the Institute of Control Sciences, as well as a supervisor of Berezovsky's doctoral dissertation, and Berezovsky became a

FIGURE 3.   Berezovsky and Petr Aven, 1998. East News.

frequent visitor to the Aven home in the 1970s. Nine years younger than Berezovsky, Aven was something of a wunderkind. He earned his doctorate in economics at Moscow State University in 1980, at the age of only twenty-five, and went on to become a senior researcher at the Systems Research Institute of the USSR Academy of Sciences. Immediately after the Soviet collapse, Aven joined Yeltsin's new team of economic reformers, led by Egor Gaidar (a fellow student of Aven at Moscow State University), as head of the new Committee on Foreign Economic Relations and then, after the Russian Federation was formed at the end of 1991, minister of foreign economic relations. Aven would provide Berezovsky with crucial connections to Yeltsin's inner circle and use his position to further Berezovsky's business projects.

An Unlikely Beginning

Unlike the Berezovskys, Putin's parents, Vladimir Spiridonovich Putin and Maria Ivanovna Shelomova, were of humble origin, with scant education.[24] Vladimir Spiridonovich's forebears were serfs from the Tver region of Russia. Putin's grandfather, Spiridon Ivanovich Putin, was the first of the Putin family not to have been born under the yoke of serfdom, which ended in 1861 under the reformist Tsar Alexander II. Vladimir and Maria married in 1928, when they were both seventeen, and moved to Leningrad a few years later. During World War II, Vladimir served in a People's Commissariat of Internal Affairs (NKVD) battalion behind German lines and was severely wounded. (He would limp for the rest of his life.) His son, Vladimir Vladimirovich Putin, was not born until 1952, when Maria, who had barely survived the siege of Leningrad, was almost forty-one. Putin's two brothers, born earlier, had both died of illness. Like Berezovsky, he was raised an only child. Vladimir Spiridonovich worked as a toolmaker in a Leningrad factory that made subway and railroad cars. According to Putin's former elementary school teacher Vera Gurevich, "His father was very serious and imposing. He often had an angry look. The first time I came to see him, I was even frightened . . . And then it turned out that he was very kindhearted."[25]

After the ravages of war and Stalinism, Soviet citizens did not take life for granted. Just as Berezovsky's parents did, the Putins doted on their only child. Putin's ex-wife Liudmila observed that "he was their sun, moon and stars. They did everything they could for him."[26] As a child, Putin recalled: "I did not go to kindergarten. I was an only child, and my parents were very worried about me, and so kept a close eye on me. Mama even did not work for a while, in order to spend all her time with me."[27] Maria Ivanovna found employment that would allow her to spend her days with her little son. She worked nights in a bakery, unloading trays of bread, and as a night security guard in a secondhand store. The Putins were so protective of their son that he did not start school until he was almost eight, in 1960. He spent most of his time playing in the courtyard of their building. According to Putin: "Mama sometimes stuck her head out the window and shouted, 'Are you in the courtyard?' I always was."[28]

The Putins' living quarters were confined to one room in a fifth-floor communal apartment, shared with two other families. A single gas stove for the families to prepare meals, along with a sink, was in the hallway. And near the stairs an unheated closet housed a toilet, over which residents would perch when washing by pouring water over themselves. Putin biographer Steven Lee Myers described the dwelling: "The stairs to the fifth floor were pocked with holes, fetid, and dimly lit; they smelled of sweat and boiling cabbage. The building was infested with rats, which [Putin] and his friends would chase with sticks."[29]

At Leningrad's School No. 193, Putin was a restless, inattentive student. According to Vera Gurevich: "Volodia [diminutive for Vladimir] could not sit still during lessons. He was always spinning around on his seat, peering out the window, or looking under his desk."[30] Putin also got very rough with his peers. His school friend Viktor Borisenko recalled: "He could get into a fight with anyone . . . He wasn't the strongest in our class, but he could beat anyone in a fight because he would work himself up into a frenzy and fight to the end."[31] Gurevich mentioned one incident, when she took the class on an outing and there was an altercation among some of the boys. Putin threw one of his classmates, K., on the ground, breaking his ankle: "I told Volodia that it was not necessary to use force against K., but it was necessary to just speak to him convincingly. To this, my pupil replied: 'Vera Dmitrievna, there are people who do not understand any words or do not want to understand. They understand only force.' It stuck in my head for years."[32]

After school Putin hung out in the courtyard with tough boys who were two or three years older and much bigger than he was. Viktor Borisenko described what it was like: "I remember him well in the courtyard. In elementary grades, the courtyard for Putin was a window to the world . . . The atmosphere there was terrible: unshaven dirty guys with port wine and cigarettes. Drinks, obscenities, fights. And Putin among all these punks."[33] These experiences seemed to have had a significant effect on the formation of Putin's personality. Tellingly, Gurevich is quoted in Putin's autobiography, *First Person*, as saying: "I think Volodya is a good person. But he never forgives people who betray him or are mean to him."[34]

When he went to secondary school and was chosen to join the Komsomol, Putin spent less time in the courtyard, and his academic performance improved. Although he achieved only average grades in math and chemistry, Putin got top marks in history and German. In the meantime, Putin, who was wiry and small in stature (around five feet six as an adult), took up martial arts, in particular sambo, which combined judo and wrestling. According to Myers: "The martial arts transformed his life, giving him the means of asserting himself against larger, tougher boys."[35] Putin would cultivate an image of physical fitness and athletic prowess well into his reign as Russia's leader.

Toward the end of his secondary school years, Putin decided he wanted to become a spy. Inspired by the hugely popular 1968 Russian television miniseries *Sword and Shield* (Shchit i mech), about a Soviet secret agent who penetrates Nazi military intelligence and later the SS, Putin walked into Leningrad KGB headquarters (the so-called Big House, *Bol'shoi dom*) and asked how he could join the KGB. The officer in charge told him that the KGB did not hire walk-ins and that he should get more education before he applied. Putin then pressed his interlocutor to suggest the best line of study for an aspiring KGB applicant and was told that law would be a good choice.[36]

Commenting on Putin's story, Russian journalist Nataliya Gevorkyan observed: "Imagine a boy who dreams of being a KGB officer when everyone else wants to be a cosmonaut."[37] But a career in the KGB was not only prestigious; it brought material rewards. KGB officers, particularly those at the senior level, lived better than their counterparts in the military, the prosecutor's office, or the police. They typically received more spacious housing and could avail themselves of comfortable rest homes and sanatoriums that the KGB made available to its employees and their families. If one were lucky enough to get a spot in the coveted foreign intelligence branch—often attained through high-level party or KGB connections—the opportunity of going abroad, denied to ordinary Soviet citizens, was a huge perquisite. In short, it is easy to see why a young man like Putin, from a poor, uneducated family, would be attracted to the KGB, whatever his ideological views.[38]

In 1970, following the KGB officer's advice, Putin entered the law faculty at Leningrad State University (LSU), which was one of the country's best universities. That said, Soviet law was first and foremost a political weapon of the state and used to maintain the regime, not to protect legal rights. Although Stalinist methods were no longer employed, individuals who challenged the state in any way were severely punished under the Soviet legal system, which was subordinate to the leadership of the Soviet Communist Party. Putin was thus gaining a higher education in a field that focused on Communist dogma, rather than on justice. Ironically, in his third year at LSU, Putin, called Put'ka by his student friends, was able to experience a nonideological pleasure: driving his own car, a Soviet-made Zaporozhets. His mother, by a stroke of incredible luck, had won the car in a lottery. In Putin's words: "Money was tight in our family, and to give the car to me was absolute madness. We could have sold it, after all, and gotten at least 3,500 rubles for it . . . But my parents decided to spoil me."[39]

At LSU, Putin forged friendships with two men who would play key roles in his future career, as part of the cohort of his allies from the security services and legal agencies in Leningrad/St. Petersburg who later followed Putin to Moscow. One was Viktor Cherkesov, who was two years ahead of Putin. After graduation from law school, followed by a couple of years in the military and the prosecutor's office, Cherkesov joined the Leningrad branch of the KGB's infamous Fifth Chief Directorate, where he gained notoriety as a ruthless persecutor of dissidents. Following the Soviet collapse in 1991, Cherkesov rose to become head of the St. Petersburg FSB (successor to the KGB), and later worked under his old friend when Putin was appointed Russian FSB chief in 1998.[40] The second close friend and classmate was Aleksandr Bastrykin, who since 2011 has headed the powerful Russian Investigative Committee, known for prosecuting high-profile political and economic cases that are important to the Kremlin's agenda.[41]

The Big House

In 1975, following his graduation from law school, Putin was formally admitted to the KGB, reportedly because of his good grades. After completing six months' training at a KGB counterintelligence school, he became a full-fledged officer in Leningrad. Putin says in his autobiography only that he worked in counterintelligence. This could mean that he worked for the Second Chief Directorate, which was responsible for the internal political control of Soviet citizens and foreigners residing in the country, as Steven Myers and other sources say. It is also possible that Putin joined his law school classmate Cherkesov in the Fifth Chief Directorate, which focused more specifically on dissidents.[42] Either way, as Myers notes, Putin "took part in operations not against the enemy outside, but against the enemy within."[43]

At this time, the Brezhnev regime had been clamping down on political dissent with increasingly repressive measures, implemented by KGB Chairman Iurii Andropov, whose trademark strategy was the incarceration of dissidents in psychiatric hospitals. Vladimir Bukovsky, the human rights activist who made the world aware of this practice, was expelled from the Soviet Union in 1976, and Alexander Solzhenitsyn had been exiled two years earlier. Leningrad was a hub of the dissident movement, in which the city's small groups of intellectuals and cultural figures spread samizdat literature (which Berezovsky consumed avidly) and staged small protests against the regime. For Putin and his KGB colleagues, these dissidents were dangerous enemies of the state.[44]

Former KGB general Oleg Kalugin, who was assigned to the Leningrad KGB as first deputy chief in 1980 after having worked abroad in foreign intelligence, described the Big House years later: "I was born in Leningrad, but it still seemed like the boondocks. Work here was not among foreigners but rather among Soviet citizens . . . the system was focused on exposing those with reformist attitudes, people who wanted to change, to improve things. These were the people the KGB was occupied with, instead of focusing on actual spies."[45] Asked once what he remembers of Putin from those days, Kalugin replied: "He brought me some papers to sign. It was not a real interaction . . . People ask me what I think of him, what I know about his life. I do not like this topic of discussion and respond that it would be better to ask his ex-wife. She lived with him for thirty years and knows him better than I do."[46]

As Putin spied on his fellow citizens, he made lifelong friendships with two coworkers in the Leningrad KGB—Nikolai Patrushev and Aleksandr Bortnikov. Patrushev would serve as Putin's first deputy after Putin became head of the FSB in 1998 and succeed him as FSB chief in August 1999. In 2008, after Patrushev assumed the leadership of Russia's powerful National Security Council, Bortnikov took over his FSB post. Both men are ruthless hardliners. In 2017, Bortnikov famously defended Stalin's purges, saying that "a significant number of criminal cases were based on factual evidence."[47] Patrushev, arguably the closest to Putin of all his allies, is also the most hostile toward the West, although he voiced reservations about Russia's 2022 invasion of Ukraine. According to Russian political analyst Tatiana Stanovaya: "His ideas form the foundations of decisions taken by Putin. He is one of the few figures Putin listens to."[48] Who would have predicted that Putin and his two friends, run-of-the-mill KGB officers in the mid-1970s, would end up wielding such power over their county?

Putin kept his KGB employment a secret from most of his acquaintances, including for a while, his future wife Liudmila, who he met in 1980 through a St. Petersburg friend. Always cautious, Putin waited for three and a half years to propose marriage. Liudmila, a flight attendant from Kaliningrad, initially found Putin "plain and dull," but she was soon drawn to his "inner-strength."[49] Once married, the two moved in with Putin's parents, as was the custom in Soviet days—because of the extreme housing shortage—and the birth of their first daughter, Masha, soon followed. The Putins' second daughter, Katerina, was born in Dresden, in East Germany, where the family moved in 1985. According to a KGB colleague there, Vladimir Usol'tsev: "Putin was the master

FIGURE 4. The Putins with their two daughters, 1991. TASS/ZUMApress.com.

of the house. This was clear . . . Liudmila simply knew her place, so to speak. She was modest, quiet. Volodia sometimes just with his eyes would tell her: 'look, I am talking, and you shut up,' or something like that."[50]

Putin was vague in his autobiography about how long he worked in counterintelligence for the Leningrad KGB, and biographers have offered conflicting accounts.[51] But an official biography, published on his sixty-ninth birthday, states that Putin remained a counterintelligence officer until after he was sent to Moscow in 1979 for training at the Felix Dzerzhinsky Higher School of the KGB, a stepping-stone for career advancement.[52] According to a study for Washington's Wilson Center, the Dzerzhinsky School devoted considerable attention to "the cultivation of what were described as 'Chekist' [a reference to Lenin's secret police, the Cheka] values: unquestioning loyalty to the Soviet Communist system and its defense from foreign and domestic adversaries."[53] A few months after his return to Leningrad, Putin was transferred to the First Department (foreign intelligence) of the Leningrad KGB, where he worked as an officer in Directorate RT, which conducted "reconnaissance from the territory of the USSR" (*razvedka s territorii*). RT officers recruited foreigners who were visiting the city and employees of foreign consulates to spy for the KGB. According to

Russian journalist Andrei Soldatov: "Directorate RT was a truly totalitarian approach to intelligence. It made the territory of the Soviet Union
a gigantic trap—all regional branches of the KGB had special depart-
ments tasked to look for ways to recruit foreigners on their soil."[54]

Deutschland über Alles

Putin's career advancement was slow. It was not until 1984 that he was
singled out for a year of study at the Andropov Red Banner KGB Institute outside Moscow and received espionage training that prepared
him for work abroad. A year later, in the summer of 1985, he was sent
to the East German industrial city of Dresden, where he could use the
German he learned in school and later perfected at the Red Banner
Institute. Dresden was not a plum KGB posting, by any measure. Had
Putin made a greater impression on his teachers at the Red Banner
Institute or on his superiors in Leningrad, he might have been sent
to West Germany under cover as a diplomat, or at least to East Berlin,
where the KGB had a much larger presence because of the close access
to the West. As one former KGB colleague observed: "In principle, Vlad-
imir Vladimirovich did the very same work in Dresden that he did in
Leningrad, only from the territory of the GDR [German Democratic
Republic]."[55]

In Dresden, Putin joined a group of eight KGB officers whose job
was to liaise with employees of the Ministry of State Security of the
GDR—better known as the Stasi, the East German political police—and
possibly recruit foreign businessmen, scientists, and students who came
to the city. As there were two others nicknamed Volodia in the group,
Putin was called "little Volodia," apparently because he was short in
height.[56] Liudmila arrived in Dresden with Maria in late October 1985.
As she later told a Putin biographer, she immediately felt at home there
because she grew up in Kaliningrad, formerly a German city, Königs-
berg, which came under Soviet control after World War II: "The same
solid, old mansions, mixed with new buildings. And then—that smell
of special coal briquettes used at home for cooking cutlets, just like in
Kaliningrad. A specific smell that is unique."[57]

Liudmila recalled that her husband had set aside some money for
her to buy something for herself on her arrival and was later "unpleas-
antly surprised" when, inside of new clothes, she purchased practical
household items. "As far as clothes were concerned," she said, "I have
sewn almost all my own clothes since the eighth grade. And Germany

was no exception."[58] Putin, by contrast, was not so restrained. Masha Gessen interviewed a former member of the radical terrorist group Red Army Faction (RAF), which the KGB was cultivating, who told her that Putin was always eager to get his hands on coveted items from the West and even managed to obtain from him a state-of-the art shortwave radio and a car stereo.[59]

Putin's biographers, both Western and Russian, have dissected his career in Dresden to ascertain exactly what he was doing at the KGB outpost. Vladimir Usol'tsev portrayed Putin as a skilled KGB sleuth: "In Dresden, Putin recruited candidates to become illegal agents. This is very hard, painstaking work . . . Putin was a good master at secret schemes."[60] Journalist Catherine Belton seems to have interviewed the same former RAF member, apparently named Klodo, who spoke with Masha Gessen. Belton concludes that Putin was leading strategy meetings with the group and giving orders, but Gessen had a different impression: "Handing out assignments to RAF radicals, who were responsible for more than two dozen assassinations and terrorist attacks between 1970 and 1998, is exactly the sort of work Putin had once dreamed of, but there is no evidence he was directly connected to it."[61] Russian journalist Dmitrii Zapol'skii, who has followed Putin's career closely, clarified Putin's relationship with the RAF: "The group in Dresden itself was clearly only a 'technical' unit, a 'cog' in the machine of the Soviet intelligence network. Putin did not play an independent role there. He only transmitted orders from his immediate superiors. I would not exaggerate his contacts with Klodo or his work along this line."[62]

However difficult it might be for Putin admirers to accept that the current leader of Russia was an unremarkable employee of the KGB, the records speak for themselves. Mark Galeotti, an expert on the Russian security services, concluded from a recently declassified KGB report on Putin that in Dresden he was acting in an administrative capacity, rather than engaging personally with potential recruits: "Technically, this was First Chief Directorate work, but in many ways it was not. He was not recruiting and running agents so much as collating reports, liaising with the East German Stasi (who gave him his own access pass) and responding to queries from Moscow."[63]

In his January 2021 documentary, *Putin's Palace*, Aleksei Navalny, who accessed Stasi archives in Dresden, described Putin's stint in East Germany thus: "Putin came to Dresden in 1985 as a petty KGB officer, an ordinary employee of the nonsecret residency—the official KGB office in East Germany . . . this was where idle employees sat at party meetings and awarded each other mementos."[64] As veteran Russian journalist Leonid Mlechin observed: "Over time, there has been a lot of talk about Vladimir Putin belonging to the group of twentieth-century superspies. In reality he was a low-ranking officer in a minor position. Putin did not make a grand career in intelligence."[65]

Gorbachev Changes Everything

Whatever Putin's work in Dresden, it was difficult for him to watch the Soviet empire in Eastern Europe crumble during his tenure there from 1985 to 1990. Soviet leaders had weathered the 1980 crisis in Poland, sparked by labor unrest at the Gdansk shipyards and the emergence of the Solidarity movement. But the Kremlin's decision not to send military troops into the country was a harbinger of its nonintervention in other Soviet Bloc countries. By the spring of 1985, following the deaths of the much-revered former KGB chief Andropov, who served as Soviet Communist Party chief in 1982–84, and his successor, Konstantin Chernenko, a younger reformist leader, Mikhail Gorbachev, was at the helm. It was not long before Gorbachev's "new thinking" in foreign policy would result in efforts to end the expensive arms race with the West and loosen Moscow's grip on the countries of the Soviet Bloc. In the GDR, the KGB soon wore out its welcome.

After the fall of the Berlin Wall in early November 1989, thousands of protestors stormed the Stasi building in Dresden on December 5, as Putin and his comrades watched from the balcony of their compound around the corner on Angelikastrasse. According to Putin's own account, when demonstrators began to gather outside the KGB building, he, as the most senior officer there at the time, called the Soviet military command in Dresden to ask for protection but was refused because orders from Moscow were required. Although he had no authorization to act on his own, Putin decided he had to protect the KGB's highly sensitive files. Putin recalled that, despite warnings from his colleagues, he went outside, accompanied by a Soviet soldier, and approached the angry mob. He told them that the compound was a Soviet military object and would be defended with firearms if anyone tried to enter. He then ordered the soldier to reload his weapon in order to demonstrate his point, and the two walked back into the building. Although the protestors did not try to enter the building, they did not leave until after Soviet paratroopers finally arrived and surrounded the compound.[66]

After Putin became Russia's president, Kremlin-sponsored television portrayed him as a hero who saved the day for his comrades by facing a crowd of thousands. In fact, subsequent eyewitness accounts revealed that there had been no more than fifteen or twenty demonstrators outside the KGB's building.[67]

Gorbachev was also making important changes at home, introducing *demokratizatsiia* (multicandidate elections for both party and state bodies), *glasnost'* (freedom to express views publicly), and *perestroika* (political and economic restructuring). He understood that the Soviet command economy was no longer viable. The country's economic situation was declining rapidly, largely due to its exorbitant military spending, and some form of privatization was called for. Two new laws, passed under Gorbachev's direction in 1987, permitted state enterprises to adopt practices used by private businesses and allowed foreign investment in Soviet firms. These changes paved the way for Berezovsky to become a businessman. In his words: "I was absolutely happy in the Soviet Union. And then this life ended, in 1989, when the institute stopped paying salaries, and I felt some sort of uncertainty, or threat, hanging in the air, and life became uncomfortable . . . I made an absolutely crucial decision: to discontinue doing science and start doing business, which was at the time called 'speculation'. . . For me a completely different life began, with risk, responsibility, and freedom."[68]

Berezovsky approached the management of AvtoVAZ with a proposal to form a joint venture with an Italian Fiat supplier, Logosystem, and in May 1989, LogoVAZ was established, with Berezovsky as general director. Badri Patarkatsishvili, a Georgian who was responsible for AvtoVAZ's spare parts distribution in the Caucasus, provided some of the start-up capital for LogoVAZ and later joined its management. As the late American journalist Paul Klebnikov noted, LogoVAZ was established to provide AvtoVAZ with state-of-the-art computer software, but before long the new firm dropped that mission and started to sell automobiles made by AvtoVAZ.[69]

AvtoVAZ was the Soviet Union's largest domestic car manufacturer, producing around seven hundred thousand cars (the brands Lada and Zhiguli) annually, and Soviet citizens, craving mobility and status, were snapping them up by any means possible. AvtoVAZ director Vladimir Kadannikov and his deputy became shareholders in LogoVAZ while keeping their positions at AvtoVAZ, so they made sure that the new joint venture was profitable. LogoVAZ bought the cars at artificially low prices set by the state and sold them on the domestic market at considerable profit. In the words of journalist David Hoffman: "The traders were effectively sucking the value out of AvtoVaz, but they were doing it with the permission of the managers inside."[70]

Within three years LogoVAZ was selling forty-five thousand AvtoVAZ cars annually, grossing revenues of nearly $300 million on these sales alone.[71] Andrei Vasiliev, editor of *Kommersant* when Berezovsky later owned the publication, made these wry observations after Berezovsky's death: "Boria [Boris] really had a brilliant intuition. When they were still working as AvtoVAZ dealers, he came and said, 'We will buy out all the Zhiguli that AvtoVAZ has for a year in advance.' They scooped up all their stash, took their mothers' savings from under pillows and mattresses, sold their wives and all invested in these tin cans called Zhiguli. At that moment, the economy switched to dollars, the ruble collapsed, and the price of the Zhiguli was fixed in hard currency . . . This is how he made his first millions."[72]

Eager to expand his business by exporting raw materials from Russia, Berezovsky traveled to Lausanne, Switzerland, in early 1991 with Nikolai Glushkov, a founding member of LogoVAZ and chief financial officer of AvtoVAZ. Glushkov, who held a doctorate in theoretical and mathematical physics, had worked for the Russian Ministry of Foreign Trade for ten years and thus had valuable experience with foreign markets. He would remain one of Berezovsky's closest allies for years to come. Berezovsky and Glushkov managed to enlist a Swiss commodities trading company, André & Cie, to go into business with LogoVAZ as a Swiss-Russian joint venture, but with Berezovsky and his partners owning the majority of the shares. In the words of Klebnikov: "For Berezovsky, the reincorporation of Logovaz represented an extraordinary achievement. The Soviet Union had not yet fallen, and here was a Russian businessman, operating without the advice of the KGB or other internationally minded parts of the Soviet establishment, setting up a sophisticated international financial structure, complete with reputable foreign partners, shell companies, and tax shelters."[73] Berezovsky later recalled that, when he started his business in 1989, he had only three thousand rubles, "half the price of a car," to his name.[74] It was not long before he would be frequenting an exclusive men's clothing store in Zurich and driving a Mercedes.

CHAPTER 2

A Meeting in St. Petersburg

> So it was in Russia in those days—it was unclear
> who was more at fault: the government or the
> financial wheeler-dealers. It was clear who the
> losers were, however: ordinary Russians.
>
> —Paul Klebnikov, *Godfather of the Kremlin*

On their return to Leningrad in January 1990, the Putins found Soviet life in turmoil. Mikhail Gorbachev's reforms had unleashed widespread ethnic discontent in the non-Russian republics, and the Soviet economy was in free fall. More importantly, a fundamental shift was occurring in people's expectations and values regarding their government. Although there were historical examples, few had anticipated that Gorbachev's cautious liberalization "from above" would ignite a revolution from below. As demands for democratic change hit a fever pitch, the KGB's dominance over society was under threat. Not long after Putin's return to Leningrad, Oleg Kalugin, his former boss, made headlines when he harshly criticized the KGB in a series of interviews with the Russian media.[1]

Putin's five-year stint in Dresden had been cut short by six months because the First Chief Directorate, not surprisingly, was reducing its staff abroad. Putin claimed in his autobiography that he had been offered a position at intelligence headquarters in Moscow, but he turned it down because "the country didn't have a future. And it would have been very difficult to sit inside the system and wait for it all to collapse around me."[2] But Putin's former Dresden boss Lazar Matveev recalled that, although Liudmila had her heart set on Moscow, Putin chose to go back to his old job in Leningrad because the Moscow offer did not include an apartment.[3] The First Chief Directorate as a rule provided housing—which was owned by the state—for all its staff, so if the agency did make an offer to Putin, it cannot have been a serious one. Obviously, the Putins could not move to Moscow without a place to live.

Liudmila Putina recalled Putin's job situation differently than her husband: "Now I can't even remember why Vladimir Vladimirovich turned down the Moscow position. It seems that they [the KGB] did not come through with what they had proposed, and the job did not have good prospects."[4] Putin's biographer Alexander Rahr observed that "a veil of mystery" surrounds the question of whether Putin actually received an offer to transfer to Moscow and suggests that Putin's superiors were displeased with the fact that Putin and his Dresden colleagues had failed to anticipate the collapse of the East German Communist leadership. As a result, Rahr wrote, Putin ended up with a minor Leningrad post: "Putin was back where he started fifteen years before—his tasks again were to spy on and recruit foreign students."[5]

With only a twenty-year-old washing machine given to them by a Dresden neighbor and a small sum of US dollars, Putin and his family had no choice but to move in with his parents, where they occupied the smaller space in a two-room apartment. In March 1990, after assuming a job monitoring foreign students at Leningrad State University—under cover as assistant rector for international affairs—Putin became a member of the KGB's "active reserve." But money was tight. Liudmila recalled: "For three months, he was not paid his salary. I remember that by the end of the third month I started getting seriously alarmed because we simply had no money. But then, everything was paid to him all at once."[6]

In May 1990, while retaining his university post, Putin became an advisor to Anatoly Sobchak, the newly elected chairman of the Leningrad City Council and a well-known democrat. According to Putin, when he told Sobchak, who had earlier been one of Putin's lecturers in the LSU law department, that he was still on the KGB payroll, Sobchak brushed it off, saying "Well, screw it." Apparently Sobchak decided that, given the political turmoil at the time, it was useful to have an assistant with a direct line to the KGB, despite Putin's subsequent claim that "although I was formally listed in the security agencies, I hardly ever set foot in the [KGB] directorate building."[7]

In fact, Oleg Kalugin said that Sobchak was actively seeking out someone from the KGB to serve on his staff.[8] This is confirmed by journalist Dmitrii Zapol'skii, who wrote *Putinburg*, a book about St.

Petersburg in the 1990s. Zapol'skii pointed out that Sobchak needed someone from the KGB to serve as his "watcher," who would keep an eye on financial flows, especially the shadowy ones, and resolve any issues that arose with the security services. Putin was singled out by Sobchak because he was not working for the KGB openly but under the guise of a university employee, so Sobchak's image as a democrat would not be tarnished.[9] As Masha Gessen put it: "This was the sort of politician Sobchak was: he talked a colorful pro-democracy line, but he liked to have a solid conservative base from which to do it . . . Sobchak—who had risen through the ranks both at university . . . and in the Communist Party—knew that it was wiser to pick your KGB handler yourself than to have one picked for you."[10]

In June 1991, after being elected mayor of Leningrad, Sobchak appointed Putin chairman of the newly formed City Committee for Foreign Economic Relations, with responsibility for attracting foreign investment. Among those working in Sobchak's office was another former student of his, Russia's future president Dmitry Medvedev; the economist Aleksei Kudrin; and Igor Sechin, a former intelligence officer, who would become known derisively as "the carrier of Putin's briefcase." Anatoly Chubais, chairman of the Leningrad Committee on Economic Reform and a vocal advocate of what came to be known as "shock therapy" also worked for Sobchak briefly before moving to Yeltsin's government. Putin later claimed, unconvincingly, that he had sent a letter of resignation to the KGB when he started working for Sobchak in 1990, but that the letter "got stalled somewhere," and thus he was still an active KGB officer when the August 1991 coup attempt occurred. So on August 20 he resigned.[11] By that time, however, it was clear that the hardline Communists in Moscow would fail to seize power. Putin, it seems, was hedging his bets, and at the last minute threw his lot in with the democrats.

Putin and his wife were vacationing on the Baltic Sea, near Liudmila's hometown of Kaliningrad, when news of the coup attempt broke on August 19. Although he phoned Sobchak that night, Putin did not fly back to Leningrad until the next day, joining Sobchak at a special session of the city council in the Mariinsky Palace and informing him of his decision to quit the KGB. Putin's timing was perfect. By August 21, the coup attempt had failed. In subsequent interviews not long after the coup, Putin disclosed his KGB past. But he insisted that he had only been a foreign intelligence officer and had played no role in the KGB's nefarious domestic operations.[12]

FIGURE 5.   Anatoly Sobchak and Putin, early 1990s. AP photo/Dmitry Lovetsky.

Berezovsky was also on holiday, in the Seychelles with his girlfriend Elena Gorbunova, when the coup attempt was launched. Like most Soviet citizens, they were caught completely by surprise and did not know what to expect as they flew back to Moscow. But when it became clear that Yeltsin, a former party apparatchik now shouting the slogans of democracy, had emerged victorious, Berezovsky saw new, boundless opportunities to pursue his business goals. Putin had a different reaction. He was later to say that the Soviet collapse and the demise of the KGB came as an unpleasant shock: "During the days of the coup, all the ideals, all the goals that I had had when I went to work for the KGB, collapsed. Of course, it was incredibly difficult to go through this. After all, most of my life had been devoted to work in the agencies."[13]

Money, Money, Money

According to Putin biographer Chris Hutchins: "Anatoly Sobchak's dream was to make the new St Petersburg [renamed as such in September 1991] the financial capital of Russia; a project that would require an organizer with an abundance of skill and nerve. Putin might be a political novice, but he had a degree in international law, spoke a couple of languages, ran an efficient office and appeared to be almost nerveless."[14] Sobchak, by all accounts, considered Putin an invaluable member of his team, appointing him deputy mayor of the city at the end of 1991 and delegating much of the decision making to him. Karen Dawisha, author of the seminal book *Putin's Kleptocracy*, noted, "Foreigners who did business in Russia universally reported that if you wanted to get something done in the city, you worked through Putin, not Sobchak."[15]

Meanwhile, in September 1991, Berezovsky told a Russian newspaper that LogoVAZ had received a $20 million syndicated loan from six Russian banks for AvtoVAZ to manufacture ten thousand cars for sale domestically at European market prices.[16] And thanks to his friend Petr Aven, who became minister of foreign economic relations in the new Yeltsin government, LogoVAZ was able to expand its business further. The company got a license to export raw materials, such as oil and aluminum, which were Russia's main sources of hard currency. Russian firms that obtained foreign trade rights through government connections were able to acquire these commodities at low state prices and sell them at much higher prices abroad.[17]

Berezovsky, who once told Aven "I will not stop until I earn a billion dollars," was on a roll.[18] In 1992, LogoVAZ created a joint venture with an Oklahoma oil company called GHK Corp and the Russian oil producer Samaraneftegaz for the export of Russian oil. Exports of oil and other raw materials also brought traders huge returns because they avoided taxes by hiding their profits abroad. Aven told Klebnikov in May 1992, "We have no idea how much money passes through without paying taxes."[19]

Aven would resign his post in December 1992 amid charges that Russia's earnings from exports were being illegally siphoned off; he promptly joined a company he had been responsible for regulating— Alfa Group, which was making a fortune exporting oil and metals. He would later tell an interviewer: "When I was minister, Boria [Berezovsky] clung to me everywhere I went. He carried my bags, was at my home every day. One time we spent the night in the same place. When I got up at half past seven, Berezovsky, already dressed, though with a sleepy face, rushed to escort me to the car, in the rain, carefully holding an umbrella over me. But as soon as I was fired, he immediately disappeared."[20] In fact, Aven and Berezovsky remained friends until the Alfa Group had a dispute with Berezovsky over the acquisition of the newspaper *Kommersant* in 1999, and Alfa Group CEO Fridman accused Berezovsky of threatening him.

Putin and Berezovsky were first introduced, by Aven, in October 1991, just two months after the coup attempt. Aven and Berezovsky brought GHK chief Robert Hefner and Oklahoma's governor, David Walters, to St. Petersburg to meet Sobchak, a meeting that Putin had arranged at Aven's request. After the group sat down to hear Sobchak talk, with Putin and Berezovsky on either side of the mayor, Berezovsky, who had eaten a big lunch with wine, nodded off to sleep. According to Aven, Putin was incensed and refused to shake Berezovsky's hand when he left. Putin even took Aven aside and said: "I did everything for you. For him to behave like that—to sleep at such a meeting . . . Don't call me anymore and don't count on my help . . . [Berezovsky] better not show up again in our city. If I meet him, I'll break his legs."[21]

Berezovsky remembered the meeting differently, claiming that it was Sobchak, not Putin, who expressed anger to Aven. According to Berezovsky, he developed a cordial relationship with Putin after this first meeting, stopping by his office whenever he visited St. Petersburg: "I can't say that our acquaintance turned into some kind of very close friendship. But it continued to evolve and ultimately grew into friendship . . . the relationship became very trusting, and from the beginning developed quite rapidly, as did everything in Russia."[22]

LogoVAZ had begun to import foreign cars—Mercedes and Volvos—so Berezovsky approached Putin with the idea of a service center for them in St. Petersburg. Putin "responded with great enthusiasm" to the proposal. Berezovsky would later remark to Masha Gessen, unconvincingly, that Putin was the first bureaucrat he met who did not take bribes.[23] But both Putin and Sobchak seem to have benefited personally from the deal; the two were soon driving Mercedes to work at the mayoral offices in the Smolny Institute.[24]

It is not surprising that Berezovsky, a Jewish scientist-turned-entrepreneur, was courting a former low-level KGB officer, who had spent several years fighting Soviet dissidents in Leningrad. Nor is it hard to understand why Putin would play such an important role in the new democratic government of St. Petersburg. As the exiled human rights activist Vladimir Bukovsky observed bitterly after returning to Moscow following the 1991 Soviet collapse: "For Russia, the result was a shoddy tragicomedy in which former second-rate party bosses and KGB generals played the part of leading democrats and saviors of the country from communism."[25]

Bukovsky urged Yeltsin to institute a Nuremberg-style reckoning with the crimes of the past regime, but this, of course, never happened. As a result, the revolution sparked by Gorbachev's reforms and the emergence of Yeltsin as Russia's president was not enough to overcome the country's deep-seated culture of authoritarianism, a culture that for decades had deprived Russian people of any tradition of self-governance. Everybody wanted to make money in the Yeltsin years. But instead of a capitalist system governed by the rule of law, Russia was becoming a country where bribery and violence combined to stifle free competition. In this environment, it was only natural that Putin and Berezovsky would be scratching each other's backs. The knives would not come out until much later.

Brokering Deals in the Mayor's Office

Looking back at the early 1990s, Petr Aven described what it was like to be living in Russia: "What had seemed out of reach became possible: money, travel, books. Just yesterday everyone received almost the same salary and spent ten years hoarding dollars; one could visit Poland only with permission from the district [party] committee; the most important books were obtained only through samizdat. Now there were huge new opportunities, new unthinkable prizes, the most important of which . . . were wealth and power, merged together."[26]

Putin, the straight-shooting KGB officer turned democrat, who only occasionally sipped vodka, was hardly immune to these allures. Responsible for issuing export licenses and regulating foreign joint ventures in St. Petersburg, Russia's largest trading city, he found ample opportunity to reap the rewards of the new Russian economy, often by corrupt means. Sobchak, who made frequent trips abroad to meet with foreign leaders, gave Putin free rein in running the powerful mayor's office, even leaving him with a stack of signed blank official documents, to be filled out as decrees by Putin when the need arose.[27] In addition to Putin, Sobchak hired numerous other former Communist Party officials and KGB officers to work for him. This created an atmosphere of impunity in the St. Petersburg government. As Myers observed of Sobchak: "To secure his power, he needed the apparatchiks, not the democrats. This would be a central dilemma in Russia for years to come."[28] Not surprisingly, this situation put Sobchak at odds with the democratically elected City Council, which began unsuccessful efforts to impeach him in 1992.

The first of many scandals that occurred around Putin at the time involved the gambling industry, one of the many responsibilities that Sobchak handed over to his deputy. As Putin recounted in *First Person*, the city gained 51 percent control of the casinos by offering free rental of municipal buildings to casino owners but somehow missed out on getting any of the gambling profits. Putin explained that the cash had been "diverted" and that "ours was a classic mistake made by people encountering the free market for the first time." Many assumed that some of the casino profits were diverted toward the city hall and ended up in the hands of Putin and Sobchak. As Putin noted: "Later, particularly during Anatoly Sobchak's 1996 election campaign, our political opponents tried to find something criminal in our actions and accused us of corruption."[29] No criminality was ever proven. But years later, the investigative news site *The Insider* interviewed Franz Zedelmeier, a German businessman whose company was in charge of security at the St. Petersburg branch of Credit Lyonnais in the early 1990s. Zedelmeier claimed that every week or ten days Sobchak would bring to the bank a suitcase full of cash for transfer abroad.[30]

The notorious oil-for-food scandal created a much greater political controversy, even threatening Putin's job. A food shortage, caused in part by the worst harvest in a decade, became dire in St. Petersburg after the Soviet collapse, and the government did not have funds to pay for food imports. (Inflation was so out of control that people were selling cigarette butts for a ruble apiece.) The city even introduced ration cards for milk, meat, and sausage. In late 1991, Petr Aven and Acting Prime Minister Egor Gaidar granted Putin's request for the legal authority to issue licenses for the export of raw materials (oil products, metals, timber, copper, aluminum, and cement) located in the St. Petersburg region. The licensed intermediary companies were to barter or sell the raw materials abroad in exchange for food products. But the only food imports received in the exchange were 128 tons of vegetable oil. In 1992, a commission of deputies from the Leningrad City Council, led by Marina Sal'e, conducted an investigation of the scam and found that over $100 million worth of exports had disappeared without any accounting.[31]

The contracts, doled out by Putin with no competitive bidding, were signed without dates, names, and registration numbers, and the values of the raw materials to be sold were vastly understated. When Sal'e and another commission member asked Putin for detailed documentation on the contracts and the fate of the deliveries, he refused, claiming "this information is a commercial secret." Journalist Oleg Lur'e estimated in a piece for *Novaia gazeta* that the firms engaged in "saving St. Petersburg from starvation" earned around $34 million in profits.[32]

When the St. Petersburg legislators demanded Putin's dismissal because of the apparent scam, Aven protected Putin from losing his job.[33] (This may partly explain why Aven became one of Putin's favored oligarchs, enjoying occasional one-on-one talks with the Russian president.) Both the St. Petersburg mayor's office and the Kremlin managed to put the brakes on the Sal'e investigation, and the uproar eventually simmered down. Sobchak, who ignored demands for Putin's removal by the Leningrad City Council, even showed his confidence in Putin by making him first deputy mayor in June 1994.[34]

A Part-Time Mafioso

It was later revealed that Putin had given export contracts to a number of his friends, including those with mafia connections, who sold the raw materials and deposited the proceeds in offshore accounts. One example was a license to export more than $30 million worth of oil products that Putin gave to the St. Petersburg firm Nevskii Dom, owned by his friend Vladimir Smirnov, a businessman and a close associate of the notorious Vladimir Kumarin, leader of the Tambov crime group. The oil products ended up in Britain, and the money disappeared.[35]

Smirnov and Kumarin (who also went by the name Barsukov) became co-owners of the St. Petersburg Fuel Company, which in 1994, thanks to Putin, received exclusive rights to supply St. Petersburg with gasoline, along with the permission to establish a network of gas stations.[36] Smirnov, who would eventually become head of Russia's atomic energy agency, partnered with Putin and some German financiers in August 1992 to establish the now infamous St. Petersburg Real Estate Holding Co., known as SPAG. Officially SPAG was a joint Russian-German venture to attract investment in St. Petersburg real estate. In reality, SPAG was a vehicle for laundering money from South American drug cartels and the Tambov crime group, with city hall as a middleman. In 1994, Putin signed an affidavit giving Smirnov voting rights over the shares in SPAG owned by the St. Petersburg government. Putin served on SPAG's advisory board until after he was elected Russian president in 2000, thus encouraging investment in the company and providing it with respectability.[37]

Kumarin—called the "night governor" of St. Petersburg, because of his powerful influence on the city's politics and business—has since 2009 been serving a lengthy prison sentence for extortion and murder (including the killing of parliamentarian Galina Starovoitova in 1998). Apparently in the hopes that Putin would eventually order his release, Kumarin denied ever knowing Putin.[38] But numerous sources, including Sobchak's daughter, Ksenia, have disputed Kumarin's claim. Ksenia Sobchak said on Dozhd' television in 2016: "Everybody knew Kumarin. I personally was there at several meetings when he was with Putin . . . I was a little girl and they [my father, Putin, and Kumarin] would be together at a table. This happened a lot." Pointing out that Kumarin would have a lot to reveal about Putin, Sobchak observed that Kumarin did not realize that Putin's decision to keep him behind bars would never change.[39]

The alliance that the St. Petersburg government forged with organized crime and the security services was on clear display when Ilya Traber, one of the city's most powerful mobsters, gained control of St. Petersburg's vital seaport—which handled all freight traffic for European Russia—and the city's oil terminal. Putin's support was crucial to Traber's efforts, because he issued licenses to Traber and his friend Gennadii Timchenko, reportedly a former employee of the KGB, which gave them a monopoly over oil exports through the oil terminal. The journalist Catherine Belton, who interviewed several of Traber's former associates for her book *Putin's People*, notes that the alliance between Traber and Putin "troubled even businessmen." Citing a former senior KGB official, Belton claims that "with the help of Putin's men in City Hall, the seaport became a major hub for smuggling drugs from Colombia into Western Europe."[40]

Traber was known in St. Petersburg as "the Antiquarian" because he made a fortune in the early 1990s as an antiques dealer. (One of his partners in that business was Putin's close friend Nikolai Shamalov, whose son would marry and later divorce Putin's daughter Katerina.) Dmitrii Zapol'skii recalled in a 2017 interview that the home of Sobchak and his wife Liudmila Narusova, which Zapol'skii visited, was filled with Traber's antiques.[41] Much later, Putin would also avail himself of Traber's talents. According to a 2017 investigation by Aleksei Navalny, Traber renovated a lavish secret island villa for Putin in the Gulf of Finland in 2011–13.[42]

In 2016, Spanish prosecutors issued an international arrest warrant against Traber as part of their investigation of money laundering by the

Tambov and Malyshev crime organizations. Later, during a 2018 trial of the ten-year money laundering case in Madrid, Traber, who was not a defendant because Spanish courts do not try people in absentia, was cited as a member of the Tambov group. He reportedly was so angry that he threatened the lead investigator, Jose Grinda, and his family with reprisals.[43]

In *Putinburg*, Zapol'skii provided his take on how the city operated with Putin and Sobchak at the helm: "In the early nineties, a new economic model of a gangster state emerged in St. Petersburg, under which any initiative immediately fell under the control of bandits and their curators in the special services. Not a single gangster, not a single organized crime group was able to emerge without the approval of authorized operative officers of the KGB and its successors." According to Zapol'skii, when Putin first assumed the role of Sobchak's deputy, he was viewed by the officers of the St. Petersburg security services with derision, because of his unimpressive KGB resume. But their opinion changed as Putin became "the supervisor who oversaw the flow of money and power in the swamp city of St. Petersburg."[44]

In moments of crisis, Putin turned to trusted friends from the "power organs"—the military, police, and security services. One such crisis occurred in October 1993, when Liudmila Putina was involved in a serious automobile accident. The Putins had been staying at their dacha in Zelenogorsk while their city apartment was being renovated. Katerina, age seven, was home sick but late in the morning persuaded her mother to drive her to school so she could appear in a school play. As Liudmila recalled, they had to rush to get there in time. Just as they were nearing the school, her car crossed an intersection and was hit broadside by another vehicle. Katerina had only bruises, but Liudmila was knocked unconscious and suffered extensive injuries, including spine and skull fractures.[45]

At the time of the accident, Putin was escorting Ted Turner and Jane Fonda around St. Petersburg. The pair was visiting the city because Turner was considering staging the 1994 Goodwill Games there. Fonda later recalled that when Putin told them his wife had been in an accident, Turner urged him to go to the hospital, but "Vladimir Putin wouldn't do it. He stayed with us."[46] Putin says in his autobiography that he went briefly to the hospital emergency room, where a doctor assured him that his wife would be fine, so he left without seeing her.[47]

Putin had already dispatched his aide Igor Sechin to the crash site to retrieve Katerina and that night he called on the prominent physician

Iurii Shevchenko to transfer Liudmila from the local hospital to the Military Medical Academy, where she had a spinal operation the next day.[48] After weeks of rehabilitation, Liudmila required further treatment that was not available in Russia. So Putin's friend Matthias Warnig, a former Stasi officer who had known Putin in Dresden and had recently opened the St. Petersburg branch of Dresdner Bank, helped out. Warnig got Dresdner Bank to pay for Liudmila to be airlifted to a clinic in Bad Homburg, Germany, as well as to cover some of her expenses there.[49] Warnig's good deed paid off. He later was invited to join the boards of Bank Rossiia and VTB Bank, along with those of the oil giant Rosneft and Rusal, the massive aluminum producer.[50]

As Liudmila Putina was recovering, the other driver involved, twenty-one-year-old Sergei Levkin, accused her of causing the accident by illegally going through an intersection at high speed. A prolonged legal battle ensued, lasting over two years. Finally, thanks to the efforts of a lead investigator with the St. Petersburg Department of Internal Affairs, the court ruled that Levkin was responsible for the accident. Although Levkin only received a suspended three-year sentence, he reportedly was ordered to pay Putin's wife fifteen million rubles (over $500,000) in damages.[51] Levkin's legal team was clearly no match for the resources Putin was able to muster.

Berezovsky Gets His Krysha

When it came to moneymaking, Berezovsky had no more scruples than Putin. He persuaded Petr Aven to double the customs duties on imported cars, which made domestic brands sold by LogoVAZ more popular. (Berezovsky promised Aven a share of LogoVAZ in return for the favor but in the end gave Aven only a six-month stint as a LogoVAZ consultant, driven to work in a white Mercedes.)[52] LogoVAZ also managed to buy large fleets of AvtoVAZ cars on consignment (with 10 percent down), repaying the company at the agreed ruble price more than two years later, when the rapidly declining ruble had become worth much less. As Hoffman observed, AvtoVAZ turned into a "gold mine" for Berezovsky, who later told Hoffman: "I understood one important thing. At that time, an enormous number of people wanted to buy cars. It didn't matter if they lacked an apartment. It didn't matter if they lacked clothes. *But if only there would be a car*!"[53]

In addition to the huge profits he was making with LogoVAZ, Berezovsky came up with a new venture, which took advantage of the privatization scheme introduced in 1992 by the state at the instigation of Anatoly Chubais, a member of Yeltsin's cabinet. Vouchers with a face value of ten thousand rubles were distributed to all Russians. They could then be exchanged for shares in the state companies that were being privatized or sold. Instead of creating millions of shareholders, the result was that the ownership of Russia's valuable property ended up in the hands of shrewd businessmen, who bought up vouchers and used them to acquire enterprises that were auctioned at bargain-basement prices. As Hoffman noted: "The voucher had opened a door, and beyond it was a wonderland of unregulated securities, surrogate money and wild finance, a period that was a perfect illustration of what happens when the market has no rules."[54]

Berezovsky's new scheme involved a company, the All-Russian Automobile Alliance, which he established with much fanfare in late 1993 to manufacture a "people's car" for domestic sale. Kadannikov, the respected director of AvtoVAZ, was chairman, and Berezovsky general director, of the company, which began issuing so-called bearers' certificates for public purchase at $10,000 each. Although similar to shares, the certificates did not include the holder's name, which it made it difficult to get future dividends, and trading it for a genuine share was discouraged. Nonetheless, between December 1993 and mid-1994, the public purchased $50 million worth of bearers' certificates. The project never got off the ground, and the proposed factory to produce the cars was never built.[55]

Like other powerful Russian businessmen, Berezovsky needed a *krysha* to protect him and his colleagues from the gang violence that had become an everyday occurrence in Russia. (Translated as "roof," *krysha* covered a wide range of services, including physical protection, settling disputes, and lobbying.) As Khinshtein pointed out, the automobile business was especially vulnerable to criminals: "In Togliatti [home of AvtoVAZ] not a single car could leave the gates of the factory unless local bandits received their percentage of sales."[56] In late 1993, after LogoVAZ parking lots were attacked several times and a grenade exploded in one of its show rooms, Berezovsky fled briefly to Israel, where he managed to get citizenship, although he had no intention of residing there permanently. Israel would become a safe haven for Berezovsky when things got rough in Russia.[57]

The root of the gang warfare was a conflict between Russia's two main criminal groups, the Chechens and the so-called Solntsevo gang, a Slavic group from the southwest part of Moscow. It was widely rumored that

Chechens with mafia ties were employed for the physical protection of Berezovsky and LogoVAZ and that Berezovsky's business partner Badri Patarkatsishvili, a Georgian, had contacts with the criminal underworld in the Caucasus.[58] But whatever the truth of the rumors, Berezovsky's security detail did not manage to prevent an attack that came close to killing him. (Berezovsky's precipitous conversion to Russian Orthodoxy, accompanied by a visit to Patriarch Aleksei two months earlier, did not protect him either.)[59] On June 7, 1994, Berezovsky was in the backseat of his Mercedes leaving LogoVAZ headquarters in central Moscow when a bomb exploded in a nearby parked car. His driver was killed, and his bodyguard lost an eye. Berezovsky's partner, Elena Gorbunova, was supposed to have accompanied Berezovsky in the car, but luckily, she had become impatient waiting at LogoVAZ for him to leave and departed on her own ten minutes earlier.[60] Berezovsky was so badly burned that he had to fly to Switzerland for several months of treatment. Those behind the attack were never found, but Berezovsky initially blamed it on competitors in the auto industry. (He would later falsely attribute the bombing to Vladimir Gusinsky, the television magnate, along with Gusinsky's political ally Moscow mayor Iurii Luzhkov.)[61]

Berezovsky already employed men from the former Ninth Directorate (guards) of the KGB, along with some Chechens, to provide security for him and LogoVAZ, but the bombing incident and his increasing public visibility apparently convinced him of the need for more extensive protection. A former MVD officer named Sergei Sokolov, who ran a security company called Atoll, claimed that he was hired to head Berezovsky's security detail in 1995. Sokolov was subsequently the source for a secret 1997 FSB report alleging that Atoll provided Berezovsky not only with physical protection but also with intelligence. According to the report, Sokolov received $1 million from Berezovsky for the purchase of sophisticated surveillance equipment to be used against commercial competitors and other opponents.[62] After Berezovsky became part of Yeltsin's entourage, media reports about Atoll spying on members of Yeltsin's family and government figures would cause a scandal and draw the attention of Russian law enforcement.

Berezovsky Penetrates Yeltsin's "Family"

By 1993, Berezovsky ambitions had extended beyond making money. Just as he had earlier discarded academic distinction for business success, Berezovsky now aspired for political influence. His lavish LogoVAZ

FIGURE 6.   Berezovsky meets with Yeltsin, 1994. TASS/ZUMApress.com.

Club on Novokuznetskaia Street in Moscow became the go-to meeting place for important politicians and businessmen, who would gather there to discuss the political and economic situation in the country and share meals at the club's restaurant. Alex Goldfarb, Berezovsky's close aide and friend, described the club: "A visit there was proof of one's status. The quality of the wine and the artistry of the chef were legendary . . . Over the bar, which also served as a waiting room, hung the first HDTV in Moscow. There was a white grand piano, played occasionally by one of Boris's old friends, an elderly Jew in a white suit. In the corner stood a stuffed crocodile, for reasons unknown."[63]

The consummate goal for Berezovsky was an entrée to Yeltsin and his inner circle. This opportunity came in late 1993, when, on the advice of Aven, a young journalist named Valentin Iumashev approached Berezovsky to inquire if he would be willing to finance the Russian publication of Yeltsin's second book, *Notes of a President* (Zapiski prezidenta), which Iumashev had ghostwritten. Iumashev, who later married Yeltsin's daughter Tatiana, was deputy editor of the journal *Ogonek*, which intended to publish the book, but lacked the necessary financing. Yeltsin's personal bodyguard at the time, Aleksandr Korzhakov, later told Paul Klebnikov that Iumashev brought Berezovsky to him, and he, Korzhakov, then introduced Berezovsky to Yeltsin. Berezovsky and AvtoVAZ chief Vladimir Kadannikov each contributed $250,000 to the publication of the book.[64]

The official launch of Yeltsin's book took place on June 12, 1994, just five days after the violent attack on Berezovsky, at the exclusive President's Club, which Berezovsky had been invited to join as a result of the book deal. He was the first businessman to be accepted into the club. Berezovsky, with his wounds painfully visible on his face and hands, decided to attend the celebration in order to demonstrate to the Russian president just how bad the violence had become. He succeeded in his purpose. Elena Gorbunova noted that "of course, Boris Nikolaevich was impressed."[65] According to another source, Yeltsin was horrified. Two days later, he signed a decree "On Urgent Measures to Protect the Population from Banditism and Other Manifestations of Organized Crime."[66]

The President's Club, at 42 Kosygin Street, featured tennis courts, where Yeltsin played regularly; a swimming pool; saunas; a bar; and a restaurant. Among the members were FSB chief Mikhail Barsukov and Yeltsin's bodyguard Korzhakov, along with a few of Yeltsin's favored advisors, businessmen, and cultural figures.[67] Berezovsky began to meet with Korzhakov there on a regular basis. By all accounts, Korzhakov, who was standing next to Yeltsin on a tank in August 1991 when Yeltsin and his followers thwarted the coup attempt and later wrote a self-serving book about his experience working for Yeltsin, had tremendous sway with the Russian president.[68] A former officer in the KGB's Ninth Directorate, Korzhakov had been Yeltsin's bodyguard since the late 1980s and had become his political advisor, gatekeeper, and tennis partner, as well as the monitor (some say abettor) of Yeltsin's prodigious alcohol consumption. Yeltsin recalled in his memoirs: "With each month and each year the political role of the Federal Guard Service, and specifically my chief bodyguard, Aleksandr Korzhakov, was growing. Korzhakov fought with everyone who didn't submit to his influence and anyone he considered 'alien.'"[69] Korzhakov became so powerful that, as Yeltsin wrote, in the spring of 1996, when Yeltsin's doctors expressed grave concerns about Yeltsin's heart and urged an operation, they sent their collective letter to Korzhakov, who did not show it Yeltsin until later.[70]

Berezovsky cultivated a close relationship with Korzhakov, but the latter turned out to be an unreliable and manipulative interlocutor, who would be fired by Yeltsin in 1996, in part at Berezovsky's instiga-tion. In a 2002 interview Berezovsky dismissed Korzhakov as a "court clown," who insinuated himself into Yeltsin's bodyguard so he could spy on Yeltsin for the KGB.[71] But in the mid-1990s Berezovsky, like everyone else in Russia's political and financial world, went to Korzha-kov when he needed something from the Kremlin.

In late 1994, Korzhakov helped Berezovsky persuade Yeltsin to priva-tize the state-owned Channel One and offer it to a group of financiers, including Berezovsky, without an auction. Berezovsky was able to con-solidate most of the shares and gain control of the new station, called by the acronym ORT, for *Obshchestvennoe rossiiskoe televidenie* (Public Russian Television). In order to resolve the conflicts among the exist-ing advertisers, who had been siphoning off profits from the state, Berezovsky decided to start from scratch and impose a three-month moratorium on advertising. The moratorium, which naturally aroused the ire of the advertisers, was announced on Channel One on Febru-ary 20, 1995, by Vladislav Listev, Russia's hugely popular television anchor, who was set to become the new executive director of ORT in April. Just days later, on March 1, 1995, the thirty-eight-year-old Listev was fatally gunned down in the stairwell of his Moscow apartment. The murder of the much-adored newscaster shook the country to its core.[72]

Berezovsky, who was in London with Russian Prime Minister Viktor Chernomyrdin at the time, flew home immediately on his private jet, only to learn that the police were about to search his office because he was a suspect in the murder. In mid-February, Berezovsky had met with two police officers, who introduced him to a stranger claiming to know the person responsible for the car bombing outside LogoVAZ. Berezovsky had paid the stranger $100,000 as a fee to prevent a further attempt to kill him, but apparently the payment was a setup, designed to frame him for the Listev murder. In fact, Berezovsky had his security men videotape the transaction and then handed the tape over to police. He later used this recording as part of the evidence he presented to Yeltsin in an appeal to successfully persuade the Russian president of his innocence.[73]

Although there were other suspects, including advertising execu-tive Sergei Lisovskii, the Listev killing was never solved, and the case was closed in 2009. Paul Klebnikov, in his highly critical 2001 biography of Berezovsky, elaborated on the theory that Berezovsky's $100,000 payment was evidence that he hired Listev's killers.[74] But Klebnikov suggested that Berezovsky's motive was Listev's declaration of a moratorium on Channel One's advertising, when in fact the moratorium was Berezovsky's decision, and Listev initially opposed the idea. Not surprisingly, after Berezovsky fled Russia in 2000, his guilt became widely accepted as fact in the country. As Russian journalist Aleksandr Politkovskii, husband of murdered journalist Anna Politkovskaya, noted in 2018: "Berezovsky became a fugitive, and it's always easy to blame a crime on a fugitive."[75] Significantly, in a 2021 interview, Listev's widow insisted that Berezovsky had nothing to do with the murder of her husband. She said there was never a conflict between Listev and Berezovsky and that the two had very cordial relations.[76]

The continuous intrigue and internecine conflict, often instigated by Korzhakov as Yeltsin descended into poor health and alcoholism, makes one wonder how the Kremlin even functioned at this time. The St. Petersburg government, of course, had its own share of dysfunction, with the city's crumbling infrastructure, corruption, and violence, but Putin was adept at managing the various clans that were competing for economic riches and political influence. Unlike Berezovsky, who was fighting enemies right and left, Putin had a solid "Petersburg team" (Sechin, Medvedev, Kudrin) he could depend on. He also retained his connections with invaluable former KGB colleagues like St. Petersburg FSB chief Viktor Cherkesov. That said, both he and Berezovsky faced the political uncertainty posed by the upcoming 1996 elections—Sobchak's run for re-election in St. Petersburg and Yeltsin's bid to retain the Russian presidency. These contests would prove crucial to the ambitions of Putin and Berezovsky as each sought to carve his path forward amid the tumult of Russian politics.

CHAPTER 3

Elections and Beyond

> Public opinion is being persuaded that it has only
> the option of a lesser evil, as if besides the "party
> of power" that wants to see Yeltsin re-elected and
> the Communist Party, there are no other forces
> able to rule Russia today.
>
> —Mikhail Gorbachev, July 1996, *Memoirs*

Just as Berezovsky was gaining a foothold in high-level Kremlin circles, the Yeltsin presidency began to unravel. By early 1996, Yeltsin had already had a series of heart attacks and was continuing to consume alcohol copiously, despite his doctors' warnings of the ill-effects on his health. According to Korzhakov, on the day of his first coronary, in July 1995, Yeltsin had shared with Mikhail Barsukov two liters of Cointreau—"a deathly dose of sugar for the pancreas"—to celebrate Barsukov's appointment as the new FSB chief.[1]

Although Yeltsin had been a hero in 1991, the Russian public was now disillusioned with his presidency. Despite—or because of—Yeltsin's reforms, the Russian economy was performing badly. The country's GDP remained in the negative, annual inflation was close to 100 percent, unemployment was rising, and disposable incomes continued to drop. Close to a quarter of the population was living below the poverty line, while Russia's wealthy elite was getting richer. The war in Chechnya, launched by the Kremlin in December 1994 because Yeltsin had come to believe that Chechnya's declared independence from Russia would lead to a breakup of the entire country, had been a complete fiasco. Contrary to the Kremlin's assumptions, the Russian military proved incapable of prevailing decisively against the militant separatists and ended up getting bogged down in a conflict that resulted in the deaths of at least six thousand Russian soldiers, along with an estimated hundred thousand Chechens. As Yeltsin biographer Timothy Colton noted, Yeltsin's military gambit might be compared with the Bay of Pigs, Vietnam, and Iraq, except that "the butchery and squalor seen on the television news were not in some distant land, but in a corner of Russia."[2]

The parliamentary elections in December 1995 reflected the public mood. The Communist Party of the Russian Federation (CPRF), led by Gennady Zyuganov, captured 22.3 percent of the proportional vote, while the ultranationalist Liberal Democratic Party received over 11 percent. The party whose formation Yeltsin had sponsored, Our Home Is Russia, led by Yeltsin's prime minister, Viktor Chernomyrdin, won only a little over 10 percent of the vote. Zyuganov was now considered the front-runner in the presidential race scheduled for June 1996. Yeltsin's deputy prime minister Anatoly Chubais, the force behind the effort to build market capitalism in Russia, had become a political liability, with the Communists even demanding that he be jailed on the grounds that he was selling off what rightfully belonged to the Russian people. In January 1996, at the urging of Korzhakov, Yeltsin fired Chubais. He also dismissed his liberal foreign affairs minister, Andrei Kozyrev, replacing him with the former foreign intelligence chief Evgeny Primakov, a hardliner who would soon ally himself with Yeltsin's opponents.

As Yeltsin himself later recalled, psychologically he reached a low point at the beginning of 1996: "Naina, my wife, was categorically opposed to my running for office again. I, too, felt as if the constant stresses were completely wearing me out and squeezing me dry. And perhaps for the first time in my life, I felt as if I were almost completely isolated politically. It wasn't just a question of my 3-percent approval rating in the polls . . . Rather, I stopped feeling the support of those with whom I had begun my political career, the people with whom I had embarked on the first parliamentary elections and then the presidential race."[3]

Berezovsky to the Rescue

But Yeltsin had not lost the support of the oligarchs, who were thrown into a panic over the prospect of a Communist winning the presidency. Berezovsky was attending the World Economic Forum in Davos, Switzerland, in early February 1996, when he had a conversation with George Soros, the Hungarian-born billionaire. The two had met when Berezovsky contributed $1.5 million to the Soros Foundation for

Russian scientists. Soros told Berezovsky that Yeltsin had no chance to win the election and advised Berezovsky to leave Russia before the Communists took over and he got killed.[4] Soros's words did not have the intended effect. Instead, they spurred Berezovsky into action on behalf of Yeltsin's candidacy. Having observed how Western politicians and CEOs at Davos were pandering to Zyuganov as if his election was assured, Berezovsky decided then and there to unite with fellow oligarchs at Davos so they would use their financial resources to turn the tide in favor of Yeltsin.

Berezovsky returned to his room at the Hotel Fluela and immediately phoned up one of Russia's wealthiest businessmen, Vladimir Gusinsky, who was at the same hotel, with an invitation for a drink. Berezovsky and Gusinsky had an intense rivalry. Gusinsky owned Most Bank, as well as the popular independent television station NTV, which was a competitor to Berezovsky's channel, ORT. In late 1994, Most Bank and AvtoVAZ Bank, in which Berezovsky had a significant share, had competed to provide banking services to the Russian airline Aeroflot. Thanks to Berezovsky's connections with the Kremlin, AvtoVAZ Bank had won out. Korzhakov claimed later that Berezovsky had spread poisonous gossip about Gusinsky, including allegations that Gusinsky was plotting with Moscow mayor Iurii Luzhkov to have Luzhkov replace

FIGURE 7.   Berezovsky and Vladimir Gusinsky, January 1998. East News.

Yeltsin as Russia's president. (Gusinsky was not helped by the fact that NTV was highly critical of the Kremlin's war in Chechnya, providing Korzhakov with an excuse to send his thugs to harass and threaten Gusinsky and his security team in December 1994.)[5]

Gusinsky needed little persuading before he consented to stop feuding with Berezovsky and join forces with him. As part of their agenda, the two agreed that the war in Chechnya had to be stopped and that Yeltsin needed to rein in both the military and the security services.[6] Berezovsky then invited other Davos oligarchs, including Mikhail Khodorkovsky of Menatep Bank and Vladimir Vinogradov of Inkombank, for a meeting, in which they decided to pool their financial assets in order to rescue Yeltsin's campaign. Also in attendance was Chubais, now jobless. Chubais was asked by the oligarchs to form an analytical group to advise Yeltsin's campaign in parallel to the group led by First Deputy Prime Minister Oleg Soskovets, Korzhakov, and FSB chief Barsukov that was officially in charge. According to Berezovsky, they turned to Chubais because the financial elite trusted him: "We knew that when he had been a civil servant he was completely honest with all of us. Perhaps this was the main thing—we never doubted his decency. Plus there's his intelligence, strength and organizational abilities. He was the only solid figure."[7] Thus, at Berezovsky's instigation, the so-called Davos pact was formed.

Of course, they first had to convince Yeltsin to go along with their plan. On his return to Moscow, Berezovsky contacted Viktor Iliushin, Yeltsin's trusted chief of staff, and asked him to arrange a meeting between the Russian president and the oligarchs. At the meeting, which took place at the Kremlin a few weeks after the Davos gathering, there were six businessmen in attendance—Berezovsky, Gusinsky, Vinogradov, Khodorkovsky, Vladimir Potanin, president of Uneximbank, and Aleksandr Smolensky of SBS-Agro (Stolichnyi) Bank—along with Chubais, who seems to have done most of the talking. Chubais explained to Yeltsin that his campaign was in dire straits, and he was sure to lose the election unless he energized his electoral operation with the involvement of the businessmen and Chubais himself. Yeltsin was at first defensive, telling the group that they had the wrong information, but in the end, he said to Chubais: "Anatoly Borisovich, I am grateful for your input."[8]

Following the meeting, Berezovsky had a short one-on-one talk with Yeltsin, which he had arranged through Yeltsin's wife, Naina, to iron out the details of the plan. Berezovsky also told Yeltsin that Korzhakov wanted the election to be called off because Yeltsin's chances were so low and warned Yeltsin that such a move might result in civil war.[9] Berezovsky's warnings about Korzhakov were soon borne out. On March 17, at the urging of Korzhakov and Soskovets, Yeltsin had his aides draft an operational plan to dissolve the Duma—which had just passed a resolution repealing the 1991 Belovezha Accords that marked the official end of the Soviet Union—as well as to postpone the presidential elections until 1998 and ban the Communist Party. Despite the strong objections of Anatolii Kulikov, minister of internal affairs, Yeltsin stuck with the plan until he was finally persuaded against it by his daughter Tatiana D'iachenko and Chubais, who argued fiercely with Yeltsin for an hour. Yeltsin recalled in his *Midnight Diaries*: "And finally I reversed a decision I had *almost* already made. To this day I am grateful to fate, and to Anatoly Borisovich Chubais and Tanya."[10]

The Chubais analytical group began operating at full force. Chubais, who was being paid a hefty salary of at least $50,000 a month by the oligarchs, recruited top-notch media specialists, political experts, and pollsters to determine which voters to focus on and how to craft the messages. Large sums of money were directed at television advertising, which played a crucial role in swaying voters toward Yeltsin, especially given the Zyuganov campaign's minimal television presence. According to some sources, the bulk of the money for the campaign did not come directly from the oligarchs but rather from a hidden scheme through which their banks purchased government bonds at a deep discount and resold them at market prices. The profits, or portions of them, were then used for Yeltsin's re-election.[11] Other sources say that the tycoons contributed to a "black treasury" for the campaign as payment for the 1995 loans-for-shares auctions they had been allowed to win and for future privatization deals.[12]

The Big Payoff

However the Yeltsin campaign was financed, its results were positive. In the first round of the presidential election, held on June 16, 1996, Yeltsin won 35 percent of the vote; Zyuganov, 32 percent; Aleksandr Lebed, a popular general, 15 percent; and liberal democrat Grigory Yavlinsky, 7 percent. But a second-round runoff between Yeltsin and Zyuganov had to be held, and in order to assure a Yeltsin win, the endorsement of Lebed was essential. Berezovsky had already met with Lebed in early May and promised that the Yeltsin team would secretly fund his campaign in order to siphon off votes from the Communist camp. Lebed also accepted Berezovsky's offer of a government post in exchange for endorsing Yeltsin after the first round of elections. According to Chubais, this offer was entirely Berezovsky's idea. As a result, on June 18, Lebed issued a statement of support for Yeltsin's candidacy, and Yeltsin announced that Lebed would be his new National Security Council secretary.[13]

The next day, June 19, Korzhakov made a bold move against the Chubais group, a move that would bring about his downfall. He had his security guards arrest two of Chubais's top campaign aides as they left the Russian White House with $50,000 in cash, supposedly to pay concert artists for campaign performances. Berezovsky was holding court at the LogoVAZ Club with Chubais, Gusinsky, and others when the group heard the news. According to NTV president Igor Malashenko, who was also present: "The two coolest heads, as usual, were Boris [Berezovsky] and Goose [Gusinsky]. They sat down with Chubais to review our assets."[14] Those assets included both NTV and ORT, which were put to good use, with broadcasts late that evening portraying the arrests as a coup attempt by the security services. As Berezovsky later recounted: "While deciding what to do, we formulated, for the first time, the following idea: we always lose to the security services if we act secretly. But as soon as we confront them openly, the situation will change."[15]

Berezovsky telephoned Tatiana D'iachenko, who arrived at 1 a.m. with Valentin Iumashev, her future second husband, and stayed at the club through the night, drinking coffee nonstop. Korzhakov's men were ominously surveilling the building, but the group figured rightly that they would not go so far as to enter with Yeltsin's daughter there. The next morning, Chubais went to see Yeltsin, who had been apprised of the situation but had slept through the night. Yeltsin immediately fired Korzhakov, Barsukov, and Soskovets in a nationally televised address.[16]

On July 3, 1996, Yeltsin was re-elected as Russia's president with 54 percent of the vote, versus Zyuganov's 40 percent. But in the meantime, on June 26, he had suffered a severe heart attack, which was kept secret from the public, and would be semi-incapacitated for the next several months. This meant that, with Korzhakov finally out of the picture, decisions would be made by the Family—a term used in Russian political parlance to describe Yeltsin's team, composed of Tatiana, Iumashev, and his close advisors. On July 16, Yeltsin brought Chubais back to the Kremlin as chief of the Presidential Administration, while Chernomyrdin remained prime minister.

Had it not been for Berezovsky's successful efforts to get financial backing for Yeltsin's campaign from Russian businessmen and the favorable coverage of Yeltsin on ORT and NTV, Yeltsin would probably have lost his bid for re-election. As the editor of *Ekho Moskvy* (Echo of Moscow), Aleksei Venediktov, later observed: "Berezovsky knew how to unite people who could not unite . . . And so, in Davos, he included the outcast Chubais . . . Berezovsky's contribution to the election of Yeltsin in 1996, as the organizer of these people, was enormous."[17] Even Chubais, who would soon fall out with Berezovsky, grudgingly acknowledged years later: "Of course, Berezovsky's magnetism was colossal. His vivid, strong intellect, his instant reactions, his ability to generate original solutions . . . He played one of the most important, if not the key, roles in the 1996 elections."[18]

On the night the results of the second round of the election were counted, members of the campaign staff went to the LogoVAZ Club. Naina Yeltsina was also there, and they celebrated until early morning. While sitting on the open veranda with Tatiana and Iumashev, Berezovsky poured himself a glass of brandy and took a sip. When he put the glass down on the table, it suddenly shattered into tiny pieces. Berezovsky mused later: "I don't believe in mysticism, but I believe that so much energy had built up over these months, that it suddenly burst out, and broke this glass."[19]

Defeat for Putin's Boss

Despite Sobchak's support for Yeltsin during the August 1991 coup attempt, as well as during the October 1993 storming of the Russian parliament, he was viewed with suspicion by the Russian president, who sidelined Sobchak politically after the coup plotters were defeated. Yeltsin's coolness toward Sobchak was in large part a result of his concern about Sobchak's political ambitions. The handsome, telegenic Sobchak was a member of the intelligentsia, who dressed smartly and spoke eloquently. He and his attractive, self-confident wife, Liudmila Narusova, interacted easily with foreign dignitaries and clearly enjoyed the limelight. (According to one source, Narusova became a liability for Sobchak, because "she acted more like Raisa Gorbachev than Naina Yeltsina.")[20] Yeltsin, a former construction worker with a lot of rough edges, resented Sobchak mingling with Western leaders, especially after word reached him that Sobchak questioned his competence and wanted to run for president himself.[21]

Not surprisingly, Korzhakov, ever resourceful, had intervened, at one point calling the head of Sobchak's security detail, Viktor Zolotov, to say "don't work with Sobchak anymore. We know what he's up to."[22] Zolotov, a fellow veteran of the KGB's Ninth Directorate, did not comply. In 1995, Korzhakov arranged for the appointment of a new prosecutor general, Iurii Skuratov, who agreed to investigate Sobchak for corruption. Sobchak, meanwhile, had made it clear that he would not compete with Yeltsin for the Russian presidency but would run for governor (the renamed mayoral post) of St. Petersburg in the May 1996 election. But Korzhakov and his cronies, including Barsukov and Soskovets, lent their support to Sobchak's competitor, Vladimir Iakovlev, and undermined Sobchak by publicizing the fact that he was under criminal investigation.[23]

Their efforts did considerable damage to Sobchak's image, already problematic because of his difficulty in communicating with working-class voters. Also, Sobchak spent so much time either traveling abroad or hosting international festivals and exhibitions at home that he did not accomplish a great deal to improve the lot of the average *piterskie* (inhabitants of St. Petersburg). The St. Petersburg writer Mikhail Vil'kobrisskii, recalled once hearing the mayor give a report at the Union of Industrial Enterprises: "The only completed investment project for that year was the second phase of the construction and commissioning of a crematory. During this era of economic reform, the death rate went up, and there was no money for burials, so the city authorities found an adequate solution."[24]

Contrary to what some of his biographers have written, Putin did not run Sobchak's re-election campaign. He assumed Sobchak's mayoral duties so the latter could devote himself fully to his re-election. As a former member of Sobchak's campaign staff recalled: "Putin was entrusted with the management of the city. He did not have time to do anything else, which is why his participation in the election campaign was so minimal."[25] Putin confirmed this in the documentary film produced by Ksenia Sobchak: "Sobchak made it clear that he did not want his staff involved in his campaign. He said 'I have a campaign team who will run my campaign. You just keep doing your jobs.'"[26]

Sobchak's wife, Narusova, took charge of her husband's re-election bid, along with Aleksandr Prokhorenko, a former professor at Leningrad State University and a member of the St. Petersburg Legislative Assembly. By all accounts, they were not up to the task. The campaign was completely disorganized and ran out of money—a sharp contrast to Vladimir Iakovlev's campaign, which was flush with cash from supporters in Moscow and able to hire professional consultants. Putin later said that after the first round on May 19, 1996, when Sobchak emerged with 28 percent of the vote and Iakovlev 21 percent, he and Aleksei Kudrin tried to "jump into the fray, but by then it was hopeless."[27] In the June 2 runoff, which followed an exceedingly poor performance by Sobchak in a televised debate between the two contenders, Iakovlev had the support of Communists and nationalists who lost in the first round. He defeated Sobchak, with 47.5 percent of the vote to Sobchak's 45.8 percent. Narusova later admitted that it had been a mistake for her to run her husband's campaign and explained: "My logic was this: if Tatiana D'iachenko could take a key role in Yeltsin's campaign, then why was I any worse?"[28]

Putin claimed that he called Iakovlev a "judas" for running against Sobchak and portrayed himself as a solid supporter of the incumbent mayor.[29] As chairman of the St. Petersburg branch of the pro-Kremlin party Our Home Is Russia, he also sent a letter to Yeltsin, Skuratov, and Chernomyrdin protesting Skuratov's investigation of Sobchak.[30] But Dmitrii Zapol'skii, who was helping the Sobchak effort, recalled Putin's role differently: "Rumors that Putin had animosity toward Iakovlev are false. I repeatedly heard from both Iakovlev and Putin that Putin never considered Iakovlev a traitor, and Iakovlev valued Putin's skills."[31] According to Zapol'skii, Putin and his allies in the mayor's office actually ended up privately switching their support to Iakovlev. Zapol'skii remembers being called to Putin's office on a Saturday morning to lend a hand late in the campaign. Putin, Aleksei Kudrin, and Igor Sechin had already been there for several hours. Zapol'skii was surprised by what he observed: "Sobchak's staff was not nervous because Sobchak might lose. No, they were worried that he would win." He concluded that "there was a higher command [from the Kremlin]: drown Sobchak."[32] A former Putin associate in St. Petersburg said much the same thing to journalist Catherine Belton years later: "It's totally possible that Putin was following the orders of the Kremlin . . . If you supposed that this was a special operation to liquidate Sobchak as a contender, then everything becomes clear."[33]

In a 1999 book about his campaign, Sobchak barely mentions Putin, except to defend him: "Putin, throughout this whole story, showed himself to be a highly decent person. He not only did not betray me, like many others, but also came to my defense and sent a letter to the highest authorities . . . protesting the rumors and slander against Sobchak."[34]

Did Sobchak really believe that Putin was loyal to him? Or, with Putin rumored to be Yeltsin's designated successor by this time, was Sobchak simply trying to stay on Putin's good side?

A Move to Moscow

Putin says in his autobiography that his relations with Iakovlev "didn't deteriorate" because of the election campaign and that Iakovlev even offered to have him stay on as his deputy governor. Putin declined the offer because he had signed a statement saying he would leave the St. Petersburg government if Sobchak lost.[35] But there might have been another reason for Putin's refusal. Zapol'skii claimed that Putin had been assured by members of Yeltsin's team that his future would be taken care of: "I think that at the time Putin already knew that if Anatolii Aleksandrovich [Sobchak] lost, he [Putin] would receive a very sweet job in the Presidential Administration—oversight of foreign property. And this meant colossal, huge money. This position was already reserved for him."[36]

In fact, the exact nature of Putin's promised post in Moscow was not determined until two months after the gubernatorial election. When Chubais was appointed to head the Presidential Administration in July 1996, he rescinded his predecessor's offer to make Putin a deputy chief of staff on the grounds that the proposed position no longer existed. (This may have been why Putin seemed to disparage Chubais in his autobiography, saying "he's so hard-nosed, like a Bolshevik.")[37] Chubais then left it up to Kudrin, newly appointed to run the president's Main Control Directorate, to find another spot for Putin. With the help of his friend Aleksei Bolshakov, a first deputy prime minister, Kudrin got Pavel Borodin, head of the President's Administrative Directorate, to bring Putin on board as his subordinate in August 1996.[38]

Whatever Putin's role in Sobchak's defeat, Yeltsin had other reasons to want Putin on his team. During his time in the mayor's office, Putin gained valuable experience in dealing with private businesses in Russia and abroad and with the mafia clans that controlled many of these enterprises. Also, his extensive ties with the law enforcement, security, and military bodies were a huge plus for the Yeltsin government. As Putin told his biographer Blotskii: "I was not the top leader in the city, but I must say that the sphere of my duties was very broad. In addition, I worked closely with the power organs, with all of them. As a result, I know all about them from the inside, thoroughly. And this is the greatest experience!"[39] For members of Yeltsin's administration having someone on their team with direct lines of communication to these bodies, as well as many years of service in the KGB, would be an important benefit.

The confirmation of Putin's appointment came at an opportune time. Just days earlier, on August 12, the Putins' dacha had burned to the ground as a result of a faulty heater in the sauna. Putin made a dramatic rescue of his daughter Maria and his secretary, who was visiting with her husband for the night, from the second floor of the dacha. He lost a briefcase containing the family's savings, $5,000, in the fire. But Putin prevailed on the builders to reconstruct the dacha at no cost, and his wife took the blow philosophically: "After that experience, I realized that houses, money and things shouldn't add stress to your life. They aren't worth it. You know why? Because at any minute, they could all just burn up."[40]

On their arrival in Moscow in mid-August, the Putins took up residence in a government-owned apartment in the same high-rise building as Kudrin and his family. According to Kudrin: "Vladimir Vladimirovich often came to visit us, as neighbors, with his daughters. The girls played with my Labrador. I think that's why they got Koni [Putin's Labrador] for themselves."[41] An acquaintance of Putin and Sechin, whom Putin brought to Moscow as his deputy, reported that Putin was unhappy when he found out that Sechin's apartment was 317 square meters, while his was only 286. But there was no question that the move to Moscow enhanced the Putins' lifestyle. That winter they would spend several weeks skiing in Davos, together with the family of Nikolai Shamalov, the future father-in-law of his daughter Katerina.[42]

Managing Kremlin Property

Putin's new boss, Pavel Borodin, was a former Communist Party apparatchik, who had been mayor of Yakutsk before joining the Yeltsin administration in 1993. Borodin had met Putin in St. Petersburg on a couple of occasions, but he was reportedly unenthusiastic about bringing Putin on board because of his known connections with the security services.[43] As for Putin, in one early interview he gushed about Borodin: "Frankly speaking, for me personally, the first phone call from Borodin was amazing. I did not expect it! Yes, we discussed immediate questions. And nothing more. But the fact that he showed attention, concern, was unexpected. That I did not expect, such a call from Borodin!"[44]

After assuming his post, which included managing all Kremlin property, Borodin became known for playing fast and loose with those assets—vast real estate holdings, factories, aircraft, art, and palaces, valued at over $600 billion. According to Yeltsin biographer Timothy Colton: "Borodin spent the next six years on Yeltsin's behalf meting out perks—offices, apartments and dachas, travel and vacation vouchers, hospital stays, and even books and cellphones—to lawmakers, bureaucrats and judges."[45] Borodin bragged many years later that his department eventually had ninety-six thousand employees and an annual budget of $2.5 billion.[46]

Just as Putin was starting his new job, Borodin's department awarded a contract for renovating the Kremlin without competitive bidding to a company called Mercata, a filial of the Swiss construction firm Mabetex, which had earlier won construction contracts in Yakutsk when Borodin was mayor there. In 1999, Borodin would become the focus of a money-laundering and bribery investigation by Swiss prosecutors, who revealed that the cost of the vast renovation was overvalued by

FIGURE 8.   Pavel Borodin, September 1998. AP photo/Ivan Sekretarev.

30 percent, which was siphoned off by Borodin and his cronies and deposited in Swiss bank accounts.[47]

Putin's responsibilities included overseeing contractual and legal affairs relating to the Kremlin's properties abroad. Felipe Turover—a young official in the Banca del Gottardo, which held the Swiss accounts of Mabetex and later assisted Swiss prosecutors in their investigation of Borodin—told *Novaia gazeta* in a December 1999 interview that, when Putin got his hands on all these vast holdings, he created front companies to retain the assets: "Thus property abroad was thoroughly plucked before the state got its hands on it."[48] Turover's allegations were never verified and, luckily for Putin, he left Borodin's Administrative Directorate in March 1997, before the Mabetex scandal broke. He was replaced in his post by his deputy Sergei Chemezov, a KGB colleague from Dresden.

Berezovsky in the Limelight

Around the time that Putin arrived in Moscow, Berezovsky was in Chechnya with Security Council secretary Aleksandr Lebed, conducting peace talks with members of the Chechen separatist movement, led by Aslan Maskhadov, a military commander. On August 30, 1996, after hours of negotiations, Lebed and Maskhadov signed a peace agreement in Khasavyurt, Dagestan, near the Chechen border. The agreement, which provided for the withdrawal of Russian troops by the end of the year and deferred the question of Chechen independence until the end of 2001, paved the way for the signing of a formal treaty by Yeltsin and Maskhadov in the Kremlin in May 1997. Berezovsky later said that he had opposed the terms of the peace that Lebed negotiated, but after a few months of further meetings with Chechens, he realized that "Lebed had made the right decision and we had to retreat in order to get our act together, to take a new approach to solving the problem at its new stage."[49] As for the Chechen leaders, Akhmad Kadyrov, who would later become the republic's president, credited Berezovsky with stopping the war and saving Chechens from genocide.[50]

Russian military leaders and MVD chief Anatolii Kulikov, whose internal troops had a large presence in Chechnya, were furious over the Khasavyurt Accords. In his 2002 memoirs, published just after Lebed was killed in a helicopter crash, Kulikov called Lebed a traitor who surrendered Russia to terrorists.[51] But the Russian people were largely supportive of the peace. Indeed, Lebed enjoyed such a boost in popularity that he even started alluding to himself as a possible successor to

Yeltsin and in a late September interview suggested that Yeltsin should cede power to his prime minister until after his planned heart surgery in November. This did not go down well with Yeltsin's team, including Berezovsky. Soon television channels ORT and NTV, which had been portraying Lebed as a hero, did an about-face and began linking Lebed with fascist organizations. Kulikov, capitalizing on the displeasure Lebed's political ambitions were causing the Kremlin, gave a press conference on October 16 in which he accused Lebed of plotting to seize power by means of a special "Russian Legion," a military force that would be directly under the National Security Council. The next day Yeltsin announced Lebed's dismissal. Chubais later recalled that, before Yeltsin's announcement, the government had beefed up security around the Kremlin, including armored personnel carriers, to an extent not seen since the arrest of Stalin's police chief Lavrenty Beria in June 1953.[52]

Berezovsky was a direct beneficiary of this latest round of internecine Kremlin conflict. He wisely sided with Chubais and Chernomyrdin in urging Lebed's removal, mainly because Lebed had teamed up with his enemy Korzhakov and endorsed Korzhakov's candidacy for the Duma as a delegate from Tula. As a result, Berezovsky was rewarded with the post of deputy secretary of Russia's Security Council at the end of October 1996. Yeltsin had already appointed Ivan Rybkin, former speaker of the Duma and dependably loyal to the Kremlin, to replace Lebed as head of that body. Berezovsky, as Rybkin announced, was put in charge of the "financial interaction" with Chechnya. But, given that the state treasury was bare, Berezovsky would have to encourage the Russian private sector and foreign businessmen to invest in the turmoil-fraught republic.[53]

As Yeltsin's former son-in-law Leonid D'iachenko noted in 2021, Berezovsky's goal was "to provide the Chechens with special economic opportunities in exchange for formal loyalty to Moscow and rejection of the idea of secession from Russia." This entailed direct interactions with Chechen leaders, a dangerous challenge for Berezovsky. In the words of D'iachenko: "The military and special services were involved in Chechnya. But there was an urgent need for a civilian who was able to 'sort out' questions and not be afraid to bring information unpleasant for the Chekists and the military to the very top. This person, moreover, had to have the personal courage to actually go to Chechnya, to negotiate in the very den of the bandits . . . The chance to get shot or become a prisoner was real for Berezovsky. After all, he often traveled without serious protection. Yes, he knew many influential Chechens. But was this a guarantee?"[54]

Although Berezovsky's appointment to the Security Council was an affirmation from the Yeltsin government of his value as an advisor and negotiator, he still felt the need to blow his own horn. When interviewed by *The Financial Times* at the beginning of November 1996, he foolishly bragged that he and six other businessmen—Potanin, Gusinsky, Khodorkovsky, Smolensky, Aven, and Fridman—controlled 50 percent of the Russian economy (a gross exaggeration) and credited his group with engineering Yeltsin's re-election. He also made it clear that he and other moguls used their television and newspaper ownerships to advance their own agendas. Even worse, *The Financial Times* went on to quote Chubais as having said: "They [the leading businessmen] steal and steal and steal. They are stealing absolutely everything, and it is impossible to stop them."[55]

Not surprisingly, *The Financial Times* piece gave Berezovsky's detractors (and there were many) an opportunity to disparage him. *The St. Petersburg Times* noted: "Berezovsky's track record as a Russian businessman . . . has not been distinguished by success managing companies," and quoted Andrei Piontkovsky, at the time director of the Moscow Center for Strategic Studies: "Berezovsky has earned his wealth, not thanks to capitalism, but thanks to the existence of bureaucrats who sign the documents he needs."[56] The next month, *Forbes* magazine came out with a scathing profile of Berezovsky, portraying him as "a powerful gangland boss" who collaborated with Chechen criminals and was the prime suspect in the Listev murder. The article, which was unsigned, also claimed, falsely, that Berezovsky's partner Nikolai Glushkov had been convicted of theft in 1982.[57] Berezovsky and Glushkov sued *Forbes* for libel in a London court and in 2003 won a retraction from the magazine as well as payment of legal fees. According to Berezovsky, the Russian security services, together with Korzhakov, had furnished the material for the article, whose author was revealed to be Paul Klebnikov. Klebnikov's biography of Berezovsky, *Godfather of the Kremlin*, was published in 2000.[58]

Business under the Table

Whatever falsehoods were said about Berezovsky, it cannot be denied that he profited financially from backroom deals with Kremlin associates. The story of Sibneft is a good example. In 1995, Berezovsky began a collaboration with a twenty-nine-year-old oil trader named Roman Abramovich, whom he met while cruising the Caribbean on Petr Aven's yacht in December 1994. Abramovich proposed to Berezovsky that the two of them partner in creating a vertically integrated oil company, combining production and refining, which came to be called Sibneft. Although he had no experience with oil, Berezovsky liked the idea and took it to Korzhakov, Yeltsin's daughter Tatiana, and Prime Minister Chernomyrdin, who gave their support because Berezovsky told them he would use his oil profits to fund the television channel ORT, an essential asset for Yeltsin's presidential campaign. Despite the difference in their ages, Berezovsky and Abramovich soon became close, seeing each other almost daily. Berezovsky's partner Elena Gorbunova and Abramovich's then wife Irina became friends, and the two families went on holidays together during the years 1995–98.[59]

Sibneft was officially created by a presidential decree in August 1995 and, thanks to Berezovsky's lobbying, was included in the loans-for-shares auction at the end of December. After other bidders were persuaded to either withdraw or offer lower amounts, Berezovsky and

FIGURE 9. Berezovsky and Roman Abramovich, June 2000. TASS Archive/Diomedia.

Abramovich won, with a bid of $100.3 million, the right to provide a loan to the Russian government secured by 51 percent of Sibneft stock. Through subsequent cash auctions in 1996 and 1997, the two men, along with Patarkatsishvili, gained a controlling interest of 89 percent in Sibneft. Abramovich would later claim that in fact Berezovsky and Patarkatsishvili never acquired shares in Sibneft and were only facilitators of the deal. Their dispute would be argued in a much-publicized 2011–12 trial in a London court.[60]

Another of Berezovsky's financial schemes would also feature in a subsequent London court case, this time as a result of criminal charges by Russian authorities who pursued Berezovsky in exile. Sometime in 1994, Berezovsky set his sights on profits from the Russian airline Aeroflot and used his clout with the Kremlin to get the airline to transfer its accounts to AvtoVAZ Bank, which also handled LogoVAZ accounts and listed Berezovsky as a major shareholder. Then, as Berezovsky all but admitted in an interview with *Kommersant*, he engineered the 1995 appointment of the malleable Marshal Evgenii Shaposhnikov, a former defense minister, as director-general of Aeroflot and managed to get several high-level LogoVAZ employees hired to work under him. Among them was Glushkov, who joined Aeroflot in late 1995 as first deputy director for finance.[61]

Aeroflot had a lot of problems when Glushkov took over its finances. Not only was its fleet of aircraft decrepit; proceeds from ticket sales trickled into hundreds of foreign bank accounts that belonged to 150 regional offices. Even worse, much of the revenue was siphoned off by staff at Aeroflot offices, almost a third of whom were intelligence and FSB officers. Glushkov and Berezovsky wanted to transform Aeroflot into a Western-style company with a centralized payment system, so in June 1996, Shaposhnikov directed all Aeroflot offices abroad to send their revenues to a Swiss company called Andava, which would serve as a deposit center. Because injections of Western capital were needed, along with expertise in organizing loans, another Swiss firm, Forus, was enlisted as a financial consultant to Aeroflot and an intermediary with foreign banks. The firm became the depository for payments to Aeroflot by foreign airlines for flights over Russian territory.[62]

The optics were bad, to say the least. Berezovsky and Glushkov had set up Forus in 1992 as a financial company trading currencies and, although Glushkov assigned his Forus shares to Berezovsky before assuming his Aeroflot post, he continued to be on Forus's board of directors. Both men also had substantial shares in Andava, established in 1994 as a centralized treasury for AvtoVAZ. Interviewed four years later, Glushkov said rather lamely: "Back at that time we did realize that the situation might look dubious, but it was okay from the viewpoint of Aeroflot's business interests." According to Glushkov, Aeroflot's operations became profitable, with its stock rising from $7 to $150 a share by 1998, and passenger turnover increased by nearly a million.[63]

Not surprisingly, the Russian security services were unhappy with the remaking of Aeroflot. A source of easy money for their employees had been cut off. Glushkov recalled later that Korzhakov "said he would screw my head off and put me in jail . . . if I continued to violate the rights of the FSB."[64] In 1999, after foreign intelligence chief Evgeny Primakov became Russian prime minister, a criminal investigation would be launched into Aeroflot's finances. Allegations of fraud against Berezovsky and Glushkov persisted for years, as did litigation, until finally a British court put them to rest in 2018, with the judge concluding that there was no evidence the two had misappropriated funds from Aeroflot.[65]

In 1997, Russian political analyst Lilia Shevtsova described the Russian political regime as a system based on personalized, paternalistic rule, rather than on collective decision making, which even the totalitarian Soviet regime had practiced. Powerful political insiders, she wrote, were weakening legitimate political institutions and creating a "shadow politics," hidden from the public, and this provided "fertile soil for the corruption of power and the criminalization of politics." The regime depended on the loyalty of the president's entourage and the power structures, rather than on public support. Yeltsin "won a democratic election, but only in the guise of a pitifully sick man, providing a smoke-screen for the clans clashing behind his back."[66]

Ominously, Shevtsova observed that the security services and police were now more powerful than they had been in Soviet times. She was describing the perfect storm for the emergence of an authoritarian leader who would gain public confidence as a spokesperson for popular interests, while undergirding his power with the crucial support of the security and law enforcement agencies. The groundwork had been laid for Putin's future presidency.

CHAPTER 4

Behind Kremlin Walls

> As the Kremlin brotherhood grew accustomed
> to armored limousines and official bodyguards,
> to having every door open for them and no one
> monitoring their behavior, they lost all sense
> of limits. They began discrediting potential
> opponents and economic rivals: as in Soviet times,
> only the servile survived.
>
> —Lilia Shevtsova, *Putin's Russia*

Following his heart operation in November 1996, Yeltsin remained in the hospital until the end of December and then was hospitalized again in January because of pneumonia. He would continue to have periodic health crises until he left office. According to Yeltsin's former press secretary Sergei Medvedev, after 1996 Yeltsin was "a completely different person and a completely different president: sick, old—in essence, broken-down and passive."[1] Although Timothy Colton insists that Yeltsin's ill health was exaggerated by the media, he concedes that Yeltsin's trademark "swagger and stamina" were gone, and "he was given to verbal faux pas and dizzy spells."[2] Yeltsin himself admitted in his memoirs how much he had declined: "I was already a different 'I,' a different Boris Yeltsin. I had suffered a lot, as if I had returned from the land of the dead. I couldn't go on solving problems as I used to, by mustering all my physical strength or charging head-on into sharp political clashes. That wasn't for me anymore."[3] Yeltsin would continue to make the major decisions, but he relied increasingly on his daughter Tatiana and Valentin Iumashev as intermediaries and purveyors of information.

Berezovsky had never been in the habit of going to Yeltsin directly when he needed something; he consulted instead with Iumashev and more often Tatiana, whom he addressed using the familiar form of you (*ty*), or even as "Taniusha." According to Boris Nemtsov, "Berezovsky sat for hours in the offices of either Valia [Iumashev] or Tatiana, and, as a modern-day Rasputin, exerted an almost mystical influence."[4] By all accounts, Tatiana was receptive to Berezovsky and valued his opinions, but on occasion, he crossed a line and sparked her anger. Thus, in March 1997, Yeltsin decided to recruit Nemtsov, the charismatic and highly capable thirty-eight-year-old governor of Nizhnii Novgorod, as first deputy premier, alongside Chubais. Yeltsin dispatched Tatiana to persuade Nemtsov, who had signaled to Chubais that he was reluctant to join the Yeltsin government. But, as Nemtsov later recalled, Berezovsky beat Tatiana to the punch, flying by plane to Nizhnii Novgorod to inform Nemtsov that he, Berezovsky, had decided to appoint him first deputy premier. Later Tatiana arrived after a seven-hour drive and was livid to learn that Berezovsky had just been there. "You should have seen her face," Nemtsov wrote. "She screamed with indignation about how that devil Berezovsky had listened in on the conversation about my appointment, jumped on a plane, and flew to Nizhnii. And she had driven by car."[5]

Good Cop/Bad Cop

At this point Putin was still a relatively minor player in Kremlin affairs and may not have even met Tatiana, although he had interacted with Iumashev, who replaced Chubais as chief of staff when the latter became first deputy prime minister in March 1997. Chubais selected fellow St. Petersburger Aleksei Kudrin as deputy minister of finance to serve under him, which left vacant Kudrin's position as head of the Main Control Directorate (GKU). Kudrin, who would eventually be referred to as "the personal accountant of the president," recommended to Iumashev that Putin be his replacement. Putin portrayed the move as a welcome change, although he had been working under Borodin for only seven months. He told Kudrin that he found the job boring: "It was not my thing. It was not lively work in comparison with what I had done in Petersburg. Yes, Petersburg was not the center, not the capital, but the work there was of a different quality, more energetic."[6] Putin may also have had an inkling that Borodin was headed for trouble.

Putin's past employment in the KGB proved useful in his new post. The GKU was the government's financial watchdog, tasked with oversight of business sectors and government bodies to ensure that malfeasance was not occurring with state funds. This meant that the GKU had access to vast amounts of sensitive financial information, which it was authorized to pass on to law enforcement officials and prosecutors. Putin became a point man between the Kremlin and the security and law enforcement bodies. In May 1997, Putin told journalist Elena Tregubova that Yeltsin had given his office a mandate to fight corruption in the Ministry of Defense and large state-owned enterprises and agencies. Special teams of employees from the GKU, the FSB, MVD, and Ministry of Finance were scrutinizing the budgets of these powerful bodies for possible corruption.[7]

Putin tackled his new job with apparent zeal. Within two months he had examined the budgets of a third of the country's eighty-nine regions and republics and charged 260 officials with infractions. By the next September, he had disciplined 450 officials for budgetary abuse. But, as Myers noted, he was careful not to step on toes: "Putin learned quickly that service in the Kremlin required delicacy and discretion in interpreting how far to take his investigations."[8] Thus Putin covered up a scandal involving the notoriously corrupt former defense minister Pavel Grachev (known as Pasha Mercedes), who was accused of complicity in the illegal transfer of weaponry, because Grachev knew too many Kremlin secrets.

Nemtsov recalled that Putin once sent him information suggesting that there was corruption among people working for Chubais and ended with the comment "I report at your discretion." Nemtsov telephoned Putin: "You wrote that Chubais is a thief, and everyone around him is a swindler. In that case, you should have concluded 'I think that it is necessary to initiate criminal proceedings.' Instead, I see a strange phrase: 'I report at your discretion.' What am I to make of this?" Putin responded without a pause: "You are the boss, you decide." "A classic example of the behavior of a security officer," Nemtsov concluded. "In general, he was not noted for anything scandalous, but he did not manage to do anything outstanding either."[9] In fact, Putin seems to have wisely grasped that such cautious behavior was the only way to survive—and get ahead—in the highly dysfunctional and unpredictable Kremlin. Such wisdom eluded the mercurial Berezovsky.

Putin's seeming cautiousness did not mean that he lacked ambition. Quite the contrary. He had already decided that, in keeping up with other members of the Kremlin elite, he needed to finally get a higher degree. Putin says in his autobiography that in 1990 he began work on a dissertation at LSU, when he was still employed by the KGB: "I chose a topic in the field of international private law and began to draft an outline for my work."[10] But nothing came of it. Then, suddenly, in 1997 he produced a 218-page dissertation, titled "Strategic Planning of the Reproduction of the Mineral Resource Base of a Region under Conditions of the Formation of Market Relations: St. Petersburg and Leningrad Region" and was awarded a candidate of economic science degree (slightly lower academically than a US PhD) by the St. Petersburg Mining Institute.[11]

How could Putin, who never attended the Mining Institute, have found time to do the required research and writing on this completely new subject? According to Olga Litvinenko, the daughter of Vladimir Litvinenko, who was rector of the Mining Institute, her father wrote Putin's dissertation. The production of dissertations was a lucrative business, she said, which Vladimir Litvinenko and other faculty members used to supplement their modest salaries. The standard price for a candidate's thesis was around thirty thousand euros, but Putin had helped her father get his position as rector in 1994, so he may not have been charged. Olga, who later became estranged from her father, claimed that she was with him at their dacha when he put together Putin's dissertation during the summer of 1997. She recalled that he brought a photocopier to the dacha and spent most of the time copying pages from books and cutting and pasting them onto blank A4 sheets, occasionally adding his written commentary. Putin did not make an appearance at the dacha to see how things were going, but he did show up to successfully defend his dissertation after being given prepared remarks.[12]

Several of those who worked with Putin in Sobchak's office also received higher degrees from the Mining Institute. Among them was Igor Sechin, who would eventually serve as Putin's top advisor when the latter became president. A former intelligence officer, Sechin was educated as a philologist specializing in French and Portuguese, but he wrote his 1998 dissertation on the economics of oil pipelines. (He later became head of the Russian oil company Rosneft.) Viktor Zubkov, a future prime minister (2007–8) defended his dissertation in 2000 on the subject of the taxation of Leningrad mineral resources. As *The Insider* wryly observed of Putin and his St. Petersburg colleagues: "All of them, regardless of their education, suddenly became specialists in the field of mineral resources of the Leningrad region."[13]

Putin's dissertation went largely unnoticed until 2005, when two researchers at the Brookings Institution in Washington, DC, managed to get a copy from a Moscow library. They found that in the key section

FIGURE 10. Putin awarded honorary membership in the Faculty of Law, St. Petersburg State University, January 2000. Yuri Kochetkov/AFP via Getty Images.

of the work, on strategic planning, more than sixteen pages of text were taken verbatim from the Russian edition of a 1978 American business school textbook titled *Strategic Planning and Policy*.[14] When asked about the plagiarism in 2006, Litvinenko responded that he had "followed Putin's academic work from the very beginning." He added that the first draft of Putin's thesis was rejected, and the academic committee recommended that he rework it, but "within a few months he returned with a completely revised version that took note of the criticisms and was accepted for defense." This was proof, Litvinenko said, that Putin did the work himself.[15]

As of 2023, Litvinenko, who managed Putin's 2000 and 2004 presidential campaigns in St. Petersburg, was still rector at Putin's alma mater, now the St. Petersburg Mining University. Putin apparently did not begrudge him for doing such a sloppy job with his dissertation. Like many of the Russian president's favorites, Litvinenko has prospered financially under the Putin regime. In 2021, he made the *Forbes* Billionaires List as owner of almost 21 percent of PhosAgro, a Russian chemical holding company that produces fertilizers and phosphates. *Forbes* estimated his assets to be worth $1.5 billion.[16] The Russian online news site MBX Media reported in March 2021 that since at least as far back as 2014 Litvinenko has failed to disclose for tax purposes millions of dollars of earnings from PhosAgro, but Russian tax authorities have turned a blind eye.[17]

The Lure of Oil

By the spring of 1997, Berezovsky was riding high, literally—flying back and forth to Chechnya to meet with Chechen leaders and work on the peace deal with Russia, signed by Yeltsin and Maskhadov on May 12. He had already played a key role in negotiating a hostage crisis, begun when Chechen forces commanded by separatist Salman Raduev kidnapped twenty-two members of Russia's MVD forces on December 14, 1996. Berezovsky flew to Grozny and, following talks with First Deputy Prime Minister Movladi Udugov and field commander Shamil Basaev, secured the release of the hostages. In June 1997, Berezovsky made his private jet available to fly four Russian journalists home to Moscow after they were held in Chechnya for three months.[18] And in August 1997, he was instrumental in gaining the release of three NTV reporters abducted in May, reportedly for a huge ransom.[19] These efforts would later lead to accusations that he had encouraged Chechen terrorists.

Despite the fact that Maskhadov was elected handily as Chechnya's president in January 1997, his efforts to establish a working secular government faced huge obstacles, as evidenced by the many kidnappings. Chechnya's economy was in a shambles after the war, and hardline Islamic separatists like Raduev rejected any Russian presence in the republic. A top priority for the new Chechen government was to resuscitate the oil pipeline that ran through Chechnya from Baku, Azerbaijan, to Novorossiisk on the Black Sea, so that the republic could get oil tariffs and transit fees. Chechnya's integration into the oil market would provide much-needed resources for the restoration of its economy. The signs were positive. Berezovsky said at a press conference on May 13, 1997, that "Russia was interested in having a section of the Caspian pipeline pass through its territory [Chechnya]," and in July Azerbaijan president Gaidar Aliev signed an agreement with Russia that endorsed shipping oil from Baku through Chechnya.[20]

Berezovsky's interest in the Caspian pipeline had as much to do with his potential financial gain as it did with Chechnya's economic recovery. He wanted to use the pipeline to gain control of the Russian government oil giant Gazprom. With this goal in mind, Berezovsky flew in early June 1997 to Budapest, where he convinced George Soros to back a plan for him to become Gazprom's chairman with an initial investment of $1 billion in the company. On June 14, the day after Chernomyrdin and Maskhadov signed an agreement to open the pipeline, Soros met in Sochi with Berezovsky and Prime Minister Chernomyrdin to seal the Gazprom deal.[21] But when Soros went to see Nemtsov in Moscow, Nemtsov persuaded Soros against the Gazprom plan on the grounds that it represented another backroom deal by robber barons. Nemtsov insisted that the government now wanted fair play. Alex Goldfarb was present when Soros broke the bad news to Berezovsky at the LogoVAZ Club: "Boris could barely control himself. As soon as George left, he exploded: 'How could he do it? We shook hands! Did he really believe those clowns? Doesn't he know that Nemtsov's sole role is to act as "Chubais with a human face" for foreign consumption? I personally recruited him for that role back in March when we still were one team.' "[22]

In August 1997, Boris Nemtsov's deputy Sergei Kirienko announced that talks with Chechnya about the pipeline were deadlocked because Chechnya was demanding "impossible" tariffs. This prompted a rebuke from Berezovsky, who was quoted by *Nezavisimaia gazeta*, a newspaper he now owned, as saying that the Russian Ministry of Finance was sabotaging the deal. After more deliberations, Nemtsov declared on September 15 that Chechen territory would not be a part of the Caspian pipeline because Moscow had decided to transmit the oil through Dagestan.[23]

After Berezovsky died, Nemtsov recalled that Berezovsky had at one point paid him a visit to inform him that Chernomyrdin and Gazprom Chairman Rem Viakhirev had decided that he, Berezovsky, would head Gazprom's board of directors. Nemtsov "could not believe his ears" and phoned up Chernomyrdin and Viakhirev, who reluctantly confirmed what Berezovsky had said. Nemtsov then told Berezovsky that his Gazprom plan would happen "only over my dead body," to which Berezovsky responded: "I will destroy you. I will launch the Channel One television, all my media resources, so that you are no more." Nemtsov added that "indeed, Boris Abramovich achieved much of what he threatened."[24]

Internecine Conflict

Berezovsky had other irons in the fire. One involved the government telecommunications company Sviazinvest, which Vladimir Gusinsky was hoping to take over when it came up for auction on July 25, 1997. A year earlier, Gusinsky had received the go-ahead from Yeltsin's privatization minister, Alfred Kokh, to prepare for the auction by bringing in investors and speaking to security and defense officials, who depended on Sviazinvest for their secure communications. Berezovsky suggested to Gusinsky that if he won the auction, Berezovsky might be interested in becoming a partner. As Gusinsky later told David Hoffman: "Berezovsky has to be number one everywhere. He has to be the best man at every wedding, the grave digger at every funeral. If something happens somewhere without Berezovsky, he is full of anxiety."[25]

Unfortunately for Gusinsky and Berezovsky, with the arrival of Nemtsov into the government, the rules of the privatization process had changed. As with Gazprom, Nemtsov and Chubais wanted to end the practice of deciding in advance of auctions which oligarch would get the prize. The pair was determined that the auction for Sviazinvest would be open to all competitors, including Vladimir Potanin, who had already enlisted Soros as an investor. But neither Gusinsky nor Potanin wanted to face the uncertainty of an open auction, so they tried to get Chubais to agree to a deal in which Gusinsky would get Sviazinvest and Potanin would acquire the next big company that came along. On July 23, Berezovsky flew with the two men on Gusinsky's private jet to see Chubais, who was vacationing near St. Tropez in the south of France. In an attempt to persuade Chubais, Berezovsky allowed that, of course, the eventual goal was normal competition, but it was a mistake to suddenly introduce such a drastic change. When that did not work, Berezovsky made threats: "You are igniting a war. You don't want it, but it is going to happen."[26]

Valentin Iumashev argued with Chubais and Nemtsov for hours, pointing out that it was unreasonable to turn the tables on Gusinsky after he had spent so much time doing the groundwork for the privatization of Sviazinvest. "What's going to happen after Gusinsky loses?" Iumashev asked them. Noting that Gusinsky and Berezovsky controlled much of the media, Iumashev gloomily predicted that "in a month we will no longer have a government of young reformers."[27] But Chubais and Nemtsov hung tough. And, despite a last-minute attempt by the oligarchs to agree between themselves on what their auction bids would be, Potanin ended up the winner. Berezovsky and Gusinsky then unleashed their fury. Sergei Dorenko, an anchorman on ORT, whose show was watched by millions of Russians, accused Potanin of using money from shady shell companies to finance his bid. Appearing subsequently on *Ekho Moskvy*, which Gusinsky owned, Dorenko suggested that there was a conspiracy behind the deal. Gusinsky's newspaper *Segodnia* followed up with an article raising further questions about the suspicious origins of Potanin's money and about his questionably close relationship with Kokh.[28]

A few days later, on August 1, 1997, Berezovsky told Tatiana D'iachenko on the phone that the night before he, Gusinsky, and Mikhail Fridman had a very difficult meeting with Chubais, which lasted until 3:30 a.m. Berezovsky said that Chubais had mistakenly thought Potanin was honest and was "very shaken" when he learned from Berezovsky and Gusinsky about Potanin's underhandedness. Adding that Potanin was not the only one "who doesn't play by the rules," Berezovsky told Tatiana that Alfred Kokh must leave his post.[29] According to Nemtsov, Berezovsky also pressured Yeltsin's family (presumably Tatiana and Iumashev) to complain about him to Yeltsin, who then summoned Nemtsov to his office sometime in August and asked with irritation: "Are you really unable to do all this without such an uproar?" Nemtsov explained passionately that "this is a war in which either they win, or we do." Yeltsin was silent and then finally said: "They are nobody. I don't know them."[30]

Kokh resigned several days after Berezovsky's talk with Tatiana, but Berezovsky's lobbying was unsuccessful in getting Chubais to nullify the results of the auction. So he upped the ante considerably on September 13, when *Nezavisimaia gazeta* published a devastating front-page attack against Chubais, which portrayed him as a cynical, power-hungry schemer, who was enabling Potanin to create a private super-monopoly. Around the same time, there were reports on ORT that Potanin organized orgies with stripteasers for Nemtsov. Nemtsov's mother was so upset that she called her son and asked him whether the reports were true. Nemtsov advised her "not to react to such nonsense." But as Nemtsov later wrote: "Berezovsky and Gusinsky were doing everything to create a zone of public alienation around us, so that we would either resign from our posts or the president would fire us."[31] All this was too much for Yeltsin, who called business leaders to the Kremlin and urged that the public attacks against Chubais and Nemtsov cease.[32]

FIGURE 11.   Boris Nemtsov and Anatoly Chubais, 1999. Sergey Fomin/Alamy.

Alex Goldfarb recalls trying to convince Berezovsky that the conflict was dangerously close to bringing down the government, asking him, "why such a fuss about a phone company for Gusinsky?" Berezovsky retorted angrily: "That's not the point. I don't care whether Goose [Gusinsky] gets it or not . . . It's about whether Tolya [Chubais] can have it his way because he decided that he is the state. Fucking Bolshevik." As Goldfarb realized, "the fight was not between Gusinsky and Potanin. They were just surrogates for the two epic figures of Yeltsin's reign: Chubais and Berezovsky, the ultimate technocrat and the super-tycoon. It was a political clash of opposing views on the role of the oligarchs in the new Russia."[33]

Berezovsky should have realized that he would pay a heavy price for indulging in revenge. Chubais and Nemtsov visited Yeltsin on November 4 and urged Yeltsin to dismiss Berezovsky from his position as a deputy secretary of the National Security Council. Yeltsin needed little persuasion. As he explained in his memoirs: "Why did I fire Berezovsky in November? My motivations are probably more difficult to explain than it might seem at first glance. I never liked Boris Berezovsky, and I still don't like him. I don't like him because of his arrogant tone, his scandalous reputation, and because people believe that he has special influence on the Kremlin. He doesn't. I never liked him, but I always tried to keep him on my team."[34] On November 5, 1997, the Kremlin announced that Berezovsky had been fired.

Berezovsky struck back. He and Gusinsky received documents showing that Chubais and members of his economic team had been paid close to a half million dollars as an advance on a book they were writing about privatization. They acted on the information immediately. On November 12, an investigative journalist named Alexander Minkin, who was close to Gusinsky, reported on *Ekho Moskvy* about the book revenues, saying that they were a veiled form of a bribe and money laundering. The scandal cost Chubais dearly. Although he retained his post as first deputy prime minister, Yeltsin took away his finance portfolio. But whatever short-term satisfaction Berezovsky and Gusinsky got from their latest attack on Chubais, the long-term repercussions for them would hardly be worth it. The warning to them from Sergei Lisovskii, who had worked on the 1996 Yeltsin campaign, would prove prescient: "If you destroy Chubais, you will eliminate yourself in several years' time, because in the long run, Chubais will never sink you, never jail you—he has created you as Russian capitalists. And anyone else in his place will treat you very cruelly."[35] Nemtsov would later say bitterly: "We had a liberal democratic government with Chernomyrdin and others. We had a real chance to move the country in a democratic direction. And when Berezovsky decided to destroy our government, and succeeded, what did we get? We ended up with a KGB government."[36]

Rescuing Sobchak

Although Putin remained out of this Kremlin conflict, he had his own problems. Korzhakov and Barsukov had been fired, but Russian Prosecutor General Iurii Skuratov and MVD chief Anatolii Kulikov were continuing the investigation of Putin's former boss Sobchak for corruption during the period Sobchak served as mayor. One particular accusation involved Sobchak contracting with a construction/real estate company, Renaissance, for the renovation of several city-owned apartment buildings. Renaissance later sold apartments to officials in the mayor's office, including Putin and Kudrin, at reduced prices. Equally scandalous was that Renaissance pressured the residents of a communal apartment next to Sobchak to relocate, so that the mayor could take it over and expand his living quarters. In April 1997, the Duma passed a resolution calling for the prosecutor general to complete the investigation of Sobchak, and three of Sobchak's former staff members were later arrested in St. Petersburg.[37]

The newspapers were full of speculation about the Sobchak case, and one article, published by *Novaia gazeta* in June, seemed ominous for Putin and Kudrin as well. The author, Pavel Voshchanov, unleashed a devastating critique of Sobchak, detailing how he had dipped into the city's coffers for his personal benefit and describing his penchant for hugely expensive Italian clothes and his connections with gangsters. But then Voshchanov pointedly added that "Sobchak did not forget about his subordinates, who now hold high positions in the Kremlin." As if to predict that these Kremlin officials would not be touched, he lamented: "We know that if someone is close to power, if he is comfortable in its tangled corridors, nothing threatens him. Any sin of his will be overlooked."[38]

As Voshchanov suggested, Putin and Kudrin were protected by the Kremlin. Nonetheless, Sobchak knew a great deal about their illegal financial machinations, particularly Putin's. Who could predict what he might say to prosecutors under pressure? Sobchak's wife, Narusova, began visiting Putin regularly in Moscow during the summer, conveying to him that her husband would soon be arrested and leaving Putin with the impression that Sobchak might not keep quiet if that happened.[39] Lest Sobchak incriminate his former subordinates, he had to be protected from prosecution. This proved to be a complicated task, in which several Kremlin figures participated.

Iumashev revealed in an interview years later that Chubais, Nemtsov, and Kudrin repeatedly told him that the Sobchak situation was urgent and something needed to be done. Iumashev paid a personal visit to both Skuratov and Kulikov, asking them to let up on Sobchak, but to no avail. The only person who could possibly put a stop to Sobchak's prosecution was Yeltsin, but he still deeply resented the former St. Petersburg mayor and thus had no motivation to protect him. "I knew that Boris Nikolayevich would never, under any circumstances, call the prosecutor general," Iumashev said. "I did not even try to have a conversation with Yeltsin on this topic."[40] Yeltsin recalled in *Midnight Diaries*: "I kept repeating the same thing to the people who came to Sobchak's defense—Chubais, Yumashev, Nemtsov: 'If there is any suspicion, it has to be investigated and proven whether the man is guilty or not.' "[41] Skuratov says in his memoirs that he visited Yeltsin in September to inform him about the Sobchak case, and Yeltsin calmly told him to do what he had to do.[42]

The situation reached a crisis point on October 2, 1997, when Chubais got a phone call from Narusova, who put her husband on the line.

Sobchak was frantic because the media was predicting his immediate arrest. Chubais reassured him: "Don't worry, Anatolii Aleksandrovich, the situation is completely under control. I had a conversation on this subject with the head of the Presidential Administration, Iumashev. He assured me that without his consent and the consent of Boris Nikolaevich [Yeltsin] no actions will be taken against you." Chubais told Sobchak that he would be meeting with Iumashev that day, and Sobchak's problem would be first on their agenda.[43] Alarmed, Chubais then called Nemtsov, who was with Yeltsin at the time. Nemtsov urged Yeltsin to do something to prevent Sobchak's arrest, but Yeltsin resisted until finally Nemtsov told him that Sobchak had a serious heart condition and might die in custody. According to Yeltsin, he then relented slightly, asking that a message be sent to Skuratov saying "you can't harass a sick man."[44]

But Skuratov later wrote that he did not hear from Yeltsin until October 7, when Yeltsin sent him an official order saying only, "it is necessary to calm down the activity of the [investigatory] group."[45] In the meantime, Sobchak had been summoned for questioning by St. Petersburg prosecutors on October 3, and he complained of heart pain. Putin quickly arranged for Sobchak to be transported to the Military Medical Academy hospital, where Putin's doctor friend Iurii Shevchenko diagnosed a heart attack. After a few weeks, the investigation team became impatient and decided to send some Moscow cardiologists to verify Sobchak's heart ailment. Desperate to avoid this medical scrutiny and Sobchak's possible arrest, Putin came up with a plan. On November 7, a holiday, officers under the command of Putin's friend Aleksandr Grigor'ev, first deputy head of the St. Petersburg FSB, transported Sobchak via ambulance to Pulkovo Airport, where he "ran up the stairs" to board a chartered jet from Finland and was flown to Paris.[46] By the time Sobchak returned to Russia from exile in June 1999, the charges against him had been dropped, and Skuratov was under a shadow.

Skuratov was outraged when he learned later that it was Putin who had orchestrated Sobchak's escape: "Just imagine: a team of investigators, including from the FSB, is working. And then an official from the Presidential Administration arrives and, going beyond his authority, and not trusting the investigators, including those from the organization where he served and would soon head, practically crushes the investigation."[47] But Putin's decisive action earned him great esteem from his Kremlin colleagues. Iumashev lauded him for taking such a terrible risk, saying that he had warned Putin he would have to fire him if the plan did not work because Yeltsin would disapprove of him breaking the law. Chubais concurred: Putin had "put his head on the block." In the words of the political observer and publisher Gleb Pavlovsky: "There were a lot of talkers around the Kremlin who were not ready to carry out any project, but this—the logistics of Putin's accomplishment! He didn't just declare loyalty, he did the best he could and succeeded."[48] Even Yeltsin, despite his dislike of Sobchak, was impressed: "Later, when I learned about what Putin had done, I felt a profound sense of respect for and gratitude toward him."[49]

As for Putin, in his autobiography, he denied playing a role in Sobchak's escape: "His friends—I think they were from Finland—sent him a medevac plane, and he was flown to a hospital in France . . . Frankly, I didn't even know the details."[50] But later he acknowledged that he had orchestrated it: "I just considered it my duty to help Anatoly Alexandrovich. And here's why: if I knew, or at least I suspected, that he was to blame for something, I would not lift a finger. But I wasn't just sure, I knew, I just knew for sure, one hundred percent, that he was innocent."[51] To save himself and others, Putin had prevented Sobchak's prosecution for bribery and financial crimes that Putin knew Sobchak was guilty of. And in doing so, he had used the security services to break the law. Yet this was perceived by Yeltsin and his team as an act of courage and loyalty and would help Putin earn the presidency.

Trouble at the Top

If it were not for its long-term ramifications, Putin's rescue of Sobchak would have been a minor incident compared with what else was going on in the country at the time. By the end of 1997, the Russian government was deeply in debt, both foreign ($123.5 billion) and domestic ($95 billion). Falling oil prices, due to a financial crisis in Asia, contributed to budget shortfalls, as did the fact that most of the oligarchs were delinquent on their taxes. In addition, as David Hoffman points out, the conflict between Berezovsky and Chubais had "paralyzed the political elite, undermined the confidence of investors and left Russia unprepared for the approaching disaster."[52] But political drama in the Kremlin continued, with Berezovsky, who remained a close advisor to Yeltsin's chief of staff, Iumashev, and controlled influential media outlets, often the catalyst.

In February 1998, Berezovsky suffered a spinal injury resulting from an accident while speeding on a snowmobile at night. After treatment in Switzerland, he was back in Moscow by March and began meeting with Iumashev, Tatiana, and other members of Yeltsin's team to discuss getting rid of Chernomyrdin, who they all agreed had lost his usefulness as prime minister. With Yeltsin's ability to govern increasingly in doubt, the post of prime minister, next in line to the succession, was crucially important. Although Yeltsin obliged the group by firing Chernomyrdin on March 23, his choice of Sergei Kirienko as Chernomyrdin's replacement displeased Berezovsky, who began lobbying against the Duma's approval of the nomination. Kirienko, a thirty-five-year-old former banker and minister of energy, was from Nizhnii Novgorod and close to Nemtsov. The last thing Berezovsky wanted was a reformer of Kirienko's ilk taking charge as prime minister.[53]

Berezovsky's audacity did not sit well with Yeltsin, to put it mildly. In a speech at a private awards ceremony for Russian cosmonauts in mid-April, Yeltsin unexpectedly brought up a recent telephone conversation he had had with Berezovsky. Berezovsky, he said, was intriguing to influence the formation of a new government, and if he didn't stop, Yeltsin warned, he would be exiled from the country. According to the journalist who broke the story, Berezovsky wanted his ally Ivan Rybkin, former secretary of the National Security Council, to replace Chernomyrdin. A source in the Duma told the journalist that Berezovsky had also hatched a backup plan whereby the Constitution would be amended so that, in the case of Yeltsin's incapacity, his successor would be not the prime minister but the chairman of Russia's Federation Council, Egor Stroev, who was close to Berezovsky. Iumashev reportedly tried to do damage control after Yeltsin's outburst by asking the cosmonauts to refrain from repeating what he said, but the word got out.[54]

However much Yeltsin disliked Berezovsky, the oligarch's political clout was formidable. Two weeks later Yeltsin was compelled against his will to approve the appointment of Berezovsky as executive secretary of the Commonwealth of Independent States (CIS), a regional intergovernmental association that was formed in 1991 and comprised twelve of the fifteen former Soviet republics. (Ukraine and Georgia later left the alliance, and Turkmenistan changed its standing to an associate member.) With Russia as its driving force, the CIS aimed at cooperation on such issues as trade, collective security, and combatting organized crime and terrorism. But by the time Berezovsky entered the picture, there was such deep dissension among members, with some seeking closer cooperation with Russia and others leaning toward the West, that experts were predicting the organization's demise.

Berezovsky had been lobbying for the CIS post, without Yeltsin's knowledge, by appealing personally to each of the government leaders for their support. When Ukrainian president Leonid Kuchma nominated Berezovsky at a CIS meeting in Moscow on April 29, 1998, and all the other heads of state voiced their enthusiastic agreement, Yeltsin was caught completely off guard. He asked them to consider other candidates on the grounds that Berezovsky was too controversial a figure politically in Russia. Finally, Yeltsin summoned Berezovsky for a private discussion and was persuaded to go along with the appointment.[55]

Berezovsky threw himself into the job with his usual zeal. Interviewed on NTV on June 8, 1998, he reported: "Over the last six weeks I have been trying to figure out what the Commonwealth is all about today. I have traveled through all the CIS states, met with all the CIS presidents, and gained a picture that accurately shows where we are now."[56] He stressed that economic problems should have priority but noted that real cooperation was not possible until regional conflicts, like those in Abkhazia, Chechnya, and other places, were addressed. Acutely aware of nationalist sentiments, Berezovsky also made it clear in subsequent statements that, for the CIS to succeed as an organization, whatever restrictions were imposed on its member states, they should not impinge on the states' independence.[57]

Ekho Moskvy editor Venediktov later praised Berezovsky for his success with the CIS: "He was never in Moscow. We couldn't get him for an interview because he was flying around to the various capitals, trying to persuade the presidents [of CIS states] that Yeltsin was great and Russia was great . . . He managed to convince the presidents to come together, to stop the disintegration process. This was really his accomplishment. No one else did it . . . And, in general, he was respected."[58] Berezovsky was asked by Venediktov in September 1998 if he saw his CIS position as a stepping-stone to a greater political role. Berezovsky seems to have taken the question seriously, responding that he had no such ambitions, particularly regarding the presidency, because of the strong Russian nationalist sentiment in the country: "I believe that it is wrong for a Jewish person to claim to be at the helm of a state like Russia today."[59]

Putin Moves Up

In the meantime, Putin had also received a new position, and a promotion. In May 1998, Yeltsin appointed him first deputy director of the Presidential Administration, with responsibility for relations with

Russia's eighty-nine regions. The regional governors were elected and thus had considerable independence, posing a potential political threat to Yeltsin. Putin already had a lot of information on their financial dealings from his work heading the GKU, so he was well suited to be a watchdog over the regions on behalf of the Kremlin.[60] Putin recalled in *First Person* that he had found the GKU job so boring—a complaint similar to what he said about his first Kremlin post—that he was considering leaving to start a private practice as a lawyer. So his promotion was a real boon: "I developed relationships with many of the governors at that time. It was clear to me that work with the regional leaders was one of the most important lines of work in the country. Everyone was saying that the *vertikal*, the vertical chain of government, had been destroyed and that it had to be restored."[61]

Putin only stayed in this job for a little more than two months. As it turned out, Yeltsin had bigger plans for him, much bigger. Putin later claimed that it came as complete surprise when, in mid-July, Prime Minister Kirienko asked to meet him at the airport as Kirienko arrived from seeing Yeltsin in Karelia and then congratulated Putin on his appointment as director of the FSB. "I can't say I was overjoyed," Putin recalled. "I didn't want to step into the same river twice." In fact, Liudmila Putina recalled that she and her husband had talked about him taking the FSB job three months before he was formally offered it, and he had told her that he would not accept it.[62] Whatever his reluctance, Putin must have understood that his new position was a huge step forward in his career.

The security services had been in the throes of reform ever since the KGB was disbanded in late 1991, with numerous reorganizations and leadership changes. Everybody who favored democracy, presumably including Yeltsin, wanted the new security services to abide by the law and observe people's rights, but in the environment of bandit capitalism that arose in post-Soviet Russia, this was difficult to achieve. An even greater problem was that many KGB officers either held on to their jobs or entered into private security. The latter developed into a burgeoning business that included technical surveillance and gathering kompromat on rivals, as well as maintaining ties with the Russian mafia. Other KGB veterans joined the so-called active reserves, serving in government, media, or university positions while reporting back to their superiors in the security services, as Putin did before the August coup.[63]

Although Yeltsin, himself a former Communist apparatchik, had metamorphosed into a democrat, his weak leadership and consequent

low popularity made him increasingly dependent on his security services. As the journalist Tregubova put it: "Yeltsin, who was losing control not only over his own country but also over his own family, which
was bogged down in dubious friendships with oligarchs who were shaking the political boat with all their might, apparently lost faith in the
effectiveness of democratic levers of government and was increasingly
inclined to rely only on the old, proven levers of the special services."[64]
While continually claiming that he wanted to reform the FSB, Yeltsin
did just the opposite. He had allowed Korzhakov, a former KGB general,
free rein to go after his enemies until he was forced by the Family to
get rid of him. Mikhail Barsukov and his successor at the FSB, Nikolai Kovalev, had been KGB veterans. And now, instead of appointing a
civilian with democratic credentials to replace Kovalev, Yeltsin turned
to Putin.

Yeltsin said in his memoirs that he decided it was time for Kovalev
to go because Kovalev had an antipathy toward business: "He couldn't
help himself. He simply despised people with money."[65] The fact that
Kovalev was investigating banks and businessmen made the president
and his team uneasy. As *Komsomol'skaia pravda* observed: "Many people
close to the president were concerned that the FSB chief did not bow
to anyone in particular and did not swear loyalty to the Boss at every
turn and constantly stressed that he took no part in political games. So
they impressed little by little on the president: He is not reliable, he is
not one of us, and in terms of personal loyalty he is the wrong man."[66]

Kovalev was an experienced general with a devoted following at FSB
headquarters. As a mere lieutenant colonel, Putin did not have the
same gravitas, and his appointment did not go over well with his new
subordinates. Putin's work as an intelligence office abroad was also
scoffed at, because he had been sent to East Germany, considered a
backwater.[67] Putin himself admitted that he was "greeted cautiously"
when he arrived at the FSB, but he insisted that his rank was irrelevant
because he had left the KGB several years earlier and thus was the first
civilian leader of the security services, "even though nobody paid attention to that."[68]

Berezovsky told Alex Goldfarb that Iumashev came to him in June to
ask him his opinion of Putin as a possible FSB chief, explaining that the
top criterion for the job was loyalty. Berezovsky responded, "I support
him 100 percent." According to Goldfarb, "Boris liked the idea of putting a lieutenant colonel over multistar generals; the newcomer would
not be a part of the old-boy network, and would in fact be snubbed by

the top brass, which should only strengthen his loyalty to the Kremlin."[69] But of course, Putin had his own network of former KGB cronies whom he would bring into the FSB. In his first press interview as FSB chief, he said clearly: "It is important not only to retain but also to arrange an influx of fresh personnel—and this is our job."[70]

Yeltsin later wrote: "Putin went about reorganizing the FSB very intelligently . . . Although the reorganization meant that a number of officers had to be retired, it proceeded calmly and, I would say, cleanly. Putin's structure would prove to be quite workable."[71] It was most certainly workable for Putin. When he cleaned house at the FSB, firing around two thousand senior staff members, including Kovalev's old-guard, Putin replaced many of them with allies from the Leningrad KGB. Viktor Cherkesov became his first deputy, while Nikolai Patrushev was appointed a deputy FSB chief and head of the FSB's newly created Department of Economic Security. Former Leningrad KGB official Viktor Ivanov, who had worked with Putin in Sobchak's office, was placed in charge of internal counterintelligence. And Sergei Ivanov, another member of Putin's team under the mayor, became head of the FSB's Department of Analytics and Strategic Planning as well as a deputy FSB chief. Others would arrive in the next year or so, providing Putin with a power base that no one in the Kremlin would dare to challenge. As Tregubova observed, when Putin took over, "the FSB, led by the Yeltsin favorite, began to resemble more and more not an anticrisis control center but a spare center of power, which Yeltsin had prepared in case the critical situation in the country developed into an irreversible one, which subsequently happened."[72]

Chapter 5

Turmoil

> It is no longer possible to imagine high Russian
> politics without Berezovsky, whether Yeltsin likes
> it or not.
>
> —*Kommersant*, April 15, 1998

Less than a month after Putin assumed the
FSB leadership, a financial crisis hit Russia like a sledgehammer. Russia
had been experiencing a drop in GDP, along with increasing inflation
and unemployment since the beginning of 1998. A decline in global
oil prices had resulted in a steep decrease in Russian export revenues,
which severely impacted Russia's foreign exchange reserves, and loss of
investor confidence had led to staggering interest rates. On August 17,
1998, the government, led by Prime Minister Kirienko, abandoned
its support for the ruble, defaulted on domestic debt, and declared a
ninety-day moratorium on repayment of foreign debt. By the end of
September, the ruble's value had depreciated 61 percent since the end
of July, making foreign loans prohibitive and causing widespread bank-
ruptcies among businesses.[1]

Enter Primakov

Yeltsin dismissed Kirienko on August 23 and attempted to replace him
with former prime minister Chernomyrdin, but the Duma, led by the
Communists, would not endorse his appointment and started preparing impeachment proceedings against Yeltsin. Putin went on television
on September 1 to deny rumors that the Kremlin was planning to use

military force to resolve the political conflict.[2] Joining the fray, Berezovsky suggested in an interview with *Ekho Moskvy* that Yeltsin should resign if he was unsuccessful in getting a cabinet approved.[3] "It is not easy to talk about these events of the autumn crisis of 1998," Yeltsin wrote in his memoirs. "It's hard because the situation changed practically every day and then every hour. Frankly, I don't remember such tension in the entire Russian political history of the 1990's, except for military coup attempts in 1991 and 1993."[4]

The crisis had a negative impact on Yeltsin's already deteriorating health. Lilia Shevtsova observed: "The leader who had made his mission Russia's return to Europe and its transformation into a flourishing democratic state ended up a politician completely dependent on his Kremlin servants, stooping to primitive intrigue and manipulation to survive . . . As Yeltsin grew weaker physically, the ostensibly superpresidential system became obviously disabled, devolving into a half-hearted Impotent Omnipotence."[5]

After days of intense discussions with advisors, Yeltsin settled on a compromise candidate, Russian Foreign Minister Evgeny Primakov. Sixty-eight-year-old Primakov was a longtime intelligence officer who had operated under cover as a journalist in the Middle East for many years. From 1992 to 1996, when he took over the Ministry of Foreign Affairs, Primakov had led the Foreign Intelligence Service, the SVR. A moderate conservative but hardly a democrat, Primakov was adept at negotiating and set about putting the country on the path to economic recovery. His assumption of the prime minister's post was not welcomed by Berezovsky. As executive secretary of the CIS, Berezovsky presented a united front with Primakov in working to keep the member countries committed to their collective partnership in the wake of the financial crisis.[6] But his relationship with Primakov had been sour since 1996, when Berezovsky and Glushkov engineered the new financial model for Aeroflot, and employees of the SVR, which Primakov had headed, lost a source of easy money.

Primakov's support from the parliament empowered him to bring in his own cabinet members and to make decisions that did not depend on consulting with the presidential staff and the Family. This meant that Berezovsky, whose political influence stemmed largely from his connections with those in Yeltsin's inner circle, saw his importance decline. According to Goldfarb: "The crowds at the [LogoVAZ] Club were gone. Its bar, with the stuffed crocodile in the corner, stood deserted."[7] Berezovsky's situation was not helped by the fact that Jews were being scapegoated publicly for Russia's economic woes, with Berezovsky often the focus. That said, the financial crisis did not have a large impact on Berezovsky's fortune—*Forbes* claimed he was worth $3 billion at this time—because he did not own a bank and revenues from Sibneft, although diminished because of the drop in oil prices, were paid in dollars. In fact, because costs were in rubles, Sibneft benefited from the devaluation. But Berezovsky's political currency was declining markedly.

Primakov's relations with Putin, despite their common background in the intelligence services, did not get off to a good start. Putin says in *First Person* that Primakov criticized him for packing the FSB with his friends from St. Petersburg. So Putin brought his senior staff to meet with Primakov and try to win him over. According to Putin, Primakov apologized for his criticism.[8] But Yeltsin's daughter Tatiana later claimed that Primakov had actually gone to her father and tried to convince him to dismiss Putin because Putin was replacing experienced FSB officers with those who were less qualified.[9]

According to Iumashev, later that year Putin requested an urgent meeting to tell him that Primakov had asked him to have the FSB wiretap liberal opposition leader Grigory Yavlinsky, who Primakov said was a spy for the United States. Putin claimed that he had refused the request and would resign if Yeltsin overruled him, because it was unacceptable for the FSB to get involved in politics. He did not want a return to KGB tactics.[10] It is hard to imagine that Iumashev took Putin's words seriously. Yeltsin and his team did not appoint Putin to head the FSB because he had democratic scruples, but rather because they wanted the FSB on their side. And the more liberal members of the government, like Nemtsov, looked down on him. Nemtsov recalled his own impressions: "No one knew much about Putin then. He was so unremarkable that even my secretary had no reaction to him. Once he called my office and my secretary refused to connect him to me until he identified himself: 'Putin, Vladimir Vladimirovich, director of the FSB.' My secretary then told me: 'Someone named Putin is on the line. He says he is head of the FSB. What should I do with him?'"[11]

Two Alarming Murders

The Kremlin apparently did not expect the FSB to put a stop to—let alone solve—the murders and assassination attempts that were occurring in the country on an almost daily basis. Several of these attacks appeared to have political motives, and one in particular raised questions about Putin's involvement. On August 20, 1998, Anatolii Levin-Utkin, deputy editor of a three-week-old newspaper, *Iuridicheskii Peterburg segodnia* (Legal St. Petersburg today), was beaten to death outside his apartment building. The paper had just published an article titled "Lt. Colonel Putin Became FSB Chief Unlawfully," which was highly unfavorable to the new FSB chief.[12] Levin-Utkin was not the author of the article— it was signed under a pseudonym--but he had contributed reporting and research.

The article discussed Putin's career in a derisive tone, pointing out that the only investment project Putin implemented during his career in Sobchak's office was the construction of a Coca-Cola plant. More to the point, the author reminded readers of Putin's "excessive gullibility" toward business when he granted gambling permits to casinos and of "irregularities" in the issuance of import-export licenses, which Putin later admitted were mistakes. But the author went further, mentioning rumors that Putin "sold out" Sobchak a few days before the 1996 St. Petersburg election after meeting with Sobchak's competitor Vladimir Iakovlev. Now that Putin was FSB chief, the author asked, would he use his office to protect Sobchak, who was still in exile, from the corruption investigation that had been initiated not only by the FSB but also by Skuratov and the MVD? The article concluded with a claim that an FSB director was legally required to hold a rank of lieutenant-general or higher upon appointment, while Putin was only a lieutenant colonel.

With his new appointment being discussed widely in the media, the last thing Putin needed was to have his past scrutinized, especially the parts involving Sobchak. According to the newspaper's editor, Aleksei Domnin, Putin's "people" called the office after the piece appeared, expressing their anger.[13] As with many other such cases, Levin-Utkin's murder aroused little attention from Russia's investigative organs, and those responsible were never brought to justice.

Three months later, on November 20, 1998, Galina Starovoitova— a prominent St. Petersburg parliamentarian, anticorruption crusader, and human rights activist—was brutally murdered. Starovoitova was an anthropologist, known for her scholarly work on ethnic groups, as well as for her advocacy on behalf of ethnic minorities.[14] A candidate for governor of the Leningrad region, she had just arrived from Moscow when she was gunned down in the stairwell of her St. Petersburg apartment by two unidentified assailants. Her press secretary, Ruslan Linkov, who was with her at the time, was wounded but survived. Starovoitova's

FIGURE 12.   Galina Starovoitova, August 1998. AP photo/Str.

murder not only caused a huge outcry in Russia and abroad; it created a furor in the Kremlin. Yeltsin was reportedly so upset when he heard about it that he was hospitalized the next day, and he recalled in his memoirs that "the news came like a stab to my heart."[15] MVD chief Sergei Stepashin immediately announced that the murder was "a case of honor for the FSB, MVD, and Procuracy," and the three agencies formed a special investigative group to find the culprits.[16] The investigation would continue for over twenty years, leading to the prosecution of several men connected with the Tambov crime group for carrying out the murder. But those who actually ordered the crime were never identified.

Starovoitova's killing was a political murder; no one denied that. She had acquired plenty of enemies during the course of her career. But for Putin and the Kremlin it was a political murder with a political solution: blame the Communists, who dominated the State Duma and posed a threat to Yeltsin's presidency. Yeltsin would later write that "the outbreak of Communist hysteria in late 1998 and early 1999 made it reasonable to surmise that some leftist extremists were involved in the murder."[17] Clear evidence that this was the Kremlin's strategy in the aftermath of the murder emerged in May 2000 with the publication by *Kommersant* of a leaked document from the Presidential Administration titled "Reform of the Administration of the President of the Russian Federation."[18] One section in the document proposed a public commission of inquiry that "will gradually reveal the 'communist trail' in the murder of Ms. Starovoitova and continue to use it as part of a large-scale campaign of struggle against the Communist Party." As an example, the document suggested promoting rumors that Gennadii Seleznev, the Communist speaker of the Duma, was connected to the murder, which would "sooner or later" make him more "compliant" in his dealings with the Presidential Administration.

Starovoitova had clashed openly with Seleznev and other Communists as she investigated their suspected illegalities and objected to their extremist comments.[19] And, in an interview she gave shortly before her death, she said she knew Putin and that he was "a pretty reasonable guy."[20] But her public actions had negative implications for Putin and his supporters. She was one of the few democrats to say that real reform in post-Soviet Russia required the government to be cleansed of *both* Communists and former KGB officers. Her efforts at introducing a law on lustration in 1992 and again in 1997 were unsuccessful, but she had not given up trying. She also was investigating corruption in St. Petersburg, which could have drawn attention to Putin's financial malfeasance there. In short, her murder not only served the Kremlin's goal of tarnishing the Communists by blaming them for the crime; it also rid Putin and the FSB of a troublesome political challenge.

Circumstantial evidence suggested FSB involvement. The two guns found at the scene of the crime were rare in the ordinary criminal world—they had silencers and required expertise to operate—so it was likely they came from the FSB. According to a top Russian private security expert: "Only operational or recently retired special services officers would be skilled in handling such weapons and have access to them." Also pointing to FSB complicity was the fact that Starovoitova had made the decision to fly home from Moscow at the very last minute. Those who planned to kill her would have learned of her change of plans only through wiretapping and surveillance methods that the security services used.[21] Coincidently, Cherkesov, newly appointed as Putin's deputy at the FSB, was on the flight to St. Petersburg with Starovoitova that night and appeared at the crime scene when Starovoitova's sister Olga went there to identify the body.[22]

There were also strange inconsistencies in the story of Linkov, which gave rise to media speculation that he might have been an accomplice of the killers. Prosecutor General Skuratov even told reporters that Linkov had withheld "several things that could shed light on the case."[23] Linkov was reportedly critically wounded by two bullets and stayed in the hospital for weeks. But after he was shot, he managed to make a call to police on his mobile phone and then knocked on the door of the couple across the hall, who let him in, only to watch him calling a friend at the media outlet Interfax. Why the assassins didn't kill Linkov, the only witness to the crime, was never explained. He was treated at the Military Medical Academy hospital, under the care of Iurii Shevchenko, who had earlier cared for both Putin's wife and Sobchak. (Shevchenko would be appointed Russian minister of health the next June.) According to Olga Starovoitova, one of Linkov's first visitors at the hospital was Putin, who discussed the details of the crime with him. Linkov later told journalist Andrew Meier that he had been close to Putin for a long time, meeting him often.[24]

In 2018, Boris Gruzd, the attorney for Starovoitova's family observed: "After twenty years there is no longer material evidence in the case . . . Now those who ordered the crime will be identified only by the testimony of persons at the top of the hierarchy of the Tambov group. This is the only way to determine if members of the political leadership, or party or regional officials, were behind the murder."[25] But such testimony has not been forthcoming. In April 2019, Vladimir Kumarin/Barsukov, erstwhile leader of the Tambov gang, who had been behind bars for a decade, was formally charged with being an accomplice to the Starovoitova murder. The indictment read: "Barsukov, learning of the desire of an unidentified person to stop the state and political activities of . . . Starovoitova, whose vigorous . . . activities caused deep dissatisfaction among her opponents and hatred among some of them, together with an unidentified person, decided to terminate her state and political activities by killing her."[26]

Kumarin has long denied that he had any role in the murder, and even Starovoitova's family has considered his involvement unlikely. But whatever his role, the indictment made it clear that someone in a high political position ordered the murder and that politician was powerful enough to prevent disclosure of his identity. Even if Kumarin was an accomplice, he will doubtless keep silent about who enlisted him. As one commentator noted, he "fears this unidentified politician more than the state. Perhaps because this politician is the state?"[27]

Taking Aim at the FSB

Starovoitova's murder occurred just three days after an event that created a huge public relations problem for Putin and the FSB. On November 17, 1998, FSB Lt. Col. Alexander Litvinenko, who would be fatally poisoned in London eight years later, appeared at a press conference with five colleagues, four of whom wore masks, to announce that in December 1997 Litvinenko and a fellow officer, Aleksandr Gusak, had been requested by their boss to kill Boris Berezovsky. Litvinenko, age thirty-six, had worked since the late 1980s for the KGB and its successors in military counterintelligence, anticorruption, and counterterrorism, which included a stint in Chechnya. In 1997, he joined a special unit of the FSB known by the acronym URPO, which dealt with organized crime and sometimes employed extralegal violence. Litvinenko first met Berezovsky when he was part of the team investigating the attempted murder of Berezovsky in June 1994 and started moonlighting as his part-time security guard. Then, in March 1995, Litvinenko saved Berezovsky from arrest in connection with the Listev murder by flashing his FSB badge and his revolver in front of a group of policemen outside the LogoVAZ Club and telling them to back off until his fellow FSB officers arrived.[28] Later Berezovsky would say: "That Sasha was brave enough to help me without any regard for his own safety or position was a gesture that I deeply appreciated . . . We were not exactly friends at that stage, and we mixed in very different social circles, but, after these extraordinary events, we trusted one another."[29]

To show his gratitude, Berezovsky took Litvinenko with him on a trip to Switzerland and invited him to spend time at the LogoVAZ Club.[30] He also introduced Litvinenko to Korzhakov (with whom Berezovsky was still on good terms) and other top security officials. Litvinenko had decided that the corruption and illegal violence he was witnessing within the FSB had to be reported to the big bosses, but his information fell on deaf ears. Korzhakov recalled later that he had not been impressed by Litvinenko, whom he described as "unshaven, shaggy-haired, with worn, unpolished shoes," and concluded, after asking around the FSB, that Litvinenko was making stories up.[31]

Litvinenko's whistle-blowing reached new heights after he told Berezovsky in March 1998 about the order from his URPO bosses to kill the oligarch. Berezovsky reported the plot to then FSB chief Kovalev, who summoned Litvinenko and his colleagues to hear them out but ended up trying to persuade them, with warnings about the consequences, to drop their complaint. So Berezovsky approached Evgenii Savost'ianov, the first deputy chief of the Presidential Administration, and at Savost'ianov's instigation, the military prosecutor's office began an investigation. All those involved, including URPO chief Evgenii Khokholkov and Litvinenko, were put on temporary leave from the department.[32]

Word of the alleged plot soon leaked out, although it did not have much resonance at the time. Then, in May 1998, Aleksandr Khinshtein, a journalist who had close contacts within the security services, published an article titled "Boris Abramovich, I Have Been Ordered to Kill You."[33] In recounting the details of the case, Khinshtein questioned why Litvinenko waited for three months to inform Berezovsky and what the supposed purpose would have been in killing Berezovsky. Also, Litvinenko's bosses knew that he was close to Berezovsky, so why would they ask him to do the job? In sum, Khinshtein wrote: "Even a layperson can see how many inconsistencies are contained in Litvinenko's accusations. This is more like an attempt to settle scores with a demanding leader than a 'fight for the truth.'" This would be the FSB's argument going forward.

Having given his seal of approval to Putin's FSB appointment, Berezovsky apparently anticipated that Putin would be more receptive to the allegations of Litvinenko than Kovalev had been. He thus arranged for Litvinenko to see Putin right after the latter assumed his new post in July 1998. Although Putin feigned interest in what Litvinenko told him, he did nothing more than place Litvinenko under surveillance, and in October the military prosecutor's office closed the case. Unwilling to let the matter drop, Berezovsky decided that Putin needed a push. So he took the bold and ill-fated step of writing an open letter to Putin, which was published by *Kommersant* on November 13, 1998. In the letter, Berezovsky described the murder plot, naming those involved, and then went on to chide Putin: "I am astonished that no due assessment was given to the URPO bosses' activity after your appointment as FSB director." He noted that criminals were everywhere in the government bureaucracy, including the FSB, and ended his letter with a dramatic plea: "I am asking you to use your powers to restore constitutional order."[34]

Putin responded four days later, issuing a curt statement saying that the chief military prosecutor was in fact investigating the case, but, if Berezovsky's allegations were found to be untrue, he would face charges for bearing false evidence against FSB officials.[35] That same day Litvinenko and his fellow FSB officers staged their sensational press conference, led by Litvinenko, who spoke about corruption in the FSB and the order to kill Berezovsky. Although Litvinenko made it clear that the order was given before Putin took over as FSB chief, he also told his audience: "I have made several attempts to get through to Vladimir Vladimirovich and present all these facts to him, but we did not have such an opportunity. We were simply denied access to him."[36] Of course, Litvinenko had met with Putin, but apparently he and Berezovsky wanted to give Putin the opportunity to claim that his subordinates were acting without his knowledge.

Putin went on the warpath. He was not about to let the FSB's reputation be publicly tarnished or his leadership abilities questioned, even indirectly. On November 18, Putin issued a lengthy statement, published by *Kommersant*, in which he stressed that his agency would not hesitate to fire any employee engaged in criminal activity and would inform the prosecutor's office. But the allegations brought by Berezovsky, he said, were based on verbal statements of certain FSB officers who could be motivated by personal interests and ambitions. Furthermore, in going to the media with his claims, Berezovsky could be seen as pressuring those conducting the investigation. Putin repeated his earlier warning to Berezovsky about making false allegations and added that *Kommersant* might also be prosecuted for slander.[37] The next night, in a television interview, Putin ridiculed Litvinenko and his comrades for their amateurish press conference and noted that he had received a call from an ex-wife of one of them—who turned out to be Litvinenko's former spouse—saying that her ex-husband was behind in his alimony payments. Putin also said that the men themselves had engaged in illegal operations.[38]

In going public with the purported murder plot and supporting Litvinenko's press conference, Berezovsky apparently did not anticipate the FSB chief's angry reaction. Also, because Berezovsky was known as a schemer who exaggerated his own importance, many observers doubted the allegations. Khinshtein was particularly scathing in an article for *Komsomol'skaia pravda*: "Dr. Goebbels taught that the more monstrous the lie, the easier it is to believe. Boris Berezovsky clearly proved this."[39]

Putin seemed to be under little pressure to get to the bottom of Litvinenko's claims, even from Yeltsin. Yeltsin reportedly summoned Putin to his dacha on November 20 to demand a resolution of the scandal, but the murder of Starovoitova that very evening soon overshadowed the issue. Putin, who considered Litvinenko and his fellow whistleblowers traitors, dismissed them from the FSB in December, and, although he had disbanded URPO, he replaced it with a new FSB unit that had the same unbridled powers.[40]

In December, Putin had another meeting with Yeltsin, which he mentioned in an interview with Elena Tregubova later that month. Putin told Tregubova that the president "spoke very kindly to me, and I feel that I have his full support." Yeltsin had even ordered a pay increase of 25 percent for FSB employees. But, Putin added, Yeltsin had made it clear he would not run for a third term, and the new president could choose his own person to run the FSB. With his future uncertain, it was evidently not in Putin's interest to burn bridges with Berezovsky. When Tregubova asked him about the murder plot, Putin responded with uncharacteristic sympathy: "Personally, I cannot exclude that these people really frightened Boris Abramovich. He had been a target of assassination before. So it was only natural for him to think that another attempt was in the making."[41]

Skuratov Gets Tough

The new year brought more trouble for Berezovsky. On January 19, 1999, Prosecutor General Skuratov began investigating him for embezzlement of Aeroflot funds.[42] The next day, Khinshtein published a sensational piece claiming that the private security company Atoll, allegedly owned by Berezovsky, had "a warehouse of surveillance equipment that would do honor to any state's security services." And the equipment, Khinshtein wrote, had been used to spy on the president's family.[43] In early February, officers from the prosecutor's office and the FSB raided the offices of Sibneft and Atoll looking for eavesdropping equipment. Two days later, the headquarters of Aeroflot were searched. And the next week, Khinshtein, the obvious beneficiary of secret documents from Skuratov's investigators and the FSB, reproduced transcripts of phone conversations between Berezovsky and Tatiana D'iachenko, as well as between Berezovsky and others, including ORT television commentor Sergei Dorenko, that had allegedly come from Atoll's secret recordings. The conversations themselves did not reveal anything sensational, but, according to Khinshtein, the message was clear: "Atoll spied not only on opponents of the tycoon but also on his friends, for future necessity."[44] For his part, Berezovsky denied that he had anything to do with Atoll and called the whole affair a provocation.[45]

FIGURE 13.   Iurii Skuratov, March 1999. AP photo/Mikhail Metzel.

Skuratov had received an indirect assurance of support for his criminal probes from Primakov and must have been further encouraged when Primakov, announcing an amnesty program for thousands of Russian prisoners, noted pointedly that it would "open up places for those who will soon be imprisoned for economic crimes."[46] Berezovsky even told David Hoffman that at some point he confronted Primakov with proof that Primakov had personally ordered the investigations.[47] Whatever Primakov's role, Skuratov needed little encouragement in his pursuit of Berezovsky. As he made clear in his subsequent memoirs, he did not hold the oligarch in high regard: "Berezovsky is a man who revels in power. He is like a drug addict with a needle: money, connections, positions are just means to get the next dose of the drug."[48]

Like others in the government, Skuratov deeply resented Berezovsky's friendship with Tatiana D'iachenko and Iumashev: "After meeting with Berezovsky, Tatiana would go directly to her father and present Berezovsky's proposals. And Yeltsin would be impressed that his daughter had such valuable ideas and judgments."[49] Some of Skuratov's bad feelings against Berezovsky had doubtless been fueled by Korzhakov, who had backed Skuratov's appointment as prosecutor general and worked with him in moving against Sobchak, among others. Also, Skuratov had opposed the Russian military's 1996 retreat from Chechnya, which Berezovsky had backed, and he objected strongly to Berezovsky's negotiations with Chechen separatists, because he thought they encouraged radical elements within the republic's leadership.[50]

Whatever motivated his decision to move against Berezovsky, Skuratov had a higher priority. While Berezovsky's mounting legal problems preoccupied the Russian press, Skuratov was secretly pursuing a case with implications for the Kremlin that went far beyond the criminal pursuit of a renowned oligarch. During a televised meeting with Yeltsin in November 1998, Yeltsin had asked Skuratov: "What cases of corruption have you brought to the courts?"[51] Little did Yeltsin know that Skuratov had been secretly collaborating with a Swiss prosecutor, Carla del Ponte, in an investigation of Mabetex, the Swiss company that had been involved with the Kremlin renovations. Del Ponte had visited Moscow in May 1998 and told Skuratov that she had documents showing that Mabetex, along with its sister company Mercata, had bribed top Kremlin officials, including Pavel Borodin, to win construction contracts and that the money had been laundered through Swiss banks. After subsequently receiving these documents from the Swiss ambassador to Moscow, Skuratov started a secret criminal investigation in October 1998.

The case was kept under tight wraps, with only Skuratov's deputy and Primakov informed, until del Ponte ordered a search of Mabetex on January 25, 1999, and telephoned Skuratov the next day to tell him that thousands of incriminating documents had been discovered. Word somehow leaked to members of the Kremlin, prompting Nikolai Bordiuzha, who had replaced Iumashev in December 1998 as head of the Presidential Administration, to call Skuratov to his office on February 1. Colonel General Bordiuzha, a KGB veteran, had been chief of the Russian Border Guard before becoming head of the National Security Council in September 1998. Yeltsin later revealed that he appointed Bordiuzha to lead the Presidential Administration while remaining in his Security Council post at Iumashev's suggestion. With the opposition to Yeltsin in the Duma preparing to go on the offensive, Iumashev felt that "the office of the president needed some force behind it, at least for show."[52]

On receiving the summons from Bordiuzha, Skuratov recalled, "I knew suddenly that something bad would happen." And he was right.

After inquiring about the Berezovsky case, Bordiuzha asked, "What about Mabetex?" When Skuratov replied that it was under investigation, Bordiuzha said: "I have a video. Let's watch it together."[53] The now infamous videotape, which had reportedly been made several months earlier and was given to Bordiuzha by Iumashev, featured a nude man, who appeared to be Skuratov, cavorting in bed with two prostitutes.[54]

Now Skuratov understood: someone had listened to his January telephone call with del Ponte, and the Family was attempting to stop his investigation. Bordiuzha suggested that Skuratov resign "because of health reasons," and Skuratov agreed, writing a letter of resignation to Yeltsin. But after checking himself into the Central Kremlin Hospital, where he stayed for a few weeks, Skuratov began to reconsider. Knowing he would have the support of the Federation Council, the upper chamber of the parliament, which would have the final say on his fate, he decided not to resign after all. The investigation of Mabetex continued. The first deputy prosecutor general, Iurii Chaika, reported in a secret communication to the Federation Council on March 10 that work on the Mabetex case was "intensifying" and had been transferred to his office's Directorate for the Investigation of Especially Important Cases.[55]

The Kremlin went into full battle mode, and late in the evening of March 16, 1999, the sex video aired on the state television channel RTR.[56] The next day, Skuratov appeared before the Federation Council and asked for the support of its members, who had already received copies of the scandalous tape. The vote was 142 to 6 for keeping him in office. On March 18, 1999, Skuratov had a meeting with Yeltsin, who was recuperating in the hospital from a bleeding ulcer. Primakov and Putin were also present. Putin had already paid two visits to Skuratov in an effort to persuade him to resign, at first commiserating with him, but then subtly threatening that Skuratov himself could come under investigation for shady financial dealings. Now it was Yeltsin's turn, and he told Skuratov that the scandalous film would not again be shown publicly if he resigned from his post. "This was already elementary blackmail, frank and undisguised," Skuratov later wrote. "I was silent and looked at the president, while out of the corner of my eye I noticed that Primakov and Putin were watching me with interest: Putin—harshly, with an unpleasant grin, Primakov—sympathetic."[57]

Yeltsin managed to pressure Skuratov to sign yet another letter of resignation, to be postdated April 5, the day before the Federation Council met again. If he did not agree to this, Skuratov feared, "drastic measures would have been taken against me, including physical elimination—either a hitman's bullet or a huge truck loaded with bricks hitting my car. These methods had been mastered to perfection." Although in Yeltsin's presence Primakov advised Skuratov to accede to Yeltsin's request, he approached Skuratov as the latter was about to drive away in his car and told him: "Iurii Ilyich, you know, I'll leave soon as well. I can't work here anymore."[58]

Clearly, Yeltsin and the Family—which now included Putin as a provisional member—considered Skuratov's probe to be a grave threat. As they had learned, del Ponte told Skuratov that credit cards belonging to Yeltsin and his two daughters were issued through the Banca del Gottardo and paid for by none other than Behgjet Pacolli, the head of Mabetex. According to del Ponte, "The president almost never used his cards, but his daughters used them a lot."[59] Skuratov was also investigating Leonid D'iachenko, Tatiana's former husband. According to Skuratov, D'iachenko and Tatiana had pressured Yeltsin to help Berezovsky and Roman Abramovich get control of Sibneft. D'iachenko then became a trader of Sibneft oil and got very rich, hiding his fortune in the Cayman Islands.[60]

Skuratov defiantly continued his investigations of Mabetex, hosting del Ponte in Moscow on March 23, so they could discuss new details of Swiss bank accounts held secretly by Russian officials, just as Skuratov's men were conducting searches of Borodin's office.[61] As for the sex video, instead of causing the intended outrage in the parliament, it aroused sympathy for the beleaguered prosecutor and anger at Yeltsin for his hypocrisy. Skuratov's ally Korzhakov told *Moskovskii komsomolets*: "If they don't leave Skuratov alone, I'll tell everything: how Yeltsin's secretaries ran out of his office with lipstick smudged over their faces; who was given apartments from us and why; where I took Boris Nikolaevich in a Volga with blacked out windows . . ."[62] Emboldened, Skuratov announced in an April 1 interview on NTV that he had requested Yeltsin to investigate information from del Ponte about numerous Russians, some "very well known," who were using Swiss banks to hide dirty money.[63]

Not surprisingly, the Family fought back. On April 2, 1999, Putin appeared on television with MVD chief Stepashin to declare that a careful examination had verified that the man in the scandalous videotape was in fact Skuratov. (They did not say who had made the video.) Furthermore, the two men added, the prostitutes in the video had contacted their agencies and reported that they had been paid by people who were under investigation by the Prosecutor General's Office as bribes to Skuratov. That same day, Yeltsin announced that Skuratov had been "suspended" because he was under criminal investigation for "abuse of office," allegedly accepting the services of prostitutes as bribes.[64] But Skuratov could not be forced to leave his office until the Federation Council affirmed his dismissal.

Skuratov later wrote that he experienced a shock to see Putin playing a role in the fabrication of the case against him: "He knew full well that I had not violated the law and that the Mabetex case really existed."[65] But, as former Putin advisor Andrei Illarionov suggested, Putin had additional motives for attempting to destroy Skuratov's career: "For Putin himself, this was another step in a desperate struggle for his own survival. If Skuratov had remained in his post, following the Mabetex case, Skuratov would definitely return to the Sobchak case and, therefore, to the Putin case."[66]

More Travails for Berezovsky

Meanwhile, Berezovsky appeared to be under siege. Yeltsin had announced on March 4, 1999, that he was dismissing him from his position as executive secretary of the CIS for "exceeding his authority."[67] Having a wealthy Jewish oligarch as an official member of his team was not something Yeltsin wanted to draw attention to, particularly after Russia's financial meltdown. He had appointed Berezovsky to lead the CIS the year before because the other member states had pushed for his candidacy. "To this day," Yeltsin later wrote, "the presidents of the commonwealth say that he was the strongest CIS executive secretary ever."[68] But apparently the criminal investigations of Berezovsky and pressure from both Nikolai Bordiuzha and Primakov, whom Berezovsky had been criticizing publicly, persuaded Yeltsin that Berezovsky had to go.

A further blow to Berezovsky came on April 6, when Skuratov's office issued a warrant for his arrest, along with Glushkov, on charges that they had stolen $250 million from Aeroflot by funneling it through the Swiss firm Andava.[69] Luckily for Berezovsky, the Family stood by him. Stepashin, asked by reporters on April 8 about the prosecutor's orders to search for Berezovsky, who was in Paris at the time, declared: "Why do we have to search for him, he will come here on his own."[70] Surprisingly, Berezovsky's archenemy Chubais, no longer employed by the Kremlin but still enjoying considerable authority with the Yeltsin team, told the press on April 12 that "the excessive activities of the

Office of the Prosecutor General regarding Berezovsky have been a deliberate political move," adding that Skuratov should resign.[71] When Berezovsky returned to Moscow on April 14, the warrant against him had been miraculously revoked.

By this time Berezovsky had an important ally—Aleksandr Voloshin, who had replaced Bordiuzha as head of the Presidential Administration in mid-March 1999. (Bordiuzha was reportedly fired—and removed as secretary of the National Security Council—because his confrontation with Skuratov had not produced the desired results.) Voloshin, a 1978 graduate of the Moscow Institute of Transport Engineers, had met Berezovsky when he worked as a civil servant providing information to automobile exporters. He became an asset manager for Berezovsky in the early 1990s and continued to assist Berezovsky with numerous business ventures after establishing a financial consulting firm in 1995. According to journalist Oleg Lur'e: "After getting close to Berezovsky, the career of the former engineer's assistant took off like a supersonic jet."[72] Considered a "liberal technocrat," Voloshin got a job, on Berezovsky's recommendation, as Iumashev's assistant in the Presidential Administration in late 1997, and the next year was appointed deputy chief of the PA for economic policy.[73]

As Yeltsin's new chief of staff, Voloshin clashed continually with Berezovsky's nemesis Primakov and, according to media reports, wrote daily memorandums to Yeltsin criticizing the prime minister's handling of economic matters. When the Federation Council again refused to approve Skuratov's resignation on April 21, Voloshin was dispatched to speak to the senators in order to persuade them otherwise. His speech was a disaster, and he left the building without even waiting for the vote. Nonetheless, Skuratov, after being officially fired by Yeltsin the next day, allowed his duties to be assumed by his first deputy, Iurii Chaika. The Federation Council would finally approve Skuratov's dismissal in August 1999.[74]

In publicly discrediting Skuratov, Putin had helped Berezovsky, along with other members of the Yeltsin clan. And Berezovsky was grateful. In fact, Putin had extended an olive branch to the oligarch by showing up unexpectedly at a birthday party for Elena Gorbunova on February 22. Berezovsky recalled Putin's gesture a year later: "It was my wife's birthday, and I decided not to invite any of my acquaintances from the top echelons in order not to put them in an awkward position. To my surprise Putin came to that birthday party. Before that, he had never attended any such birthday parties—neither my wife's nor my own. So he came and said 'I don't care at all what Primakov may think about me. I am here because I think it is right.'"[75]

Did Berezovsky not suspect that Putin's gesture had a motive? The Family had decided that they needed Berezovsky on board with them in the impending struggle over Yeltsin's succession. Yeltsin was hanging on to power by a thread. If the Family allowed Berezovsky to be pursued by prosecutors, Yeltsin would lose a powerful advocate, who controlled key media outlets, including ORT and the newspapers *Kommersant* and *Nezavisimaia gazeta*. As for Berezovsky, his financial and political interests, like those of other oligarchs, would be irrevocably damaged if Primakov and the Communists managed to wrest power from the Yeltsin camp. As one observer put it: "Berezovsky had succeeded in combining his own interests so closely with those of the Yeltsin family that it would have been impossible to disentangle his personal fate from the political fortunes of the president. Like it or not, Yeltsin had become the protector of the oligarch from the arm of the law."[76]

According to both Masha Gessen and Alex Goldfarb, Berezovsky began to meet privately with Putin around this time. Gessen says that they saw each almost daily to discuss strategies against Primakov and, later, the question of Yeltsin's successor.[77] Goldfarb describes one meeting, held in mid-April 1999 outside a disused elevator shaft at the back of Putin's office for maximum privacy. Primakov had to go, the two men agreed. But who should take his place and eventually become president? After discussing two possible candidates for prime minister, Stepashin and Nikolai Aksenenko, minister of railways, Berezovsky asked Putin if he would consider becoming Yeltsin's heir apparent. Putin quickly dismissed the idea, saying, incredibly, that he what he really wanted was "to be Berezovsky."[78]

Khinshtein considered Goldfarb's story, which came from Berezovsky, completely implausible: "The director of the most powerful security agency afraid that he could be overheard and so conducting secret negotiations in this sealed-off area . . . And Putin admitting that he dreamed of being Berezovsky?"[79] He was right to be skeptical, given Berezovsky's proclivity to exaggerate his influence in Kremlin circles. In fact, Berezovsky's hubris may well have prevented him from realizing that Putin did not have a high opinion of him. Interestingly, Liudmila Putina told her German friend Irene Pietsch that Berezovsky was "enemy number one," because he was "born under the star of David." On another occasion, she remarked that Berezovsky was to blame for many of Yeltsin's unwise decisions and, to Pietsch's discomfort, again brought up his Jewish heritage, adding: "I don't understand how Tatiana [D'iachenko] can get on so well with Berezovsky! She's such a smart, sober-minded woman. Besides, she's a Capricorn."[80] Did Putin share his wife's views of Berezovsky? Whatever the nature of the alliance between him and Berezovsky at this point, it would soon begin to unravel.

CHAPTER 6

An Heir to the Throne

> Everybody in Russia who did not spend the last
> decade staying in bed has willingly or unwillingly
> violated the law.
>
> —Boris Berezovsky, July 18, 2000, the day he
> resigned from the Duma

By 1999, Berezovsky had been living with his third (common law) wife, Elena Gorbunova, for around six years. Gorbunova, a Russian beauty twenty-one years younger than Berezovsky, had been briefly married to the playwriter Mikhail Shatrov and met Berezovsky in 1989 when she was a student working as an apprentice at LogoVAZ.[1] She gave birth to a daughter, Arina, in 1996 and a son, Gleb, in 1997. With four children from his two previous marriages, Berezovsky, fifty-three, was now the father of six. By all accounts, he adored his children. But Berezovsky's political agenda left him little time to spend with them. His obsession with politics was accompanied by a seemingly insatiable need for publicity. Hardly a day went by without a press interview or a story about Berezovsky in the press.

Putin, by contrast, maintained a low public profile. Now forty-six, he and Liudmila were living with their two daughters outside Moscow in a six-room home at the dacha complex in Arkhangelskoe, reserved for members of the Kremlin inner circle. Because of security concerns related to Putin's leadership of the FSB, both daughters were home-schooled, and Liudmila cut off communications with her close German friend Irene Pietsch. Outwardly, the Putins led a modest life, but they did not fail to enjoy the regular pleasures of the south of France and the Swiss Alps. Putin himself also traveled weekly to St. Petersburg during the spring and summer of 1999 to visit his father, who had been diagnosed with stage four cancer.[2]

Stepashin Gets the Family's Blessing

With Skuratov's flames at least temporarily extinguished, the Family now focused on getting rid of Evgeny Primakov, whose alliance with the Communists in the Duma and the Federation Council presented a major obstacle to the political and economic agenda of the Yeltsin clique. Although not disloyal to Yeltsin, Primakov was a liberal in the Soviet tradition and had socialist proclivities that were incompatible with Yeltsin's fervent anti-Communism. According to an opinion poll conducted in the spring of 1999, Primakov also enjoyed the approval of two-thirds of the electorate, which offered him an incentive to press for his own policy views if he and Yeltsin disagreed or even to decide to run for president. As Khinshtein put it, "In contrast to the eternally sick president surrounded by a palace clique, Primakov saw his popularity grow by leaps and bounds."[3]

Yeltsin and his team wanted a prime minister who would be beholden to them and show unwavering loyalty. But who would take Primakov's place as prime minister, a key stepping-stone to the presidency? Everyone in Yeltsin's circle, it seems, was feverishly endeavoring to promote the "right" candidate. With the presidential election looming in 2000, the pressure was intense. In Shevtsova's words, "the weaker the president grew, the more acute became the Family's need to find a successor they could rely on after his departure."[4]

The candidate favored by Chubais and Iumashev was MVD chief Sergei Stepashin, considered a democrat despite having held law enforcement posts, including chief of Russia's security services in 1994–95. Although he was blamed by many for the FSB's botched attempt to rescue 1,500 hostages held by Chechen separatists in the town of Budennovsk in the summer of 1995, Stepashin had always demonstrated fierce loyalty to Yeltsin, and that meant a lot to the Family.[5] But the opinion of other members of Yeltsin's team had to be considered, and there was by no means a consensus. According to Stepashin, Yeltsin had been seriously considering as his successor Railways Minister Nikolai Aksenenko, whom Berezovsky and Abramovich had been pushing for.[6] But Chubais rushed to Yeltsin's country residence at the last minute and persuaded him that the loyal and "moderate" Stepashin was much better suited for the prime minister's job.[7]

To complicate matters, Yeltsin was wildly unpopular and facing impeachment on five charges by the Duma, which had scheduled a vote on the matter for May 15, 1999. Dismissing Primakov before the impeachment vote was risky, because it could increase the possibility of the impeachment resolution passing. But Yeltsin took a gamble and on May 12 announced Primakov's resignation while naming Stepashin acting prime minister. This caught Duma members completely off guard and prevented them from overcoming their differences in time to muster the two-thirds majority necessary for any of the five articles of impeachment to pass. A week later, the Duma, to avoid giving Yeltsin an excuse to dissolve the parliament, approved Stepashin as prime minister.[8]

Chubais was delighted over Stepashin's appointment. Speaking at the Carnegie Endowment for International Peace in Washington, DC, in May 1999, he said that Stepashin represented "a new generation of Russian politicians" who would bring stability to Russian political life. Despite his portrayal in the Western media as a spymaster, Chubais said, Stepashin was "definitely not a Communist." Primakov, by contrast, attracted Soviet-era Communist figures who wanted to reverse Yeltsin's economic reforms, which was why Yeltsin had to dismiss him. Apparently to counter widespread reports that Berezovsky had helped to engineer Primakov's dismissal, Chubais made a point of telling the group that Berezovsky's role in Primakov's firing was "much lower than he [Berezovsky] would hope."[9] But of course, in sponsoring the incessant media attacks against Primakov, Berezovsky did his part.

Yeltsin later wrote that he had never intended for Stepashin to become Russia's president and had appointed him prime minister as a buffer between Primakov and the real successor, Putin. Stepashin, according to Yeltsin, was just a placeholder until the time was ripe to introduce Putin, whom Yeltsin had already decided upon as his successor. But Iumashev, who was a constant presence at Yeltsin's side, had a different story. He told Yeltsin biographer Timothy Colton that Stepashin was a serious candidate until he seemed unable to handle the crises the Kremlin was facing—the upcoming Duma election and Chechnya.[10] Iumashev confirmed this in a later interview: "Yeltsin really believed that Stepashin could become his successor. But at some point, the president realized that it was a mistake and it would have to be corrected."[11]

If the plan was to have Putin be the successor, Yeltsin did not inform Stepashin, or anyone else for that matter. He admitted as such in his memoirs: "It was too early to put Putin in. Someone else had to fill the gap . . . This role had to be entrusted to the nice, decent Sergei Vadimovich Stepashin. Of course I would try to explain to him that the question of the future, of the presidential elections, was still open. And he, too, would have a chance to show himself . . . Stepashin, and of course many other people, would assume that he was the government's main candidate for the 2000 presidential elections."[12]

Operating on the belief that he was a serious candidate to succeed Yeltsin, Stepashin quickly stepped into the role of statesman and seemed to do a reasonably good job. On June 19, 1999, he attended a summit of the G8 countries in Cologne, Germany, where the main topic of discussion was the armed conflict in Kosovo and the implementation of the United Nations peace accord between NATO and Yugoslavia. Stepashin appeared at a press conference after the first day of meetings and discussed Russia's participation in the settlement of the Kosovo crisis, despite its support for Serbian president Slobodan Milosevic.[13]

The next month Stepashin made his first trip to the United States to pursue arms control, encourage investment in Russia, and resolve other problems in order to improve Russian-American relations after tensions had arisen over Yugoslavia. On July 23, he had a long interview with *CBS News*, in which he displayed an impressive knowledge of issues. Asked whether he planned to run for president in 2000, Stepashin said that his first goal was to stabilize the economic and political situation in Russia and to ensure a favorable outcome for the Duma elections. "And then," he said, "I think closer to the winter, we'll see—time will tell."[14]

Stepashin was reportedly well received both at the G8 summit and during his visit to the United States.[15] But, according to one Russian account, this was a drawback for him: "In the opinion of many experts, the results of the prime minister's PR actions did not strengthen his power. It could have been foreseen that, if he managed to accumulate serious political weight, Yeltsin and his entourage would immediately feel sharp pricks of jealousy and begin to look for shortcomings in his activities."[16] In other words, the Family wanted Yeltsin's heir to be someone who could be controlled.

Chechnya Heating Up

A daunting challenge for Stepashin was the deteriorating situation in Chechnya, which the Kremlin had failed to address effectively. Instead of following up on the 1997 peace agreement signed between Yeltsin and Aslan Maskhadov by bolstering the Maskhadov government and allocating funds to improve living conditions for Chechens, the Kremlin appeared to do little as radical militant Islamists backed their elected leader into a corner. The kidnapping of MVD Major-General Gennadii Shpigun in early March 1999 prompted the Kremlin, Stepashin in particular, to threaten Russian military intervention if Shpigun was not released and acts of terrorism not brought under control. It was at this time, according to what Stepashin revealed to the press in January 2000, that the Kremlin began planning for a limited incursion into Chechnya. But the plan was only to create a "security zone" that extended to the Terek River, close to the northern border of Chechnya, not to engage in "large-scale hostilities" with Chechens.[17] Primakov, who as foreign intelligence chief in 1994 had opposed the first Chechen war, reportedly objected fiercely to this plan, but his removal in mid-May allowed it to go forward.[18]

Stepashin met Maskhadov on June 11 in Ingushetia, the Russian region bordering Chechnya to the west, and implored Maskhadov to "separate yourself from the bandits." If he did not, Stepashin told Maskhadov, "then you are finished."[19] During the next weeks, the situation heated up further, with skirmishes between Russian and Chechen troops and missiles fired from Russian helicopters along the border with Dagestan. Maskhadov's radical Islamist opponents, including Shamil Basaev and Movladi Udugov, seemed to be pushing Chechnya into conflict by stirring up adherents of Wahhabism, which espoused a pure form of early Islam and especially appealed to radical militant youth.[20]

Following the Shpigun abduction, Maskhadov gave an interview in which he blamed Berezovsky for the crisis his government was facing, because Berezovsky had in the past negotiated with Chechen criminals and paid them in order to get hostages released: "All those Berezovsky trips, all those bags of money, playing with criminals, as well as opponents [of the legitimately elected president] leads right to this result."[21] Although he was no longer secretary of the National Security Council, Berezovsky remained in contact with Chechen politicians and had several telephone conversations with Udugov in the spring of 1999, followed by a meeting with him in Moscow. Udugov, a former foreign minister in Maskhadov's government, proposed a plan to Berezovsky: led by Basaev, Wahhabis from Chechnya would begin military attacks against neighboring Dagestan, which would provoke Russian troops to move in and cause the collapse of the Maskhadov government. Given

FIGURE 14.   Chechen president Aslan Maskhadov. Reuters/Alamy.

that Maskhadov and his allies wanted Chechnya to become fully independent and eventually integrated with the West, Russia would be far better off with an Islamist government in Grozny, which would be staunchly anti-Western. Thus, Udugov proposed, after a limited military action in Dagestan, the Kremlin would install him and Basaev as Chechnya's leaders.[22]

Berezovsky later told Alex Goldfarb that he had not been keen on this proposal, because an Islamic state on Russia's doorstep "might have unpredictable consequences." But he nonetheless went with the plan to Prime Minister Stepashin, who said "he would take it from there." At the beginning of September 1999, when the conflict in Dagestan was well underway, Berezovsky discussed the situation with Putin, by this time the new prime minister, but warned him not to start a full-fledged war in Chechnya, which he said would never end. Berezovsky suggested instead that they should try to bring Basaev and Udugov back into a coalition government with Maskhadov, so the two sides could "neutralize" each other. After hearing him out, Putin responded: "Stop your contacts with Chechens. No more phone calls, nor messages, no small favors. You cannot imagine what my people are telling me about you.

If I believed 1 percent of it, we would not be talking here." Berezovsky promised he would follow Putin's instructions.[23]

Putin's statements in his autobiography appear to confirm that Berezovsky raised concerns about further military action and suggested an alternative: "In my view, his [Berezovsky's] proposals on Chechnya are not realistic or effective. Frankly speaking, that is why nothing that he has proposed is being implemented."[24] But Berezovsky would later be accused of supplying Udugov with funds to finance a raid by Basaev and the Arab warrior al-Khattab into Dagestan that took place in early August. Also, he was reportedly present at meetings in Nice between Voloshin, an active proponent of the raid, and Basaev in early July. So, whatever his rethinking of the plan later, he may well have contributed to its implementation.[25]

Mudslinging

The Yeltsin team had reason to encourage Chechen rebel warlords to incite a conflagration with the Russian military. Absent a crisis, the team's plan for a successful transition from a Yeltsin presidency to one controlled by its handpicked successor was far from certain. Moscow mayor Iurii Luzhkov, head of the Fatherland (Otechestvo) Party, was highly popular and considered a likely contender for the presidency. Luzhkov had used his authority over Moscow's economy to forge ties with some of the country's most powerful banks and media outlets, as well to build alliances with many of the regional governors.[26] At one point, members of the Yeltsin group had sent Berezovsky as an emissary to give Luzhkov an offer: if he agreed to grant them legal immunity and guaranteed the results of privatization, Yeltsin would support him as his successor. Luzhkov declined the offer. In the words of journalist Mikhail Zygar: "Luzhkov was sure that the Family was in trouble, beyond salvation . . . [He] was reluctant to join the fight on the side of those he considered to be the losers. He wanted to associate himself with the winners."[27]

Luzhkov began courting Primakov, whose poll ratings were impressive, especially in comparison with Yeltsin's dismal ones. An alliance between the two men presented the Yeltsin forces with an existential threat. Yeltsin later described the situation:

> By the summer of 1999, the slow rapprochement of Primakov and Luzhkov had begun . . . Together he [Luzhkov] and Primakov could obtain an overwhelming advantage in the Duma elections,

especially because Primakov knew how to make a good deal with the Communists . . . But how to stop them? . . . In July I repeatedly talked to Sergei Stepashin about this situation . . . It was clear to me that the final round of a pitched political battle was approaching . . . Stepashin was able to reconcile some people for a time, but he wasn't going to become a political leader, a fighter, or a real ideological opponent to Luzhkov and Primakov in the Duma elections. A new political party had to be created, and the prime minister had to be changed.[28]

Although he had opposed Yeltsin's impeachment, Luzhkov was becoming increasingly aggressive in criticizing the Yeltsinites. And he had managed to gain the support of Vladimir Gusinsky, who controlled both NTV and the widely read newspaper *Segodnia*. At the end of May, the popular political commentator Evgenii Kiselev appeared on the NTV show *Itogi* with a chart displaying the president's political elite (using the hitherto unpublicized term "Family") and suggested that its members were engaged in corruption and hiding their ill-gotten funds abroad. Yeltsin later said that the show was like a "stab in the back from people I thought were of my mind," and put him into a state of shock.[29] To make matters worse, the Mabetex scandal reemerged on July 14, with the formal announcement by Swiss prosecutors that they had opened a criminal money-laundering investigation into Pavel Borodin, his wife, and twenty-two other unnamed senior Russian officials. When one of the investigators was asked whether Yeltsin or his daughter were being investigated, he responded "Not yet."[30]

Tatiana D'iachenko, in an interview ten years later, recalled the Family's panic:

> An enormous well-equipped propaganda machine was working against Papa. NTV, the Moscow television channels, newspapers, magazines . . . Their aim was a simple one: to win the elections in the year 2000 . . . When it became clear that Papa did not want to support the Primakov-Luzhkov tandem, the people were inundated with stories about the Family, about stolen billions, credit cards, castles in Germany and France, houses in London, and so on.[31]

The Kremlin decided to retaliate, pressuring the state-owned Vneshekonombank to renegue on a loan agreement with Gusinsky's Media-Most company and then announcing that the company was insolvent. In a July 13 newspaper interview, Berezovsky, who was just completing the purchase of Kommersant Publishing House, claimed that Media-Most owed more than a billion dollars in loans and was thus forced to engage in "political racketeering." By supporting Luzhkov, Berezovsky said, Gusinsky was "openly confronting the Kremlin and the president" and was "acting in the same way as the Communist Party that he criticizes."[32] After ORT repeated the claims about Media-Most, Kiselev suggested on *Itogi* that NTV was the victim of a smear campaign engineered by Berezovsky and Aleksandr Voloshin, who was now chairman of the board of ORT.[33]

According to Khinshtein, Berezovsky had begun to craft a strategy for a media counterattack at the end of June, when he assembled a small group of close allies on his yacht for a cruise on the French Riviera near St. Tropez. Among the guests were Badri Patarkatsishvili, Nikolai Glushkov, and Sergei Dorenko, who until March had hosted a weekly news commentary program, *Vremia*, on ORT. Khinshtein described the scene:

> It was there, swaying on the waves of the Mediterranean Sea, that Berezovsky described his ingenious venture, announcing that Dorenko would soon return to ORT in order to raze Primakov and Luzhkov to the ground. "And how will the Family look at this?"— they asked him. Boris Abramovich only grinned in response: "The Family will do everything that I propose. They have no other choice, otherwise they will be finished."[34]

Putin contributed to the effort by initiating an FSB investigation into Luzhkov's wife, businesswoman Elena Baturina, and her brother Vladimir Baturin, owners of two firms that produced plastics and were allegedly suspected of illegally transferring millions of rubles abroad through fictitious foreign contracts.[35] Luzhkov reacted with a fierce counterattack, appearing on NTV's *Itogi* on July 18 to denounce Berezovsky for being behind the illegitimate case against his wife, along with the Presidential Administration. Asked how that could be, since Berezovsky was not in charge of the FSB, Luzhkov retorted: "Unfortunately the FSB now works for the Kremlin and not the country." After Luzhkov insisted that the FSB had been instructed to find "something criminal" in his wife's business, Putin and the Family apparently decided to back off from the attack on Baturina. The prosecutor's office announced within days that there was no case against her.[36]

Stepashin opposed the Kremlin's use of the media for mudslinging against its political opponents. At a government meeting on July 19, 1999, he observed: "I watched television last night. The channels do nothing but attack each other. They do not cover important events, as if there are no problems other than their own in the country."[37] But his moderate strategy and his attempts to mediate between the presidential team and its opponents did not sit well with the Family. According to Nemtsov, both he and Chubais thought Stepashin was doing a good job as prime minister: "He was a considerably mild man, accommodating and honest. We were convinced that he would not act foolishly. For Russia, such a president would mean a step forward." But, Nemtsov said, those close to Yeltsin convinced the president that he needed someone who would ensure that he and his family were protected legally: "The members of Yeltsin's circle were indifferent about how the new president would lead the country. They were only concerned about themselves."[38]

Fending Off Investigations

Although he was not implicated in the Mabetex case, Berezovsky was still on the radar of law enforcement bodies. At the request of Russian prosecutors, Swiss police had raided the offices of Andava and Forus, the two companies that had handled Aeroflot's foreign transactions, in early July. And on July 14, Iurii Chaika, interim prosecutor general, extended the investigation of the Aeroflot case by another six months. Khinshtein reported that Berezovsky and his colleagues faced charges of money laundering and embezzlement. But he added: "Do not think that Berezovsky is sitting with his arms folded waiting for a Black Maria to call at his doorstep. The Kremlin staff and other power structures have lately stepped up their pressure on the Prosecutor's Office."[39]

Chaika and Skuratov had been classmates at the Sverdlovsk Institute of Law in the early 1970s. When Skuratov became prosecutor general in 1995, he brought Chaika to Moscow to serve as his first deputy, commenting in an interview that Chaika was "a very energetic, demanding, and tough person in the fight against crime."[40] Chaika pursued the Mabetex investigation after Skuratov took temporary absence from his post in February, and Skuratov had counted on his support when the Kremlin demanded his resignation, asking Chaika to investigate the source of the sex tape. But on April 2, when Skuratov got the news that

the Kremlin had arranged for the Moscow prosecutor's office to initiate a criminal investigation of him, he learned that Chaika had turned
against him and was backing the probe. "I had known Chaika for a
long time, considered him my comrade, a like-minded person," Skuratov recalled. "The betrayal on his part was a heavy blow for me, which
I experienced painfully."[41]

The Kremlin had reportedly promised to reward Chaika by keeping
him in Skuratov's job on a permanent basis. But in late July, he was
forced to step down because of a scandal involving his son Artem. In
March 1999, Artem Chaika had loaned his father's car (complete with
official flashing lights) to a couple of armed bandits from Ingushetia,
who were stopped by the police, arrested, and charged with extortion of
a Moscow businessman for $100,000. As one source put it, "The likeli-
hood that Chaika could stay on as prosecutor general after such an incident was virtually zero."[42] Nonetheless, Putin did not forget the debt
the Family owed Chaika. After he became prime minister on August 9,
Putin appointed Chaika minister of justice. Chaika has remained a
key member of Putin's team ever since, surviving even worse scandals
involving him and his family. He became Russian prosecutor general in
2006 and was implicated in Russian attempts to interfere with the 2016
US presidential elections.[43]

Skuratov himself was in limbo, prevented from working in his office
but still supported by the Federation Council, so not officially dismissed. He wrote in his memoirs that in the late summer of 1999,
Berezovsky, apparently with the Family's approval, paid him a visit and
asked him to publicly renounce his struggle against Yeltsin's entourage. In return, Berezovsky said, the Family would support him if he
chose to embark on a political career and run for election to the Duma.
Skuratov told Berezovsky that he might consider some sort of a compromise if the Kremlin admitted publicly that the sex tape was a fabrication. Ten days later, the two had another meeting, during which
Berezovsky dangled another offer: if Skuratov resigned, the tape would
be disavowed and Skuratov would be given a special appointment as
Russian coordinator of relations with foreign law enforcement authorities. Skuratov thought seriously about accepting but decided in the
end that he would be betraying his colleagues who had worked for
many months on the investigations. Surprisingly, he was grateful for
the offer: "I confess, despite all the hostility, that it made me respect
Berezovsky."[44]

Calling Vladimir Putin

Berezovsky also made another overture on behalf of the Family. In mid-July 1999, he flew in his Gulfstream jet to the south of France and paid a visit to Putin, who was vacationing at a hotel in the seaside resort of Biarritz with Liudmila and their two daughters. According to Goldfarb, Berezovsky said to Putin as the two had lunch: "Boris Nikolaevich sent me. He wants you to become the prime minister." Putin responded: "I am not sure that I am ready for that," and suggested instead that he be given Gazprom to run. After more coaxing by Berezovsky, Putin finally acceded but insisted that the offer had to come from Yeltsin himself. Berezovsky agreed, noting that he had been sent to sound Putin out because Yeltsin "does not want to hear no for an answer."[45] Just before the presidential elections Berezovsky gushed to an interviewer about how he respected Putin, and added that "there's one other trait that distinguishes Putin from all the others . . . Putin had never struggled for power, he only accepted Yeltsin's proposal."[46]

Interviewed by Petr Aven in 2014, Iumashev gave a different account of Berezovsky's visit to Putin. Iumashev claimed that Berezovsky had heard that Voloshin was discussing Putin as prime minister when events in Dagestan started heating up. So, without saying a word to anyone, Berezovsky rushed to the vacationing Putin and told him, "A decision has been made, Vladimir Vladimirovich, you will be the next president."[47] In fact, the appointment was still uncertain as late as August 6 when Iumashev, Tatiana, Voloshin, and Chubais deliberated intensely for several hours, without Yeltsin present. Yeltsin had met with Putin on August 5 and tentatively offered him the job of prime minister, but Voloshin had persuaded Yeltsin to wait over the weekend before making a final decision. Chubais was so opposed to Putin becoming prime minister that he organized a meeting with a group of oligarchs to get their support on Sunday, August 8, and asked Aven to go to Putin and advise him against taking the position. Aven duly arranged to meet Putin that same afternoon at Putin's dacha, but when Putin arrived, forty minutes late, he leapt out of the car shouting, "I have already agreed!"[48]

According to Yeltsin, Stepashin, Putin, Voloshin, and Aksenenko, the first deputy premier, had assembled in his office at 8 a.m. that morning. There he informed them that he had signed a decree removing Stepashin as prime minister and appointing Putin in his place. Stepashin at first refused to accept the decree but then backed down. Putin recalled only that the meeting was "very unpleasant," because Stepashin did not take the news well.[49]

The next day, August 9, 1999, Yeltsin announced Putin's appointment on national television. In itself, this might not have been considered a hugely significant event. Putin was, after all, the fourth prime minister to be appointed in the last sixteen months. But, after reminding his audience that there would be a presidential election in less than a year, Yeltsin declared Putin his designated successor: "I have confidence in him. And I want those who go to the polls next July to be confident in him as well and make him their choice. I think he has enough time to show himself."[50]

Chubais later said that he had backed Stepashin because he had a greater chance than Putin of being elected president: "I fought for my point of view to the end. Right up to that moment when Yeltsin informed Stepashin of his removal."[51] Chubais had good reason for this assessment. Stepashin's approval ratings had risen from 19 percent in May to an impressive 42 percent by early August. But for Yeltsin and the other members of the Family, Stepashin was a weak prime minister. Berezovsky later said: "I think Stepashin is a liberal, of course, but he failed to show such willpower or such courage as Putin has shown. Putin did risk a lot as he was coming to grips with Primakov and Luzhkov, because the two guys were the undisputed leaders in that race. As regards Stepashin, he got scared and began to shuffle between the Kremlin and Primakov, Luzhkov and other political forces."[52]

In other words, Stepashin was hesitant to go along with extreme solutions in order to defeat Yeltsin's opponents. When he gave his parting speech to the cabinet on August 9, Stepashin made what seemed like a veiled warning. He stressed that the government must act legally and adhere to the constitution and that the upcoming parliamentary elections must take place as scheduled. He added that "our people will not be deceived by anyone, no matter who wants to do so."[53] Later, just before the Russian presidential election, Stepashin would be more explicit in his concerns about violations of the law. Speaking at the National Press Club in Washington, DC, in March 2000, Stepashin noted that in Russia "the institution of press censorship was being restored," and warned that "whoever is putting thoughts into Mr. Putin's head [about reviving censorship] . . . has to be stopped."[54]

Outside observers saw a threat as well. *The Moscow Times* editorialized that "the anointment of Putin—a KGB hack who has never held an elected office—sends the strongest signal to date that his [Yeltsin's] regime is contemplating a dangerous adventure."[55] Communist Duma leader Viktor Iliukhin told the paper that he feared Putin would act against the constitution and cancel elections. But others just considered the Putin appointment a sign of the Kremlin's incompetence. "It's hard to explain madness," Boris Nemtsov told *Ekho Moskvy*. "The people have grown tired of watching an ill leader who is not capable of doing his job." Journalist Iulia Latynina was perhaps the most scornful: "Monday morning [August 9], it finally became clear who will not become Russia's president in the year 2000. It will not be Vladimir Putin . . . The only thing worse for Putin [than this appointment] would be an endorsement from a Russian lesbian association."[56]

More Challenges for the Family

It was perhaps not a coincidence that on August 7, the day before Yeltsin confirmed his decision to appoint Putin as prime minister, warlords Basaev and Khattab invaded the Russian republic of Dagestan with 1,500–2,000 armed Islamic militants and declared their goal of establishing an Islamic state in the republic. Stepashin, after being told by Yeltsin that he was going to lose his job, flew to Dagestan on August 8 with the army's chief of staff, General Anatolii Kvashnin, and authorized a full-scale bombing of the villages occupied by Chechen rebel forces. He warned that the situation was very difficult and that "we could really lose Dagestan."[57] But, as he later made clear, Stepashin was opposed to Russian forces going beyond the Terek River: "In August of that year [1999] we told Mr. Putin that it was not desirable that we move any further forward because that might result in some negative implications."[58] Putin and the Family, however, had a greater adventure in mind.

On becoming prime minister, Putin asked Yeltsin to grant him "absolute power" to conduct the necessary military operations in Chechnya, which Yeltsin did. Then Putin issued an ultimatum to the Russian military: the Chechen invaders had to be repulsed from Dagestan in two weeks. A combination of heavy Russian bombing of occupied villages and lack of support among local Dagestanis for the Islamic republic envisaged by Basaev and Khattab allowed this goal to be achieved. By August 23, Chechen rebel fighters had withdrawn, and Putin, accompanied by reporters, flew to Dagestan a few days later to celebrate the victory by handing out medals to fifty of the fighters. In his remarks Putin warned about the enemy's plans and "acts of provocation to be expected in the near future." As Steven Myers observed, Putin's remarks "contained the seeds of caution—and, some believed, forewarning—that the conflict had not ended with Basayev's retreat back into Chechnya."[59] In fact, within less than two weeks, Putin's prescience would be starkly demonstrated.

While fighting had de-escalated in the North Caucasus, the Kremlin faced daunting political challenges at home. Despite Putin's impressive command of the situation in Dagestan, most pundits deemed him a nobody, just another example of Yeltsin's impulsive decision making. Polls in August showed that only 1 percent of respondents would vote for a Putin presidency, confirming the concerns of Chubais.[60] Meanwhile on August 17, Primakov, who had been courted by the Communists, formally joined the powerful Fatherland-All Russia Alliance, a coalition with Russia's regional governors formed by Luzhkov two weeks earlier. Primakov was widely regarded as the country's most powerful politician, with polls showing he was trusted by close to 50 percent of respondents. With Primakov on board, more governors were expected to jump on the Fatherland-All Russia bandwagon. Political experts were predicting a victory for the political bloc in the December parliamentary elections and a win for Primakov if he became a candidate in the presidential election scheduled for mid-2000. As Iumashev recalled: "At that time, Putin was opposed by the Primakov-Luzhkov tandem, whose joint ratings were off the charts. The most successful mayor with a budget larger than the total budget of two-thirds of Russia. And the political heavyweight, the favorite of the people and all the special services, Yevgeny Maksimovich Primakov. The entire political elite lined up for them. The governors and presidents of the republics raced to support the future prime minister and president. Businesses were waiting in line to offer money for the election campaign to Primakov and Luzhkov."[61]

The new alliance posed an existential threat to the Yeltsin team. Although the bloc's platform opposed a return to a Soviet-style economy, run by the state, it did advocate greater government control over business, along with curbs on presidential powers, which would put an end to the prevailing Yeltsin system of crony capitalism.[62] And Luzhkov himself had publicly spoken of reallocating shares of some companies to those who lost out in the original privatization process. In the words of author Vasif Guseinov: "The thing that frightened the Family and its entourage the most was the redistribution of property that would surely take place if either Luzhkov or Primakov became president."[63]

ЕВГЕНИЙ
ПРИМАКОВ

ЮРИЙ
ЛУЖКОВ

FIGURE 15.   Evgeny Primakov and Iurii Luzhkov, August 1999. Reuters/Alamy.

Alarm bells sounded even louder for the Yeltsin team when more stories on Kremlin corruption began to make headlines. On August 19, 1999, an account of massive Russian money laundering via the Bank of New York appeared in *The New York Times*. According to the report, "Investigators say the transactions seem to add up to one of the largest money laundering operations ever uncovered in the United States, with vast sums of money moving in and out of the bank in a day."[64] On August 25, the leading Italian newspaper *Corriere della Sera* reported that Yeltsin's family was being investigated by the Swiss for using credit cards that were billed to Mabetex, which also allegedly transferred one million dollars to a Hungarian bank account for the use of Yeltsin's family. Then on September 3, the paper published a list of twenty-four Russians who were being probed by Swiss authorities for money laundering through Mabetex. Pavel Borodin, Putin's old boss, was at the top of the list, along with his family members, and former deputy prime minister Oleg Soskovets was also included.[65] The impact of these revelations was huge, leading to calls in the West for a suspension of the billions of dollars of International Monetary Fund lending to Russia and demands by Russian politicians that those who looted state assets be jailed.

Yeltsin was reported to be in panic mode, as his advisors struggled to respond.[66] On September 3, he had a meeting with the new FSB chief, Nikolai Patrushev, to discuss the Bank of New York scandal. After the meeting Patrushev told reporters that the case was purely political and connected with upcoming US elections. "It is simply ridiculous," Patrushev said, "to talk about sums of $15–20 billion that were supposedly laundered." As for the Swiss credit cards held by Yeltsin and his family, Patrushev said he did not discuss those "rumors" with the president.[67]

That same day, Yeltsin's chief of staff, Aleksandr Voloshin, held a briefing for journalists to address the corruption scandals. According to Elena Trebugova, the Kremlin had been conducting secret meetings to decide how to react, but when Voloshin stepped forward, he did not deny the accusations. All he could say was that "the proper response to what is happening will follow in the near future. Russia will not be wronged anymore." Tregubova was incredulous: "This could in no way be called an adequate response to the flow of compromising evidence that has harmed the reputation of not only the government but the entire country."[68]

A Dramatic Change of Subject

Public attention was diverted from the scandal the very next day, September 4, when the first in a series of devastating bombings occurred in the city of Buinaksk, Dagestan. A powerful truck bomb exploded at Apartment House No. 3, which housed soldiers, mainly Dagestani, of the Russian army's 136th Motor-Rifle Brigade, along with their families. Fifty-eight were killed, and more than hundred wounded.[69] An earlier, much smaller bomb attack had taken place on the evening of August 31 in an underground shopping center at Moscow's Manezh Square, killing one person and injuring dozens. But that attack, for which two Dagestani terrorists would eventually be convicted, was downplayed by the authorities. Appearing remarkably complacent, FSB chief Patrushev assured a journalist that there was no necessity for additional security measures to be taken in Moscow.[70]

Russian authorities immediately attributed the Buinaksk attack to al-Khattab, who they said had used Wahhabi Chechen rebels to carry it out and was hiding in Chechnya. In March 2001, six organizers and perpetrators would be tried and sentenced to varying degrees of imprisonment by the Dagestani Supreme Court, with two others prosecuted later. But, as John Dunlop has pointed out in his deeply researched book on the 1999 bombings in Russia, the version of the bombing put forth by Dagestani prosecutors cannot be trusted, given the clear violations of legal procedure during the investigation and trials. Dunlop provides evidence suggesting that, while some of those convicted were guilty as charged, the FSB and certain elite units of the MVD were aware of the terrorists' plan and abetted it. Officers of these agencies thoroughly examined the truck that carried the explosives from Chechnya when it reached a checkpoint and let it pass through. Dunlop concludes that "elements among the FSB and the regular police wanted the terrorists to succeed in their plans, most likely because they had been ordered to do so by their superiors."[71]

These superiors included FSB chief Patrushev, one of Putin's closest allies.[72] At the helm of the MVD was the recently appointed Vladimir Rushailo, a veteran internal affairs officer, who, as deputy chief of the MVD's organized crime division, had formed ties with numerous businessmen, including Berezovsky. Berezovsky had been a generous donor to a special foundation Rushailo set up for the financial support to employees of the organized crime division. It was allegedly because of Berezovsky's influence that Rushailo was appointed to replace Stepashin as MVD chief when the later became prime minister. Rushailo was thus referred to as "Berezovsky's falcon."[73]

Of the two men, Patrushev carried by far the most weight. The FSB was a more powerful agency than the MVD, and Patrushev had a direct line to Putin. He could be counted on to implement Putin's plans. But what were those plans? If the goal was to distract the Russian public from the mounting reports of Kremlin corruption and to enhance support for the new prime minister's government, it was not achieved by the bombing in Buinaksk. Because the majority of the victims were not ethnic Russians, there was not the huge outrage in the country that would occur after the subsequent bombings. A second bomb—with explosives powerful enough "to turn the basic part of the city into dust"—had been set to go off that same night near a military hospital in Buinaksk. But it was unexpectedly discovered by local police and defused by military sappers. (As with the first bomb, the truck that transported the explosives from Chechnya had its contents examined by militia, in this case at more than one checkpoint, but was not detained.)[74] So in the end, the Buinaksk bombing was portrayed by the Russian media as just another episode in the continued fighting and violence in Dagestan. More earthshaking terrorist events would soon follow.

CHAPTER 7

Putin's Path to Victory

> Those explosions were a crucial moment in the
> unfolding of our current history. After the first
> shock passed, it turned out that we were living
> in an entirely different country, in which almost
> no one dared talk about a peaceful, political
> resolution of the crisis with Chechnya.
>
> —Human rights activist and Duma member Sergei
> Kovalev, February 2000

Putin was preparing for a trip to New Zealand to attend the annual Asia-Pacific Economic Cooperation Forum when, just after midnight on September 9, 1999, a powerful explosion demolished a nine-story apartment at 19 Gurianova Street in Moscow, killing 100 people and wounding 690. Given the importance of the high-level forum, which would include US president Bill Clinton, Putin went ahead with the trip, flying from Moscow on September 11. When Clinton asked him about the Chechen situation, Putin said that the Chechen terrorists were financed by Al-Qaeda and confided that the Russian military was about to launch an invasion of the republic.[1]

A second bombing on September 13, which killed 124 and wounded around 200 at an eight-story apartment building on Kashirskoe Highway in Moscow, caused Putin to cut short his trip and fly back to Moscow. He gave a fiery speech to the Duma upon his return on September 14, in which he declared: "Those who organized and launched a whole series of brutal terrorist attacks have far-reaching plans . . . Their goal is to demoralize the government, undermine the foundations of the state, interfere with the normal operation of state bodies, and sow panic among the population." Stressing that not just the terrorists but the sources of the terrorism needed to be eliminated, Putin singled out Chechnya, where, he said, the authorities were protecting bandits. To address the problem, Putin said, the Khasavyurt Accords, which had led to the withdrawal of Russian troops from Chechnya, needed to be reassessed. Thus, although he did not announce plans for the Russian military to enter the republic and spoke instead of a cordon sanitaire around Chechnya, Putin seemed to be laying the groundwork for an invasion.[2]

The day after Putin's speech, September 16, another powerful explosive device was denoted, at an apartment building in the city of Volgodonsk. Miraculously, only eighteen people were killed, but at least eighty-nine were hospitalized, included several children. (It would later be revealed that the chairman of the Duma, Gennadii Seleznev, had advance knowledge of the bombing, but how he obtained the information was never explained.) Within less than a week, Russian forces had amassed on the border in numbers comparable to those deployed for the first invasion of Chechnya in 1995. And Putin was becoming more belligerent publicly, vowing famously on September 24 to "rub out the terrorists in the crapper."[3]

Putin's response to the bombings was well received among the Russian people, who had been thrown into a panic by the possibility of further devastating attacks. As American scholar Henry Hale observed: "Given the USSR's cookie-cutter approach to housing design, the apartment buildings that had been obliterated, shown over and over on Russian television, looked just like the kinds of apartment complexes in which millions of Russians lived. Anyone's residence could be next."[4] And, despite the fact that not only Chechen president Maskhadov but also the invaders of Dagestan, Basaev and Khattab, disavowed these terrorist bombings, the public seemed to go along with Putin's claim that Chechens bore the responsibility.

Berezovsky, meanwhile, had been hospitalized for hepatitis on September 10. Four days later, he got an unpleasant shock. In an article that opened with the question "Were the Moscow explosions prepared in the Kremlin?" Aleksandr Khinshtein published excerpts of June–July telephone conversations Berezovsky had with Udugov and Chechen Minister of Internal Affairs Kazbek Makhashev. The conversations appeared to concern prisoner exchanges, as well as payments of money that Berezovsky had promised the men, and there was a possible reference to the planned incursion into Dagestan. Khinshtein ended his piece by castigating Berezovsky for consorting with the enemy Chechens, drawing the conclusion that Berezovsky financed their August foray: "Why does Berezovsky need a war in Dagestan? Because when the regime changes, he and his accomplices will be in prison. Today the 'family' has no other legitimate ways to preserve power."[5]

The political opposition was quick to pick up on the story. On September 15, NTV, owned by Luzhkov supporter Gusinsky, featured clips of the telephone conversations. Outraged, Berezovsky went straight to the press, holding a news conference at Interfax on September 16, while, in Goldfarb's words, "his face and the whites of his eyes were still yellow from hepatitis."[6] Berezovsky claimed that—although he had had many conversations with Udugov, Makhashev, and other Chechen leaders while in the National Security Council and afterwards—the conversation presented recently in the media had been falsified. He also reminded his audience that Gusinsky himself had once requested that Berezovsky intervene when one of his journalists had been kidnapped by Chechens. And he went on to say that the government was now reaping the consequences of its failure to address the buildup of fortifications in Dagestan by Wahhabi extremists for more than two years: "The secret services were aware of it. Let us name the heads of all the secret services within that period: Stepashin, Kovalev, Kulikov, Primakov and Trubnikov [Viacheslav Trubnikov, Primakov's successor as head of the Foreign Intelligence Service] . . . These people knew exactly what was happening. They let the situation develop, and we are overcoming this situation at the cost of numerous fatalities." Furthermore, Berezovsky said, the Kremlin took no action to mitigate the economic situation in Chechnya after the 1997 peace agreement: "One cannot keep armed hungry people unemployed, without any hope for the future. Of course, things had to explode. We created the situation through our own inaction."[7]

Berezovsky was treading a thin line by criticizing the past actions of the security services. In listing the names of security and law enforcement chiefs who were aware of the volatile situation in Dagestan, Berezovsky pointedly did not include Putin. But it was clear that, as head of the FSB until August, Putin was among those responsible. Interestingly, it was the "weak" Stepashin who took Berezovsky's statements about the Dagestan conflict even further. When asked in mid-September by a journalist whether Berezovsky might have been negotiating with Chechen extremists in order to ignite a conflict that would propel Putin into the forefront as a leader, Stepashin replied cryptically: "That certain agreements were made in order to destabilize the situation and bring it under emergency rule, that is a possible version of events, according to what was published in *MK* . . . It is necessary to check when this recording was made, what the conversation was about, to summon, if necessary, people for questioning."[8] Although he denounced Basaev and Khattab for murders and hostage taking, Stepashin was not discounting the claim that Berezovsky and the Yeltsin clan had planned to use an armed conflict as a pretext for declaring emergency rule, thereby causing a postponement of parliamentary and presidential elections.[9]

Stepashin's departure from the official Putin line emerged more clearly when he was interviewed on NTV on October 1 and asserted in no uncertain terms that he opposed a full-scale operation in Chechnya: "We call it a war on terrorism, but it is quite obvious—when artillery and aviation are used, and the troops have already approached the Terek River—that this is an all-out war . . . How will this war end? Destruction of militants and terrorists, that is clear. But tens of thousands of people live there . . . This is a humanitarian problem." Stepashin went on to say that, in his personal view, it was wrong to burn bridges with Maskhadov: "Yeltsin's agreement with Maskhadov was signed. We recognized him as the legitimate president. There should be no double standards. Leave at least a small loophole! You can't corner people and at the same time try to reach an agreement with them."[10] That very day, Putin declared that Russia no longer considered Maskhadov the legitimate ruler of Chechnya. Close to a hundred thousand Russian ground troops entered Chechnya, and Putin confirmed that "combat operations in Chechnya are already under way." Air strikes on Grozny, begun more than a week earlier, had already caused nearly eighty thousand civilians to flee the republic.[11]

In an effort to defend his reputation, Berezovsky enlisted Vitalii Tretiakov, the editor-in-chief of *Nezavisimaia gazeta*, to weigh in with a piece on October 12. "Boris Berezovsky has long been chosen by many to be the one to blame," Tretiakov wrote. "This is not very fair, because they all sinned together, and they want to send one to the slaughter." According to Tretiakov, Berezovsky should not have been singled out for organizing the war in Dagestan, because it was an operation approved by the entire Yeltsin leadership: "It is quite obvious that the Chechens were lured to Dagestan—they were allowed to get involved in this business in order to provide a legitimate reason for the restoration of federal power in the republic and the beginning of an active phase of the struggle against the terrorists gathered in Chechnya. Obviously, it was an operation by the Russian special services (not to be confused with the bombings of houses), and it was politically sanctioned at the very top."[12]

Official Narrative Challenged

Although Tretiakov made of point of noting that apartment bombings were not part of the Kremlin plan, others conflated the Dagestan incursion and the subsequent terrorist attacks, attributing both to the Kremlin. Thus Aleksandr Lebed, who had brokered the Khasavyurt Accords, and was now governor of Krasnoyarsk, told the Paris newspaper *Le Figaro* on September 29 that he was "convinced" that the Yeltsin government was behind the apartment bombings: "Any Chechen field commander set on revenge would have started blowing up generals," Lebed said. "Or he'd have started striking Internal Affairs Ministry and Federal Security Service buildings, military stockpiles, or nuclear power plants. He wouldn't have targeted ordinary, innocent people. The goal is to sow mass terror and create conditions for destabilization, so as to be able to say when the time comes, 'You shouldn't go to the polls, or you'll risk being blown up along with the ballot box.'"[13]

Russian journalists were also questioning the official version that Chechens had masterminded the bombings, in part because of evidence that the Russian security services had received advanced warning of the attacks. *Novaia gazeta* reported that on September 8, its offices had received detailed information about the planned bombings and passed it on immediately to the MVD, to no avail. And a journalist for *Obshschaia gazeta* reported on September 16 that the respected State Duma deputy Konstantin Borovoi had received directly from a GRU officer on September 9 details of plans, including several names, for further terrorist bombings in the wake of the explosion that had just occurred. Borovoi conveyed the information to the FSB and the National Security Council, but there was no response.[14]

As John Dunlop pointed out, the anti-Yeltsin newspaper *Moskovskii komsomolets* was in the forefront of reporting that questioned the official version, arguing in a series of articles that the execution of the attacks required such lengthy planning and expertise that it had to have been carried out by professionals from the security services rather than rebels from the North Caucasus.[15] Questions were also raised in the press about the explosive material, which the authorities initially said contained hexogen (in bags marked as sugar) as the key ingredient, although they later denied this. Hexogen, as journalists pointed out, could be obtained only from facilities that were closely guarded by the FSB and other law enforcement agencies. Then there was the revelation that a man identified by authorities as having rented storage space for explosives in Moscow had been operating under the false identity of a dead man from the Karachaevo-Cherkessia region of the North Caucasus. This led to speculation that the security services had helped the actual alleged terrorist, Achimez Gochiiaev, with the production of his false documents.[16]

Then came a bizarre incident in Ryazan on September 22, when a powerful bomb was discovered unexpectedly by residents of an apartment building. The bomb, in the form of three sacks of explosives and a detonator, was confirmed by local FSB experts as containing the explosive hexogen. The three individuals who planted the bomb and drove away in a white Zhiguli were soon apprehended, and local law enforcement officials were celebrated on nation-wide television for saving so many lives. But after it was revealed that the would-be bombers were Moscow-based FSB agents, who were subsequently released and disappeared, the story changed. FSB chief Nikolai Patrushev claimed that the sacks of apparent explosives, which had been hastily transported to Moscow, actually contained only sugar and were placed in the building as part of a "training exercise" to test the vigilance of the local citizens.[17]

Not surprisingly, the press voiced skepticism, especially because the local Ryazan authorities continued to insist that the bags of sugar had contained hexogen. As the popular online newspaper *Lenta.ru* observed, "One can only guess what the inhabitants of the 'mined' Ryazan apartment house think about such 'exercises,' and how many more reports about the heroic prevention of explosions, the detection of weapons, etc., refer to 'exercises' and not to real terrorists."[18] The Ryazan fiasco clearly lent credence to the theory of FSB involvement in the bombings. In the scathing words of Andrei Piontkovsky: "After the 'exercises' in Ryazan, no one can say where the line is between training and provocation, between provocation and terrorist attack. But it is obvious that the [apartment] explosions achieved the goals set by their authors." He added that "the lieutenant colonel of the KGB with thieves' vocabulary, who miraculously ended up at the head of a great country, is in a hurry to take advantage of the effect produced . . . Putin is deliberately bombing Grozny in order to make it impossible to negotiate with Maskhadov, in order to make all Chechens, one and the same, enemies of Russia."[19]

Despite the serious questions about the incident raised in the press, the public—and even politicians opposed to Yeltsin—seemed willing to go along with the official version. It was as if the horror of the FSB actually planning to murder so many innocent people in Ryazan—and the logical inference that the FSB had therefore orchestrated the earlier bombings—was too much to contemplate. Although no Chechens had been identified among the alleged perpetrators of any of the attacks, the results of a poll published on September 28 showed that 64 percent of the respondents favored a massive bombardment of Chechnya if there were further terrorist acts.[20]

Residents of the Ryazan apartment building who tried to take the matter to court were successfully deterred from doing so by the FSB, and a brief investigation by the Prosecutor General's Office ended without conclusion in early 2000. There would be subsequent probes by determined Russian journalists such as Pavel Voloshin, a reporter for *Novaia gazeta*. Among his many discoveries, Voloshin was able to identify a Russian soldier who claimed that before the bombings he had been assigned to guard a military warehouse near Ryazan that stored sacks of hexogen.[21] Responding to Voloshin's revelations, some members of the Duma called for an investigation of the September attacks, but the Duma voted against the proposal in March 2000. Duma deputy and human rights activist Sergei Kovalev would later, in 2002, create an independent investigative commission, but with no results in the end.[22]

Berezovsky's Brainchild

Did Berezovsky suspect that the FSB was behind the apartment bombings? Although he would eventually accuse Putin publicly of orchestrating the attacks, while still in Russia Berezovsky did not question the official narrative. He even gushed about Putin's remarkable character and abilities, telling journalist Nataliya Gevorkyan in late November 1999: "I believe Putin has two qualities that will enable him to become Russia's leader. In the first place, he upholds and tries to promote liberalism in Russia. Secondly, he is a man of great willpower."[23]

The Family's silence in the face of allegations of FSB involvement in the bombings convinced journalist Iulia Latynina that suspicions about Putin were unfounded: "There is one simple consideration: it was not the Lubianka [FSB headquarters] that staged Putin. Putin was brought on by the Family, incl. Boris Abramovich Berezovsky. He was presented as a submissive puppet, and if at that moment [Roman] Abramovich, Yeltsin, [Tatiana] D'iachenko, Iumashev, or Berezovsky suspected even for a second that there was a force of such magnitude behind Putin that was blowing up houses, they would have thrown him out like hot potatoes."[24] But if the Family had addressed the evidence of Putin's culpability and "thrown him out," they would have suffered grave consequences. Not only would they have handed the Primakov-Luzhkov alliance a victory in the Duma elections; they would have lost their handpicked heir to the presidency, whom they needed desperately to protect them from the legal consequences of their corruption.

And the corruption allegations were not going away. Skuratov was still at bay, although he was under severe pressure—including police searches and interrogations—to stop talking publicly about the scandals. In a mid-September interview with the Italian newspaper *La Repubblica*, he confirmed reports that Mabetex had paid $10 million in kickbacks for its Kremlin renovation contract and that billions of dollars from an IMF bailout in 1998 had been sold to a small group of Russian private banks at preferential exchange rates.[25] Yeltsin's repeated efforts to fire Skuratov were stymied by the Federation Council, which on October 14, 1999, refused to sack him for the third time.[26] Even worse, on that very day, a spokesperson from the Banca del Gottardo announced that, at the request of the Mabetex construction company, the bank had acted as a guarantor of credit cards issued to Yeltsin and his two daughters.[27]

Meanwhile, the US press had reported that Yeltsin's then son-in-law Leonid D'iachenko—whom Skuratov had been investigating—held two Bank of New York accounts in the Cayman Islands, containing more than $2 million. According to one American official: "This isn't the end of the embarrassing kompromat likely to emerge in this case. It's likely just the beginning."[28] In early October, *The New York Times* added more to the story: "Dyachenko is an oil trader. But he is more than that. He is a participant—if not a key figure—in a network of politically blessed companies that ship Siberian oil products to Ukraine and to Eastern Europe . . . The officials of those companies, and Mr. Dyachenko's benefactors, include two Russian tycoons who are among Mr. Yeltsin's strongest supporters, Boris A. Berezovsky and Roman Abramovich."[29]

Duma Deputy Iurii Shchekochikhin was so scandalized by the revelations that he wrote an open letter to Tatiana D'iachenko, published in *Novaia gazeta* on October 11: "Recently, I was a witness at a hearing in the US Congress on corruption in Russia, and, believe me, I felt embarrassed when the president of the Bank of New York said that your husband has two accounts with this bank for about two million dollars . . . It was a shame to remember how the Presidential Administration had assured us that the Family did not have a single penny abroad."[30] Chubais was also singled out for attack. In early October, *Moskovskii komsomolets* featured a scathing article that portrayed him as the creator of Russia's "bandit capitalism" by monopolizing the American aid allocated for the implementation of privatization.[31]

Taken together with the formidable political force of the Fatherland-All Russia coalition, the corruption allegations put the Family's succession plans in jeopardy, even as Putin was demonstrating his might against the Chechens. But Berezovsky had already been devising a rescue plan. As he lay in the hospital with hepatitis in September, Berezovsky called in his aides, along with Sergei Dorenko, to devise a plan for creating a new political party that would ally itself with the Kremlin. Berezovsky then met with Yeltsin's team at Aleksandr Voloshin's dacha to present his project. Writing a decade later, Yeltsin's daughter Tatiana—now Tatiana Iumasheva, having married Valentin Iumashev in 2001—described Berezovsky's pitch: "Berezovsky zealously, noisily, and emotionally convinced us that the future president could not cope without a party, that every president should have a party. And one of Yeltsin's serious mistakes was that he did not make his own party."[32] Voloshin was resistant to the idea, but finally was persuaded and asked his first deputy to assist with the project on behalf of the Kremlin.[33]

Thanks to Berezovsky's initiative, a new, pro-Kremlin political movement, Unity, was formed by thirty-nine provincial governors on September 22, 1999. It would be the forerunner of what today is Putin's United Russia party. Tatiana Iumasheva observed: "United Russia doesn't like to remember Berezovsky's role in the emergence of Unity. But history is history. We must not forget those who stood at its origins. Otherwise it resembles the *History of the CPSU* [Soviet Communist Party], which was painstakingly rewritten every time its next founder turned out to be an enemy of the people."[34] Berezovsky and his men had personally approached regional leaders and persuaded them that it would be a mistake to have Primakov as president because he would turn Russia back into a Communist state. As Goldfarb noted, they had the same message in every provincial capital: "Just wait until Primus [Primakov] gets into the Kremlin! He will bring back his Soviet cohorts, the old-time apparatchiks, the veterans of central planning, the bureaucrats. He will take away your local elections, your rights and privileges."[35]

The founders of Unity decided that it was too early to enlist Putin as its leader; they would wait until the bloc gained political momentum. So they chose Sergei Shoigu, minister for emergency situations, who announced at Unity's first congress on October 2 that the party's goal was to hand power over "to real representatives of Russia's regions and therefore of Russia itself, to sweep away Moscow-dwelling politicians." The bloc was built, he said, "by people who are tired of hypocrisy and lies."[36] But, as Henry Hale pointed out, Unity was different from traditional political parties: "Unity's chief aim was *not* to provide representation for the president in the parliament but to be a decoy in the war to defeat the virulently anti-Kremlin Fatherland-All Russia Party, drawing away enough votes for the latter to finish below political expectations [in the Duma elections]. That is, Unity was a *presidential election tactic,* not primarily a parliamentary party project."[37]

Berezovsky and Roman Abramovich provided the main funds for Unity, although other wealthy businessmen contributed hefty amounts. According to Zygar, "the average check from an oligarch was for $10 million, and Unity raised a total of about $170 million."[38] Both Berezovsky and Abramovich also registered in October as independent candidates for the Duma—Abramovich from the remote arctic Chukotka district and Berezovsky from the North Caucasian republic of Karachaevo-Cherkessia, which was impoverished but rich in mineral resources. Berezovsky had established relationships with numerous businessmen there and presented himself to voters as a successful capitalist who could turn their economy around. He promised to build a new ski resort, a car assembly plant, and construction companies, as well as to establish a charitable foundation to support the republic's poor. Berezovsky told potential voters at one meeting: "I came here with one purpose—to help not only you but me. Because rich people can't live where there are a lot of poor people." To demonstrate his commitment to the area, he bought a two-story house in Cherkessia. An added bonus for both Berezovsky and Abramovich was that Duma deputies had immunity from prosecution.[39]

Although not led by Putin, Unity's message was clear: support the prime minister because he is leading the struggle against Chechen terrorists. And because Putin had de facto assumed the functions of supreme commander of the military, he was not only defeating the terrorist enemies, he was restoring Russia's sense of national pride. Putin's image of toughness reinforced this message. Young and physically fit, he was the direct opposite of the ailing, alcoholic Yeltsin. Putin also had another advantage, noted by Steven Myers: "Although he owed his career to Yeltsin and the 'Family,' the fact that he had mostly worked on the margins of public scrutiny since 1996 meant he was not associated with the Kremlin's multiple failings and scandals."[40]

The Russian Media Delivers

In early October, Putin summoned top media executives to urge their support for the invasion of Chechnya; they seemed to need little persuasion. The businesses and corporations that had acquired controlling shares in print and electronic media depended on good relations with government officials. In contrast to the highly critical coverage of the first Chechen war, both television and newspapers focused on the successes of the Russian military advance rather than on the devastation of Chechen towns and villages, the waves of refugees, and the civilian death toll. According to the analyst Laura Belin: "Only a handful of publications, such as *Novaya gazeta* and *Obshchaya gazeta*, questioned the wisdom or morality of the Russian military strategy. Some newspapers that had been hostile toward the armed forces during the first war now concentrated on the same upbeat themes that dominated television newscasts. Destroyed Chechen towns and the wave of refugees fleeing the republic received far less column space." Belin added that "evidence suggests that those who set editorial policy at ORT and RTR (Russia-1) deliberately crafted Chechnya coverage so as to encourage voters to connect their approval of the war with support for Putin."[41]

ORT's Sunday evening program, *The Sergei Dorenko Show*, which was Berezovsky's brainchild, doubtless made the greatest contribution to the political rise of Unity and Putin. As mentioned above, Dorenko and Berezovsky had been planning a news program that would rival NTV's highly popular program *Itogi*, hosted by Evgenii Kiselev, which presented sharply critical news coverage of the Family, including about corruption. The plan was to first go after Luzhkov, the lower-hanging fruit, with devastating attacks and later to move against Primakov more subtly. From the moment that Dorenko's weekly show first aired on prime time in early September, his brutal, slanderous allegations against Luzhkov created a sensation, and the show soon outstripped *Itogi* in ratings. As Hale described it, "During the weeks of the campaign, Dorenko, in his trademark smirking baritone, lambasted Luzhkov for alleged misdeeds ranging from the plausible, that there is corruption in Luzhkov's Moscow bureaucracy, to the outrageous, that Luzhkov was an accomplice to the 1996 murder of US businessman Paul Tatum, to the just plain ridiculous, that he had ties to the deadly Japanese Aum Shinrikyo cult."[42]

Dorenko's smears against Primakov focused on his age, with suggestions of ill health, and his ties with the dubious spying operations of the Foreign Intelligence Service. The show's host also repeated false

FIGURE 16.   Sergei Dorenko on his nightly news program. TASS archive/Diomedia.

accusations by the Georgian security services that linked Primakov to an assassination attempt on Georgian president Eduard Shevardnadze. Noting that "in some sense *Itogi* was getting a taste of its own medicine, but a much deadlier dose," Hale points out that NTV refused to stoop to the level of the Dorenko show with similar slander. But amazingly, polls found that viewers actually trusted Dorenko more than they did *Itogi*'s commentators. "*Itogi* was the unrivaled master of television news analysis prior to September 1999," Hale writes. "Dorenko's growling hatchet job worked, not because there was no alternative, but because it won the ratings battle, going head-to-head with *Itogi*."[43]

Moskovskii komsomolets, one of the Yeltsin team's harshest critics, lamented in October: "Dorenko has achieved his goal: they talk about him in the metro, in the Duma, at the market. He is, without a doubt, a boor and a talker who plays politics. How long will all this continue and who or what will stop Dorenko and his ilk?"[44] Berezovsky was elated. Dorenko later recalled: "Berezovsky praised my work and praised it enthusiastically. He called me after almost every transmission, wailing and shouting, 'You are a genius!'"[45]

In his public comments, Berezovsky gave the impression that he had nothing to do with the content of the Dorenko show, but that was not true. Just before the December Duma elections, *Novaia gazeta* published excerpts of a bugged telephone conversation between Berezovsky and Dorenko in which they were discussing the details of the next program. In particular, Berezovsky reminded Dorenko, whom he addressed familiarly as "Seryozha," of a scheduled press conference by lawyers for the family of Paul Tatum. Tatum's family was suing Luzhkov for allegedly protecting the perpetrators of his murder by hindering an investigation. Berezovsky told Dorenko how he should explain the case to his audience and even suggested mentioning that former FSB employees were involved. But he made a point of telling Dorenko to make sure he "cut Putin off from this whole story."[46] Berezovsky would later brag: "Everyone was sure that Primakov would become Russia's next president, but nobody actually wanted him. It was my personal task to anticipate this and help the society. My instrument was the ORT channel."[47]

The combination of Putin's forceful response to the terrorist bombings, the emergence of Unity to challenge Primakov and Luzhkov's Fatherland-All Russia Party, and the brilliantly effective propaganda spewed out weekly by Dorenko caused Putin's popularity to skyrocket. Whereas September opinion polls showed that 21 percent of the population approved of his government, by mid-November the government's approval rating was 74 percent.[48] And Putin's personal approval ratings rose to 80 percent.[49] This meant that Putin's endorsement of Unity would provide the party with a huge boost in the upcoming Duma elections. So, on November 24, Putin appeared publicly to announce that "out of all the current election blocs" he would vote for Unity. Admitting that, as prime minister, he should not "state his political preferences," Putin said that, as an ordinary citizen and friend of Minister of Emergency Situations Shoigu, he could not help but respond to Unity's promise "to support the current government."[50]

A Victory for the Family

The Communist Party of the Russian Federation, led by Gennady Zyuganov, dominated the legislative process in the Duma and was the front-runner for delegates in the forthcoming elections. But with the backing of the popular prime minister, Unity emerged as a serious contender. In mid-November, before Putin's announcement, Unity had the support of 7 percent of the electorate and Fatherland-All Russia 20 percent. When the results of the Duma vote on December 19 came in, Unity had managed to capture 23.3. percent, second in place to the Communist Party, which won 24.3 percent, while Fatherland won only 13.3 percent. The Family's expectations for Putin had been confirmed.

Yeltsin, who had fallen asleep before the vote tally was complete, woke up the next morning to the good news: "The results of the vote confirmed what I had thought all these weeks: Vladimir Putin has an enormous reserve of credibility . . . We now had a very new picture. The leftist forces had ceased to be a majority in parliament."[51] Berezovsky was among the new deputies, having won a whopping 45 percent of the vote in Karachaevo-Cherkessia, where he had spent six weeks campaigning. He told the press that he intended to revive the republic's economy by lobbying for funds from the Kremlin and getting contracts for the republic's construction industry.[52] In early February 2000, he became a member of the Duma Committee on International Affairs.

By this time Yeltsin had already decided that he would step down before his term ended in July 2000. On December 14, five days before the Duma elections, he called Putin to his office and told him that he intended to resign at the end of the year. According to Yeltsin, Putin said he was not ready to take over the presidency and suggested that

FIGURE 17.   Yeltsin and Putin, December 31, 1999. Reuters/Alamy.

Yeltsin stay until the end of his term, but then agreed with the plan.[53] Putin, in *First Person*, gives the impression that he was caught completely off guard and did not want the job at all: "On the whole, it was a depressing conversation. I had never thought seriously that I might become his successor, so when Boris Nikolayevich told me about his decision, I wasn't really prepared for it." He tried to get himself "off the hook," Putin says, but it didn't work.[54]

Putin's assertion that he had no idea that he was in line for the presidency is unconvincing. Yeltsin had said publicly when he appointed Putin as prime minister that Putin was his chosen successor. Also, there had been considerable speculation in the press that Yeltsin would step down early. Although he claimed to have no aspirations for the presidency, Putin must have realized that Yeltsin's decision to resign all but assured his successful win in the presidential election. The elections had been scheduled for June 4, but Russian law required that an election had to take place three months after the presidential post was vacated. This moved the date to March 26, 2000, narrowing the window for a possible loss of support for Putin as a result of the Chechen war. As Masha Gessen pointed out at the time: "In a country fighting a war and forever vulnerable to economic collapse, six months is a long time. If the war bogs down in the Chechen mountains, public support for it will wane, as will Putin's popularity. If the price of oil drops and takes Russia's fragile economy down with it, Putin also stands to lose. In both respects, cutting in half the time left before Election Day lessens the possibility of a comeback by any of the Kremlin's opponents, all of whom depleted their treasuries during December's parliamentary election campaign."[55]

Shortly after the Duma elections, the Russian journalist Oleg Lur'e published a remarkable article in *Novaia gazeta* about a large volume of documents on high-level Kremlin corruption that were held in the Prosecutor General's Office. Many of the documents had been assembled by Felipe Turover—a former employee of the Banco del Gottardo, which had handled accounts for Mabetex, and a key witness in the Swiss investigations. A Soviet émigré, Turover had collected debts for the bank in Russia and had an insider's knowledge of those involved in Kremlin corruption, whose names he rattled off to Lur'e. When asked by Lur'e about Putin's possible role, Turover described how Putin, while working in the Yeltsin administration in 1997, had "got his paws on" much of the property abroad that had belonged to the Soviet state and Communist Party and registered these assets to various front companies.

According to Turover, "Property abroad was very thoroughly plucked before the state got its hands on it."[56]

The prosecutor's office, Lur'e told his readers, had conveniently forgotten all about the incriminating documents that it possessed. Indeed, these documents would never see the light of day, and the accusations against the Family would fade away. Four days later, at noon on December 31, Yeltsin made his surprise announcement that he was resigning and delegating Putin to serve as acting president. Putin, whose first decision was to grant Yeltsin immunity, would remain prime minister. His path to the presidency, as political commentators concurred, was assured. As *The New York Times* noted: "In August, Mr. Putin was a political nonentity, with no party, no popular support and the backing of a deeply distrusted president. Four months later . . . Mr. Putin is Russia's latest rising star, hailed at home as the architect of an uncompromising war that many Russians have welcomed as a belated if brutal attempt to restore the battered authority of the Russian state."[57]

Berezovsky, the man who deserved much of the credit for the turn of political events in Putin's favor, had been basking in glory since the Duma victory of the Unity party. David Hoffman observed from Moscow that "the outcome of the elections demonstrated that Berezovsky has reclaimed his status as a Moscow power broker . . . Unity's success may give Berezovsky a powerful new lever in Russian politics."[58] But the Family did not see it that way. According to Elena Gorbunova, after the Duma elections Iumashev, Tatiana, and Voloshin gave Berezovsky an ultimatum, which Roman Abramovich, now a Kremlin insider, conveyed: he had to leave the country so that he would not be associated with Putin's presidential campaign. They considered Berezovsky to be toxic, surrounded by scandal. "It wasn't even an insult," Gorbunova recalled. "Boria, of course, really wanted Putin to be elected." So, according to Gorbunova, he made himself scarce, spending a lot of time abroad before the March election: "He did not take part [in the campaign], did not show up in any way. He only said, 'here is your tool, ORT; use it, guys!' "[59] Zygar writes that the decision to "ditch" Berezovsky had been made in the autumn of 1999: "Berezovsky's political vanities—and especially his never-ending interviews and sweeping comments—were beginning to irk Tanya, Valya, Voloshin and Abramovich, who decided that he was doing more harm than good. Once the threat of losing their power and freedom had receded, they began to sideline their former friend."[60]

What was Putin's role in this decision? Berezovsky told Alex Gold-farb that Putin invited him to the Russian White House late on December 19, 1999, the day of the parliamentary elections, specifically to thank him for all he had done toward raising popular support for Unity and damaging the prospects of the Primakov-Luzhkov alliance. Putin's emotional words rendered Berezovsky momentarily speechless: "I want to tell you, Boris, that what you have done is phenomenal . . . I am not given to melodrama, so what I am going to say is particularly significant. I do not have a brother, and neither do you. You should know that in me you have a brother, Boris. Coming from me, these are not empty words." Berezovsky recalled that he was deeply touched and assured Putin enthusiastically that he would beat the political opposition and continue the work of Yeltsin as the new president.[61]

Given Berezovsky's proclivity to embellish the truth, his account of this meeting cannot be taken at face value. But Putin may well have decided to mollify Berezovsky with a few kind comments to keep him in line until after the presidential election. Whatever transpired between the two men, Berezovsky's role as kingmaker was over, and Putin knew this better than anyone.

CHAPTER 8

A Clash of Titans

> There is no one in the United States who cuts
> quite the figure that Boris Berezovsky does here
> in Russia. Imagine someone with the ego of a
> Donald Trump, the ambition of a Ross Perot, the
> instincts of Rupert Murdoch, and the business
> reputation of John Gotti.
>
> —Ted Koppel, reporting from Moscow on
> *Nightline*, March 2000

Putin apparently did not tell his wife about Yeltsin's plan to resign on New Year's Eve. As Liudmila Putina recounted to a Putin biographer: "I heard that Boris Nikolaevich was resigning later than many others in the country. I did not see Yeltsin's appearance on December 31, 1999, and knew nothing about it. An acquaintance called me exactly five minutes after the televised address and said, 'Liuda, congratulations!' 'And you as well,' I answered, having in mind that it was New Year's. 'No, No, Vladimir Vladimirovich has been appointed acting president of Russia.' That's how I heard that my husband was replacing Boris Nikolaevich."[1]

In *First Person*, Liudmila recalled, "I cried the whole day because I realized that our private life was over for at least three months, until the presidential election, or perhaps for four years."[2] Putin had informed his wife that he might become president back when he was appointed prime minister and warned her that it would mean "limitations" on her life. She had responded matter-of-factly that "for every politician, and for anyone who is engaged in politics, the aim, of course, should be to become president. Not for nothing do people say that it's a bad soldier who does not dream of becoming a general." But at that time Liudmila had not fully grasped the implications of being the president's wife—in particular, that she would always have bodyguards, which she did not welcome.[3]

At midnight on New Year's Eve, Putin gave a brief televised address to the nation, pledging that "there will be no power vacuum, even for a moment" and that "freedom of speech, freedom of conscience, freedom of the press, the right to private property—all these basic principles of a civilized society will be reliably protected by the state."[4] The Putins then flew by helicopter to Chechnya, accompanied by FSB chief Patrushev and his wife, and visited a military unit in the city of Gudermes. Liudmila said later that she had initially declined her husband's request that she go along, because the trip posed dangers and would mean leaving their daughters alone on an important holiday, but with reluctance she had changed her mind.[5] Yet, when asked by a journalist on their return why he had brought his wife to a war zone, Putin dismissed her presence with sarcasm: "My wife tagged along. I couldn't do anything about it."[6] Such remarks may have been a harbinger of the eventual deterioration of the Putins' marriage.

FIGURE 18. The Putins in Chechnya, January 1, 2000. AFP via Getty Images.

The President-Elect

It is not surprising that Putin decided on a visit to Chechnya for his first public appearance as president. Although his approval ratings were still high, public enthusiasm for the war threatened to wane as casualties mounted, and the Russian military had reached an apparent impasse in Grozny.[7] Western governments and human rights groups were expressing outrage about the devastating toll on Chechens.[8] And the liberal Russian media was becoming increasingly critical of the Chechnya invasion as journalists reported on the spot about innocent civilians killed by air strikes or massacred by "wilding" Russian troops.

Writing for *Novaia gazeta*, Anna Politkovskaya described the daily horrors she saw as a reporter in Chechnya. In mid-December, she described a Chechen girl dying in a hospital in Ingushetia after being riddled with bullets from a Russian plane as she fled a village near Grozny in a car flying a white flag and filled with refugees: "Everyone looks away when, worn by her struggle to keep alive, this once cheerful and carefree fourth-year student in the languages faculty at Grozny University suddenly shifts her gaze from the ceiling and stares at them as they repeat their meaningless phrases." Politkovskaya also reported on the slaughter of twenty-three farmers and their families at that same village, Alkhan-Yurt, during a Russian "check" on their residence documents. "So this is the 'fierce struggle with the Chechen fighters,'" she wrote. "The army tells us 'We are not shooting at people's homes' and the result is a devastated village and not one piece of evidence that the fighters have been there."[9]

A journalist for Radio Liberty, Andrei Babitsky, reported from Grozny in late December 1999 that he saw at least eighty corpses of Russian soldiers after a recent battle in the city and said that he had video footage confirming the deaths of other Russian servicemen as they stormed Grozny.[10] Given that the Kremlin sought to downplay Russian casualties, Babitsky's reporting was unwelcome. Even worse, he seemed to defend the motives of the rebels. On January 16, 2000, Russian forces detained him as he was leaving Chechnya, on the grounds that he had violated the military's prohibition against journalists being in the war zone. But they then denied that they knew his whereabouts to his family and colleagues, who were frantically trying to locate him. It was not until January 28 that Russian authorities admitted they had Babitsky in custody, but instead of releasing him, they claimed to have handed him over to Chechen warlords, purportedly in exchange for Russian soldiers who were held captive. Babitsky was released by his captors at the end of February, only to be arrested briefly by Russian police on charges of possessing a fake passport.[11]

Meanwhile Babitsky's cause had been taken up by the Americans, who funded Radio Liberty. The State Department condemned his treatment as a journalist and Secretary of State Madeline Albright personally intervened through her counterpart, Russian Foreign Minister Igor Ivanov. Despite the potential damage to his global image, Putin remained adamant that Babitsky was, in his view, a traitor because of his reporting: "He was working directly for the enemy. He was not a neutral source of information. He was working for the bandits."[12] The Babitsky incident was a foretelling of how journalists would be treated under Putin's presidency. As Gevorkyan said to Masha Gessen: "I knew that this was how he [Putin] understood the word patriotism—just the way he had been taught in all those KGB schools: the country is as great as the fear it inspires, and the media should be loyal."[13]

A mid-January editorial in *The Moscow Times* summed up the folly of Putin's Chechen military operations in no uncertain terms: "The aerial bombing campaigns, which have destroyed entire communities, have no clear military purpose. Instead, they are the equivalent of a terrorist factory—for what is more likely to produce a man willing to take up arms against the state than a state that kills his parents, his wife, his children? . . . As near as we can see, the only beneficiary of the war so far is Putin himself."[14]

But while the West and the liberal Russian press raised alarm bells about Putin's heavy-handed methods, the Russian political and business elite continued to rally around him. Chubais, for example, who earlier had opposed the choice of Putin as prime minister, had become one of his biggest fans. In an interview during a visit to Chechnya in late November 1999, Chubais said unequivocally, "If Putin asks me, I will do everything to support him," and denied that Putin had initiated the war in order to boost his popular standing: "He believes that his personal, human duty is primarily connected with Chechnya. Vladimir Vladimirovich, it seems to me, perceives the Chechen problem as an absolutely personal mission. He seems to be internally hurt by the fact that they attacked Russia."[15] Chubais, who later became head of the state electricity monopoly RAO UES, was a leader of the Union of Right Forces (SPS), along with Boris Nemtsov, Egor Gaidar, and others. Nemtsov, who disliked Putin intensely and opposed their party's support for him, was outnumbered when party leaders took a vote.[16]

Another Putin advocate was Anatoly Sobchak, who had returned from exile in Paris in July 1999 to announce that he would be running as a candidate to the Duma from St. Petersburg, representing the Right Cause (Pravoe delo) bloc. After encountering strong political opposition in St. Petersburg, Sobchak lost his election bid. In the words of historian Roy Medvedev, "this was a heavy blow for the brave but too restless, conceited, and ambitious politician."[17] Sobchak then volunteered to work on Putin's presidential campaign, rallying voters in the northwest regions of Russia. But his support may have been a liability for Putin. The Russian press was merciless in attacking Sobchak with stories of his corruption as St. Petersburg mayor and suggestions that the 1997 diagnosis of his heart attack by his and Putin's doctor friend Iurii Shevchenko was an excuse to get Sobchak out of the country.[18]

On February 15, 2000, Sobchak went to Kaliningrad to speak on Putin's behalf. Four days later, he was found dead in his hotel room in the city of Svetlogorsk. He had died alone, reportedly of a heart attack. Putin sent a special plane to retrieve Sobchak's body and in a telegram of condolence to Sobchak's wife and daughter he wrote: "It is impossible for me to come to terms with this loss. Anatolii Aleksandrovich was very close to me, my teacher . . . He always served as an example of decency and firmness in his convictions." At Sobchak's funeral on February 24, which was attended by all of the Kremlin's political elite, Putin, who delivered the eulogy, was seen shedding tears.[19]

Sobchak's sudden death gave rise to theories that he had been murdered. The last people in his Kaliningrad hotel room were two mafia-connected businessmen who were later killed in showdowns. Two autopsies were done on Sobchak's body, one in Kaliningrad and the other by Shevchenko, who had recently been appointed Russian minister of health. The cause of death was determined by Shevchenko to be a heart attack, but the Kaliningrad prosecutor's office carried out a three-month investigation, which proved inconclusive, into a possible "premeditated murder with aggravating circumstances." In 2012, Narusova said in an interview that her husband had not died of a heart attack and that those responsible for his death were still in power. She had documents that would prove that her husband was murdered, she added, but could not disclose them because she feared reprisals against her daughter, Ksenia.[20] Some suggested that Putin had his former mentor murdered because he knew a lot about Putin's past criminal activities in St. Petersburg. The journalist Arkady Vaksberg, who had met with Sobchak during his time in Paris, was convinced that Sobchak was poisoned on Putin's orders.[21] Not surprisingly, the questions raised by Vaksberg and others came to nothing.

Dissent and Rebuke

Although Berezovsky had been instructed by the Family to lie low during the presidential campaign, it was not in his nature to keep quiet. He continued to give interviews to the Russian and Western media, never failing to voice his support for Putin. His newspaper *Kommersant* paid for the publication and distribution of Putin's autobiography, *First Person*, which appeared just before the presidential election and portrayed Putin in the best possible light. But Berezovsky sometimes slipped and said things that appeared to demean the future president. In a late December interview, for example, Berezovsky was asked by the political strategist Stanislav Belkovsky whether Putin was another Andropov (the ruthless former KGB chairman who succeeded Brezhnev and portrayed himself as a reformer). He replied: "The present 'successor' is a child of the new system; he'll hardly dare to cancel civil rights and freedoms. After all, he was just a lieutenant colonel under Soviet rule, not a field marshal."[22]

Berezovsky also began to suggest in the press that the war in Chechnya would not lead to success. Interviewed in January by Sergei Dorenko on ORT, he opined that an effective government should be able to resolve the Chechen situation by negotiations, rather than force.[23] And just before the March elections, Berezovsky told the newspaper *Vedomosti* that he and Putin assessed the situation in Chechnya completely differently and stressed again that negotiating with the Chechens was the only way forward.[24] In early April, he urged a cease-fire and political dialogue with Maskhadov, in order to keep the death toll from rising.[25]

At least some of Berezovsky's statements must have reached Putin, and he cannot have been pleased. On the eve of the Russian presidential election, *The Economist* published an article speculating on the relationship between Berezovsky and the acting president.[26] "Maybe Mr. Berezovsky's number is up," the magazine posited. "Mr. Putin's austere, disciplined style is a world away from the indulgent, ostentatious cronyism of the Yeltsin era. Though he [Berezovsky] praises Mr. Putin publicly, the president-in-waiting has been noticeably cooler in return." The article went on to quote Putin as saying, "beware of Greeks bearing gifts," when Berezovsky endorsed him as president, but concluded: "So even if Mr. Putin loathes Mr. Berezovsky, as some say he does, and regards his influence as pernicious, there would be no point in turning on him and his chums until after the election."

The March 26 presidential elections brought no surprises. Putin won with 53.4 percent of the vote, followed by Zyuganov, with 29.5 percent, and Grigory Yavlinsky, leader of Yabloko, with 5.9 percent. As Jonathan Steele predicted in *The Guardian* two days earlier: "A pseudo-democratic seal of approval will be stamped on the lucky man on Sunday, when those Russian voters strong enough to resist the crushing hands of apathy and disgust troop off to the polling booths. But the real election took place last August when a handful of men behind closed doors in the Kremlin chose a hard-nosed apparatchik, Vladimir Putin, to take over from Boris Yeltsin."[27] Steele added that being the incumbent "in a society where authoritarian instincts run deep" gave Putin a huge advantage, especially with his backers controlling the television news. But what would happen to these wealthy supporters now that Putin's position as leader was secure?

Putin had hinted publicly that, once elected president, he would place a distance between himself and powerful business tycoons. Just before the election he spoke in more ominous terms when asked in a radio interview about his intentions for the oligarchs: "If by oligarchs . . . we mean representatives of groups that are merging or are facilitating the merging of government with capital, there will be no such oligarchs as a class."[28] The statement contrasted sharply with what Berezovsky said to the Duma just days later: "It is impossible to distance oligarchs from power. That is how the modern society is made. If he eliminates one oligarch, others will come."[29]

Putin wasted little time in going after business tycoon Vladimir Gusinsky, whose television channel, NTV, had been so critical of him, with such programs as the *Kukly* satire. Even worse, despite an admonition from the Kremlin, conveyed by Iumashev, NTV had aired a sensational talk show about the Ryazan bomb incident just two days before the presidential elections. The participants all agreed that the bomb was real, thus rekindling doubts about the official version of the September 1999 attacks.[30] On May 11, masked FSB commandos raided the offices of Gusinsky's Media-Most empire as part of a criminal investigation opened by Russian prosecutors the previous month. On June 13, after openly criticizing Putin, Gusinsky was summoned to the prosecutor's office, where he was promptly arrested and thrown into the brutal Butyrka prison without access to a lawyer for four days. The arrest prompted NTV's president Igor Malashenko, vacationing in Spain at the time, to call a press conference in Madrid and announce: "Today Russia got its first political prisoner."[31]

Putin, who was also in Spain on a postelection tour, claimed to know nothing of the arrest, but no one believed him. The Union of Russian Journalists issued a statement saying that the action against Media-Most was a politically motivated anticonstitutional act by the government with the goal of intimidating independent journalism.[32] Sergei Dorenko, who had spent months promoting Putin and destroying his opponents on television, was so outraged over what happened to Gusinsky that he raced to the NTV studios and joined an evening broadcast to denounce the security services. Putin's reaction was odd. He called Dorenko to his office a few days later and asked him "to join our team" for a large reward. Dorenko, incensed, declined the offer. On leaving Putin's office he called Berezovsky on his cell phone to shout: "What have you done, Borya? What the fuck have you done?"[33]

The condition for the Kremlin dropping charges against Gusinsky was conveyed to him by Mikhail Lesin, Putin's press minister, who visited Gusinsky in jail: Gusinsky had to sell Media-Most to Gazprom, the state-owned gas monopoly. This left Gusinsky with no choice. He consented to Putin's terms and was released from jail. As Gusinsky explained to David Hoffman: "I was indeed a hostage. When you have a gun to your head, you have two options: to meet the condition of the bandits or take a bullet in your head."[34] On July 18, after agreeing to sell his empire for $300 million in exchange for forgiveness of his debts and the dismissal of criminal charges, Gusinsky left Russia for Spain. But he then had second thoughts and tried to back out of the deal. Finally, after months of negotiations and further arrest warrants issued from Russia, Gusinsky relented. By April 2001, NTV and the news publications *Itogi* and *Segodnia* were in the hands of Gazprom, which immediately closed *Segodnia*. Gusinsky never returned to Russia, making his home in Israel.[35]

More Trouble in Paradise

After the March election, it had seemed to Berezovsky that Putin would pursue a democratic agenda in Russia, despite the war in Chechnya. Putin retained Yeltsin allies Chubais and Voloshin on his staff, and his new prime minister, Mikhail Kasyanov, was a respected technocrat and a free market economist. Berezovsky at some point ran into Boris Nemtsov and commented: "There is nothing left to do . . . Putin has been elected. Everything is under control. Now I am bored. I don't know what to do with myself." Nemtsov responded: "Boria, you shouldn't be bored. Putin will change very quickly. He will never forgive you for the fact that you saw him as weak and helpless and graciously supported him." Nemtsov recalled that "Berezovsky looked at me like I was crazy . . . But I think that he later cursed hundreds of times the day his decision to support a man from the FSB."[36]

As if fulfilling Nemtsov's prophecy, Putin set out in the first week after his May inauguration to rein in the leaders of Russia's eighty-nine regions by issuing a decree that organized the country into seven zones, with each supervised by a specially appointed presidential envoy. The significance of this bold plan could not be overstated. It seriously weakened the powers of the elected governors by giving Putin's representatives control over regional bodies—such as defense, security, police, and justice—including appointing the heads of these bodies. In addition, the seven envoys would have oversight over the governors themselves and act as intermediaries between the Kremlin and regional leadership. As *Kommersant* noted, this reorganization was only the beginning; the

FIGURE 19.   Berezovsky at the Federation Council, June 28, 2000. Alexander Natruskin/Alamy.

next steps would involve giving the Kremlin the power to sack governors and deprive them of their automatic right to be members of the
Duma's upper house, the Federation Council.[37] Indeed, Putin then
introduced a law that ended ex officio membership for regional executive and legislative heads in the Federation Council. The law was passed
in July, with some compromise, against the strong objections from Federation Council members.[38]

Berezovsky was alarmed when Putin announced his plan to overhaul
Russia's system of regional government. In France at the time, he called
up Alex Goldfarb, who was in Moscow, and asked him to do some background research on the concepts of federalism and democracy. On his
return to Moscow, Berezovsky got together with Goldfarb and other
allies to draft a lengthy letter to Putin explaining that the planned
reorganization was undemocratic and a throwback to Soviet times. On
May 31, after going to see Putin and making no headway in convincing
him against his plan, Berezovsky published the letter in *Kommersant*.[39]
Goldfarb had warned Berezovsky not to do it: "Boris, if you go down
this road, I predict in a year from now you will be an exile in your cha-
teau, or worse, sitting in jail."[40] But Berezovsky would not be dissuaded.

Berezovsky's letter began respectfully: "As with many people in the
country, I am convinced in the sincerity of your intentions and will to
make Russia powerful and prosperous and create welfare and wellbeing
for its citizens." Berezovsky then went on to point out, with considerable detail and legal analysis, the ways in which Putin's plans violated
the constitution, breached democracy, and damaged Russia's existing federal system. The letter was such a departure from Berezovsky's
enthusiastic support for Putin that *Moskovskii komsomolets* speculated
that he was faking his opposition to the Putin plan: "Since it is cus-
tomary among the people to believe that 'what is good for Berezovsky
is death for Russia,' Boris Abramovich's protest will be taken as a sign
that the reform is useful after all."[41]

Then came the news of Gusinsky's arrest. According to Goldfarb:
"It shook Boris more personally than the federalism fight. The latter
might be an honest mistake by a president who wanted an efficient
government. The former was clearly an act of revenge." Once Putin
had returned from Spain, Berezovsky went straight to see him, telling
him that the arrest of Gusinsky was senseless vengeance that damaged Putin's reputation internationally. But Putin's only response was
to remind Berezovsky that Gusinsky had been number one on Berezovsky's enemies list.[42]

In early July, Berezovsky, determined to rein in Putin, announced that he was forming a new political party and had already enlisted members of the Duma to join. Such a party was needed, he said, because the government was heading in an authoritarian direction.[43] In an interview with *Time Magazine* the next week, Berezovsky said he had no doubt of Putin's desire to have Russia be a democratic country, but that "the route he has chosen for this is absolutely fallacious." Therefore, Berezovsky went on, in order to limit Putin's political power, it was necessary to create an opposition party composed of the business elite.[44]

Repercussions against Berezovsky for his public criticisms of Putin were swift. A criminal case for tax evasion against AvtoVAZ was opened on July 12, 2000. Berezovsky claimed he no longer had a financial interest in the company, but he still had ties with its management, so the investigation was an indirect blow. Two days later, Berezovsky was called for questioning as a witness in the Aeroflot case, and Russia's chief investigator in the case was reportedly going to Switzerland at the end of the month to get documents that Swiss authorities had seized from Andava and Forus, the two companies founded by Berezovsky that provided financial services for the airline.[45]

Under increasing pressure, Berezovsky held a news conference in Moscow on July 17 to declare that he was resigning from the State Duma because he "did not want to participate in Russia's destruction." He outlined three reasons for his decision: (1) his disagreement with the Russian president's attempt to tighten control over the regions; (2) the Kremlin's lack of attention to the needs of Karachaevo-Cherkessia, where there was political conflict; and (3) Putin's campaign against the business elite. Berezovsky made it clear that, by giving up his Duma seat, he would be on equal footing with other oligarchs who did not enjoy parliamentary immunity. He also said pointedly: "Putin believes that economic and political progress can be achieved by centralizing power. But this is fundamentally wrong."[46] Khinshtein later observed that a turning point had come for Berezovsky and his relations with Putin: "Berezovsky outplayed himself. He did not notice how he finally crossed the Rubicon. From now on, a return to peaceful coexistence was no longer possible, and Berezovsky, reluctantly, rushed to the attack. On his last breath, he flew around to see a dozen governors, urging them to fight against the regime; he did not even hesitate to call—after everything that had happened between them—Luzhkov. (The mayor of the capital, with great pleasure, responded to Boris Abramovich by telling him what he thought about him; for censorship reasons, I will not quote this monologue.)"[47]

Berezovsky and Gusinsky were not the only oligarchs under threat. The powerful tax police had opened a criminal case against Lukoil, headed by Vagit Alekperov, and was conducting sweeping inspections of Moscow banks. Vladimir Potanin's mining company, Noril'sk Nikel', was also being investigated by the prosecutor's office. (Both Alekperov and Potanin had publicly protested Gusinsky's arrest.)[48] Noting the growing number of cases, *Moskovskii komsomolets* observed in mid-July: "It looks like we are facing a 'hot summer.' According to our laws, it is very easy to imprison a person. The head of a large company can easily end up behind bars with no explanation. In the meantime, the 'oligarch' will languish in prison while the authorities try to concoct some sort of accusation."[49]

On July 29, Putin held a televised meeting at the Kremlin with twenty-one of Russia's most powerful business tycoons. While he reassured the elite gathering that he did not intend to reverse the privatizations that took place under his predecessor, he said that there needed to be new rules and new understandings between the government and businesses because their relations had been "excessively politicized." Putin spoke to the men in a mildly chiding tone: "I want to draw your attention to the fact that you built this state yourself, to a great degree through the political or semi-political structures under your control. So there is no point in blaming the reflection in the mirror. So let us get down to the point and be open and do what is necessary to do to make our relationship in this field civilized and transparent."[50] The thrust of Putin's message to the oligarchs could not have been clearer: stay out of politics or face serious repercussions.

Berezovsky was conspicuously absent from the Kremlin meeting. Instead he had an interview that day at the LogoVAZ Club with the Russian journalist Yevgenia Albats. Berezovsky was remarkably restrained when asked about Putin, insisting that the new president was a conscientious liberal politician who had simply made some mistakes because of his inexperience and retelling for the umpteenth time the story of Putin's surprise appearance at his wife's birthday party. "I have no doubts that Putin feels a moral obligation to those people he regards as his comrades or friends," Berezovsky added. He also made a point of saying that businessmen had a responsibility to participate in politics, which was a direct contradiction of what Putin told those at the Kremlin gathering.[51]

True to his word, Berezovsky followed up on his plan to create a political movement with a statement, published on the front page of *Izvestiia* and signed by nine leading political and cultural figures, of "constructive opposition" to the Kremlin's authoritarian tendencies. The specifics of the movement and its goals were not clear, but Berezovsky said that, with enough support, it could become a political party.[52] Given Berezovsky's much tainted reputation, it was doubtful that his movement would make much headway, but it was yet another thorn in Putin's side.

A Submarine Goes Down

On August 12, 2000, the *Kursk*, a Russian nuclear submarine carrying cruise missiles, was eighty-five miles off the Murmansk coast of the Barents Sea when it sank to the bottom after an explosion resulting from the spontaneous discharge of a practice torpedo. After a second explosion occurred, only 23 sailors out of the 118 abroad were still alive. Putin's inadequate response to the crisis was a public relations disaster. For several days, as the desperate sailors hoped to be rescued and their anxious families awaited news, Putin was seen on television enjoying a vacation at his Sochi residence, jet-skiing on the Black Sea, and hosting a barbecue.[53] Rescuers did not reach the *Kursk* until sixteen hours after the accident and then were unable to open the escape hatch. It was only after five days had passed that the Kremlin authorized the assistance of the British and Norwegians, who managed to open the hatch, but by this time all the sailors had died. According to Goldfarb, Berezovsky, who was at his Cap d'Antibes villa on the French Riviera at the time, reached Putin by phone on August 16 and urged him to go immediately to the submarine base on the Barents Sea, or at least back to Moscow, warning Putin that he could be seriously damaging his reputation. Putin was not receptive, waiting until August 19 to return to Moscow.[54]

Meanwhile both ORT and NTV were broadcasting interviews with the distraught mothers of the dead sailors, along with reports of the Russian navy's inadequacies and Kremlin indifference. Putin was furious. With Aleksandr Voloshin at his side, he met with Berezovsky in Moscow on August 20 to tell him that he needed to give control of ORT to the government and suggested that if Berezovsky did not comply, he would end up in prison like Gusinsky. Although earlier that summer he had said publicly that he would sell his ORT shares to the government, Berezovsky defiantly refused Putin's demand. Noting that Yeltsin would never have shut off media critics, he added, "You are destroying Russia." Finally, Putin turned his cold gaze on Berezovsky and said: "You were one of those who asked me to be president. So how can you complain?" This would be the last time that the two met.[55] (During testimony in 2011 at the London trial of Berezovsky's case against Roman Abramovich, Voloshin would claim that neither he nor Putin pressured Berezovsky to sell his ORT shares.)[56]

Afterwards Berezovsky went back to his office and wrote Putin a letter, pointing out the Russian leader's mistakes yet again. Putin was becoming an autocrat, Berezovsky wrote, finding "solutions to complex problems by simple means," but it would not work. On giving the letter to Voloshin, Berezovsky realized that his relationship with Putin had reached a dead end.[57] Two days later, he announced that a fund-raising drive he initiated had collected over a million dollars to aid families of the deceased *Kursk* sailors; he added that he would set up a commission to investigate the causes of the disaster.[58]

Putin did not travel to Severomorsk, headquarters of Russia's Northern Fleet, to meet with the families of the *Kursk* victims until August 22, a full ten days after the tragedy occurred. According to a transcript of the closed meeting, published later by *Kommersant*, it did not go well.[59] Putin, faced with tears and angry shouts, tried to explain why he had not come earlier: "I asked the military if there was anything I could do to help, and they firmly said no!" When Putin promised compensation for the families, one woman wailed: "We are experiencing such grief. People are already sobbing . . . We don't need money. We need them alive. Children had fathers; wives had husbands. They believed that the state would save them." Putin responded by blaming others for the disaster. He claimed that the economic turmoil caused by his predecessors' policies had deprived the military of the funds necessary to maintain rescue equipment, and that the media had lied about the disaster in order to discredit the government. The minute foreign help was offered to the *Kursk*, Putin said falsely, it was accepted, "and that means, the television lied, lied, lied."

The next day, Putin appeared on state television and acknowledged responsibility for the tragedy. But he also vented his anger at those who "take advantage of this calamity in an unscrupulous way." In a clear reference to Berezovsky, Putin said that some of those helping the sailors' families, even collecting a million dollars, have for a long time contributed to the decline of the military and the government. "It would be better if they sold their villas on the Mediterranean coast of

France and Spain," Putin added. "Then they would have to explain why all this property is registered in fake names and legal firms. We would ask them where they got the money."[60]

In the end, Putin did not suffer a great loss of public confidence because of his handling of the *Kursk* tragedy. Although his approval ratings dropped from 73 to 65 percent in the immediate aftermath of the crisis, they soon bounced back.[61] But Putin was thin-skinned, and this was the first crisis he had faced, so he experienced the media attacks personally and focused his revenge on Berezovsky. On August 27, Putin summoned Berezovsky's business partner Badri Patarkatsishvili to his office and asked him what kind of "strange game" Berezovsky was playing. He told Patarkatsishvili, who thought he might be arrested on the spot, that he wanted him and Berezovsky to "clear out" of ORT and suggested that Patarkatsishvili meet with his minister of the press, Mikhail Lesin, who had negotiated the Gusinsky buyout, to discuss the sale of their ORT shares.[62]

Feeling the pressure, Berezovsky reverted to a previous tactic—an open letter to Putin, which appeared in *Kommersant* on September 5. Berezovsky wrote that he rejected the Kremlin's demand that he transfer to the state his holdings (49 percent of the shares) in ORT television: "If I agree to the ultimatum, television information will cease to exist in Russia and will be replaced by television propaganda, controlled by your advisors." Noting that the president was unhappy with ORT's coverage of the *Kursk* submarine disaster, Berezovsky alleged that the Kremlin was resorting to threats and blackmail to wrest control over ORT from him, offering him a choice between relinquishing his shares or following Gusinsky to jail. But, he said, "you know me quite well and therefore should not be surprised to learn that I will not submit to your ultimatums." Instead, Berezovsky wrote, he was transferring his ORT shares to a group of prominent journalists and intellectuals.[63]

Desperation

Had Berezovsky quietly sold his ORT shares to the government and ceased speaking out in the media about Putin's failings, he might possibly have made a tenuous peace with the Russian president and remained in Russia. But he seemed to hope that by publicizing his dispute with the Kremlin and demonstrating the danger for democracy posed by a Kremlin takeover of ORT, pressure might be brought to bear on Putin. An article in *Kommersant* on September 5 suggested this.

Pointing out that Putin was heading to the United Nations summit in New York, the author noted that he might face questions about press freedom from other world leaders: "For the West, Berezovsky is a much more odious figure than Gusinsky. But if there really is not a single nonstate Russian TV channel left in Russia, the Western establishment is likely to temporarily forget about its antipathy toward the oligarch and agree conditionally to consider him another victim of the Putin regime's struggle with independent media."[64]

In fact, Putin was questioned about Berezovsky during a dinner with the media, hosted by Tom Brokaw, on September 8, 2000. Asked why his government would harass Berezovsky, given that the oligarch had helped in the selection of Putin as Boris Yeltsin's successor, Putin responded angrily: "Did he really? He wanted you to believe that" and did not answer the question.[65] In a one-on-one with Larry King, Putin said that freedom of the press in Russia was not under threat and that the real issue with Gusinsky and Berezovsky was simply that they had incurred debts. He also told King that he always wore the Orthodox cross his mother had given him, which was almost lost in a fire at his dacha.[66]

Andrei Piontkovsky later scoffed at the story of the cross, which Russians had already heard countless times in different versions and was intended to show Western audiences that Putin had a human side. "The interview with Larry King helps shed light on why Western leaders are so taken with Putin," Piontkovsky noted. "The export-model Putin is vastly different from the version for domestic consumption. When abroad, Putin doesn't threaten to wipe anyone out in the outhouse, and he doesn't go into self-revealing hysterics, shouting 'Television is lying! Television is lying! Television is lying!' The export Putin doesn't use [a crude expression] when talking with women. This kind of behavior is only acceptable at home, with his own lackeys. Especially as the lackeys love it."[67]

If Berezovsky was counting on support from the Russian public as a victim of Putin, it was wishful thinking. Albats probably reflected the views of most well-informed Russians when she commented harshly in *The Moscow Times* on Berezovsky's most recent letter to Putin.[68] The only rationale behind Berezovsky's public and private adventures, she wrote, "has been self-enrichment at the expense of subverting all the noble desires that he presumably is fighting for now." He himself created the situation he was now in, with little to offer in bargaining with the Kremlin: "Once again, Berezovsky has proved that he is good at short-term tactics, but no good at strategic thinking." Lilia Shevtsova later observed: "Though the most restive tycoon said all the right things about the threat to democracy, no one in Russia thought he was sincere. Everyone remembered his role in the evolution of the Yeltsin regime and assumed he was only trying to save himself and his empire now."[69]

Some independent journalists accepted Berezovsky's offer to become trustees of his shares in ORT, despite his reputation of being more a manipulator of the media than a defender.[70] But Berezovsky lamented in a presentation at the International Press Center in Washington, DC, on September 20 that "it is easier for me to speak in the West than at home because the Americans understand me much better." Russians, he said, have a slave mentality. He went on to say that his political opposition to Putin was not meant to topple him from power but to offer the Russian leader alternative strategies.[71] Back in Moscow in mid-October, Berezovsky raised his pitch, warning that "the whole might of the state machinery is being used to prevent the formation of an opposition."[72]

On October 17, Berezovsky was grilled for two hours by Russian prosecutors on the Aeroflot case and afterward announced that "the whole case is pure politics, first by Primakov and now by Vladimir Putin."[73] The next day he was locked out of his lavish state dacha in Aleksandrovka, which he had rented for his family since 1994. As if Berezovsky needed any further reminder of the Russian president's wrath, Putin gave an interview to *Le Figaro* on October 26 in which he responded to a question about Berezovsky by suggesting that the oligarch was trying "to scare the political leadership" with blackmail. Putin then made a pointed warning: "We wield a big stick, called 'palitsa' in Russian, which can clinch an argument with one fell swoop. We have not used it yet, we are simply holding it in our hands, and that has had some resonance already. But if we are provoked, we will have to use it."[74]

By this time, Berezovsky had headed to his French villa, where he soon received an order from Russian prosecutors to appear for questioning in Moscow on November 15, 2000. According to a deputy prosecutor, Berezovsky could expect "very serious charges of embezzlement" involving the $700 million of Aeroflot funds that had gone through the bank accounts of Forus and Andava. Nikolai Glushkov, Berezovsky's business partner and onetime deputy director of Aeroflot, had also been summoned, but his appearance had been postponed because he was in the hospital.[75]

Alex Goldfarb arrived at Cap d'Antibes on November 12, 2000, to discuss a planned Berezovsky foundation for political opposition to

Putin. He was surprised the next day when Berezovsky announced that he would be flying to Moscow to answer the Russian prosecutor's summons. Goldfarb literally pulled Berezovsky out of his car as he was about to leave for the Nice airport, saying: "Boris, are you insane? Didn't they tell you that they would put you in jail if you did not give up ORT? Why are you going there?" Goldfarb got Elena Bonner, Andrei Sakharov's window, on the phone to talk with Berezovsky. With Bonner's help, Goldfarb and Berezovsky's wife, Elena, managed to dissuade the oligarch from returning to Russia.[76]

Instead, a depressed Berezovsky wrote a long statement for the Russian press, published on November 15, in which he said that he would not return to Moscow for questioning by prosecutors. He had been compelled to choose, Berezovsky wrote, "between becoming a political prisoner or a political emigrant." He went on to say that "as a candidate for Russia's presidency, Putin had seen nothing wrong with using the profits of Swiss firms cooperating with Aeroflot for purposes of financing the Unity bloc or his own presidential campaign." Yet now, Berezovsky added, Putin was using the Aeroflot case against him because ORT had told the truth about the *Kursk* tragedy. He ended the letter by predicting that, if Putin continued to use the security services to stifle freedom, "his regime will hardly last until the end of the first constitutional term."[77]

Consigned like Trotsky to permanent exile, Berezovsky would become more extreme in pursuing a vendetta against Putin in the following years. But what he said in this letter, openly accusing Putin of corruption, helped to seal his fate. Berezovsky's predictions of the demise of Putin's regime, which would open the way for his own triumphant return to Russia, would prove to be a fantasy—like wishing on a star.

CHAPTER 9

The Outcast versus the Tyrant

American policy must reflect the sobering
conclusion that a Russian government which does
not share our most basic values cannot be a friend
or partner and risks defining itself, through its
own behavior, as an adversary.

—John McCain, November 4, 2003

Berezovsky could not avoid scandal, even
on a personal level. It was widely rumored that he and Elena Gorbunova were separating because Berezovsky had taken up with a young
Russian fashion model before his departure from Russia.[1] Whatever
the truth of the rumors, the couple stayed together. Gorbunova and
their two young children, Arina and Gleb, moved to Cap d'Antibes
at some point during the summer of 2000, and the next year, they
accompanied Berezovsky to Britain, where he requested political asylum. Berezovsky's second wife, Galina Besharova, had moved with the
two children from their marriage to Israel but would later take up residence in Britain as well.

Having left Russia for good, Berezovsky needed to reorganize his
business commitments and finances—a complicated endeavor, given
that his departure was sudden and he had made no advance plans.
With this in mind, Berezovsky and his partner Badri Patarkatsishvili
arranged to meet Roman Abramovich on December 6, 2000, at Le
Bourget Airport outside Paris to discuss their joint business affairs.
The three, who arrived separately on private jets, reached a stalemate on
financial arrangements with Sibneft and Rusal, an aluminum company
that Berezovsky and Patarkatsishvili also claimed ownership in, along
with Abramovich and Oleg Deripaska. According to Berezovsky's later

testimony, Abramovich made it clear to his interlocutors that he was fully integrated into the Kremlin's leadership team and had influence with the Russian prosecutor general. Berezovsky suspected that he was trying to blackmail him and Patarkatsishvili into complying with his requests.[2]

Berezovsky's suspicions were confirmed when Abramovich met with him and Patarkatsishvili at Cap d'Antibes two weeks later and, acting as Putin's emissary, pressured them to sell their interests in ORT to him. (Abramovich would later deny that this meeting took place.) According to Berezovsky, he was compelled to agree because his close friend and business associate Nikolai Glushkov had been arrested and imprisoned at Lefortovo on December 7, the day after the meeting at Le Bourget Airport. Abramovich told them that if they did not sell their ORT shares, Glushkov would be in prison for a very long time. The price, $175 million, considered by Berezovsky to be much undervalued, was non-negotiable. Berezovsky and Patarkatsishvili felt that they no choice but to agree. Berezovsky recalled: "I saw now that I had been wrong to trust Mr. Abramovich. At the conclusion of the meeting, I made clear to him that I knew he was blackmailing me, and that he had betrayed me. I told him 'It's the last time that I will meet you, Roma, I never want to see you again.'"[3]

In fact, Glushkov was not released from prison and in April 2001 was caught trying to escape. (He would remain incarcerated until March 2004.) Berezovsky and Patarkatsishvili's continued concern about Glushkov and their fear that their shares in Sibneft would be expropriated led them to give up all claims to the oil company in return for a $1.3 billion payment from Abramovich. Patarkatsishvili, who had left Russia for good in March 2001, handled the direct negotiations with Abramovich that spring. Abramovich would later insist that the payment was not for shares in Sibneft, which he said Berezovsky and Patarkatsishvili had never owned, but rather a final payment for the two men's services to the company, including Berezovsky's use of his influence with the Kremlin for the benefit of Sibneft.[4]

Meanwhile, Berezovsky's friend Alexander Litvinenko had been engaged in his own battle with the Kremlin. In March 1999, when Putin was still head of the FSB, Litvinenko was arrested on trumped-up charges of exceeding his authority by physically attacking a police suspect and sent to Lefortovo prison, where he was placed in solitary confinement for thirty-six days and beaten. At his trial in late November 1999, the judge found Litvinenko not guilty on all counts, but he was rearrested in the courtroom on new, equally spurious charges. It was not until Berezovsky went directly to then Prime Minister Putin and appealed to him to intervene that Litvinenko was released in late December 1999. But he was placed under FSB surveillance and his passport was confiscated, so Litvinenko knew that it was only a matter of time before he would be back in jail, or even worse, murdered by the FSB. Putin apparently considered Litvinenko a traitor because of his 1998 public accusations against the FSB.[5]

With the help of his friend Yuri Felshtinsky, a journalist based in the United States, Litvinenko flew to Georgia at the end of September 2000 and later met up with his wife, Marina, and son, Anatoly, in Turkey. Alex Goldfarb, enlisted by Berezovsky to assist the Litvinenkos, drove them to Ankara, where they tried unsuccessfully to get political asylum at the US Embassy there. After consulting Berezovsky, Goldfarb flew with the Litvinenkos to London on November 1 and managed to persuade British authorities to take the family in. A British lawyer who had been hired for Litvinenko was quoted as saying that Litvinenko "fears for his life also because he knows about a lot of things, including the explosions of the apartment buildings in Moscow last year."[6] Berezovsky arranged accommodation for the Litvinenkos in Kensington, where they stayed for the next two years before moving to a home in London's Muswell Hill, which Berezovsky bought for them. Henceforth, Berezovsky provided financial support for the family and, once he himself had moved to Britain, hired Litvinenko to work with him on a campaign to bring about Putin's political downfall.[7]

Putin Asserts His Grip

Putin had seen the crucial role that television played in shaping public opinion during the year leading up to his election and, particularly after the *Kursk* affair, he realized that control over television was now essential to preserving his political power. Russia's newspapers and Internet media outlets were independent and freely criticized the Kremlin, but a majority of Russians got their news from television. The Russian president and his supporters moved in on the networks. Once Abramovich had gained Berezovsky's 49 percent stake in ORT, he apparently ceded his authority over the station to the Kremlin. The state gas monopoly Gazprom managed to gain control of NTV in 2001 by calling in a $281 million loan it had given to Gusinsky in 1998. And the only other independent station, TV6, which was owned largely by

Berezovsky, was shut down by the Kremlin in January 2002 for alleged financial violations.[8] Unlike Yeltsin, who had often been the victim of merciless television coverage, Putin would not only be protected from negative publicity; he would use television as a propaganda tool to promote his personality cult, which was well underway by the end of 2001.

The cult of Putin was furthered in other ways. Portraits of the president appeared in all military bases and government offices, and new textbooks describing Putin's childhood were introduced in Russian classrooms. As Shevtsova noted, "Putinomania gradually became an element of Russian life."[9] None of this had happened under Yeltsin, whose tenure as Russian leader was a marked departure from this Soviet tradition of leadership cults.

Putin also had a firm grip on the Kremlin power organs—run by the so-called *siloviki*—which were crucial to keeping his people in line at all levels. Patrushev's FSB was filled with Putin loyalists from the Leningrad/St. Petersburg security services in its senior ranks. The agency's role was not confined to counterintelligence and counterterrorism but also included investigating economic crimes, and corruption allegations were a powerful tool for going after political enemies. The Prosecutor General's Office was in the safe hands of Vladimir Ustinov, unswervingly loyal to the new Putin regime. As one source expressed it: "Vladimir Ustinov turned out to be a very useful Prosecutor General for Vladimir Putin and his entourage. Unlike his predecessor, Iurii Skuratov, he did not show any attempts to investigate the activities of the highest state officials and clearly followed the changing environment . . . Under Vladimir Ustinov, the prosecutor's office turned into an obedient instrument of the ruling regime."[10] In addition to closing the Mabetex case and going after Gusinsky's NTV, Ustinov took charge of investigations of the 1999 apartment bombings, the *Kursk* tragedy, and major terrorist incidents that occurred later.

Putin's close ally, St. Petersburg KGB veteran Evgenii Murov, was placed in charge of the Federal Guard Service (FSO), the agency that protected the Kremlin. Under Murov, who would hold his post for the next sixteen years, the FSO could be counted on to be loyal to Putin. Within the FSO was the Presidential Security Service (SBP), the personal guard of Putin, led by Viktor Zolotov, who had protected Anatoly Sobchak before going into private security. Zolotov, a KGB offspring whose connections with the St. Petersburg mafia were widely known, reportedly was a judo partner of Putin's when the latter was at the mayor's office, and the two became close. In 2016, Putin would appoint Zolotov chief of the newly created National Guard, with close to 340,000 troops under him.[11]

Leningrad native Igor Sechin, perhaps the closest to Putin of all his associates, could be considered a silovik because he served as a military translator in Africa in the late 1980s, when such positions were undercover for the Soviet intelligence services, and he subsequently allied himself with the hardliners on Putin's team. After working under Putin in Sobchak's office, Sechin had followed him to Moscow in 1996 and occupied various positions, some directly under Putin, in the Yeltsin administration. According to the author Thane Gustafson: "In every one of Putin's jobs, as Putin moved up the hierarchy, Sechin was there, guarding the entrance to his office, managing Putin's life."[12]

Once Putin became president, he appointed Sechin deputy chief of the Presidential Administration and in 2004, Sechin also became chairman of the board of directors of Rosneft. Former KGB officer Yuri Shvets described Sechin as "a secretive and mistrustful person who has a peculiar habit of turning documents on the table upside down when somebody enters his office."[13] Mikhail Zygar noted that Sechin was the "spiritual leader" of the siloviki and added: "Sechin understood better than anyone Putin's psychology. He knew that for Putin there was nothing worse than a traitor. To betray him personally and to betray Russia were for Putin almost the same."[14]

As for the military, in March 2001 Putin took the bold step of appointing a civilian, Sergei Ivanov, as minister of defense. A trusted friend of the president, Ivanov hailed from St. Petersburg, where he had worked with Putin in the KGB during the 1970s. Ivanov spent the bulk of his career in the Foreign Intelligence Service before being appointed by Putin to serve as his deputy when Putin headed the FSB in 1998. Looking back on Putin's early presidency, the political scientist Richard Sakwa observed: "Under Putin, the *siloviki* flaunted themselves as the guardians of Russian state interests, and their influence seeped out of narrowly defined security matters into business relations and the information sphere, as well as into foreign policy."[15]

Approaches to the West

Although Putin seemed an unlikely world leader when he first appeared to the public as prime minister in August 1999, he soon made his mark on the global stage, traveling to eighteen countries in his first year as president, often with Liudmila in tow. A high point on his

Figure 20.   George Bush and Vladimir Putin with their wives, Crawford, Texas, November 2001. AP photo/American-Statesman, Taylor Johnson.

path to international prominence came when Putin met US president George Bush in Slovenia in June 2001. The two got on so well that Bush famously said of Putin: "I looked the man in the eye. I found him to be very straightforward and trustworthy. We had a very good dialogue. I was able to get a sense of his soul; a man deeply committed to his country and the best interests of his country."[16]

Later, after the September 11 World Trade Center bombings, Putin gained even more of Bush's trust when he telephoned the US president and offered help in the fight against terrorism. In November 2001, Putin and Liudmila paid a visit to the Bushes at their ranch in Texas, where Putin continued with his charm offensive: "Being here I can feel the will of these people, the will to cooperate with the Russian Federation, the will to cooperate with Russia. And I can assure you that the Russian people fully share this commitment and is also committed to fully cooperating with the American people."[17] *Time Magazine* observed in December 2001: "The West now seems infatuated with Putin. The Russian President appears a paragon of liberalism, democracy, sophistication and championship of human rights. Nice to have such an ally."[18]

It did seem, at this point, that Putin was not merely playacting, that, despite his initial antidemocratic reforms and the brutal war in Chechnya, he was enticed by the idea of Russia cooperating with the West in pursuit of a stabilized world order, with the Cold War far behind. After all, he had even mentioned the possibility of Russia joining NATO shortly before the Russian presidential elections in March 2000.[19] Richard Sakwa observed that Putin initially faced the same choice that Gorbachev and Yeltsin faced when they assumed Russia's leadership: "Would Russia join the existing US-led liberal international order, adapt to its norms, conventions and power hierarchy, or would it try to maintain its autonomy as a great power and separate political civilization, even if this generated conflict with the dominant power system?"[20]

If Putin really was considering the idea of a rapprochement with the West, he would have soon realized that it was completely incongruous with the type of regime he was creating. US efforts to nurture democracy in the former Soviet Bloc and discussions of including Eastern European nations in NATO were an anathema to the Kremlin, which had no intention of establishing political pluralism or a strong civil society in Russia. After Yeltsin's chaotic attempts at democracy, Russian people were not demanding such changes, as long as they did not suffer economically. They preferred stability above all. It would not be long before Putin and his team would consider NATO to be Russia's greatest threat.

In contrast to Putin, Berezovsky's image in the West—just as in Russia—was that of a corrupt oligarch, a self-promoter, and a has-been Kremlin powerbroker. *The New York Times* described him in early 2003 as a "Soviet-era mathematician and oligarch of robber-baron capitalism, onetime Kremlin kingmaker and now plain old self-exiled billionaire."[21] Some, such as George Soros, thought even worse of Berezovsky. In a lengthy 2000 article, Soros even suggested that Berezovsky was behind the September 1999 bombings: "From Berezovsky's point of view the bombings made perfect sense. Not only would such attacks help to elect a president who would provide immunity to Yeltsin and his family but it would also give him, Berezovsky, a hold over Putin."[22]

Not long after the World Trade Center attack, Goldfarb and Berezovsky went to Washington, DC, to promote their new International Civil Liberties Foundation and Berezovsky's efforts to form a liberal political movement against Putin. There they experienced firsthand the impact of Putin's alliance against terror with the Bush administration. Goldfarb recalled, "It was clear to me that from now on, we would be viewed in Washington as an enemy of a friend." As they were leaving the State Department, Berezovsky lamented Putin's good luck and opined: "I wonder whether the Americans understand that he is not their friend at all. He will play them and the Muslims against each other, exploring every weakness to his advantage."[23]

The Bombings Revisited

In October 2001, Berezovsky moved with Gorbunova and their children into a seven-bedroom, ten-thousand-square-foot mansion in Surrey, and Berezovsky established offices at 5 Savile Row, in London's Mayfair district, about a forty-five-minute commute from his home. (That same month, Berezovsky's name was put on Russia's list of wanted criminals in connection with the Aeroflot case.) Berezovsky later told *The New York Times* that since fleeing Russia he had been able to spend more time with his children, after years as "not a very good father": "For the first time in my life I visit their school. I know exactly what my five-year-old boy and seven-year-old girl are doing."[24]

According to his son Gleb, he and Berezovsky's other children found their father to be "always an attentive listener, who at the same time tried to impart his knowledge to us."[25] But Berezovsky devoted most of his time to his all-consuming cause of bringing about Putin's downfall. Having played an outsized role in Kremlin politics for several years, he apparently could not resign himself to the obscurity of exile, helplessly watching the man who had forced him out of Russia accumulate power. In May 2001, Berezovsky had hosted the liberal Duma deputy Sergei Iushenkov at his French villa, along with another prominent parliamentarian, Vladimir Golovlev, to discuss the formation of a new Russian opposition party, Liberal Russia. The party would sponsor candidates for the 2003 Duma elections who would run on an anti-Putin platform. At the first congress of Liberal Russia, held in Moscow in December 2001, Berezovsky was elected in absentia as one of the co-chairmen of the party, along with Iushenkov and others. He would also provide several million dollars in financing.[26]

Berezovsky began seeing a lot of Litvinenko, who, together with Yuri Felshtinsky, was finishing a sensational book, *FSB vzyrvaet Rossiiu* (published in English as *Blowing Up Russia*) about the FSB and its history of terrorism, including the September 1999 bombings. Excerpts from the

FIGURE 21. Alexander Litvinenko with his daughter Sonia, son Anatoly, and Berezovsky at Berezovsky's mansion outside London. Shutterstock.

book, which would appear in Russian and English in early 2002, were published in *Novaia gazeta* on August 27, 2001, creating a sensation.[27] (In Russia itself the book was banned, so it could only be accessed online, at the website Grani.ru.) Although the book did not provide definitive proof that the FSB was behind the bombings, it provided persuasive circumstantial evidence of FSB involvement.

Even the cautious, respected human rights advocate Sergei Kovalev, while concurring with others that the book's sources were often unverified, had praise: "We undoubtedly need the book; it is more than useful, it is simply necessary . . . As for the version about the participation of special services in these explosions, about the organization, I'm afraid to believe in this version, but this does not mean that we reject it . . . I must say that the Ryazan episode is indeed the best chapter in the book; it is a very neatly made compendium of all existing public statements of this kind and a completely logical analysis."[28]

Berezovsky had hitherto refused to say, publicly at least, that the FSB was behind the bombings. This was hardly surprising, given that he had been one of Putin's main supporters in his ascent to the presidency. Also, Berezovsky had been credibly accused of encouraging the incursion of Chechen rebels into Dagestan in August 1999, which was seen as a precursor to the bombings. So he was treading on thin ice when, on December 14, 2001, he appeared via video from London at a conference in Moscow sponsored by his International Civil Liberties Foundation and stated that he was now convinced of the FSB's culpability in the 1999 acts of terrorism. But he did not go so far as to blame Putin: "The only thing I cannot tell for sure is whether or not Putin gave the orders in those operations or commanded them."[29]

While Berezovsky's comments drew a lot of attention, they were greeted with the usual skepticism. According to *The Wall Street Journal*, "Observers say this latest salvo in Mr. Berezovsky's increasingly quixotic campaign against the Kremlin reveals the desperation of a man who once was one of the most powerful players in Russian politics, but has seen his influence wane under Mr. Putin."[30] *The New York Times* interviewed Berezovsky about his claims in February 2002, a week after FSB chief Patrushev had accused him of providing financial support to Russian terrorists. Berezovsky said that Patrushev's accusations were made in response to the investigations of the 1999 bombings and promised that within weeks he would have documentary evidence of the FSB's complicity. Noting that "the unsolved explosions that brought terror to Russia . . . stand as an enduring and troubling mystery," *The New York Times* speculated on whether "Mr. Berezovsky is simply trying to orchestrate a political crisis for Mr. Putin to win political asylum in Britain."[31]

The next month, on March 5, Berezovsky appeared at a large gathering in a London auditorium to present the documentary film *The Assassination of Russia*, based on the book by Litvinenko and Felshtinsky and produced by two Frenchmen with his financial help.[32] Elena Bonner introduced the film, emphasizing its importance for a debate about what had actually occurred in the Ryazan incident. The powerful film focused on what was described convincingly as a planned terrorist bombing of an apartment building by the FSB that was inadvertently thwarted by the building's inhabitants. Several of those who lived in the building were interviewed for the film and vigorously objected to the FSB's claim that it had only been carrying out a "training exercise." Also, the film made it clear that, despite the assertions of Russian authorities that Chechen terrorists had carried out the apartment bombings, two years later they had come up with no proof of Chechen involvement. Putin, the film's narrator said, could get to the bottom of the mystery by ordering an official investigation, but that could threaten the legitimacy of all those in power in Russia, including Putin himself.

Reviews of the film in Russia were predictably mixed. *Moskovskii komsomolets*, long a fierce Berezovsky critic, scorned the film: "The grandiose revelations advertised by Berezovsky turned out to be another bluff. Despite his sworn promises, the oligarch did not provide any real evidence of the involvement of the FSB in the explosions of houses in Moscow."[33] Not surprisingly, Berezovsky's newspaper *Kommersant* considered the film significant: "For the first time, documentarians brought together all the facts and details related to the 'Ryazan case,' lined them up chronologically, and gave back-to-back contradictory 'testimonies' in this case of the country's top officials, including the then Prime Minister Putin."[34]

Among those who attended the London screening were Iushenkov and another prominent parliamentarian, Iulii Rybakov, who was not a member of Liberal Russia. The men hoped to distribute the film in Russia and perhaps even find a television channel that was willing to air it. Their plans were thwarted at every turn. Russian customs officials confiscated the hundred copies that Rybakov brought with him from London, and he subsequently received death threats. No Russian television had the courage to show the film, although it did make it into the hands of eager Duma deputies, and there was considerable demand on the street for the thousands of pirated copies.[35]

In April 2002, Iushenkov went to Washington, DC, where he and Goldfarb distributed the film and screened it for the staff of the Senate Foreign Relations Committee and the Kennan Institute, part of the Woodrow Wilson Center. After they got a less than lukewarm reception at the State Department, Iushenkov told Goldfarb: "This is to be expected. Just imagine that we'd come to Washington, say in 1944, to complain about Stalin. We wouldn't get a sympathetic hearing, would we? Uncle Joe was Roosevelt's favorite ally, so he could get away with anything."[36] With Putin on the side of the United States in the war on terror the Americans were not about to rock the boat because of allegations about Putin's possible crimes.

However circumstantial the evidence against the FSB, the Putin regime was unable to refute it. And, for all its forensic skill and investigatory power, the FSB had arrested and prosecuted only two persons, both from Karachaevo-Cherkessia, who had acted as paid middlemen in transporting the explosives. The organizers and perpetrators of the plot were never found, and the alleged *zakazchik* (the one who gave the order), the ethnic Saudi jihadist al-Khattab, who resided in Chechnya, had no apparent motive. As General Lebed had earlier pointed out, it was not in the interests of radical Islamic leaders to bomb apartment buildings housing poor Russian citizens.[37]

Violence in Russia

Equally damning for the FSB were the murders of those who publicly questioned the official line. Iushenkov, who, as co-chairman of the Kovalev Commission, had pressured the Kremlin to furnish answers about the bombings, was shot to death outside his apartment building in April 2003 by a gunman who claimed that he had been hired by a leader of Liberal Russia named Mikhail Kodanev.[38] Earlier, a split had arisen in the party when Berezovsky made overtures to the Communists, which Iushenkov and his supporters opposed, and Kodanev had sided with Berezovsky. Also, Iushenkov was warned by a high government official that the Kremlin would not allow the party to register for the 2003 elections if Berezovsky was a member. All of these circumstances supposedly provided Kodanev with a motive to kill Iushenkov. But Berezovsky later explained that there was no rift between them, and that Iushenkov, with Berezovsky's agreement, had deliberately publicized the conflict so that Liberal Russia would not have problems registering for the elections.[39] Kodanev maintained his innocence, and the case against him was flimsy, to say the least. Berezovsky said the murder charges were "just like something out of 1937."[40] Nonetheless, Kodanev received a twenty-year prison sentence. In 2018, he was released from prison after publicly saying that Berezovsky had ordered Iushenkov's murder, adding to the string of killings that the Kremlin had attributed to the oligarch by this time.[41]

Iushenkov's murder was not an isolated case. Vladimir Golovlev, who had visited Berezovsky in France along with Iushenkov, was walking his dog on a street near his Moscow home when he was shot dead by an unidentified assailant in August 2002. Berezovsky's reaction was immediate. The murder, he said, "is a message to the political classes of Russia that anyone who crosses the red flags of the existing powers will be killed."[42] Just two months after Iushenkov's death, in June 2003, another member of the Kovalev Commission, Duma deputy and investigative journalist Iurii Shchekochikhin fell violently ill from a substance that eventually caused all of his organs to fail and his skin and hair to peel off. He died on July 3. Because the doctors withheld his medical records, Shchekochikhin's family was never able to learn more about the poisonous substance and how it entered his body.[43]

The deaths of these two key members were a huge setback for Kovalev's commission, which already faced obstacles in being denied access to key witnesses and documents. Then, in October 2003, the commission's attorney and key investigator, Mikhail Trepashkin, was arrested after the Russian press reported on a discovery that he had made. The FSB had claimed that the perpetrator of the Moscow apartment bombings was a man from Karachaevo-Cherkessia named Achemez Gochiiaev, who had fled into hiding. Trepashkin found out that Gochiiaev was the wrong man, and the actual criminal—described by Dunlop as the "Mohamed Atta in the Moscow bombings"—was a former FSB officer who was conveniently killed in a car accident in Cyprus after Trepashkin located him.[44] As a result of these misfortunes, Kovalev's work ground to a halt, although Litvinenko and Felshtinsky, who had collaborated with Trepashkin on the bombings case, continued to probe the matter, with Berezovsky supporting them.

Litvinenko and his family had received formal political asylum in Britain in May 2001, but Berezovsky's status was still uncertain, and Russian authorities were hounding him. In October 2002, the Russian prosecutor general charged Berezovsky, Patarkatsishvili and their former business associate Iulii Dubov with fraud relating to a purchase by LogoVAZ of thousands of cars from AvtoVAZ in 1994–95. A month later the Russian government officially requested Berezovsky's extradition from Britain to face the charges. After further pressure from Russia, Berezovsky was very briefly arrested in March 2003 by British authorities, along with Dubov. The two claimed the charges were politically motivated and were released after each paid $160,000 in bail pending a court hearing, which took place on April 2. During the brief court hearing, which extended the proceedings until May, Berezovsky learned that his asylum appeal had been denied by the Home Office because of the extradition demands.[45]

Russia's decision to request Berezovsky's extradition may have been spurred on by his announcement on November 1, 2002, that his International Civil Liberties Foundation would support Akhmed Zakaev, a representative of the Chechen government in exile, who was also facing extradition from Britain to Russia. Zakaev, accused by the Kremlin of terrorism and mass murder because of his support for the Chechen cause, was released from custody by a British court after putting up bail in December 2002 and, like Berezovsky, had to go through an extradition hearing. Then, suddenly, the unexpected happened. In September 2003, the judge in Berezovsky's case announced that Berezovsky had been granted asylum, and the Russian extradition request was denied. MI5 had learned of a plot to kill Berezovsky by stabbing him with a poison pen. The man who had been recruited by Russia's Foreign Intelligence Service as the assassin, Vladimir Terluk, had approached Goldfarb and Litvinenko in London in March 2003 and told them of the plot, asking them to provide him with financial assistance and help in gaining asylum in Britain. Terluk later confirmed his story to British police.[46] To protect Berezovsky when he traveled outside Britain, the Home Office provided him with an alias identity—Platon Elenin.

In Zakaev's case, a key prosecution witness made a surprise appearance in court to announce that he had been tortured by the FSB into making false accusations against the Chechen leader. Another accuser was shown by Zakaev's lawyers to be lying on the witness stand. In November 2003, Judge Timothy Workman threw out the extradition case against Zakaev, concluding that the Russian government was not pursuing an antiterrorist operation in Chechnya but a war, and it was seeking Zakaev's extradition to prevent him from negotiating a peace deal.[47] According to Mikhail Zygar, the British decision to refuse the extradition of Berezovsky and Zakaev was a heavy blow to Putin, especially given his cordial relations with Prime Minister Tony Blair: "Putin simply could not believe that Blair had no influence over the British judicial system."[48]

Putin may have been especially sensitive to condemnation from the Berezovsky camp abroad because of the challenges he was facing at home. On October 23, 2002, forty Chechen terrorists stormed the Dubrovka Theater in central Moscow, taking over nine hundred hostages. Three days later, without the government having conducted serious negotiations with the terrorists, Russian special forces pumped poisonous gas into the theater, killing close to two hundred hostages, along with their captors. Questions were raised immediately in the Russian press about the regime's handling of the incident, including how a band of terrorists with explosives had gathered in Moscow unnoticed by the security police.[49] According to Zygar: "For Putin this was a catastrophe. Not only was the war he had promised to end three years earlier not over, but it had come to the capital. People close to him recalled that Putin was not only upset—he was convinced that this was the end of his political career."[50] But instead of incurring political damage, Putin saw his approval rating increase from 77 percent in October to 82 percent in December.[51] The public was apparently so outraged by

Chechen terrorism that its support for Putin and military action in Chechnya became stronger.

Two years later, on September 1, 2004, militants under the direction of Shamil Basaev seized some 1,200 children, parents, and teachers in a middle school in Beslan, a town in the southern republic of Ossetia. Again, the crisis was mishandled terribly by the FSB. Instead of earnestly pursuing negotiations with the hostage takers, the FSB ended the standoff by opening fire on them, causing 333 deaths, including 186 children. The authorities were later criticized for allowing the attackers to get through checkpoints and for using excessive force when they ended the siege. But, as the former Kremlin foreign policy official Andrei Kovalev noted, Putin again turned the tragedy to his advantage: "He used it both to ratchet up tension inside Russia and in international affairs and to launch a further assault on democracy. 'We are dealing,' he [Putin] declared, 'with the direct intervention of foreign terrorism against Russia. With total, brutal, and full-scale war.'"[52]

In its 2004 annual report on Russia, the Committee to Protect Journalists noted "an alarming suppression of news coverage during the Beslan crisis" and reported that several journalists were prevented by security agents from going to Beslan, including Anna Politkovskaya. Politkovskaya was on her way to cover the crisis for *Novaia gazeta* when she drank tea that had been poisoned on the flight and became so violently ill that she had to be hospitalized. According to the report, this reflected a larger trend of media suppression by the Putin regime: "Using intelligence agents and an array of politicized state agencies, Putin pushed for an obedient and patriotic press in keeping with his ever tightening grip on Russia's deteriorating democracy . . . Critical reporting on the president's record, government corruption, terrorism, and the war in Chechnya has become rare since Putin took office. Overt pressure by the Federal Security Service (FSB), bureaucratic obstruction, politicized lawsuits, and hostile corporate takeovers have enabled the Kremlin to intimidate and silence many of its critics."[53]

Kremlin control over the media had helped to ensure Putin's victory in the March 2004 presidential elections with 71.9 percent of the vote. (The Communist candidate, Nikolai Kharitonov, Putin's closest challenger, received 13.8 percent.) On the surface, the election appeared democratic, but as Western election observers pointed out, "The state-controlled media comprehensively failed to meet its legal obligation to provide equal treatment to all candidates, displaying clear favouritism towards Mr. Putin."[54] That said, Putin continued to enjoy genuine popularity in his country. His approval ratings in March 2004 were above 80 percent. Thanks to a surge in the price of oil, the Russian economy had rebounded solidly from the decline of the 1990s, with significant growth in income and consumption. Ordinary Russians, now better off, were grateful to their president.

The Downfall of Khodorkovsky

Putin had also achieved an important victory over the oligarchs with the arrest in October 2003 of Mikhail Khodorkovsky, who was viewed by the Russian president and his siloviki as a threat to their political and financial dominance. Born in 1963, Khodorkovsky, the owner of the oil company Yukos, was much younger and more financially successful than Berezovsky. (In 2003, his net worth was estimated by Forbes at $8 billion, making him the richest man in Russia.) But as with Berezovsky, Khodorkovsky's ambitions went beyond wealth. Not only did he believe that the economy should be free from state control; he strove to extend his activities and those of Yukos into social and political spheres. In December 2001, Yukos established the Open Russia Foundation, which soon had branches all over the country. The aim of the foundation was to further the development of civil society in Russia by promoting social welfare, public health, and education. Khodorkovsky also made extensive donations to US nonprofit institutions and gave frequent lectures and speeches in Russia and abroad. Richard Sakwa, author of a book on the Yukos affair, writes, "The goal, as Khodorkovsky put it, was to help create a 'normal country,' but it also transformed his image from robber baron to international philanthropist."[55]

Yukos entered the media market in early 2003 when it purchased *Moscow News* and hired an outspoken Kremlin critic, Evgenii Kiselev, as its editor. In addition, Khodorkovsky donated millions of dollars to opposition political parties Yabloko and the Union of Right Forces, as well as to the Communists. And he even had discussions with members of United Russia about the possibility of making changes in the constitution to introduce a "French-style presidential-parliamentary republic." Not surprisingly, Khodorkovsky's undertakings deeply rankled the Kremlin. Open Russia, Sakwa notes, "came to be seen as a type of opposition party . . . the regime feared that it could mobilize an anti-Putin movement."[56] According to Zygar, "people close to Khodorkovsky said that he saw himself as a future prime minister inside a new government."[57]

Khodorkovsky's relations with Putin became especially strained after a televised meeting between Putin and business leaders in the Kremlin on February 19, 2003. With the approval of Voloshin, still head of the Presidential Administration, and the meeting's organizer, Gazprom chairman Dmitrii Medvedev, Khodorkovsky gave a presentation titled "Corruption in Russia: A Brake on Economic Growth." Claiming that the country's corruption was systemic, amounting to $30 billion a year, he noted that it was prevalent in transactions between the government and private business and cited as an example the acquisition by Rosneft of the oil company Severnaia Neft. According to Khodorkovsky, the state grossly overpaid for the company, and the surplus payment went as kickbacks to those involved in the transaction, including government officials. The Russian president was visibly angry. This amounted to a direct attack on his government and business elite. Khodorkovsky's advisor, former KGB general Aleksei Kondaurov, recalled: "If it were not for Mikhail Borisovich's speech at a meeting with Putin in February 2003, I don't exclude the possibility that our fate might have turned out differently. I don't blame Khodorkovsky. He did as he saw fit. He understood the risks, and so did I. I thought the risks were more serious than he thought."[58]

As with Berezovsky, Khodorkovsky's boldness had severe consequences. After the meeting, the FSB, in collaboration with Prosecutor General Ustinov, stepped up an investigation of Yukos begun in 2002, with a focus on gathering kompromat. Igor Sechin, who would become chairman of Rosneft's board of directors in 2004, was reportedly orchestrating these efforts behind the scenes. He had been involved with the Rosneft deal to acquire Severnaia Neft and so naturally took umbrage at Khodorkovsky's criticism of the transaction. Sechin also led the siloviki faction of Putin's team that backed more state control over the economy. With Khodorkovsky out of the picture, Rosneft would be able to snap up Yukos assets, which is in fact what happened.[59]

While Khodorkovsky was determinedly pursuing financial deals, including a proposed merger of Yukos with Abramovich's Sibneft, danger signs appeared. First came the publication in May of a report by Stanislav Belkovsky, head of the Council on National Strategy, titled "The State and the Oligarchy." The report claimed, among other things, that Khodorkovsky was organizing a coup with some other oligarchs. In June 2003, Aleksei Pichugin, a former KGB officer responsible for economic security at Yukos, was arrested on what later proved to be spurious murder charges, and at the end of the month prosecutors searched the Moscow headquarters of Yukos. A few days later Platon Lebedev, chairman of Khodorkovsky's Menatep Group, which owned Yukos, was seized by police from his hospital bed and charged with fraud and tax evasion. Searches continued throughout the summer, and Khodorkovsky was called for questioning as a witness.[60]

When Berezovsky had faced a criminal investigation and aggressive calls from prosecutors to report for questioning, he knew that his arrest was imminent and fled Russia. But Khodorkovsky had reason to believe that he could stay in the country without being arrested. In contrast to Berezovsky, Khodorkovsky had a highly favorable image in the West and a lot of support from Western policy makers, especially in the United States. He spoke in Washington at both the US-Russia Business Council and the Carnegie Endowment on October 9, 2003, appearing confident and assured. He also had been told (falsely, it turns out) that President Bush had raised the Yukos case with Putin at the Camp David summit in September. In addition, Prime Minister Mikhail Kasyanov had informed Khodorkovsky after Lebedev was arrested that Putin wanted him to know that he, Khodorkovsky, had no reason to worry. Voloshin had also assured Khodorkovsky that he was safe from arrest. Apparently both these men had underestimated the authority of Sechin, the prime mover against Khodorkovsky.[61]

As it was under Yeltsin, accusations of financial malfeasance, or other criminal acts, served as weapons to fight political enemies. But, unlike Yeltsin, Putin had complete dominance over the law enforcement agencies, so the accused had no recourse. Khodorkovsky was a sitting duck. At dawn on October 25, the FSB's antiterrorist unit, Alpha, conducted a raid on Khodorkovsky's private jet as it made a stop to refuel in Novosibirsk. Khodorkovsky was taken into custody for allegedly not complying with a summons to appear at the prosecutor's office. After being flown to Moscow, Khodorkovsky was imprisoned without bail to await his June 2004 trial for tax evasion, embezzlement, and other offenses. In May 2005, a Moscow court sentenced him to nine years in a labor colony. (The sentence was later reduced to eight years.) As for Yukos, after the Russian government claimed the company owed $27 billion in taxes and froze its assets, most of it was eventually acquired by Rosneft.[62]

Predictably, Berezovsky portrayed Khodorkovsky's arrest as a cause for alarm in the West over the increasingly dictatorial nature of the Putin regime. In early November, just as Putin was about to attend a summit of the European Union in Rome, Berezovsky urged Western leaders to speak out against Putin's lawlessness. Writing in *The Daily*

Telegraph, he pointed out that "the West needs to pay equal attention to Mr. Putin's attacks on democratic institutions in Russia as it does to the fight for global security."[63] Later that month, he wrote in *Le Monde* that Western statesmen should stop giving legitimacy to Putin as a leader and compared him to Stalin: "At one time, the West supported Stalin. Everyone remembers what the consequences of that policy were for the West and the consequences for us."[64]

Berezovsky was preaching largely to deaf ears. However much Western leaders might have liked to see democracy in Russia, regime change was not on their agenda. Senator John McCain spoke out fiercely against the Russian president after Khodorkovsky's arrest, urging President Bush to rescind Putin's invitation to the June 2004 G8 summit in King Island, Georgia.[65] But McCain's advice was ignored. Putin attended the summit, and while encouraging the Russian president to see the benefits of becoming a cooperative global partner by respecting human rights in his county, Western leaders appeared to accept Putin for what he was.

CHAPTER 10

The Kremlin on the Offensive

> You may be able to shut one man up, but the
> noise of protest all over the world will reverberate
> in your ears, Mr. Putin, to the end of your life.
> May God forgive you for what you have done,
> not only to me but to my beloved Russia and her
> people.
>
> —Alexander Litvinenko, statement made shortly
> before his death on November 23, 2006

With politically active oligarchs like Berezovsky and Khodorkovsky out of the way and a landslide election victory in March 2004, Putin was in a position to run the Kremlin like a fiefdom. He did just that, appointing his allies to head key state-controlled companies and merging money and political power as never before. As Andrei Piontkovsky observed after Putin finished his second presidential term: "The right to property in Russia is entirely conditional upon the property owner's loyalty to the Russian Government. The system is tending to evolve not in the direction of freedom and postindustrial society, but rather back toward feudalism, when the sovereign distributed privileges and lands to his vassals and could take them away at any moment."[1]

The contributions of a few million dollars that Berezovsky made to Yeltsin and his team in the 1990s—for Yeltsin's book and the election campaigns—were paltry compared to what Putin would receive as fealty from his tycoons in the following years. Exiled Russian entrepreneur Sergei Kolesnikov recalled: "So every businessman dreams about giving presents and gaining protection. And if you give a present to the president, it's like having God himself watching your back."[2] Kolesnikov was involved with funding the construction of "Putin's palace," the billion-dollar presidential retreat on the Black Sea, using donated funds that were funneled into an investment company called Rosinvest. By 2022, Putin's personal wealth—some of it stashed away in offshore accounts held by others—was estimated to be between $70 and $200 billion.[3]

It seemed that the more money and power Putin accumulated, the greater the need to protect it by eliminating all vestiges of Yeltsin's democracy. In December 2004, a new law was passed ending the popular election of regional governors, who would henceforth be appointed by regional parliaments on recommendations from Putin. The governors would no longer be accountable to the people they governed but to the Russian president. At the time this law came into force, the so-called Orange Revolution was occurring in Ukraine. With Putin's ability to control political events outside Russia's border limited, he had further incentive to tighten his political grip over his country.

Upheaval in Ukraine

The Orange Revolution threw Putin and his comrades for a loop. Ukraine's president, Leonid Kuchma, had been in office since 1994 and was not running for a third term in the country's scheduled October 2004 presidential elections. Instead, he was supporting the candidacy of his prime minister, Viktor Yanukovich, the Kremlin's preferred choice. The main opposition candidate, democratic reformer Viktor Yushchenko, favored closer ties with the West, including NATO and European Union membership, and thus was considered undesirable by the Kremlin. So the Putin team pressured Russian businesses to contribute large sums of money to the Yanukovich campaign and sent advisors to Ukraine to help strategize. In fact, Putin was so intent on achieving a Yanukovich victory that he even traveled to Kyiv on the eve of the election and urged voters to back his chosen candidate.[4]

The Kremlin's efforts were for naught. After a runoff election in November, Yanukovich won narrowly, but the flagrant voter fraud set off mass protests by Yushchenko supporters, and a second runoff, held in late December, gave Yushchenko a victory with almost 52 percent of the vote, versus Yanukovich's 44 percent. While for Putin the election was a humiliating defeat, it was a triumph for Berezovsky, who, according to Goldfarb, had contributed around $40 million to the Yushchenko campaign. After the election, he and Goldfarb set up an office of his International Civil Liberties Foundation in Kyiv, which, in Goldfarb's words, would be used "as a bridgehead for a similar peaceful revolution in Russia."[5]

FIGURE 22.   Ukrainian president Viktor Yushchenko and Prime Minister Yulia Tymoshenko. Mykola Lazarenko/AFP via Getty Images.

Berezovsky was eager to play a role in Ukraine's new politics and even spoke of moving to the country. He had reportedly pushed Yushchenko into making Ukrainian politician Yulia Tymoshenko his new prime minister and intended to make major financial investments in the country. But he faced strong obstacles. Russia's outstanding criminal charges against Berezovsky meant that if he went to Ukraine, the Kremlin would pressure Ukrainian authorities to extradite him to Russia, which would place the new government in an awkward position. So the Yushchenko government denied Berezovsky's request for a visa.[6] Berezovsky's financial contributions to Yushchenko's campaign were also controversial, given his reputation for shady financial deals. In October 2005, Berezovsky met in London with members of the Ukrainian parliament (Verkhovna Rada) who were investigating possible illegal financial contributions to Yushchenko's campaign. Berezovsky admitted that he had funneled millions of dollars into Ukraine but insisted that the money was to support the democratic process in the country, and not specifically for Yushchenko's election.[7]

None of these problems stopped Berezovsky from giving advice to the new government in Kyiv, whether sought after or not. In May 2005, he wrote a letter to Tymoshenko, emphasizing that his main goal was to have Ukraine influence political change in Russia. He discussed proposed business projects in Ukraine that would generate profits to be used to further the aims of the Orange Revolution and urged Tymoshenko not to make concessions to Russia: "In general, your biggest mistake—both yours and V. Yushchenko's—consists in your overestimation of the power of Putin's Russia. If you made fewer overtures to Russia . . . and were more methodical, the regime in Russia could be changed within a year, two years at most."[8]

Berezovsky felt strongly that, in order to move forward, the new Ukrainian government had to address its past and finally get to the bottom of a crime that had plagued the country for several years: the gruesome September 2000 murder of the journalist and editor Georgiy Gongadze. Fraught with political intrigue, the case had been investigated on and off with little success because it was repeatedly sabotaged by various Ukrainian officials. A key piece of evidence was a recording of a conversation sometime before the murder between then President Kuchma and former interior minister Iurii Kravchenko about getting rid of Gongadze, who had been highly critical of the Kuchma government. The recording had been secretly made by Kuchma's bodyguard, Mykola Melnychenko, who then fled the country and gained asylum in the United States.[9]

At some point Berezovsky's people, including Litvinenko and Felshtinsky, contacted Melnychenko and obtained copies of the tapes. Berezovsky, who had agreed to provide Melnychenko with security protection, told Ukrainian lawmakers during the October meeting that his foundation had transcribed some of the tape recordings and handed over copies of tapes and the transcripts to Ukrainian law enforcement authorities.[10] Melnychenko flew back to Kyiv in December 2005 to speak with Ukrainian investigators and members of the parliament. But by this time, he had apparently been pressured, possibly by the Russian security services, to hold back some of his evidence against Kuchma. Melnychenko claimed that the Yushchenko camp had told him to "lay off" Kuchma, and he later split with the Berezovsky group, after accusing its members of falsifying some of his tapes. In the end, Berezovsky's involvement with the Gongadze case was unsuccessful in helping to expose those behind the murder, which to this day remains unsolved.[11]

Putin Empowered

Berezovsky's efforts on behalf of the Orange Revolution must have deeply rankled the Russian president. What Putin and his colleagues doubtless feared was what Berezovsky envisaged—that democracy in

Ukraine would be contagious and spread to Russia, a fear that would motive the Kremlin's military aggression against Ukraine in 2014 and 2022. Their deep concern about political threats from abroad was aggravated by the eastward expansion of NATO in March 2004, when six countries were admitted as new members: Bulgaria, Slovenia, Slovakia, and the three Baltic states that had previously been part of the Soviet Union—Lithuania, Latvia, and Estonia.

When Putin met George Bush for a summit in Bratislava, Slovakia's capital, in February 2005, it was clear that their once friendly relationship had cooled and that Putin, who sniped at Bush more than once during their exchanges, had lost interest in cooperating with the West. As Secretary of State Condoleezza Rice observed, "This Putin was different than the man who we had first met in Slovenia."[12] The next month, addressing a joint session of the Duma and Federation Council, Putin made his now infamous statement that "the collapse of the Soviet Union was the greatest political catastrophe of the century."[13] However much Putin had wanted to be a member of the Western leaders' club when he first became Russia's president, he now seemed to be convinced that his political survival at home depended on aggressively protecting Russia's depleted empire and striving to gain hegemony over what Russia had lost in 1991. As Lenin observed, "foreign policy is a continuation of internal policy," and Putin believed that his ability to control domestic politics depended on being tough abroad.

Liudmila Putina had accompanied Putin to Bratislava, where she spent time sightseeing with Laura Bush and the wife of Slovakia's president. But her trips abroad with her husband would become less frequent. According to Sergei Pugachev, a banker who was close to the Putins, Liudmila was unhappy about her husband's re-election: "She said she had agreed to four years, no more than that. He had to persuade her to stay."[14] In an interview with three Russian newspapers in June 2005, Liudmila lamented that she and her daughters rarely had a chance to talk to Putin: "He doesn't come home until half past eleven or twelve at night. I tried to persuade him that it is necessary not just to work but also to live . . . He works too hard. Everyone in the family knows this." She also said that her involvement in projects as the president's wife centered around her desire for world peace and communication among different countries: "Probably every woman has a desire to save the world. After all, a woman gives birth to children, and she wants to keep them alive, wants them to live in peace."[15] Her goals would increasingly diverge from those her husband was pursuing.

To ensure that his cohort was solidly behind him, Putin had made changes at the top. Voloshin, once Berezovsky's advocate, resigned as head of the Presidential Administration in October 2003, shortly after Khodorkovsky's arrest. His sympathies with Khodorkovsky and his pro-business orientation had put him at odds with Putin's crackdown on Russia's financiers.[16] Dmitry Medvedev, the longtime loyalist from Putin's St. Petersburg clan, assumed Voloshin's post. Four months later, the last remaining member of the Yeltsin old-guard, Prime Minister Mikhail Kasyanov, was fired along with Putin's entire cabinet. Kasyanov later became a vocal critic of Putin and joined the democratic opposition. Under Putin he had pushed for much-needed reforms of Russia's financial system—including further privatization of state enterprises—as well as for an ambitious program of modernizing Russia's outdated infrastructure, such as roads and rail transport. But he ended up achieving only tax reforms and a lower inflation rate.[17]

Putin's new prime minister, Mikhail Fradkov, had a security background, having served abroad in posts reserved for the KGB, and later as director of the Federal Tax Police. (Putin would subsequently, in 2007, appoint Fradkov to head the Foreign Intelligence Service.) Patrushev would remain as head of the FSB until 2008, while Patrushev's longtime KGB/FSB subordinate Rashid Nurgaliev assumed the leadership of the MVD, the regular police forces, in 2003. Minister of Justice Chaika swapped places with Prosecutor General Ustinov in June 2006, thus ensuring that Putin's agenda of criminal investigations would be rigorously followed. In short, Putin continued to have all his bases covered when it came to security and law enforcement, the pillars of his regime.

Berezovsky Throws Caution to the Wind

On January 23, 2006, Berezovsky's sixtieth birthday, his nemesis Aleksandr Khinshtein, who fed on sources in the Russian security services, published a sensational, damning piece about him. Khinshtein described an interview with Nikita Chekulin, a former director of a Russian scientific institute, who had earlier claimed publicly that he had been recruited by the FSB and had direct knowledge that the FSB had transferred hexogen from military facilities to secret recipients, presumably to be used for the 1999 apartment bombings. Chekulin had made an appearance at the screening in London of *Assassination in Russia*, on behalf of Berezovsky's team. He then had a falling-out with

Berezovsky and told Khinshtein that the story about hexogen was false and that Berezovsky and Litvinenko had invented it. Also, Chekulin claimed that Berezovsky had fabricated a murder plot against himself in order to gain asylum in the UK.[18]

In mentioning a murder plot, Chekulin was referring to the allegations of Vladimir Terluk that he had been recruited to kill Berezovsky in 2003. Like Chekulin, with whom he was acquainted, Terluk seems to have been persuaded by the Russian security services to take back his original story and thus provide further ammunition for a Kremlin disinformation campaign against Berezovsky. Later, in April 2007, the state-owned television channel RTR would feature a program intended to implicate Berezovsky in the Litvinenko poisoning. The program included a taped interview with Terluk (in silhouette under the pseudonym Pyotr), alleging that Berezovsky offered him large sums of money in 2003 to tell his false story to British authorities. In response, Berezovsky filed a defamation suit against RTR and Terluk, and in March 2010 he was awarded a judgment of 150,000 British pounds by a British court.[19]

Berezovsky's tendency toward extreme comments about Putin and the Kremlin tested the patience of British authorities. To commemorate his sixtieth birthday, Berezovsky threw a lavish bash at Blenheim Palace, arranging for a plane to bring thirty of his oldest friends from Moscow to celebrate with his exiled London friends and his family. The next day, apparently roiled by Khinshtein's slanderous article, Berezovsky gave two inflammatory media interviews. He told *Ekho Moskvy* that he had been working for a forceful seizure of power in Russia for the past year and a half. "The current regime," Berezovsky said, "will never allow fair elections, so there is only one way out—a change, a forceful interception of power." He went on to point out that no one could have predicted the 1991 collapse of the Soviet Union, and "Putin's regime is much weaker in terms of force than the Communist one was." Berezovsky elaborated on his plans with Agence France-Presse (APF), saying that power would be taken from Putin by an elite coup d'état, which would then inspire people to take to the streets. Claiming that his fortune had tripled to billions of dollars over the past five years, Berezovsky said that he would finance the coup with his personal funds.[20] His statements were so incendiary that even Litvinenko thought Berezovsky had gone too far, telling a British academic: "I warned him that he cannot talk about changing the political regime in Russia by force but he ignores me. They will get him. He is not careful enough."[21]

It was not until a month later that the British government, probably pressured by the Kremlin, reacted to Berezovsky's statements. In a written statement to the House of Commons on February 23, 2006, British Home Secretary Jack Straw gave a stern rebuke to Berezovsky: "Advocating the violent overthrow of a sovereign state is unacceptable, and I condemn these comments unreservedly." After noting that his government respected Russia's constitution and territorial integrity and valued its partnership, Straw went on to warn Berezovsky that his refugee status could be reviewed at any time and that "we will take action against those who use the UK as a base from which to foment violent disorder or terrorism in other countries."[22]

Berezovsky responded to Straw's warning in early March, with a letter in which he walked back his statements about overthrowing Russia's government by claiming they had been misconstrued. "In none of the interviews I have given or published articles have I supported a 'violent coup' and even less 'instigation of violent riots or terrorism,'" he wrote. "In the interview you mentioned, I used the expression 'forceful interception of power,' which accurately reflects the meaning of bloodless ways to replace authoritarian political regimes with democratic ones, as happened, for example, in Georgia and Ukraine." Berezovsky went on to say: "I highly appreciate the decision of Her Majesty's Government to grant me political asylum in the United Kingdom, but I do not perceive, I hope, like you, that this dooms me to a vow of silence about the unconstitutional actions of the Putin regime."[23]

Meanwhile, the Kremlin lashed out against Berezovsky as never before. On March 2, the Russian Prosecutor General's Office announced criminal charges against him under article 278 of the Russian Criminal Code, which prohibits "actions aimed at the forcible seizure of power." New documents requesting his extradition had been conveyed to the Home Office a day earlier.[24] The Russian media dutifully chimed in. At the end of February, the state television's First Channel aired a press conference held by Alu Alkhanov, president of the Chechen Republic and a Kremlin ally, who accused Berezovsky of financing Chechen terrorists. *Izvestiia* speculated that Berezovsky would face a British court for promoting a violent government overthrow and could be extradited to Russia as a result. And *Moskovskii komsomolets* raised questions about Berezovsky's mental health.[25]

With his business investments at increasing risk after his January remarks, Berezovsky announced in mid-February 2006 that he intended to sell his ownership in the Kommersant Publishing House to his partner Badri Patarkatsishvili. He told *The New York Times* that pressure from the Putin government had made it impossible for him to operate business in Russia.[26] Just months later, Patarkatsishvili would sell Kommersant to Alisher Usmanov, a metals magnate with close Kremlin ties. Although Patarkatsishvili insisted that there was "no political subtext" involved in the $300 million deal, media observers saw the sale as a move by the Kremlin to gain control over independent media outlets ahead of the 2007–8 elections.[27]

In the end, the Kremlin's persistence in pressuring the UK government to extradite Berezovsky proved futile. On June 1, 2006, Judge Timothy Workman issued a judgment in which he denied the Russian prosecutor's March request because, he said, Berezovsky had political asylum in the UK and returning him to Russia would violate provisions of the Geneva Convention that protected those with asylum status.[28]

The Kremlin Unleashes Its Fire

The Russian government did not comment on the Berezovsky ruling, but Putin and his team were not standing idly by. If British authorities would not cooperate with Moscow in pursuing those labeled criminals and terrorists by Russia, another strategy was needed, and this entailed enacting laws that would provide the Kremlin with a legal justification for retribution against enemies outside Russia. In March 2006, the Russian parliament approved an antiterrorism law that authorized *both* the armed forces and the FSB to take action against terrorists abroad. This law was followed in July 2006 by an amendment to the law against so-called extremism that expanded the list of actions constituting extremism to include not only terrorist activity but a wide range of other offenses, such as slander and advocating violence against Russia's territorial integrity.[29]

The vague language of these laws gave the FSB license to act without constraint beyond Russia's borders, alarming Russians exiled in Britain who feared that they might be on the Kremlin's hit list. The famed Soviet-era dissident Vladimir Bukovsky and KGB defector Oleg Gordievsky drew attention to the danger in a letter to *The Times* in July 2006: "The stage is set for any critic of Putin's regime here, especially those campaigning against Russian genocide in Chechnya, to have an appointment with a poison-tipped umbrella [a reference to Georgii Markov, a Bulgarian dissident who was stabbed with an umbrella in London in 1978]."[30]

As one of Putin's fiercest critics and an outspoken advocate of the Chechen cause, Litvinenko was especially concerned. Berezovsky later told British police: "Sasha mentioned loads of times that this legislation of course was designed in the first place to get rid of us—him, Zakaev and myself."[31] Russian authorities had filed new criminal charges against Litvinenko in June 2002—for allegedly committing illegal acts of violence when he was serving as an FSB counterterrorism officer—and they reportedly made one unsuccessful attempt to extradite him before he gained British citizenship in 2005. Sir Robert Owen, who presided over the 2015 Litvinenko inquiry, would later observe: "Just as the evidence suggests that the FSB's anger at what some at least of its members appear to have regarded as Mr. Litvinenko's betrayal of his old organization did not diminish on his departure from Russia, so it is reasonable to speculate that such feelings of betrayal in fact increased over the following years."[32]

This was an understatement. Not only did Litvinenko co-author two books (financed by Berezovsky), one accusing the FSB of organizing the 1999 bombings and the second, *The Gang from Lubianka*, documenting the FSB's involvement in organized crime and terrorism; he was also consulting for British intelligence, MI6, and helping Spanish authorities gather evidence on Russian mafia figures in Spain. Worst of all, Litvinenko published an article for the *Chechen Press* in July 2006 in which he claimed that Putin was a pedophile and had destroyed tapes of himself having sex with underage boys. It is no small wonder that Litvinenko's photograph was being used for target practice at a Russian special forces training center.[33]

Litvinenko was deeply shaken by the murder of the crusading Russian journalist Anna Politkovskaya in Moscow on October 7, 2006. Politkovskaya, who had visited Litvinenko in London not long before she was killed, shared his deep contempt for Putin and his strong sympathy for the Chechens. She campaigned relentlessly in her writings against the unspeakable horrors that the Russian military inflicted on the Chechen people. Speaking at London's Frontline Club on October 19, Litvinenko told his audience: "I know for certain that the murder of a journalist as prominent as Politkovskaya could only have been ordered by one person, Putin."[34]

Although Litvinenko worried that he might be the Kremlin's next victim, he did not suspect that Andrei Lugovoi, who had been a part of Berezovsky's circle for a long time, was the designated hit man. A former KGB officer, Lugovoi had first met Berezovsky in 1993, while working for Yeltsin's guard agency and providing security for Deputy Prime Minister Egor Gaidar. In 1996, Berezovsky hired Lugovoi to oversee security for his television station, ORT, where Patarkatsishvili was deputy director. In the summer of 1998, Lugovoi accompanied Berezovsky to Chechnya, where Berezovsky negotiated for the release of hostages, and in 1999 he was at Berezovsky's side, along with Litvinenko, when Berezovsky campaigned for election to the Duma in the North Caucasus.[35]

After he left ORT in 2001 to start a private security business, Lugovoi visited Berezovsky at Cap d'Antibes on numerous occasions to organize security and later provided similar services for members of Berezovsky's family, including his son-in-law Egor Shuppe. Lugovoi also assumed protection for Patarkatsishvili when the latter was at his residence in Georgia. In July 2004, Lugovoi visited Berezovsky in London and the following year traveled with him to Israel and Kyiv. According to Lugovoi: "For a long period of time I was at the heart of Mr. Berezovsky's and Mr. Patarkatsishvili's life. Mr. Berezovsky has not denied this, and neither could he. I was entrusted to carry out many covert surveillance

FIGURE 23. Andrei Lugovoi, March 2009. AP photo/Misha Japaridze.

and other sensitive tasks relating to Mr. Berezovsky's personal and romantic life, even his medical affairs—liaising for him with doctors and the like."[36] Lugovoi had even flown to London for Berezovsky's sixtieth birthday on the oligarch's private plane and shared a table with Litvinenko and his wife, along with Goldfarb and Akhmed Zakaev.

By 2006, Lugovoi was traveling to London regularly and meeting with Litvinenko to discuss various business plans. It is not clear when Lugovoi had been enlisted to work secretly for the FSB, but it was probably not long after Berezovsky's falling-out with Putin and involved a seemingly fabricated story about Lugovoi's arrest. Lugovoi claimed that he had served jail time for trying to assist Berezovsky's colleague Glushkov escape from prison in 2001. But Glushkov had long suspected that Lugovoi was part of a plot to keep him behind bars longer, while making Lugovoi trusted by the Berezovsky camp. The ruse clearly worked, enabling Lugovoi to further insinuate himself into Berezovsky's circle and eventually forge a friendship with Litvinenko. When former KGB officer Yuri Shvets tried to warn him about Lugovoi, Litvinenko had responded that he trusted Lugovoi because "he served time in jail for Boris Berezovsky."[37]

When Litvinenko met Lugovoi and his accomplice Dmitrii Kovtun in the Pine Bar of London's Millennium Hotel on the afternoon of November 1, 2006, a pot of green tea was sitting on the table. Unbeknownst to Litvinenko as he poured the tea into a cup, one of the two men had slipped drops of polonium-210, a highly lethal poison, into the pot. The rest of this tragic story is well known. Litvinenko became violently ill and died in the hospital, after three weeks of agony, on November 23. It did not take long for the police to identify Lugovoi and Kovtun as the probable killers, but they had already fled to Russia.[38]

Aftermath

For Berezovsky, the ramifications of Litvinenko's poisoning were huge. Having brought Litvinenko and Lugovoi together, he probably felt remorse, along with fear that he was next in line to be killed. As it turned out, earlier on the day of the poisoning Litvinenko had met with an Italian associate named Mario Scaramella, who had been working with him on the investigation of Russian organized crime in Spain. Scaramella had given Litvinenko emails from a Russian intelligence source indicating that the Kremlin was behind the recent slaying of Politkovskaya and was planning also to kill Litvinenko and Berezovsky.

Suddenly realizing the significance of the emails after he left the Millennium Hotel, Litvinenko went to Berezovsky's office to photocopy them. He then urged Berezovsky to have a look at the copied messages, but Berezovsky was hurriedly preparing to fly off to South Africa that night and was too rushed to give them attention.[39]

While still in South Africa, Berezovsky learned of Litvinenko's illness and, after speaking on the telephone with both Litvinenko and his wife, understood that his friend was in grave condition. The day after his return to London in mid-November, Berezovsky went to the hospital to visit Litvinenko with Goldfarb, and his worst fears were confirmed. Litvinenko's hair was falling out, and he was in terrible pain, barely able to speak. A toxicology report confirmed that Litvinenko had been poisoned, but it was not until after Goldfarb enlisted a renowned toxicologist that polonium-210 was discovered to be the culprit.

Polonium-210, a highly radioactive substance, was the smoking gun in Litvinenko's case. Undetectable by ordinary Geiger counters because it emits alpha, as opposed to gamma, radiation, the poison is extremely difficult and dangerous to produce. In Russia it was made and stored at only one nuclear facility, which was guarded by the FSB. The fact that Lugovoi and Kovtun left traces of polonium—detected by special instruments—everywhere they had been during their London visit confirmed that they were the FSB-enlisted poisoners of Litvinenko. Lugovoi had even contaminated two chairs in Berezovsky's office when he stopped by to pick up football tickets that Egor Shuppe had procured for him on October 31 and had a glass of wine with Berezovsky.[40] The Kremlin denied involvement in the poisoning and later refused to allow Lugovoi to be extradited to the UK for prosecution, thus plunging relations with the British government, which were already sour, to a new low.

In early February 2007, Berezovsky received a telephone call from Lugovoi, who had been named publicly as a suspect in Litvinenko's murder immediately after the latter's death. (Lugovoi and Kovtun gave a press conference in Moscow on November 24, denying their culpability.) Lugovoi asked Berezovsky if he believed the accusations against him. Berezovsky was noncommittal, suggesting that Lugovoi should come to London and talk to the police in order to resolve the matter and offering to pay for a lawyer. Lugovoi not only refused the offer but also turned the tables on Berezovsky. In May 2007, after the British had issued an international warrant for his arrest, Lugovoi gave another press conference with Kovtun, in which he announced that Berezovsky had poisoned Litvinenko in collusion with MI6 because Litvinenko was blackmailing the oligarch with threats to reveal that he was a secret MI6 spy. He also claimed that he and Kovtun had been framed by being contaminated with polonium.[41]

The theme of Berezovsky's alleged connivance in Russian murders was, of course, not new. Even Putin, when asked about the Litvinenko murder during a February press conference, had hinted that Berezovsky was involved by saying that "runway oligarchs hiding in Western Europe" who sought to harm Russia were the real enemies.[42] The idea that Berezovsky would have Litvinenko poisoned, let alone by polonium, was laughable. True, Berezovsky's relationship with Litvinenko had been under strain because, when Litvinenko began to do work with MI6, Berezovsky had ceased paying him. Litvinenko was unhappy about Berezovsky's decision, but the two were by no means estranged. The Litvinenkos continued to live in the house Berezovsky provided for them, and Berezovsky carried on paying Anatoly Litvinenko's tuition at the City of London School. Litvinenko stopped by Berezovsky's office at least once a month.[43] As Berezovsky suggested in a later interview, Lugovoi could have easily poured polonium into his wine glass when he visited Berezovsky's office the day before Litvinenko's poisoning, but the Kremlin wanted Berezovsky to be a villain, rather than a victim: "they needed a demon, who is behind all the conspiracies, on whom any political assassination can be blamed."[44]

In fact, Egor Gaidar, the architect of Yeltsin's liberal economic reforms, had already laid the groundwork for the Kremlin's version of Litvinenko's death—that the poisoning was a provocation against Russia, which had nothing to gain by Litvinenko's death. On November 24, just a day after Litvinenko died, Gaidar fell ill while attending a conference in Dublin. He spent the night in the hospital, where doctors suspected either gastroenteritis or complications from diabetes, and returned a day later to Moscow to receive additional medical treatment. Then, on November 29, when news of Gaidar's hospitalization broke, Anatoly Chubais told journalists that he was certain that Gaidar had been poisoned because his death, like the deaths of Politkovskaya and Litvinenko, "would be highly favorable to supporters of an anticonstitutional change of power in Russia."[45] That same day, in response to get-well wishes from George Soros, Gaidar faxed a letter to him (published later on a Russian website), in which he noted that Berezovsky had advocated cooperation with international terrorists and was intent on damaging Russia's relations with the West as a means of undermining

Putin's power. Gaidar suggested that Soros remind people in the West about Berezovsky's ruthlessness and immorality.[46]

A week later, Gaidar wrote a piece in *The Financial Times* saying that "adversaries of the Russian regime" were behind his poisoning.[47] Other politicians chimed in to agree, linking the crime to the murders of Politkovskaya and Litvinenko. And all repeated the same Kremlin line—that such crimes could not be attributed to the Russian leadership because they damaged the Kremlin's interests. Berezovsky's name was not mentioned publicly until Russian television journalist Nikolai Svanidze revealed that Gaidar had told him that Berezovsky was the adversary of the Kremlin who had carried out these crimes. This prompted a harsh rebuke from Alex Goldfarb, who said that the Kremlin had been caught red-handed in the Litvinenko case and that it was regrettable that a respected economist like Gaidar would be helping the Kremlin to deceive people with false propaganda. In an interview with Yevgenia Albats in June 2007, Gaidar got his revenge on Goldfarb by saying, falsely, that Goldfarb was an expert in nuclear chemistry and thus had probably poisoned Litvinenko himself. A Kremlin campaign against Goldfarb would continue for years.[48]

As the Russian commentator Andrei Illarionov pointed out, the version of Berezovsky as the culprit in Gaidar's illness was far-fetched. Why did it take several days for the alleged poisoning to become known? Why were there no comments or reports about the episode by doctors, either in Dublin or Moscow? Why did both the Irish police and Ireland's Foreign Office insist that there was no reason to think that Gaidar's illness had resulted from foul play? And if he had been severely ill from poisoning, why was Gaidar back in his office two days after he returned to Moscow? Illarionov concluded that there was no poisoning. Chubais and Gaidar had come up with this false story in order to demonstrate their loyalty, as leaders of the Union of Right Forces (SPS) Party, to Putin.[49]

Putin's Iron Fist

Gaidar's emergence as an outspoken promoter of the Kremlin's line was indicative of the insidious nature of Putin's authoritarian rule as it turned democrats into sycophants. Under Yeltsin, Gaidar had been a vigorous and courageous defender of Western political and economic ideals, even criticizing the war in Chechnya. But he was silent when Putin began dismantling democratic reforms and moved against Khodorkovsky. As sociologist Vladimir Shlapentokh observed: "The political evolution of Gaidar as a public figure from a champion of democracy and Western values to a pitiful advocate of any move in the Kremlin is a sad story . . . Gaidar's recent public behavior reveals how far Putin's regime will go in order to intimidate the cream of the Russian people."[50]

Nonetheless, there were those like Boris Nemtsov, who had become a scathing public critic of Putin and his regime. In a July 2007 article for *Vedomosti*, for example, Nemtsov enumerated the reasons why life in Putin's Russia had become "disgusting": the suppression of the media, shameful government corruption, violence against protestors, rigged elections, and the promotion of an arms race with the West. What's worse, Nemtsov wrote, the regime had done this with the approval of the majority of Russian people, who were content because they were materially better off than they had been before Putin.[51] Nemtsov had left the Union of Right Forces (SPS) Party in 2004 and would found the Solidarity opposition movement with Garry Kasparov in 2008. Beginning with his arrest for participating in a November 2007 protest, Nemtsov faced continued legal harassment from the authorities until he was tragically gunned down outside the Kremlin in February 2015.[52]

Nemtsov had courageously remained in Russia, but, as shown by Litvinenko's killing, even residence abroad was not a protection. This obvious danger did not prevent Berezovsky from continuing to recklessly challenge the Kremlin at every opportunity. In April 2007, Berezovsky, perhaps emboldened by Russia's pariah status in the UK, told *The Guardian* that he was planning the violent overthrow of Putin and had forged close ties with members of Russia's ruling elite, who planned a palace coup. Berezovsky put it bluntly: "We need to use force to change this regime. It isn't possible to change this regime through democratic means." In addition to offering ideological guidance, Berezovsky said that he would be financing the coup plotters.[53] The Russian Prosecutor General's Office responded to Berezovsky's statements by issuing new criminal charges against him for conspiring to seize power.[54]

Berezovsky backed off his April statements when asked about his plans for a revolution in Russia during a lengthy interview at the Frontline Club in early June 2007.[55] He said that the revolution would not necessarily be bloody but did not explain the specifics and was vague when asked how the Russian people could be convinced that they need political change. Asked if he feared for his life now, he responded: "If the Kremlin decides to kill me, I do not have any chance to survive . . . But I am strong psychologically and I sleep well."

Ironically, not long after his Frontline appearance Berezovsky was again targeted for assassination. In June 2007, Scotland Yard learned of a plot to kill Berezovsky, and police later arrested an armed hitman, an ethnic Chechen named Movladi Atlangeriev, in the lobby of Berezovsky's office building. The incident reportedly caused an uproar in Whitehall. But because of concerns about a further deterioration in relations with the Kremlin, it was decided to simply expel Atlangeriev, who had known ties to the FSB, back to Russia. Later, after being kidnapped and beaten in Moscow, he disappeared.[56]

By this time, relations between Russia and Britain had deteriorated further. When Putin first became Russia's president, the official British assessment had been that "he was essentially a liberal modernizer by instinct who may at times be inclined to use authoritarian methods." But this assessment, of course, had proved wrong. Russia's continued attempts to have Berezovsky and Zakaev extradited and its refusal to cooperate with the British investigation of the Litvinenko poisoning were key sources of tension between the two countries, causing Britain to expel four Russian diplomats in July 2007, after which the Kremlin retaliated by ordering four British diplomats to leave Russia.[57]

Russia's tensions with Britain reflected the growing belligerence toward the West on Putin's part. Thanks to high oil and gas prices, his country's economic growth had been robust for several years, contributing to a new confidence within the Kremlin about Russia's role as a global actor. At the same time, "color revolutions" in former Soviet states, along with the expansion of NATO, had led Putin and his colleagues to increasingly see the West, in particular the United States, as a threat to Russia. Putin's landmark speech at the Munich Security Conference in February 2007—defensive and confrontational at the same time—expressed a litany of complaints about the US domination of world affairs, ranging from its ballistic missile defenses to the inclusion of the Baltics in NATO and Western financial support of Russian political opposition groups.[58]

Meanwhile, Putin was managing a conflict over power and profits between the two main siloviki clans that erupted openly in October 2007 when FSB officers arrested a senior deputy to Viktor Cherkesov, head of the antinarcotics agency. Cherkesov, who was allied with Putin's bodyguard Viktor Zolotov, had come under attack by a rival group headed by Patrushev and Igor Sechin. His response was to write an open letter, which appeared in *Kommersant*, in which he deplored the fighting among Russia's security services, saying that it threatened the stability of the regime. In a subsequent interview, Putin rebuked Cherkesov (without mentioning his name) for airing his grievances publicly, and Cherkesov was eventually moved to a lesser post. By 2008, the clan warfare had died down, but it had left scars.[59]

Part of what had fueled the siloviki conflict was uncertainty over the scheduled presidential elections in March 2008. Some hardliners wanted Putin to have the Duma change the constitution so that he could run for a third term, while others had their preferred candidates to succeed Putin. In the end, Putin chose his loyal protégé Dmitry Medvedev to run for the presidency, and Medvedev then announced that his prime minister would be none other than Putin. Not surprisingly, forty-three-year-old Medvedev had a difficult time extending his authority over the government. As Myers writes, "the entire system—the bureaucracy, the military, the media—had become so conditioned to [Putin's] role as paramount leader that it struggled to preserve the appearance that Medvedev was in charge."[60]

In conducting foreign affairs, Medvedev was also constrained by Putin, who vetted most of his decisions. To be sure, Medvedev had his own views and was more open to improved relations with the West than Putin was. He even dared not to veto a UN Security Council resolution in March 2011 authorizing military intervention in Libya, which made Putin furious. But, as Putin later revealed, Medvedev had agreed with him before the 2008 election that he, not Medvedev, would run again for the presidency in March 2012. This rendered Medvedev a lame duck president, with Putin waiting in the wings.[61] As Berezovsky observed: "Having no control over either the government or the parliament, Medvedev will one day ask: 'what, in fact, are my powers?' And at that moment, Sechin will doubtless respond: 'Ah, I warned you!'"[62]

Medvedev's tenure as Russia's president was not a reprieve for Berezovsky. The campaign of Kremlin lies against him continued. Just after Medvedev's 2008 election, a former official on the Prosecutor's Investigative Committee claimed in an interview that Berezovsky had ordered the killing of Anna Politkovskaya.[63] Prosecutor General Chaika had hinted months before that Berezovsky was the culprit when he said that the person who ordered the crime lived abroad and was trying to "destabilize the leadership of Russia." But this was the first time Berezovsky was publicly accused by a law enforcement source of being behind Politkovskaya's death.

Politkovskaya's son, Ilya Politkovskii, would later say that Russian investigators had pressured him and his sister Vera to endorse their allegations about Berezovsky, so that he could be extradited to Russia. But they resisted, knowing that Berezovsky was being used as a scapegoat. Although Politkovskaya's five hired killers were eventually rounded up and convicted, the *zakazchik* would never be found. As Vera Politkovskaya observed: "The person who ordered the murder will not be revealed until there is a change of regime in Russia."[64] But that possibility was becoming increasingly remote.

CHAPTER 11

A Life Falling Apart

> Berezovsky was a gambler. But at his casino the
> game was politics. And it is a fact that, if a person
> plays in a casino seriously, then sooner or later he
> will definitely lose big.
>
> —Andrei Vasiliev, former editor of *Kommersant*

On February 12, 2008, Berezovsky suffered a devastating loss. His longtime business partner and closest friend for almost two decades, Badri Patarkatsishvili, died suddenly of an apparent heart attack at age fifty-two, after collapsing in his bedroom at his lavish Surrey estate. Berezovsky had been with Patarkatsishvili just four hours before his death, at a meeting in London with Patarkatsishvili's lawyer. When he telephoned his media advisor, Lord Timothy Bell, to inform him of Patarkatsishvili's death shortly after he heard the news, Berezovsky was in tears. He later told journalist Suzanna Andrews: "He [Badri] was like my father, brother, and son—all at the same time . . . We never had any, any conflict at all." According to a mutual friend, the two men, who talked on the telephone four or five times a day, were so connected that "they were almost like lovers."[1]

As Georgia's wealthiest citizen, Patarkatsishvili had invested vast amounts of money in the impoverished country's businesses and charities. He also owned Georgia's popular independent television station, Imedi. Initially a strong supporter of Mikheil Saakashvili, who had become Georgia's president in 2004 after leading the Rose Revolution, Patarkatsishvili later fell out with him and began supporting the political opposition. At Berezovsky's urging—and against the advice of Patarkatsishvili's wife, Inna Gudavadze—Patarkatsishvili ran for the

FIGURE 24.   Badri Patarkatsishvili, right, with Berezovsky, 2005. AP photo/George Abdaladze.

country's presidency in January 2008, opposing Saakashvili. Despite promising free electricity and gas for voters if he won, he earned only 7 percent of the votes. Five weeks later, Patarkatsishvili was dead.[2]

Berezovsky had lost more than a friend. Patarkatsishvili had been running the finances of the two men for years. "I didn't pay attention to how much money we had, where the money was allocated, how Badri organized contracts. I didn't know at all," Berezovsky told Andrews.[3] According to Andrei Vasiliev: "When Borya required money for all his projects, for politics, he took as much as he needed. And everything was controlled by Badri. At the dawn of capitalism, everyone did business this way—Khodorkovsky, Fridman, and Smolensky. But these men then changed their ways: they moved from kindergarten to the first grade, to the second, to the tenth . . . Borya, by contrast, didn't attend those classes at all."[4]

As it turned out, Patarkatsishvili shared Berezovsky's Soviet habit of making verbal financial agreements, instead of putting things down on paper; and he hid their joint assets in myriad offshore accounts and trusts in Cyprus, Panama, and the Cayman Islands. Complicating the situation was Patarkatsishvili's secret second wife in Moscow and a Georgian-American stepcousin, Joseph Kay, who claimed Patarkatsishvili had made him executor of his will and swooped down on his assets, which were estimated at between $2.6 and $6 billion. Gudavadze began a fierce battle against Kay that took place in courtrooms worldwide and even involved arrests and an alleged kidnapping.[5]

Eventually Patarkatsishvili's widow prevailed over Kay, and she regained her deceased husband's assets, but it took several years. In the meantime, she and Berezovsky had a feud. Immediately after Patarkatsishvili died, Berezovsky had Gudavadze sign papers certifying that half of Patarkatsishvili's holdings were rightfully his, because of the oral partnership agreement the two had made in 1995. By June 2008, Gudavadze had changed her mind, claiming that Berezovsky and her husband had parted ways financially in 2006 and separated their assets. In December, Berezovsky, no longer on speaking terms with Gudavadze, filed a lawsuit against Patarkatsishvili's estate.[6] He would argue that the political and legal harassment he was under from the Kremlin forced him to have Patarkatsishvili keep their joint assets in Patarkatsishvili's name only, while in reality he still was a half owner.[7]

Berezovsky badly needed his share of the money from Patarkatsishvili's estate. In addition to expenses for his large family and lavish lifestyle, his political projects now included an ambitious plan to democratize Belarus. Berezovsky had persuaded Alexander Lukashenko, the authoritarian president of Belarus, that he should take steps to move more toward the West and away from Moscow, which was creating tensions with Belarus over tariffs on Russian energy products. In an effort to improve his standing with the West, Lukashenko enlisted Timothy Bell's renowned PR firm to do "reputation management" for him in mid-2008, with Berezovsky footing the bill of $3.9 million, which Bell said later was never paid in full. Although Lukashenko made a few cautious steps toward reform, such as freeing some political prisoners, he could not bring himself to allow democratic voting. By 2009, it was clear that the project was doomed, and Bell's group left the country.[8]

A New Battle

Berezovsky had also embarked on a momentous legal struggle that would cost him millions and, some say, contribute to his untimely death. In July 2005, he announced to the Russian business newspaper *Vedomosti* that he was bringing a lawsuit against Roman Abramovich for "using blackmail and threats to force me to sell assets in Russia at a reduced price."[9] Almost two years later, in June 2007, Berezovsky filed a formal claim against his former partner for $5.6 billion in the British High Court. The following October, after spotting Abramovich in a Knightsbridge Hermes store, Berezovsky served him with court papers, saying, "I have a present for you." He later described the incident as "like a scene from 'The Godfather.'"[10]

Said to be worth over $12 billion, Abramovich had continued to enjoy Putin's favor, though he spent increasing amounts of time in Britain, where he owned several lavish homes, along with the Chelsea Football Club. He also was the owner of a Boeing 767 and the world's largest yacht—a 560-foot vessel equipped with two helipads and a submarine.[11] As noted, in 2001 Berezovsky and Patarkatsishvili had received a $1.3 billion payment from Abramovich in return for their giving up claims to Sibneft. Four years later, Abramovich sold his 70 percent interest in Sibneft to energy giant Gazprom for a staggering $13 billion. Had they not been forced by Abramovich to relinquish their shares earlier, Berezovsky stated in his lawsuit, he and Patarkatsishvili would have received half of that sum, given that their joint interest in Sibneft was split with Abramovich fifty-fifty.

Another, much smaller part of Berezovsky's claim against Abramovich had to do with shares in aluminum companies, which, according to Berezovsky, he, Patarkatsishvili, and Abramovich had acquired by using their profits from Sibneft, and then merged in 2000 with assets of the oligarch Oleg Deripaska to form a company called Rusal. Berezovsky contended that he and Patarkatsishvili together owned 25 percent of the Rusal shares, although they were controlled and legally owned by Abramovich. In 2003, Abramovich had sold shares of Rusal to Deripaska without the permission of Berezovsky and Patarkatsishvili and had not compensated them, except for a sum to Patarkatsishvili for supposedly providing services that facilitated the venture.[12]

The trial of Berezovsky vs. Abramovich at London's High Court of Justice, the largest financial case in British history, did not begin until October 2011, after extensive legal proceedings that involved round after round of appeals on procedural and factual issues and lengthy witness statements. For the trial alone, there were four thousand pages of written submissions. In the words of the presiding judge, Justice Elizabeth Gloster: "Given the substantial resources of the parties and the serious allegations of dishonesty, the case was heavily lawyered on both sides. This meant that no evidential stone was left unturned, unaddressed or unpolished."[13]

The hearings, courtroom drama at its best, continued until January 19, 2012, attracting unprecedented media coverage. According to *The New York Times*: "At a time of austerity and grim news wafting from Europe, the trial has proved to be a welcome cinematic diversion. The two oligarchs travel with large entourages that include burly bouncer-esque bodyguards sporting Secret Service-style earpieces, and comely girlfriends wielding designer handbags."[14] The journalist Peter Pomerantsev was similarly impressed: "The witnesses at court number 26 in the Rolls Building were a who's who of post-Soviet Russia: anti-Putin activists, Chechen ministers-in-exile, former heads of Kremlin administration, directors of Chelsea Football Club and a thirty-strong team of English lawyers. 'That's the last twenty years of our history stuffed into one room,' a Russian journalist said."[15]

The dispute centered on whether Berezovsky and Patarkatsishvili had in fact owned shares in Sibneft and Rusal. Abramovich's contention was that the two had never contributed financially to his commercial ventures and never were shareholders. They received payments from him for providing *krysha*, including political patronage and lobbying.[16] According to Berezovsky, he and Patarkatsishvili were actual shareholders and were paid profits as such, but Abramovich had insisted that they keep their ownership secret and allow him to control their shares because of Berezovsky's political involvement with the Yeltsin administration. "I would not have expended my own commercial connections and personal political capital, far less have made financial commitments," Berezovsky said in his witness statement, "were it not for the fact that I was to become a part-owner of the newly created company."[17]

Abramovich, in Berezovsky's account, later pressured them to sell their shares by threatening them with reprisals from the Kremlin, including against their friend Glushkov, who was languishing in a Russian jail. But Abramovich alleged that, when he and Patarkatsishvili conducted negotiations in early 2001, there was no discussion of Patarkatsishvili and Berezovsky selling him their interests in Sibneft, which they did not have, and that Patarkatsishvili had only requested a final lump-sum payment for krysha services. Abramovich also claimed that he never used Glushkov's imprisonment as a threat. He had discussed Glushkov with Patarkatsishvili, he said, only out of concern that Berezovsky's confrontational behavior toward the Kremlin would jeopardize Glushkov's situation: "Mr. Patarkatsishvili and I discussed 'how to control Boris,' i.e. how best to try and persuade Mr. Berezovsky to moderate his conduct (which I thought was quite irresponsible) so as not to worsen the relations with the Russian government even more. I remember telling Mr. Patarkatsishvili that Mr. Berezovsky behaved like a child."[18]

With Patarkatsishvili dead, there was no one to challenge Abramovich's retelling of this meeting. Patarkatsishvili had given witness statements before he died that were offered in evidence at the trial to show that his discussions with Abramovich were based on his assumption that he and Berezovsky were shareholders of Sibneft. But in cross-examining those who prepared the statements, Abramovich's lawyers cast doubt on their veracity, thereby strengthening Abramovich's claim that he had a good relationship with Patarkatsishvili up until his death, meeting with him on several occasions. (Patarkatsishvili's widow, Inna Gudavadze, had by this time aligned herself with Abramovich, who was helping her access Patarkatsishvili assets in Russia. She noticeably sat on Abramovich's side in the courtroom.) According to Abramovich, when the two got together in Israel in early 2006, Patarkatsishvili told him that he would not support Berezovsky's lawsuit against him: "I remember him saying that he thought I had treated them very fairly with regard to Sibneft. He said that no one would have paid them more."[19]

Court Testimony

The burden of proof was on Berezovsky, as the claimant, and he was the first to take the stand, testifying for six days. Things did not go smoothly. On October 6, Abramovich's chief lawyer, Jonathan Sumption, cross-examined Berezovsky and successfully backed him into a corner when he brought up the fact that Berezovsky persuaded Yeltsin's Family to approve the creation of Sibneft so he could use the profits for ORT, which proved pivotal in convincing people to vote for Yeltsin in 1996:

Q: You have in these proceedings indignantly denied the suggestion that you were corrupt; presumably therefore you disapprove of it, corruption that is?

A: I really confirm that I am not corrupt and I didn't bribe anybody . . .

Q: Now, suppose a businessman approaches an elected official and says, "I'm going to support your re-election campaign so

please will you exercise your official powers in a way that fa-
vours my business interests and those of my associates," and
the elected official says, "Yes." In your view, is that corrupt?

A: Just a second. Give me reference: where is that?

Q: Can you read my question on the screen?

A: No, no, I'm reading . . .

Just a second. (Pause) Yes, it's corrupt.[20]

At another point, Sumption asked Berezovsky about a statement he
made to the Russian journalist Nataliya Gevorkyan in a 1999 interview: "I am not a Sibneft [share] holder, and I have said that many
times, although I was lobbying for the creation of this company, and
I have strategic interests within this company and in relation to it."
Berezovsky agreed that the quotation was correct but asked Sumption
"to understand the context of everything what [sic] we're discussing."[21]
Berezovsky's point was that he denied publicly that he owned Sibneft
shares for political reasons, because of his association with Yeltsin
and the Kremlin. But Sumption's cross-examination and Berezovsky's
inconsistencies were damaging to his credibility.

The issue of why Abramovich made payments to Berezovsky and
Patarkatsishvili was crucial to the ownership question. In his witness
statement Abramovich said: "Mr. Berezovsky's demands [for payments]
were not tied to any notion of a 'share of profits'—be it of Sibneft or
any other company. Mr. Berezovsky never asked me to provide to him
any official profit and loss position for either Sibneft or any other company under my control. He only seemed to be interested in whether
I had sufficient cash available to afford his demands for payment."[22]
Berezovsky's hands-off approach was confirmed in his trial testimony,
when Justice Gloster asked him: "Was there any formal or informal
process whereby Badri or you, or staff on your behalf, would audit the
profits that were being generated by Sibneft?" Berezovsky's response (in
imperfect English) was: "I don't know anything about formal process.
I just know about regular meetings Badri [had] with Roman." When
asked by Sumption how Patarkatsishvili had ascertained Sibneft profits, Berezovsky replied: "I don't have any idea. I think, as we agreed . . .
in '95, we trust Abramovich and we didn't have time to manage the
company and send audit."[23]

These statements would be cited by Justice Gloster in her final judgment, where she commented: "If indeed there had been an express
agreement that Mr. Berezovsky and Mr. Patarkatsishvili were to be

jointly entitled to a 50% share of the net profits after tax of Sibneft and/
or Mr. Abramovich's Trading Companies, one might have expected that
at least some sort of informal audit process would have taken place."[24]
Berezovsky had explained his lack of concern for financial details and
written contracts in his witness statement. "Such oral agreements were
simply common practice at that time between Russians in Russia, where
most business dealings at the level at which I operated necessarily place
a high emphasis on personal trust."[25] As he gave his testimony, he had
difficulty conveying this point.

It hardly helped Berezovsky's case that Putin's former chief of staff
Aleksandr Voloshin testified to the court that neither he nor Putin
had pressured Berezovsky to sell ORT in August 2000 or threatened
him by bringing up Gusinsky's arrest. There was no need, Voloshin
said, to have Berezovsky sell his ORT shares because the government
had 51 percent of the shares in the television company, and Berezovsky
controlled only 49 percent, so they could appoint the director and control content and programming. They just wanted Berezovsky to stop
exercising his "informal" influence over ORT. In fact, Berezovsky had
always exerted enough control on ORT's board of directors to veto
major decisions. Justice Gloster would later say in her decision that
she found Voloshin's testimony convincing: "Although he gave evidence through a translator, I formed the impression, from the manner
in which he gave his answers, his demeanour and the content of his
answers themselves, that he gave his evidence honestly and directly . . .
his account of the meetings [with Berezovsky] was more credible than
that given by Berezovsky."[26]

Justice Gloster also accepted as truth the testimony of Putin's trusted
oligarch Oleg Deripaska, made to the court through video link. Berezovsky had stated that in March 2000 at London's Dorchester Hotel,
he, Patarkatsishvili, and Abramovich met with Deripaska and agreed
on a merger of their aluminum assets, obtained with profits from Sibneft shares, with those of Deripaska, to form Rusal. Berezovsky and
Patarkatsishvili would own 25 percent of the new company, Abramovich 25 percent and Deripaska 50 percent. Deripaska testified that there
had been no negotiations concerning Rusal at the London meeting
because he and Abramovich had already agreed on the merger, with
just the two of them Rusal owners. Admitting his intense dislike for
both Berezovsky and Patarkatsishvili, Deripaska said he attended the
meeting because it gave him an opportunity to get to know Abramovich
better, and, he added, because Berezovsky owed him money.[27] At that

time Berezovsky still resided in Moscow, so it was not clear why Deripaska felt he had to fly to London to confront him.

For his part, Abramovich said that he had flown to London for the meeting only because Berezovsky had requested it: "At that time I still regarded Berezovsky as one of the most powerful men in Russia, and when he invited me for a meeting, I would always attend."[28] To a seasoned observer of Russian politics, Abramovich's explanation must have seemed weak. By March 2000, it was clear that Berezovsky no longer had clout with those running the government, let alone with Putin. Whatever the incongruities of their narratives of the London meeting, Justice Gloster would later come down on the side of Berezovsky's detractors, concluding: "I prefer their evidence to that of Mr. Berezovsky."[29]

The judge would also interpret in Abramovich's favor a key piece of evidence introduced by the Berezovsky team—a transcript of a conversation, secretly taped by Patarkatsishvili, between Abramovich and Berezovsky at Paris-Le Bourget Airport in December 2000. In the conversation Berezovsky says clearly that he, Patarkatsishvili, and Abramovich should legalize their interest in Rusal. Abramovich responds: "We only hold 50 per cent there, so the other party has to agree," and adds that, because of taxes, such legalization would reduce their income [from Rusal]. He then says: "Besides, you will have to wait in line to receive dividends." Amazingly, Justice Gloster concluded: "Taken in context, one can see that Mr. Abramovich's comment was a response to Mr. Berezovsky's suggestion that he should become a shareholder in Rusal in order to receive payments in the future, rather than any recognition of an existing interest."[30] It would be seven months after the hearings ended in January 2012 before the judge would reveal her findings to a packed and anxious courtroom.

Putin Challenged at Home

During the Medvedev interregnum, Putin, as prime minister, had continued to pull the strings of power in the Kremlin, much to the disappointment of Western leaders, including President Barack Obama. The US ambassador to Moscow in 2010, John Beyrle, reportedly repeated a joke that had been going around Moscow: "Medvedev sits in the driver's seat of a new car, examines the inside, the instrument panel, and the pedals. He looks around, but the steering wheel is missing. He turns to Putin and asks: 'Vladimir Vladimirovich, where is the steering wheel?'

Putin pulls a remote control out of his pocket and says: 'I'll be the one doing the driving.' "[31] Putin had even prevailed on Medvedev to initiate a law changing the presidential term from four to six years.

When Medvedev announced at the United Russia party conference in late September 2011, that Putin would be the presidential candidate in the 2012 elections, it came as a rude shock to Putin's political opponents. Nemtsov, leader of the People's Freedom Party (Parnas), told a journalist that this was "the worst possible scenario for the development of my country."[32] As the news sunk in, the implications became clear: Putin, sure to win the presidential contest, could remain as Russia's leader, not only until 2018 but until 2024—all told, for longer than even Brezhnev had served! Adding insult to injury, Putin then announced that he would choose Medvedev as his prime minister, and that this swap had been agreed on before Medvedev ran for the presidency in 2008.

Lilia Shevtsova observed: "The ruling faction has demonstrated its focus on lifelong rule. They can no longer jump out of the logic of omnipotence. They cannot leave. And this is the most important result of the Putin-Medvedev swap. The authorities themselves have begun to prepare Russia for the Arab Spring."[33] The explosion of Arab uprisings that began in early 2011 had indeed caused considerable consternation in the Kremlin. Not only did Putin and his men fear that the revolts would encourage Islamist movements in the North Caucasus, where insurgency continued to fester; they had a more general concern that revolutionary sentiment would spill over into Russia as a whole. They also believed that Western powers were supporting the revolutions in order to squeeze Russia out of the Middle East and inspire the Russian people to follow the Arab example.[34]

Negative public reaction to the swap soon appeared on the Internet, where anger over the succession plan was vented on Twitter, Facebook, YouTube, and VKontakte. The discontent spread to the point where Putin was booed by crowds at Moscow's Olympic Stadium in November 2011. By that time, according to polling by the Levada Center, Putin's approval rating, although high by Western standards, had dropped to 66 percent, the lowest since 2000, and it would drop to 63 percent in December.[35] When Russia elected delegates to the Duma on December 4, the pro-Kremlin party United Russia barely retained a majority, despite the widespread election fraud that was documented by election observers.

Word spread quickly, along with calls for protests. Russians were used to manipulated elections, but coming on top of the announced swap by the Putin-Medvedev tandem, the fraud was too much for many. On the night of December 5, a crowd of nearly five thousand showed up in the center of Moscow and heard the opposition activist Aleksei Navalny speak as they waved banners saying, "Russia without Putin." Police arrested nearly three hundred people, including Navalny, who was sentenced to jail for fifteen days. After hearing of the arrests, US Senator John McCain tweeted a message to Putin: "Dear Vlad, the Arab Spring is coming to a neighborhood near you."[36] The protests continued, swelling to tens of thousands at Bolotnaia Square a few nights later.

On December 24, close to a hundred thousand demonstrators rallied on Andrei Sakharov Prospekt, where the most prominent members of Russia's political opposition spoke, including Navalny, fresh out of jail. Navalny stole the show, declaring: "I can see that there are enough people here to seize the Kremlin. We are a peaceful force and will not do it now. But if these crooks and thieves try to go on cheating us, if they continue telling lies and stealing from us, we will take what belongs to us with our own hands."[37]

If ever there was a moment when Putin's grip on power seemed seriously threatened, this was it. The authorities, clearly surprised by the huge numbers of angry citizens, were shaken. As the journalist Julia Ioffe put it: "2011 is the big wakeup call for them. This is when the color revolution finally comes to Moscow. This is Putin's biggest fear. Remember, this comes at the end of a year in which Muammar Qaddafi is toppled from power and is killed in a very public and humiliating way. And it started, again, as peaceful protests."[38] Comments like those of Senator McCain may have furthered the impression in the Kremlin that the West was helping to foment the protests.

Significantly, even some Kremlin stalwarts like Vladislav Surkov, first deputy chief of staff in the Presidential Administration, expressed sympathy for the oppositionists' cause: "To grant the sensible demands of the active part of society is not a forced maneuvre by the authorities but their obligation and constitutional duty."[39] Putin's longtime ally Aleksei Kudrin, who had recently resigned as finance minister, took to the stage at the December 24 rally and called for a rerun of the election and the dismissal of the head of the Central Election Commission. Even Medvedev, seemingly emboldened by the unrest to exert some independence from his mentor, Putin, proposed electoral reforms in his state-of-the-nation address on December 22. The measures that were subsequently adopted included: a simplified procedure for registering political parties, the restoration of single-mandate districts for half of the 450 Duma delegates, and a return to direct election of regional governors.[40]

But Putin himself never came close to acknowledging that the protestors had legitimate demands, and he offset the concessions with repression. After he won re-election as president with a solid majority on March 4, 2012, there was a large protest march on the eve of his May 7 inauguration, and close to thirteen thousand policemen were called out. At least four hundred people, including Navalny, were arrested, with some getting stiff prison sentences. Once his third presidential term got underway, Putin introduced harsher punishments for unauthorized demonstrations and in 2013 signed a law that allowed regional legislators to decide whether to have direct elections for regional governors, thus watering down the 2012 reform. As Richard Sakwa wrote: "Putin did everything in his power to ensure that the electoral insurgency model of political change, operationalized as 'colour revolutions' elsewhere, would have minimal traction in Russia."[41]

For all Navalny's charisma, for all the bravery and determination of the protestors, Putin and his hardline siloviki prevailed. There were several reasons why Russia's political unrest in 2011–12 did not turn into another Arab Spring, as Putin and his allies feared. The first is that the oppositionists did not have a united leadership with concrete, forward-looking goals. Navalny, the most popular among them, had been expelled from the liberal Yabloko Party in 2007 because of his alleged nationalistic tendencies. Second, protestors were mainly from the educated middle class, and half were under the age of forty, so they were not representative of the country as a whole. And finally, as in the past, the Kremlin controlled television broadcasting—still the main source of information for the majority of Russians—which had skilled propagandists who manipulated facts and persuaded audiences that protestors were lawbreakers supported by Western governments.

Berezovsky's Rude Awakening

After the trial of his case against Abramovich ended, Berezovsky, convinced that he had won, turned his attention to protesting Putin's upcoming election and inauguration for a third term as president. In mid-January, he posted on his LiveJournal blog an open letter to the Russian patriarch, Kirill, urging him to bring Putin to his senses and persuade him to give up power, He followed up with a letter to Putin, saying "Volodia, it is still within your power to avoid a bloody revolution." Pointing out that Putin had "driven himself into a trap," he urged Putin to leave the government immediately.[42]

On February 1, *Ekho Moskvy* published an appeal from Berezovsky on its website with the heading "To Those Not Born in the USSR." Addressed to Russia's youth, the appeal urged the new generation to become "a legitimate force to overthrow the fraudulent thieves' regime" and prevent the March 4 presidential elections. After leaders of United Russia complained and threatened legal action, the website removed the letter.[43] In late April, Berezovsky wrote a blog post offering a fifty-million-ruble award for the arrest of Putin, "a particularly dangerous criminal," on the grounds that he was committing a crime in returning to the presidency. According to the constitution, Berezovsky wrote, Putin was not permitted to serve as president for a third term, and the Kremlin had produced no legal document to justify his doing so. Thus, in taking office, he was seizing power by force. The next month Berezovsky appealed on his blog to businessmen on the Russian *Forbes* list, saying it was time to stop "licking Putin's boots" and support those rebelling against him.[44]

The Kremlin predictably responded to Berezovsky's provocations with more criminal charges against him at the end of May 2012—for calling on Russian citizens to carry out an insurrection.[45] The charges were meaningless, given that Britain would refuse to extradite Berezovsky, but they suggested that, no matter how outlandish Berezovsky's appeals to Russians, they had drawn Putin's attention. In fact, Putin might have been particularly sensitive at this time, given that his new term as Russia's president had gotten off to a such shaky start.

Powerless to retaliate against Berezovsky through legal channels, Putin must have been pleased to learn of Justice Gloster's final judgment in Berezovsky v. Abramovich, issued on August 31, 2012. The judge rejected Berezovsky's allegation that Abramovich forced him and Patarkatsishvili to sell Sibneft holdings by threatening them. She determined that the $1.3 billion Abramovich paid was a lump sum to cover the krysha that the two men provided.[46] Having also decided that Berezovsky and Patarkatsishvili had no financial interests in Rusal, the judge concluded, "It follows that I dismiss Mr. Berezovsky's claims both in relation to Sibneft and in relation to Rusal in their entirety."[47]

Justice Gloster had harsh words for Berezovsky: "The manner in which he gave, and the content of, his evidence also showed him to be a man with a high sense of his own worth, who was keen to portray himself as the central and indispensable figure in political and commercial events . . . I found Mr. Berezovsky an unimpressive, and inherently unreliable, witness, who regarded truth as a transitory, flexible concept, which could be moulded to suit his current purposes."[48] The judge found Abramovich, by contrast, "a truthful, and, on the whole, reliable witness" and praised his courtroom performance: "He did not present himself in cross-examination as a 'humble man' or as someone who was attempting to appear likeable, or to be liked. Whilst his demeanour was reserved and restrained, he made no attempt to pretend that he was anything other than a highly successful and very wealthy businessman, who had made a very substantial fortune in the challenging Russian business environment of the 1990s and early 2000s."[49]

Clearly, Justice Gloster was influenced not just by what Berezovsky said but also by how he presented himself. Masha Gessen, who attended the trial, observed: "When Berezovsky was on the stand, he was emotional to the point of being overwrought—articulate yet ridiculous in his broken English, which seemed oddly suited to the broken reality he was attempting to describe."[50] As the British journalist Luke Harding, a regular in the courtroom, pointed out, Berezovsky was at a disadvantage. Abramovich testified in Russian, with questions and answers translated into English for the court. This gave him extra time to reflect before he responded. Berezovsky, by contrast, chose to testify in his grammatically imperfect English, and thus responded more spontaneously, often without pausing to think about the impression he was giving.[51] Also, while Abramovich had obviously prepared well for the trial, Berezovsky, according to Elena Gorbunova, "did not rehearse what he would say in court because he thought that by just being himself he would win."[52]

More importantly, as Harding pointed out, Justice Gloster and the British lawyers had little concept of the world in which Berezovsky and Abramovich operated: "The English High Court was not a place to understand the way the Russians did big business deals at this time. Russians had no legal tradition; their agreements were often made orally, without formal contracts, and payments were made in cash. Participants relied on political contacts and kickbacks just as much as they did on financial acumen. This world was completely alien to the British jurists."[53] The judge, apparently unaware that television was a crucial Kremlin propaganda weapon, even refused to accept Berezovsky's contention that Putin had intimidated him into selling ORT. Writing in *The Guardian*, Harding noted that "her finding prompted seasoned Russia watchers to guffaw."[54]

Mikhail Khodorkovsky, for one, said that he had no doubt that Berezovsky was indeed a Sibneft shareholder: "I could have testified at any moment that they were partners in the late 1990s. Moreover, it was Boris who invited Roman to join him. When the merger of Yukos and Sibneft was first mooted, they talked to me as partners. There was no talk of 'political protection.' They were 50–50 partners."[55] Khodorkovsky was unable to testify, of course, because at that time he was in prison.

Gorbunova recalled that when she and Berezovsky were on the way to the High Court to hear the judge's verdict Berezovsky received a telephone call from someone who said, "you are going to lose, and Abramovich has organized a party."[56] Ignoring this message, Berezovsky arrived in the courtroom smiling and sure of a victory, saying: "I'm confident. I believe in the system." Later, clutching his face and shaking his head, he listened to the judge repudiate his entire case and malign his character. But he insisted afterwards that he did not regret his lawsuit and left open a possible appeal, saying "sometimes I had the impression Putin himself wrote the judgment." Abramovich, apparently knowing

FIGURE 25.   Berezovsky, with Alex Goldfarb (left), after London verdict was announced, August 31, 2012. AP photo/Sang Tan.

he would prevail, did not bother to show up for the verdict. He was reportedly in Monaco watching his team, Chelsea, in a match.[57]

Berezovsky did not appeal, in part because he faced huge legal bills. His lawyers did call for an investigation of Justice Gloster, claiming that she should have recused herself from the trial because her stepson, Andrew Popplewell, had been Abramovich's lead counsel when the case began and had prepared his initial defense claim in 2008. But Gloster had disclosed her stepson's involvement earlier, and the defense had not formally objected, so there was little recourse at this point.[58]

For all Berezovsky's bravado, the outcome of the trial could not have been more devastating for him. He had not only lost a court battle; the trial reinforced his image as a corrupt oligarch who would stop at nothing to enrich himself. How could he continue to claim that he was a victim of the Kremlin and lead a credible campaign against Putin? As Aleksei Venediktov expressed it: "It was not about the money, but about the fact that the entire strategy of exposing the Putin regime that Berezovsky built for twelve years collapsed. If he had been awarded only one pound but the court had acknowledged that he was honest, then the transcript would be his testimony against the Putin regime and he would have made history. But that didn't happen."[59]

In the Wake of Losses

By the time Berezovsky lost his case against Abramovich, Putin, back in the Kremlin as Russia's president, was in full battle mode. The "Reset" with the West, which the Obama administration tried to initiate, had become a distant memory. NATO's strikes against Libya, the war in Syria, and mass protests at home—which Putin accused the West of igniting—had led the Kremlin to a Cold War stance. Putin pointedly did not attend the May 2012 G8 Summit at Camp David, sending Medvedev instead. When he did meet with President Obama at the G20 summit in California in June 2012, the tension was obvious. They reached no agreement on pressing issues, such as the Syrian conflict and arms control. Obama had expected that Putin would be more amenable to improving relations with Washington after his election, but it was just the opposite.

Putin's suspicions that the West was intent on toppling his regime had only intensified. In September 2012 the US Agency for International Development was ordered to leave Russia, and the next month two American organizations supporting fair elections were also forced out. For its part, Washington also sent signals that a reset with Russia was no longer in the cards. The US Congress adopted the Magnitsky Act, a bipartisan bill signed into law by a reluctant President Obama in December 2012, which sanctioned Russian officials responsible for the death of the Russian tax lawyer Sergei Magnitsky in a Moscow prison in 2009. The Russians retaliated by enacting a law banning American adoptions of Russian children. This cycle of mutual retaliation would continue.

Meanwhile Putin began throwing himself into preparations for the 2014 Winter Olympics, to be held in the Russian city of Sochi. This was not only a project to assert Putin's and Russia's greatness; it offered him an opportunity to enrich his friends—officials and businessmen like Arkady and Boris Rotenberg and Vladimir Yakunin—by awarding them construction contracts. The Kremlin had originally announced that the cost of the Olympics would be $12 billion, but according to a report published in May 2013 by Nemtsov and his colleague Leonid Martynyuk, the cost was approaching $50 billion, much of it consisting of embezzlement and kickbacks.[60] Far away in London, Berezovsky had urged Russians to boycott the Sochi games on his LiveJournal blog.[61] But few of his countrymen would have paid attention, and this would be his last blog post. Eleven days later, the verdict in Berezovsky v. Abramovich was announced, draining Berezovsky of the fiery energy required to continue his battle against Putin.

In fact, October 2012 brought some good news for Berezovsky and for his friend Nikolai Glushkov. The two men had continued to be pursued by Russian prosecutors in connection with the Aeroflot case after Berezovsky left Britain. Glushkov, who had been released from prison in 2004, was convicted by a Moscow district court in 2006 of new charges for allegedly defrauding Aeroflot, causing him to flee immediately to Britain; the following year, Berezovsky was similarly convicted in absentia. Subsequently, Russian authorities aggressively pursued the financial assets of the two men, with some success regarding Berezovsky. In 2010, Russian prosecutors, working with a Swiss magistrate, managed to obtain on Aeroflot's behalf more than $52 million of funds held by Andava, the Swiss company linked to Berezovsky. But when these prosecutors later went to a British court seeking to enforce a 2011 Russian monetary judgment against Berezovsky and Glushkov for fraud connected with Andava, they were not successful. On October 30, a British judge granted a request by the two defendants for summary judgment and dismissed the Aeroflot claim.[62]

Berezovsky had also been convicted of alleged embezzlement of money from AvtoVAZ, for which in 2009 he had been sentenced by a Russian court in absentia to thirteen years in a penal colony. His former business partner Iulii Dubov was sentenced to nine years, also in absentia. Russian prosecutors had not been able to document the amount of the embezzlement, so charges were based more generally on what they called "damage." Berezovsky dismissed the verdict as "an attempt by the [Russian] authorities to check the reliability of Great Britain as a place for asylum."[63] Still, although Britain was protecting Berezovsky and his Russian friends from extradition, their physical safety was something that British authorities could not necessarily ensure.

The battles that Berezovsky had been waging against his Russian enemies took their toll on his relationship with Gorbunova. She had accompanied her partner of almost twenty years to the hearings in the Abramovich case and testified on his behalf, but Berezovsky had already become involved with a young Russian woman named Katerina Sabirova, whom he had first met in 2008, when Sabirova was only eighteen. At the end of 2011, he and Gorbunova discussed a financial separation, apparently amicably, and in January 2012, Berezovsky moved out of their Surrey estate, Wentworth Park. Three months later, they were forced to sell the estate. In December 2012, forty-five-year-old Gorbunova, now living in London with their two children, filed a lawsuit against Berezovsky claiming that he owed her $8 million, her share from the sale of Wentworth Park for $40 million. In addition, she claimed that Berezovsky was preparing to sell two properties in the south of France which he had promised to her. At Gorbunova's request, the judge froze $317 million of Berezovsky's funds. On January 23, 2013, Berezovsky's sixty-seventh birthday, he contested the freeze in court. Although the judge said the sum of $317 million was inappropriate, he agreed in principle to a freeze, saying: "On the evidence, Mr Berezovsky is a man under financial pressure. It is likely he will feel a more pressing need to satisfy creditors than satisfy Ms. Gorbunova."[64]

Berezovsky was indeed under financial pressure. In 2011, he had paid $150 million to Galina Besharova as part of their divorce settlement and doled out large sums of money to lawyers working on the Abramovich lawsuit. After he lost the case, he was ordered to pay Abramovich's legal costs, which amounted to $56 million. And, three weeks after the devastating verdict, when Berezovsky finally settled his case against Patarkatsishvili's family, the sum was only $150 million, rather than the billions he had expected.[65] He had been forced to put his French properties on the market, and his treasured Andy Warhol painting *Red Lenin* was in the hands of Christie's Auction House. His vintage 1927 Rolls-Royce would be the next treasure to go. Although in 2008 Berezovsky's net worth was estimated at $1.3 billion, by early 2013 his financial straits were such that he was laying off staff members, including most of his security guards.[66]

Ironically, Putin's marriage was also on the rocks, though for him the stakes were political as well as personal. When he and Liudmila finally revealed in June 2013 that they were divorcing—after months of speculation—they portrayed it as an amicable and inevitable separation, caused by Putin's devotion to his work. The Putins, who had not been seen together publicly since Putin's last inauguration, had been attending a ballet at the Kremlin Palace when a reporter from the state TV channel Rossiia 24 asked them if rumors that they had separated were true. After Putin answered in the affirmative, saying it was a mutual decision, Liudmila interjected: "Our marriage is over because we barely see each other. Vladimir Vladimirovich is engrossed in his work. Our children have grown up. They live their own lives. We all do."[67]

The Putins' announcement fueled rumors that had been circulating for years about Putin's extramarital affairs with younger women. In 2008, while visiting Italian prime minister Silvio Berlusconi, Putin had even publicly denied allegations that he was involved with the gymnast Alina Kabaeva, then twenty-seven: "There is not a word of truth in which you say. I have always treated badly those who poke their noses and their erotic fantasies into someone else's life."[68] Whatever Putin's indignation, there was a positive side to such rumors. They made the Russian leader seem more human. It was hard to imagine Putin, who never seemed to let his guard down, feeling emotion about anyone—except, of course, his political enemies.

CHAPTER 12

Berezovsky's End

It's hard to hear that Boria is gone forever. He was very fond of life in all its manifestations, made mistakes, sinned, repented, and sinned again. I was often angry with him, but now he is gone, and I am very sad.

—Mikhail Khodorkovsky, interview with *Novoe vremia*, March 31, 2013

There is no question that the loss of the Abramovich case was a terrible blow for Berezovsky, made worse by the fact that he had been so confident of victory. As Berezovsky's former wife Galina Besharova recalled in an interview with Petr Aven: "The verdict was completely unexpected, and Boria was insanely upset. How could this happen in a British court? He believed that it had been the fairest trial. It was a shock. And with this shock, of course, other reactions followed."[1] Besharova had continued to have a close relationship with her ex-husband after their divorce, and in the autumn of 2012, he moved into her Ascot mansion, Tites Park, while she remained at her London residence. (Nikolai Glushkov observed: "Galina still loved Boris. All his wives did. He was very fortunate about that.")[2]

Besharova made a point of visiting Berezovsky frequently after the verdict was announced. "I worried about him a lot and tried to support him in every sense," she told Aven. "Everyone supported him, everyone took care of him as best they could; he was constantly surrounded by attention from his older daughters and younger children. He did not want any visitors at home, did not want to answer the phone, or talk to anyone other than family." Berezovsky had at that point moved out of his London office. According to Besharova, he normally drank very little alcohol, but for the next month—before leaving on a trip to

Israel—he was consuming a bottle of whisky daily.[3] When Berezovsky's Moscow girlfriend, Katerina Sabirova, arrived for a prolonged visit in September, she too was struck by his change for the worse, noting that on some days he chain-smoked, stayed in bed all morning, and was very pessimistic: "He often said he did not know how he could go on living, what was there to live for," she recalled in a later interview.[4]

Besharova insisted that Berezovsky's despair had little to do with money: "Money was in the last place. When he was accused of being a liar, a blow was dealt to his ego, to his image. This is hard for anyone to experience. And for him, with his sensitive psyche, it was just devastating."[5] Iulii Dubov, among the few who saw Berezovsky frequently after the trial, pointed out that Berezovsky was not that bad off financially. He still had a car and driver and, although ready cash was tight, he had not lost all his financial holdings: "From a very rich man, he became just a rich man. In the end, how much does a person need for life? He had more than enough."[6]

Berezovsky's legal advisor, Michael Cotlick, concurred: "Yes, there were problems with cash. But with twelve months of intensive work, Boris could again become an extremely wealthy person. Not a billionaire, as before, but very wealthy. If lately he spoke of near-total ruin, it was rather because he wanted to give that impression. This is not true."[7] Although the media would later report on Berezovsky's vast debts, he apparently had financial assets that had not been tracked down. In August 2013, for example, Russian investigators—still pursuing the oligarch's money—learned that Berezovsky owned seven companies in Serbia, worth a total of $273 million.[8] The real issue for Berezovsky, Dubov said, was not that he lost a monetary judgment but the way it happened: "To lose, not just anywhere, but in a British court, which stood for him on the right hand of God, was a terrible blow . . . He was in love with British courts in the same way he loved girls . . . and it was incredibly damaging to his reputation."[9]

Moving Forward

Berezovsky began treatment for clinical depression at London's Priory Clinic, and Besharova was relieved to see that after a month or so he seemed to improve. At some point, she recalled, he made a full recovery: "Later we talked about the future, made plans, and he said, 'I will never go back to politics, I will do business, I have some ideas' . . . He calmed down, he no longer had a feeling of disappointment or resentment . . . That life was gone, there was no return to it, now was only the future: 'I will take care of children, grandchildren, I don't want anything else.'"[10]

Elena Gorbunova, who stayed in contact with Berezovsky despite their breakup and conflict over finances, also believed that his mental health had improved. When Aven later asked her, "there were no panic attacks, no depression?" Gorbunova responded: "No, no. Boris, as you know very well, always tried to find a way out of the situation."[11] Dubov, who spoke to Berezovsky twice in the week before he died, thought that Berezovsky's depression did not seem severe: "He made plans, was going to Israel, his friends were waiting for him there."[12] And Nikolai Glushkov dismissed Berezovsky's depression entirely: "I saw him the day that Mrs. Justice Gloster handed down her judgment in Boris's case. He was full of life even then, talking about a certain young lady who was waiting for him in the house. Latterly he had managed to resolve his financial issues."[13]

According to both Gorbunova and Sabirova, soon after Berezovsky lost the Abramovich case, he decided that he wanted to return to Russia and would write a letter informing Putin. Gorbunova said she had encouraged him to seek some sort of rapprochement with the Russian president, as did Berezovsky's mother, Anna. Gorbunova recalled that Berezovsky wrote one letter to Putin, which he gave to an emissary, later said to be a German businessman named Klaus Mangold. But the letter was not delivered to Putin until after Berezovsky's death because Berezovsky had second thoughts and told the emissary to hold off. He had begun negotiating through intermediaries with Badri Patarkatsishvili's widow and Roman Abramovich over money due to him from Patarkatsishvili's assets, some of which were frozen and held in Moscow. According to Gorbunova, Abramovich had suggested that the process would be expedited if Berezovsky wrote a letter to Putin asking to return to Russia, which Abramovich would arrange to be conveyed to the Russian president. Gorbunova said that the second letter was sent off on October 7, Putin's birthday: "He said in the letter that he had some ideas, and he would really like to somehow participate in the processes going on in the country. He had become caught up with the idea. He discussed it with me all the time."[14]

Sabirova knew of only one letter, which she thought was sent in November and which Berezovsky showed her: "He apologized to Putin and asked if it was possible to return to Russia. It was such an aberration. He asked me what I thought. I told him that he would look bad if the letter was published. And that it would not help him. He answered that he didn't care, that everyone already accused him of sins, and that this was his only chance."[15]

Dubov found it hard to believe that Berezovsky wrote a letter apologizing to Putin and asking to return to Russia. Berezovsky had never mentioned such a letter to him, he said, and never talked about going back to his home country: "Boris had a lot of crazy ideas . . . But the one thing he understood quite well was that, if he went back to Russia, he would go to jail." While conceding that Berezovsky may have written to Putin, Dubov thought that the only thing he would have proposed to the Russian president would have been some sort of a "peace deal," not a Russian homecoming. According to Dubov, British police thoroughly searched Berezovsky's computers and papers after he died, but they could not locate a copy of any letter to Putin, so the contents could not be verified.[16]

After Sabirova's departure for Moscow (her British visa expired in November), Berezovsky spent two months in Israel to continue his recovery and to see business and political acquaintances. In January, he met with Vladimir Zhirinovsky, leader of the nationalist Liberal Democratic Party, at the Israeli resort town of Eilat, and the two discussed his intended return to Russia. Apparently Berezovsky wanted Zhirinovsky to negotiate with the Kremlin on his behalf. They reportedly talked about whether Berezovsky could get any guarantees about his future there and what sort of punishments might await him. What sort of sacrifices would he be required to make?[17] Zhirinovsky later told *Ekho Moskvy* that he had suggested to Berezovsky a campaign to pave the way for him in implementing his plans: "He responded very eagerly . . . he was prepared to return to Russia under any conditions."[18]

Whatever Berezovsky's hopes were for a new future in Russia, they were not fulfilled. At approximately 3:23 p.m. on Saturday, March 23, 2013, his ex-Mossad bodyguard, Avi Navama, found him dead on the floor in the bathroom adjoining his bedroom at Besharova's home. His black cashmere scarf was tied around his neck, and a strip of the scarf's torn fabric was on the bar above the tub. Berezovsky was clad in a black t-shirt and track pants, his face deep purple. He had died at approximately 9:30 that morning. Navama, who had not seen his boss since the night before, had been out doing errands for several hours. When he went to check on Berezovsky, he found the bathroom door locked from the inside. After phoning for emergency help and calling Michael Cotlick, Navama finally kicked down the door and discovered

Berezovsky.[19] It appeared to be suicide. But Berezovsky's actions in the days leading up to his death did not suggest that he was a man about to take his own life.

Last Days

On Monday, March 18, Berezovsky made numerous telephone calls, including to his son-in-law Egor Shuppe, who was preparing to fly to Kyiv. He spoke practically every day with Shuppe, a successful businessman. His secretaries often helped Berezovsky because he no longer had an office staff, and Berezovsky asked them to book a ticket for a flight to Israel the next week. He also called his business associate Mikhail Sheitelman, who was in Latvia at the time, and arranged to meet him in Israel to discuss a new business idea. Sheitelman told Berezovsky to let him know if his plans changed and heard nothing more. The rest of the day Berezovsky spent planning for his upcoming trip, organizing business meetings and doctors' appointments. That evening he called Iulii Dubov and requested him to contact a journalist from the Russian *Forbes*, Ilia Zhegulev, who had been seeking an interview with Berezovsky.[20]

The next day Berezovsky telephoned Dubov again, to tell him that he had arranged a meeting with Zhegulev for Thursday, March 21. It would be a conversation, Berezovsky said, not an interview, and he would be talking only off the record, but the time had come for him to emerge from the shadows. Dubov recalled that Berezovsky was full of energy and enthusiasm, very different from the man who earlier had complained about everything and sought sympathy from those around him. On Wednesday, March 20, Berezovsky met with the headmaster of his daughter Arina's boarding school, along with Elena Gorbunova, and that evening had dinner at a London restaurant with Vladimir Gusinsky to discuss his proposed return to Russia and what he might expect from Putin. Gusinsky promised to lend Berezovsky money, and the two agreed to meet again in Israel. He said later that Berezovsky "felt he was no longer in the game and had lost his way . . . but he said he was ready to fight."[21]

On Thursday, Berezovsky called Zhegulev and told him he wanted to postpone their meeting until the next evening, because he had a cold. According to Navama, Berezovsky also cancelled an appointment with his psychiatrist at the Priory Clinic. He told Navama that he was feeling okay mentally and did not think it necessary to see his doctor.

He had just stopped taking antidepressants because of their negative side-effects, and Navama thought his boss seemed better. That evening, the two of them had a meal of veal chops and pasta, which Berezovsky enjoyed.[22]

The next day, Friday, March 22, Berezovsky telephoned his friend Mikhail Cherny, a businessman in Tel Aviv who had helped Berezovsky pay legal fees when he was preparing for the Abramovich trial, and asked him to book a hotel for him in Eilat, where he and Sabirova planned to vacation after Berezovsky finished three days of meetings in Tel Aviv. Later that morning, Berezovsky met with his accountants in London and then had a late restaurant lunch with Cotlick. Navama drove Berezovsky to the Four Seasons Hotel to meet Zhegulev around 7 p.m.[23]

Zhegulev published a story about the interview the next night, just after the news of Berezovsky's death broke.[24] He noted that the hotel restaurant was noisy, with the piano playing and Arab businessmen negotiating nearby. Berezovsky, dressed in a "shabby black turtleneck, a hastily tied black scarf, and a jacket," was nervous and seemed unenthusiastic about discussing his finances. But when Zhegulev asked him if he missed Russia, he was more responsive: "I want nothing more than to return to Russia. Even when a criminal case was opened against me, I wanted to go back." Berezovsky went on to say that he had greatly overestimated democracy in the West and had put too much hope in Russia's ability to develop democracy.

The conversation proceeded thus:

ZHEGULEV: "If you had stayed in Russia, you would be in prison now. Do you want that?"

BEREZOVSKY: "I don't have an answer to this question right now . . . Khodorkovsky . . . preserved himself. That doesn't mean that I've lost myself. But I have experienced many more reassessments and disappointments than Khodorkovsky. I have lost the meaning . . ."

ZHEGULEV: "Of life?"

BEREZOVSKY: "The meaning of life. I don't want to engage in politics."

ZHEGULEV: "What will you do?"

BEREZOVSKY: "I don't know what I am going to do. I am sixty-seven years old. I don't know what to do next."

Then Berezovsky said he would like to return to science, pointing out that he had been a member of the Russian Academy of Sciences.

But when Zhegulev suggested that they talk in detail about the subject, Berezovsky did not seem eager. Zhegulev wrote: "It seems that he did not really believe either in returning to his homeland or in science. Trying to encourage him, I promised that the next time I met him it would be in Moscow at the Academy of Sciences. At that, Berezovsky chuckled grimly and said, 'Exactly.'"

On his way home in the car, Berezovsky spoke on the phone with Gorbunova for about twenty minutes, mainly about their daughter Arina and her plans for study, which Gorbunova opposed. Berezovsky also talked with his son Gleb, telling him he would try to get Arina and her mother to "make peace," and affirming plans to go to lunch with Gleb the next day.[25] By 9 p.m., he arrived at his destination and went to his bedroom. He made several more calls that evening. One was to his daughter Ekaterina to congratulate her on her fortieth birthday. Another was to Sabirova to discuss last-minute details regarding their upcoming vacation. Sabirova thought Berezovsky sounded good: "His inner state was always reflected in his voice. And I got the impression that he was much better. Also, his intentions were very firm—to meet in Israel. There was no sense that something would be cancelled or rescheduled."[26]

Berezovsky then talked on the phone with Shuppe, still in Kyiv, for more than an hour about his Israel plans and how websites of whistleblowers oppose governments. Shuppe recalled: "He was absolutely normal. We had a stimulating conversation. He was in the mood of someone about to leave for a trip to Israel. I had seen him at rock bottom, when I'd really feared for him. But now I thought that maybe we'd seen the worst and we'd manage to pull him out of it."[27]

Inquest

This was the last that was heard from Berezovsky. Nothing is known about what happened before he died the next morning. When police responded to Navama's call that afternoon, they found no evidence of a violent struggle and no sign of forced entry into the home; subsequent toxicology reports showed no evidence of poison. The pathologist who conducted the postmortem concluded that Berezovsky's injuries were "consistent with hanging." Nonetheless, there was no suicide note, and in cases of violent or unusual deaths, inquests are required to determine all facts and rule out the possibility of foul play.

Although a brief inquest was conducted immediately after Berezovsky's death, the formal two-day inquest, held at Windsor Guildhall in Berkshire, did not take place until March 2014. Dr. Simon Poole, the Home Office pathologist who had conducted the postmortem, reiterated his conclusion that Berezovsky had hung himself and there was nothing to indicate foul play. But Poole's testimony was unexpectedly challenged. Berezovsky's daughter Elizaveta, who originally assumed that her father's death was a suicide, had experienced second thoughts and enlisted an eminent German asphyxiation expert, Professor Bernd Brinkmann, to examine photographs of Berezovsky's body.[28] Brinkmann testified that "the strangulation mark is completely different to the strangulation mark in hanging"—circular, instead of the typical V-shaped mark left by self-hanging. Also, Berezovsky had petechiae, or spots on his skin and eyes—a so-called congestion syndrome—that were consistent with homicidal strangulation.[29]

According to Brinkmann, Berezovsky could have been strangled from behind in the bedroom, which explained the absence of signs of a struggle in the bathroom and on the body. Then, Brinkmann continued, the corpse could have been dragged to the bathroom, where it was discovered by Navama. This theory would account for a strange fingerprint on the shower rail, which police were unable to identify, despite it being checked against numerous databases, including Interpol and the FBI.[30]

Navama testified that he called the emergency number and then Michael Cotlick before he broke down the bathroom door. This raised a question from Bedford as to why Navama, a professional bodyguard, did not do this immediately. Navama answered, "Boris became more than a boss for me, he became my friend, and I was afraid of what I might see inside." In his witness statement for the police, Navama said that Berezovsky usually woke up between 6 and 7 a.m. to eat his breakfast, which Navama would prepare. Yet on this day Navama slept until 11:30 a.m. and never checked on his boss before going out for more than two hours to do errands.[31] This was puzzling, given that, as Navama told the inquest, he thought Berezovsky had been suicidal: "He wanted to die, he was talking about it for the last six months . . . Once when he was talking about wanting to die, he held up a steak knife and asked me where he should cut. He wanted me to show him how to choke. He said, 'How to die? What is the best way?'"[32]

Noting that Navama had at one point guarded an Israeli prime minister, Elizaveta Berezovskaya would express concern in a later interview about what she saw as Navama's negligence: "For some reason the security guard slept all morning on that ill-fated day, although Papa always woke up early. After that, the guard talked on the phone with his wife for a long time, then went out for coffee, then to the pharmacy to buy cold medicine for himself, then bought groceries. He did not return until three o'clock in the afternoon, even though all the other staff was off for the day . . . It is not clear why Avi suddenly decided it was okay to be absent for so long . . . This is a big mystery."[33] Equally troublesome, she said more recently, was that Navama did not turn on the security alarm or CTV cameras before he left, although he knew Berezovsky would be alone in the house for several hours. When asked why he failed to do this, Navama's answer was, "Boris did not tell me to."[34]

Berezovsky's son Gleb shared his half-sister's doubts about Navama. He recalled that not long before he died, his father told him that he no longer trusted Avi.[35] Berezovsky himself expressed similar negative feelings about Navama to Akhmed Zakaev.[36] But others, including Michael Cotlick and Iulii Dubov, insisted that Navama was trustworthy and loyal to Berezovsky.[37] Sabirova told a journalist that, after she heard of her lover's death, she called Navama from Moscow, and "he cried, constantly repeating 'I'm sorry,' and cried again. He couldn't speak."[38]

Cotlick told the inquest that Berezovsky had talked about suicide for months and asked him for advice on how to kill himself. But Cotlick had not taken his client seriously, reasoning that because Berezovsky spoke about suicide to "almost everybody," he was unlikely to actually do it. Cotlick concluded his testimony thus: "If somebody told me before that he would end his life, I would never believe it. Looking back on the past year, I think that's the only explanation."[39]

Berezovsky's psychiatrist, Saeed Islam, testified at the inquest that Berezovsky had only moderate depression and was not "actively suicidal," and Besharova, in a written statement to the inquest, said that on Sunday, March 24, some of Berezovsky's friends were planning a visit, along with their children. She added that "suicide was not in his nature, he is not that kind of person. He would never have done this, especially knowing that the children would come."[40] Elizaveta Berezovskaya voiced a similar view and even suggested that Putin had killed her father. After she told the inquest that "a number of people" would be interested in her father's death, the coroner, Peter Bedford, pressed her as to whom she had in mind. She replied: "I think we all know. I don't think they liked what my father was saying. He was saying that Putin was a danger to the whole world and you can see that now."[41] As a result of the conflicting evidence, the coroner declared an open verdict: "It is impossible to say, given the requisite burden of proof, that one explanation holds over another."[42]

The Kremlin Speaks Out

In the aftermath of Berezovsky's death, the Kremlin painted a picture of the oligarch as a prodigal son who sought forgiveness from a wise Putin before he took his own life. On March 23, 2013, the day Berezovsky died, Putin's spokesman Dmitry Peskov announced that Berezovsky had written a letter to the Russian president two months previously: "Boris Berezovsky sent a letter personally written by him. He admitted that he made lots of mistakes and asked Vladimir Putin to forgive him," said Peskov. "He asked Putin for a chance to come back to Russia." Peskov mentioned nothing about Putin's reaction to Berezovsky's letter, adding only, "I can say that in any case information about somebody's death—whoever the person was—cannot bring positive emotions."[43]

That same day, Berezovsky's supposed letter of repentance to Putin was published by an obscure Russian blogger named Viktor Telegin on LiveJournal. In the letter, Berezovsky was a supplicant to the extreme: "I am ready to openly admit my mistakes . . . Much of what I did, said, has no justification and deserves severe censure. But I am 68-years-old [sic] . . . Isolation from Russia is killing me. I ask you, Vladimir Vladimirovich, to forgive me those misdeeds and words I said in the blindness of anger . . . Vladimir Vladimirovich, I, like the Wandering Jew, am tired of wandering the earth. Allow me to return, Mr. President. I ask you to. I beg you. Sincerely yours, Boris Berezovsky."[44]

When asked about the published letter two days later, Peskov said that it was similar to the message that Vladimir Putin received, but he could not say for certain that the letter was genuine: "It's close, but I'm not sure, I can't say."[45] It seems to have gone unnoticed that in the letter Berezovsky gave his age as sixty-eight years old, instead of sixty-seven, an unlikely mistake.

Peskov later said that the letter on the Internet was fabricated and declared that Berezovsky's actual letter to Putin would never be made public. Sergei Ivanov, Putin's chief of staff, made a similar statement.[46] But many people accepted the published letter as genuine, so it served the Kremlin's purposes. In fact, already in early March the Kremlin had leaked news of Berezovsky's repentance letter to journalists at *Vedomosti* and probably to others, thus setting the stage for Peskov's revelations and the flurry of speculation that would follow.

The journalists had also been told from other sources that Abramovich was the emissary.[47]

Meanwhile, the Russian media put its own spin on Berezovsky's death. The former FSB chief Nikolai Kovalev said on Russian television that Berezovsky, as a traitor, had got what he deserved—a nasty death.[48] On March 31, Russia's NTV broadcast a documentary titled *See Big Ben and Die*, in which it was claimed that MI6 had murdered both Litvinenko and Berezovsky. According to this theory, on learning that Berezovsky had become disillusioned with the West and planned to return to Russia, the British intelligence services decided to eliminate him so he could not reveal their secrets.[49]

In late April 2013, Putin himself spoke out about Berezovsky's letter in response to a question during his annual nationally televised call-in show, *Direct Line*: "I received the first letter from him early this year, sometime in February, I think, and the second letter arrived recently, after his death. The text was the same." Putin noted that the first letter, delivered by one of Berezovsky's former Russian business partners, was

FIGURE 26.   *Direct Line* with Vladimir Putin, April 25, 2013. AP photo/RIA Novosti, Mikhail Klimentyev, Presidential Press Service.

handwritten, while the second, brought to him by a foreign businessman, was typed, with a handwritten header. Asked about the content,
Putin seemed to endorse the Internet version: "Actually, some details
have already appeared in the media. He wrote that he had made a lot of
mistakes and caused great damage and asked for forgiveness and the
opportunity to return to his homeland."[50]

The Kremlin, apparently with Berezovsky's original letter in hand,
seems to have waited for the right opportunity—Berezovsky's death—to
reveal its existence and portray it as an unconditional surrender, regardless of what the letter actually said. As the political scientist Vladimir
Pastukhov wrote: "Its content destroys Berezovsky as a historical figure.
This is more than death, it is the erasure of his historical memory into
cosmic dust ... Everything falls into place if the idea of a letter (or a real
letter) was held in anticipation for the possibility of death, prepared in
advance as a kind of scenario, as a preapproved and agreed-on plan of
action in case an 'unforeseen' situation arises."[51]

Significantly, Russian threats on Berezovsky's life had continued
after the London arrest of a hit man in 2007. In June 2010, Litvinenko's
accused killer Lugovoi, a member of parliament who would later receive
a state honor from Putin, sent Berezovsky a black t-shirt with the words
"radioactive death is knocking at your door" printed on the back.[52]
Michael Cotlick, who had been present when Berezovsky received the
t-shirt, told the inquest that after Berezovsky's court loss to Abramovich he was no longer a danger to the Kremlin, thus suggesting that the
Kremlin had no motive to kill him.[53] But Putin's sense of threat did
not necessarily correspond to reality, and his need for revenge did not
always subside when an enemy was defeated. As Dubov said: "Putin
would not forgive Berezovsky under any circumstances. This is not
about revelations, not about the Liberal Russia party, not about his
activities here. The point is that Berezovsky made Putin the president.
This is unforgivable."[54]

Tying up Loose Ends

Putin was also asked during the April call-in show about the Boston
Marathon bombings, carried out by two Chechen immigrants twelve
days earlier, leaving 3 dead and 260 wounded. It would later emerge
that Tamerlan Tsarnaev, the perpetrator of the bombings along with
his younger brother Dzhokhar, had traveled to Russia in January 2012
under the watchful eye of the FSB and spent several weeks in the North

Caucasus with Islamic jihadists. Russian authorities had never notified their American counterparts of Tamerlan's visit, where much of his radicalization had occurred. According to one US counterterrorism official, if they had known of the trip to Russia, "it would have changed everything."[55]

The Boston bombings offered Putin an opportunity to convey an important message—that Russia and the United States were both victims of international terrorism and should join together in struggling against this evil: "I have always felt outraged when our Western partners . . . referred to our terrorists who committed brutal, bloody, appalling crimes on the territory of our country as 'insurgents'. . . . We always said that Western governments shouldn't make empty declarations that terrorism is a common threat, but actually make real efforts and cooperate with us more closely. Now these two criminals have provided the best possible proof that we were right."[56] Washington got the message. In June 2013, Nikolai Patrushev, since 2008 secretary of the National Security Council, was invited to the White House, where he met with Obama to discuss uniting efforts against global terrorism.

Putin's stature as a global leader was enhanced by the February 2014 Olympics in Sochi. But Russia's annexation of Crimea and incitement of insurgency in Eastern Ukraine the next month resulted in serious damage to his image abroad. Russia was thrown out of the G8 and subjected to Western economic sanctions. Relations between Washington and Moscow remained at a post-Cold War low until the 2016 election of Donald Trump, who was eager for a friendship with Putin. Trump not only tried to lift US economic sanctions against Russia; he sought to weaken NATO. But despite his cozy relationship with the new US president, Putin continued to fear that NATO would undermine his regime, and that internal political opposition, stirred up by democrats like Aleksei Navalny, would strengthen. These perceived threats may have given Putin the impetus to settle old scores shortly before the Russian presidential election on March 18, 2018.

Sergei Skripal was a former Russian colonel for the Russian military intelligence agency (GRU) living in the British city of Salisbury. In 1995, while posted in Madrid, Skripal had been recruited by MI6. He subsequently passed on to British intelligence the names of hundreds of agents working undercover for the GRU, along with valuable details of the GRU's overseas operations. Skripal's role as an informant was eventually discovered. He was arrested by the FSB in 2004 and two years later convicted of treason, with a sentence of thirteen years' hard labor.

In 2010, Skripal gained release from prison as part of a "spy swap" with the United States and settled in Britain. At the time of the swap, Putin issued a not-so-veiled threat: "These people betrayed their friends, their brothers in arms. Whatever they got in exchange for it, those thirty pieces of silver they were given, they will choke on them."[57]

On the afternoon of March 4, Skripal and his daughter Iulia, visiting from Moscow, were found unconscious on a Salisbury park bench after having lunch at a local Italian restaurant. They had been poisoned with Novichok, a lethal nerve agent developed in Russia. But the poisoning was carried out carelessly. Not only did Skripal and his daughter survive (after months in the hospital); the would-be assassins, two GRU operatives, were caught on CCTV cameras walking near Skripal's home before the poisoning, and traces of Novichok were found in their London hotel room. The British were quick to condemn the Kremlin for the Skripal poisonings and within days sent twenty-three Russian diplomats packing.

Why would the Kremlin wait eight years before targeting Skripal for death? By this time he had long since offered up all his secrets to British intelligence. Perhaps, as with Berezovsky, there had been earlier attempts that were unsuccessful, or perhaps Moscow had a sudden need to deter other defections by using Skripal as an example. Given that the poisoning occurred just two weeks before Putin's election, it may also be that Putin wanted to send a signal of strength to his Russian supporters and the West: the Kremlin would go after its enemies, no matter the consequences.

In keeping with this message, Litvinenko's accused killer, Andrei Lugovoi, gave an interview on *Ekho Moskvy* about the Skripal poisonings. Although he denied that Russia was responsible, he nonetheless offered a warning: "Something constantly happens to Russian citizens who either run away from Russian justice, or for some reason choose for themselves a way of life they call 'changing their Motherland.' So the more Britain accepts on its territory every good-for-nothing, every scum from all over the world, the more problems they will have."[58]

On March 12, 2018, six days after Lugovoi's interview, Nikolai Glushkov's lifeless body was discovered by his daughter, Natalia, at his home in New Malden. He was due to attend London's Commercial Court for a hearing in the Aeroflot case that very day. Police launched a murder investigation, interviewing over 1,800 witnesses and viewing 2,200 hours of CCTV footage, along with thousands of forensic samples and physical evidence. After an inquest in April 2021, the coroner

FIGURE 27. Nikolai Glushkov after being arrested in Moscow, December 2000. Pavel Smertin/ Kommersant photo via AP.

ruled that Glushkov was strangled by a third party who had attempted to make the death appear to be a suicide. The assailant had wrapped the leash of Glushkov's dog around his neck and put a small two-stepped ladder next to his body to simulate a hanging. But the ladder was upright, whereas with a self-hanging it would have been knocked over. Just as forensic expert Brinkman had hypothesized in the Berezovsky case, Glushkov was apparently ambushed from behind and rapidly subdued. As Natalia Glushkova described the scene, "it was a trashy setup of a murder."[59]

Aside from footage of a black van seen driving near Glushkov's home the night of the murder, which was never identified, the police found no clues to determine the killer. But Moscow's involvement seemed likely. In fact, Glushkov had predicted after Berezovsky died that he would be the next Kremlin target, telling *The Guardian* that the list of designated Russian victims in Britain was getting smaller and "I don't see anyone left on it apart from me."[60] As it turned out, Glushkov seems to have also suffered a poisoning not long after Berezovsky's death. In November 2013, he was staying at a hotel in Bristol when two Russians whom he had met on an earlier occasion approached him with a bottle of champagne. Glushkov accepted their offer to sit down with them and share a glass. The next morning he was so ill that he had to be taken by ambulance to the hospital.[61]

Glushkov did receive some posthumous justice from a British court. Aeroflot suddenly dropped the case against him and the Forus group, and at a hearing in June 2018, the court ordered the airlines to pay $3.9 million in indemnity costs to Glushkov's estate and to the other defendants. The judge criticized Aeroflot for the "aggressive and unsympathetic" way in which it treated Glushkov's bereaved loved ones after his death and noted: "The Forus Defendants do not shirk from asserting that neither Aeroflot nor its legal representatives ever had any real belief in the truth of the fraud allegations that they were making: 'Aeroflot's game, or the game of the Russian state acting through Aeroflot, was essentially to use civil proceedings as an instrument of political oppression.' "[62]

Fabricating a Legend

However much Putin liked to convey the message that traitors would be punished, portraying Berezovsky's death as a suicide reinforced the image of Berezovsky as a fallen enemy, in despair because he realized how wrong he had been to turn against Putin. Posthumous attacks on Berezovsky's character and his legacy as a successful businessman who had been a power broker in the Yeltsin years also served Putin's purposes. In April 2013, RT produced a documentary on Berezovsky's life, comparing him with Rasputin.[63] And Petr Aven set about interviewing Berezovsky's friends, associates, and two of his wives, for a book that would portray Berezovsky in the worst possible light.[64]

Aven's book, *The Time of Berezovsky* (Vremia Berezovskogo), composed of excerpts from thirty two-hour taped interviews, was published in Russia in 2017. In themselves, the interviews are valuable because they are firsthand accounts from people who knew Berezovsky well. But Aven encouraged those he interviewed to focus on Berezovsky's deep flaws.[65] In the book's lengthy introduction, Aven himself sets the stage: "Boris had a pathological indifference to the grief of others . . . As his social status grew it became easier for Boris not to demonstrate basic sympathy, and his indifference offended and disgusted many." According to Aven, Berezovsky did not repay his debts: "Boris still owes a lot of money to many people . . . For me, such a casual attitude toward debt is unacceptable." Later Aven tells readers: "Boris was a bad mathematician

. . . He himself never wrote a single scholarly article; they were written by the young people who worked for him."[66]

Following up in an interview with Vladimir Borzenko, who collaborated with Berezovsky as an academic, Aven asks: "If I am not mistaken, his doctoral dissertation passed by only one vote . . . What was the problem? Was the dissertation not very good or did someone else write it?" Borzenko replies that neither was the case. There was simply a lot of competition and intrigue going on. In conversation with the media magnate Vladimir Voronov, Aven notes: "there was a myth that Boris was a great mathematician. This myth was easy for me dispel because I knew it wasn't true."[67]

Aven discusses Berezovsky's business skills with Chubais, who says, "Petya, you know better than I that Boris Abramovich Berezovsky certainly was not a great businessman in the true sense of the word." "Absolutely not," Aven agrees. Chubais then elaborates: "There were businessmen who created entire giant companies from scratch. What did Boris Abramovich create? What new enterprise did he ever create?" "Nothing, nothing at all," Aven answers.[68]

Aven remarks to the billionaire Leonid Boguslavskii, who had been a fellow student of Berezovsky's and later worked at LogoVAZ: "Boris certainly did not believe in democracy. He valued his freedom but not the rights of others." Boguslavskii, who at some point had fallen out with Berezovsky, agrees.[69] But Demian Kudriavtsev, the former general director of Kommersant, refuses to play along. When Aven asserts that "Boris was an extremely authoritarian person, he was contemptuous of others' opinions and, in my view, was not a democrat at all," Kudriavtsev retorts: "This is absolutely not true. This is the reason why I didn't want to participate in your project: not only do you not understand Berezovsky, you don't even want to!"[70]

Clearly intent on confirming the Kremlin's preferred version of Berezovsky's death—that he died of suicide—Aven dwells on Berezovsky's depression. After Alex Goldfarb tells Aven that he spoke with Berezovsky by phone several times before he died, Aven inquires, "Did you have the feeling that he was depressed?" Aven asks the former Kommersant editor Andrei Vasiliev: "Was Boris in a bad mood? I've talked to different people, and many said he was depressed." When Aven directs a similar question to Dubov, "Did he give the impression of a sick person?" Dubov demurs: "Well, I'm not a doctor." Aven then presses him: "Didn't you see his depression?" But Dubov only responds, "You see, I can't really recognize depression."[71]

Ekho Moskvy editor Aleksei Venediktov expressed outrage over *The Time of Berezovsky* during a discussion of the book at the Yeltsin Center in Moscow. In their interviews, Venediktov said, Voloshin, Chubais, and Iumashev "deliberately obscured the political role of Boris Berezovsky" because "they were ashamed to admit that someone like Berezovsky, who later became a 'traitor,' was pivotal in such events as the re-election of Boris Yeltsin in 1996." Calling the book "contemptuous" of Berezovsky, Venediktov said that it aimed to portray Berezovsky as a "little demon." But, he went on, "the main point was not that he is a demon, it's that he is little. And he loses all the time." Venediktov concluded, "If Boris were alive, this book would not have appeared."[72]

After Aven's book was published, a web series, "Berezovsky—Who Is He?," based on Aven's videotaped interviews, appeared online. The ten-episode series, produced by the Russian journalist Andrei Loshak, included longer segments from the interviews and presented Berezovsky in a more balanced way than Aven's book. As Loshak observed about his film: "Unlike the rest, Berezovsky declared a fight against authoritarian tendencies—and found himself completely alone. Not a single former comrade from the mighty of this world supported him."[73] But the series had a much smaller audience than it would have had if it appeared on television, where the image of Berezovsky as a vanquished villain continued to prevail.

Berezovsky's death allowed his enemies to rewrite his history, thus giving Putin a final victory against the oligarch who had helped him to become the most powerful and longest-lasting Kremlin leader since Joseph Stalin. But Putin now lives with the knowledge that his own legacy will be that of a ruthless, authoritarian leader who launched an unprovoked military invasion of Ukraine and set his country on the road to isolation and economic decline. Berezovsky's urgent warnings from exile about the dangers of Putin's leadership, ignored for so long, will now be recognized for their prescience.

Berezovsky's flaws were many. His ambition took precedence over concerns about Russia's democratic development, and his hubris blinded him to the dangers of Putin's rise to power until it was too late. But he was far from alone in failing to recognize Putin for who he was. It was Yeltsin who left his country in the hands of a career Chekist whose ruthless disregard for human rights became apparent with the invasion of Chechnya, and the Russian people readily went along. On the occasion of Putin's inauguration as president for his second term in 2004, Anna Politkovskaya wrote: "Tomorrow a KGB snoop, who even in that capacity did not make much of an impression, will strut through the Kremlin just as Lenin did . . . It is we who are responsible for Putin's policies, we first and foremost, not Putin . . . Society has shown limitless apathy, and this is what has given Putin the indulgence he requires."[74] Two decades later, with most democratic oppositionists having been forced to leave Russia or face prison, that societal apathy prevails.

Acknowledgments

I owe a deep debt of gratitude to my friend Alex Goldfarb, a close aide and associate of Berezovsky for a number of years. I have not only relied on Alex's insightful writings about Berezovsky, which are cited throughout the book; I also have benefited from long conversations with him, which have inspired and informed me. In addition, I owe thanks to others in Berezovsky's circle and family who generously gave me time for interviews: Elizaveta Berezovskaya, Gleb Berezovsky, Michael Cotlick, Iulii Dubov, Elena Gorbunova, Marina Litvinenko, and Akhmed Zakaev. Elizaveta Berezovskaya also kindly provided me with important research material, as did Gleb Berezovsky. Additionally, Peter Morgan, creator of the London play *Patriots*, about Putin and his oligarchs, was kind enough to share his time with me to talk about Putin and Berezovsky.

I could not have written this book without the invaluable help of my literary agent, Philip Turner, who encouraged me to write the proposal and successfully found a home for the book at Cornell University/NIU Press. Philip also read the manuscript in its entirety and made many useful suggestions. My editor, Amy Farranto, has helped me greatly in improving the manuscript and has been a pleasure to work with, always patient and responsive. Jessica Landy was essential in locating photographs and obtaining permissions, just as she was with a previous book. I am also grateful to my production editor, Karen M. Laun, and my copyeditor, Carolyn Pouncy, for their indispensable role in the transformation of my manuscript into a book.

Special thanks are also due to my friend at *The Guardian*, Luke Harding, who has kindly shared his insights and information with me, and to Peter Reddaway, a mentor to me as a student at the London School of Economics. Finally, I am thankful for the encouragement of my daughter, the writer/producer Molly Knight Raskin. Molly's energy and enthusiasm for my writing, our shared interest in Russia, and her willingness to listen when I have faced problems have made me a better author and a better person.

Notes

Introduction

1. Moscow Agence France-Presse, November 15, 2000, http://www. russialist.org/archives/4638.html##4.

2. See, for example, a video of Putin speaking that surfaced on *The Independent*, March 7, 2018: https://www.independent.co.uk/news/world/europe/vladimir-putin-traitors-kick-bucket-sergei-skripal-latest-video-30-pieces-silver-a8243206.html.

3. Author interview with Marina Litvinenko, April 2014.

4. Alex Goldfarb, "A Russian View of Patriots, Peter Morgan's Play about Boris Berezovsky," *Guardian*, July 15, 2022, https://www.theguardian.com/world/2022/jul/15/patriots-peter-morgan-play-boris-berezovsky-russian-view.

1. Offspring of the Soviet System

1. Petr Aven, *Vremia Berezovskogo* (Moscow: Corpus (ACT), 2017), 62.

2. Anastasiia Egorova, "Kem i kakim on vse-taki byl?" *Novaia gazeta*, March 4, 2016, https://novayagazeta.ru/articles/2016/03/04/67671-yuliy-dubov-171-za-vsyu-svoyu-zhizn-ne-vstrechal-podobnogo-berezovskomu-a-ya-videl-mnogih-187.

3. Matthew Kaminski, "Viktor Orban: Putin Has No Personality," *Politico*, November 23, 2015, https://www.politico.eu/article/viktor-orban-putin-has-no-personality/.

4. Masha Gessen, *The Man without a Face: The Unlikely Rise of Vladimir Putin* (New York: Riverhead Books, 2012).

5. On Beria's post-Stalin "liberalization," See Amy Knight, *Beria: Stalin's First Lieutenant* (Princeton, NJ: Princeton University Press, 1993).

6. A. Khinshtein, *Berezovskii i Abramovich: Oligarkhi s bol'shoi dorogi* (Moscow: Lora: 2007), 10.

7. Nataliya Gevorkyan, "Interv'iu s mater'iu Berezovskogo: Ia plakala, kogda on rodilsia," *Vokrug novostei*, January 30, 2004, http://www.vokrugnovostei.com/Politika-i-ekonomika/Intervyu-s-materyu-Berezovskogo-Ya-plakala-kogda-on-rodilsya/.

8. Author interview with Elizaveta Berezovskaya, London, October 27, 2022.

9. Khinshtein, *Berezovskii i Abramovich*, 11.

10. Khinshtein, *Berezovskii i Abramovich*, 14–15.

11. Aven, *Vremia Berezovskogo*, 140.

12. Boris Berezovsky, *Avtoportret, ili zapiski poveshennogo* (Moscow: Tsentrpoligraf, 2013), 54–55.

13. Berezovsky, *Avtoportret*, 30–31.

14. Peter Pomerantsev, "Berezovsky's Last Days," *London Review of Books* 35, no. 8 (April 25, 2013), https://www.lrb.co.uk/the-paper/v35/n08/peter-pomerantsev/diary.

15. Elizaveta Berezovskaya's interview with Dmitrii Gordon, gordonua.com, June 29, 2018, https://gordonua.com/publications/doch-berezovskogo-mne-kazhetsya-papu-otravili-tak-chtoby-vsem-kazalos-on-v-depressii-a-v-itoge-ubili-chtoby-vse-poverili-v-samoubiystvo-250144.html.

16. Berezovsky, *Avtoportret*, 31.

17. David E. Hoffman, *The Oligarchs: Wealth and Power in the New Russia* (New York: Public Affairs, 2001), 130–31.

18. Berezovsky, *Avtoportret*, 31.

19. Hoffman, *Oligarchs*, 140.

20. Aven, *Vremia Berezovskogo*, 32.

21. Aven, *Vremia Berezovskogo*, 69.

22. Aven, *Vremia Berezovskogo*, 70.

23. Owen Bowcott, "Boris Berezovsky Pays Out £100m in UK's Biggest Divorce Settlement," *The Guardian*, July 22, 2011, https://www.theguardian.com/world/2011/jul/22/boris-berezovsky-divorce-record-payout.

24. Details on Putin's early years appear in Oleg Blotskii, *Vladimir Putin: Istoriia zhizni* (Moscow: Mezhdunarodnye otnosheniia, 2001). Also see the biography by Steven Lee Myers: *The New Tsar: The Rise and Reign of Vladimir Putin* (New York: Knopf, 2015); and Philip Short, *Putin: His Life and Times* (New York: Henry Holt, 2022). Short uses many of the sources Myers cites, including Blotskii, but also provides some new details on Putin's early life.

25. Vladimir Putin, *First Person: An Astonishingly Frank Self-Portrait by Russia's President Vladimir Putin*, with Nataliya Gevorkyan, Natalya Timakova, and Andrei Kolesnikov, trans. Catherine A. Fitzpatrick (New York: Public Affairs, 2000), 17.

26. Putin, *First Person*, 63.

27. Blotskii, *Vladimir Putin*, 25–26.

28. Putin, *First Person*, 22–23.

29. Myers, *New Tsar*, 14.

30. Blotskii, *Vladimir Putin*, 105.

31. Blotskii, *Vladimir Putin*, 68–69.

32. Konstantin Rylev, "'Zapreshchennye' fakty o Putine," *Fokus*, May 13, 2022, https://focus.ua/world/515409-zapreshchennye-fakty-o-putine-patologicheskaya-zhestokost-agressivnost-svyazi-s-kriminalom. The article cites excerpts from the first edition of Vera Gurevich, *Vladimir Putin: Roditeli, druz'ia, uchitelia* (St. Petersburg: Izdatel'stvo Iuridicheskogo instituta, 2004) that were omitted from later editions because of their negative portrayal of Putin.

33. Blotskii, *Vladimir Putin*, 68.

34. Putin, *First Person*, 21.

35. Myers, *New Tsar*, 16.

36. Blotskii, *Vladimir Putin*, 199–202.

37. As quoted in Gessen, *Man without a Face*, 52.

38. See my study on the KGB: Amy Knight, *The KGB: Police and Politics in the Soviet Union* (Boston: Unwin-Hyman, 1988).

39. Putin, *First Person*, 36.

40. "Cherkesov, Viktor," *Lenta.ru*, https://lenta.ru/lib/14169763/full.

41. Amy Knight, *Orders to Kill: The Putin Regime and Political Murder* (New York: Thomas Dunne, 2017), 44–45.

42. See Irina Stoilova, "Ital'ianskaia gazeta 'Repubblika' opublikovala v sredu pervuiu iz serii statei, posviashchennykh proshlomy presidenta Rossii Vladimira Putina," *Radio Svoboda*, July 11, 2001, https://www.svoboda. org/a/24223192.html; and Vladimir Usol'tsev, *Sosluzhivets: Neizvestnye stranitsy zhizni prezidenta* (Moscow: Eksmo, 2004), 186.

43. Myers, *New Tsar*, 25.

44. Putin biographer Philip Short writes that the KGB in cities such as Leningrad had stopped using overt repression against dissidents by the second half of the 1970s and even permitted samizdat to circulate (Short, *Putin*, 72–73). While the 1975 Helsinki Accords did result in some temporary moderation of KGB policy toward dissent, overt repression continued. Members of Helsinki monitoring groups were frequently arrested, and Nobel laureate Andrei Sakharov was consigned to internal exile in 1980 for his human rights advocacy.

45. Interview with Oleg Kalugin, *Radio Svoboda*, March 28, 2015, https:// www.svoboda.org/a/26920026.html.

46. Interview with Oleg Kalugin by Dmitrii Gordon, May 7, 2015, https:// gordonua.com/news/war/eks-nachalnik-putina-kalugin-vse-zayavleniya-o-razmeshchenii-yadernogo-oruzhiya-v-krymu-blef-putin-sam-boitsya-takogo-razvitiya-sobytiy-79494.html.

47. "Head of FSB Defends Purges, Denounces Traitors on Cheka Anniversary," *Moscow Times*, December 20, 2017, https://www.themo scowtimes.com/2017/12/20/fsb-chief-defends-purges-denounces-traitors-on-cheka-anniversary-a60002.

48. Catherine Belton, "The Man Who Has Putin's Ear—and May Want His Job," *Washington Post*, July 13, 2022, https://www.washingtonpost.com/ world/2022/07/13/nikolai-patrushev-russia-security-council-putin/.

49. Putin, *First Person*, 59.

50. Interview with Vladimir Usol'tsev, *Radio Svoboda*, November 11, 2003, https://www.svoboda.org/a/24187711.html.

51. See, for example, Myers, *New Tsar*, 24–28; and Short, *Putin*, 71–72. Also see Viktor Rezunkov, "Vladimir Putin: Kak zakalialas' stal'," *Radio Svoboda*, January 8, 2016, https://www.svoboda.org/a/27474231.html.

52. TASS, "Biografiia Vladimira Putina," October 7, 2021, https://tass. ru/info/12592215?utm_source=google.com&utm_medium=organic&utm_ campaign=google.com&utm_referrer=google.com.

53. Filip Kovacevic, "Chekism 101: An Independent Study Plan for a KGB Officer in the 1980s," Wilson Center blog, November 15, 2021, https://www.wilsoncenter.org/blog-post/chekism-101-independent-study-plan-kgb-officer-1980s.

54. Quoted in Michael Weiss, "Revealed: The Secret KGB Manual for Recruiting Spies," *Daily Beast*, December 27, 2017, https://www.thedailybeast.com/the-kgb-papers-how-putin-learned-his-spycraft-part-1. Weiss reproduces a top-secret manual used by the Andropov Red Banner KGB Institute for its students. For a description of my 1981 encounter with a probable RT officer in Leningrad, see Amy Knight, "The Two Worlds of Vladmir Putin," *Wilson Quarterly* 24, no. 2 (2000): 32–41.

55. Oleg Blotskii, *Vladimir Putin: Doroga k vlasti* (Moscow: Osmos-Press, 2002), 211 (hereafter *Doroga k vlasti*). In his biography of Putin, German writer Alexander Rahr wrote: "If you ask a KGB officer today how important an agent's job in Dresden was in 1985, the only answer is a weary smile. No career officer wanted to be sent to Dresden. There was hardly anything to spy on in Dresden as far as the GDR was concerned" (*Wladimir Putin: Präsident Russlands—Partner Deutschlands* [Munich: Universitas Verlag, 2000], 58–59).

56. Usol'tsev interview. Also see Myers, *New Tsar*, 39. After entering public life, Putin added to his height by wearing shoe lifts covered by extra-long trousers. See "Putin Makes Effort to Keep His Height Secret from Voters," *Washington Times*, March 23, 2000, https://www.washingtontimes.com/news/2000/mar/23/20000323-011028-2791r/.

57. Blotskii, *Doroga k vlasti*, 219.

58. Blotskii, *Doroga k vlasti*, 220.

59. Gessen, *Man without a Face*, 65.

60. Usol'tsev interview.

61. Catherine Belton, *Putin's People: How the KGB Took Back Russia and Then Took on the West* (New York: Farrar, Straus, and Giroux, 2020), 39–42. See also "Bombist" on the website "Putinizm kak on est'," February 18, 2021, https://putinism.wordpress.com/2021/02/18/bombist/#more-3126.

62. Dmitrii Zapol'skii interview, "Putinizm kak on est'," January 17, 2020, https://putinism.wordpress.com/2020/01/17/zapolsky/.

63. Mark Galeotti, "Putin's Declassified KGB Record Shows He Was No High-Flier, but a Solid B," *Moscow Times*, November 4, 2019, https://www.themoscowtimes.com/2019/11/04/putins-kgb-declassified-record-show-that-he-was-no-high-flier-but-a-solid-b-a68024.

64. Aleksei Navalny, "Dvorets dlia Putina" (Putin's Palace), https://palace.navalny.com.

65. L. M. Mlechin, *KGB: Predsedateli organov gosbezopasnosti: Rassekrechennie sud'by* (Moscow: Tsentrpoligraf, 2011), 628.

66. Blotskii, *Doroga k vlasti*, 260–65. Also see Myers, *New Tsar*, 50–51, for a slightly different account.

67. Ray Furlong, "Showdown in Dresden: The Stasi Occupation and the Putin Myth," Radio Free Europe/Radio Liberty, December 2, 2019, https://www.rferl.org/a/showdown-in-dresden-the-stasi-occupation-and-the-putin-myth/30302831.html.

68. Berezovskii, *Avtoportret*, 35.

69. Paul Klebnikov, *Godfather of the Kremlin: The Decline of Russia in the Age of Gangster Capitalism* (Orlando: Harcourt, 2000), 55. Klebnikov, who was the editor of *Forbes Magazine* in Moscow, would be brutally gunned down there in 2004. His killers were never found.

70. Hoffman, *Oligarchs*, 146.

71. Klebnikov, *Godfather of the Kremlin*, 93; Hoffman, *Oligarchs*, 141–45.

72. Yevgenia Albats, "Berezovskii byl chast'iu nashei zhizni: I chast'iu zhizni Putina—tozhe," *Novoe vremia*, March 31, 2013, https://newtimes.ru/articles/detail/64630/.

73. Klebnikov, *Godfather of the Kremlin*, 72.

74. Berezovsky, *Avtoportret*, 75.

2. A Meeting in St. Petersburg

1. See Bill Keller, "Another K.G.B. Officer Is Charging Incompetence and Graft," *New York Times*, September 8, 1990, https://www.nytimes.com/1990/09/08/world/another-kgb-officer-is-charging-incompetence-and-graft.html.

2. Putin, *First Person*, 85.

3. Blotskii, *Doroga k vlasti*, 280–83.

4. Blotskii, *Doroga k vlasti*, 273.

5. Rahr, *Wladimir Putin*, 68. Philip Short theorizes that Putin was called back from Dresden early to perform a special assignment on the orders of KGB Directorate Z chief Filipp Bobkov (*Putin*, 120–22).

6. Blotskii, *Doroga k vlasti*, 271–73.

7. Putin, *First Person*, 88–89. Short (*Putin*, 135) says that Putin did not start working for Sobchak until October 1990, but most sources say he was an advisor to Sobchak by May or June. See, for example, his biography on zampolit.com: https://zampolit.com/dossier/putin-vladimir-vladimirovich/. Also see Myers, *New Tsar*, 58–59.

8. Myers, *New Tsar*, 58.

9. Dmitrii Zapol'skii, *Putinburg* (Cheltenham, UK: PVL Consulting Ltd., 2019), Kindle ed., 214–15.

10. Gessen, *Man without a Face*, 97.

11. Putin, *First Person*, 91–93.

12. Myers, *New Tsar*, 62–67.

13. Putin, *First Person*, 94.

14. Chris Hutchins, *Putin*, with Alexander Korobko (Leicester, UK: Matador, 2012), Kindle ed., chap. 4, loc. 1026.

15. Karen Dawisha, *Putin's Kleptocracy: Who Owns Russia?* (New York: Simon and Schuster, 2014), 82.

16. As reported in *Kommersant vlast'*, September 23, 1991, https://www.kommersant.ru/doc/909.

17. Klebnikov, *Godfather of the Kremlin*, 95–97.

18. Khinshtein, *Berezovskii i Abramovich*, 49.

19. Klebnikov, *Godfather of the Kremlin*, 98–100.

20. Khinshtein, *Berezovskii i Abramovich*, 59.

21. Aven, *Vremia Berezovskogo*, 76.

22. Berezovsky interview with Masha Gessen, 2008, published in *Republic*, March 25, 2013, https://republic.ru/posts/l/923157.

23. Gessen, *Man without a Face*, 15–16.

24. Dawisha, *Putin's Kleptocracy*, 65.

25. Vladimir Bukovsky, *Judgment in Moscow: Soviet Crimes and Western Complicity*, trans. Alyona Kojevnikov, English ed. prepared by Paul Boutin (California: Ninth of November Press, 2019), 59. See my review of Bukovsky's book: "The Secret Files of the Soviet Union," *New York Review of Books*, January 16, 2020.

26. Aven, *Vremia Berezovskogo*, 12.

27. See the 2018 biographical film about Sobchak created by his daughter, Ksenia Sobchak, and Vera Krichevskaia, *Delo Sobchaka* (The case of Sobchak), https://www.imdb.com/title/tt8342962/.

28. Myers, *New Tsar*, 77.

29. Putin, *First Person*, 102.

30. Anastasiia Kirilenko, "Kazhduiu nedeliu Sobchak prinosil v bank portfel' kesha," *The Insider*, March 1, 2017, https://theins.ru/korrupciya/46539.

31. Dawisha, *Putin's Kleptocracy*, 106–25; Yuri Felshtinsky and Vladimir Pribylovsky, *The Corporation: Russia and the KGB in the Age of President Putin* (New York: Encounter Books, 2008), 71–82; Robert Coalson, "Marina Salye: The St. Petersburg Lawmaker Who Became Putin's First Accuser," RFE/RL, May 19, 2022, https://www.rferl.org/a/putin-corruption-accusation/31855104.html.

32. Oleg Lu're, "Kolbasa dlia Pitera," *Novaia gazeta*, March 13, 2000, https://on-demand.eastview.com/browse/doc/3464053.

33. Anastasiia Kirilenko and Iurii Timofeev, "Pochemu Marina Sal'e molchala o Putine 10 let?," *Radio Svoboda*, March 2, 2010, https://www.svoboda.org/a/1972366.html.

34. Philip Short claims wrongly that Putin was innocent of wrongdoing in the oil-for-food scandal, which Karen Dawisha documented in *Putin's Kleptocracy*. Short says that Dawisha was ill when she wrote her book and that it thus "contains errors which, had she been well, she would certainly not have let pass" (Short, *Putin*, 729n162). Dawisha died of cancer in 2018, four years after her pathbreaking book was published to great acclaim by scholars and journalists alike. Short apparently did not consult the many Russian-language sources on the oil-for-food scandal that Dawisha drew upon in her exhaustive research.

35. Dmitrii Volchek, "Delo Sobchaka: Zagadki biografii pokrovitelia Putina," *Radio Svoboda*, July 9, 2018, https://www.svoboda.org/a/29278219.html; Dawisha, *Putin's Kleptocracy*, 116–17.

36. Felshtinsky and Pribylovsky, *Corporation*, 94.

37. Volchek, "Delo Sobchaka"; Dawisha, *Putin's Kleptocracy*, 132–41.

38. Amy Knight, *Orders to Kill*, 70–74. Kumarin was charged for the murder of Starovoitova after my book was published. For an excellent, detailed

biography of Kumarin, see "Putin's List," on the Free Russia Forum: https://www.spisok-putina.org/en/personas/barsukov-kumarin-2/.

39. Dozhd', March 27, 2016, https://tvrain.ru/teleshow/bremja_novostej/lobkov_raskryvaet_sekrety_vzryvchatki-406267/. Dmitrii Zapol'skii learned from a close acquaintance of Kumarin, Irina Iakovleva, the wife of former St. Petersburg governor Vladimir Iakovlev, that Kumarin remained in contact with Putin after his imprisonment. Zapol'skii observed that the contact with Putin has not helped Kumarin much: "At least he is still alive. Not murdered, not poisoned, just locked up. Not in a golden cage, but an ordinary one" (*Putinburg*, 120).

40. Belton, *Putin's People*, 102–3.

41. Dozhd', August 24, 2017, https://tvrain.ru/teleshow/piterskie/piterskie_otets_i_syn-442938/. Also see Belton, *Putin's People*, 98–99.

42. See Mike Eckel, "Navalny Punches Even Higher with New Video Alleging Secret Island Dacha Used by Putin," RFE/RL, August 30, 2017, https://www.rferl.org/a/russia-navalny-putin-island-dacha/28705917.html.

43. Anastasiia Kirilenko, "Konets piterskoi 'prachechnoi,' " *Novoe vremia*, April 17, 2018, https://newtimes.ru/articles/detail/158697/.

44. Zapol'skii, *Putinburg*, 437–38, 445.

45. Blotskii, *Doroga k vlasti*, 351–54.

46. Kylie Mar, "Jane Fonda's Bizarre Story about Vladimir Putin Once Being Her Travel Guide," Yahoo.com, September 17, 2020, https://autos.yahoo.com/jane-fondas-bizarre-story-about-vladimir-putin-once-being-her-travel-guide-052904255.html.

47. Putin, *First Person*, 104.

48. Myers, *New Tsar*, 89–92; Putin, *First Person*, 105–10.

49. Guy Chazan and David Crawford, "A Friendship Forged in Spying Pays Dividends in Russia Today," *Wall Street Journal*, February 23, 2005, http://online.wsj.com/news/articles/SB110911748114361477.

50. "Circles of Power: Putin's Secret Friendship with Ex-Stasi Officer," *The Guardian*, August 13, 2014, https://www.theguardian.com/world/2014/aug/13/russia-putin-german-right-hand-man-matthias-warnig.

51. *Argumenty i Fakty*, March 14, 2002, https://aif.ru/archive/1724337.

52. Khinshtein, *Berezovskii i Abramovich*, 59. Aven, *Vremia Berezovskogo*, 124.

53. Hoffman, *Oligarchs*, 137.

54. Hoffman, *Oligarchs*, 214.

55. Khinshtein, *Berezovskii i Abramovich*, 80; Hoffman, *Oligarchs*, 215–18.

56. Khinshtein, *Berezovskii i Abramovich*, 88.

57. Klebnikov, *Godfather of the Kremlin*, 23. Klebnikov says that Berezovsky was accompanied by his wife, Galina, and his two youngest children, but Berezovsky already had a new partner, Elena Gorbunova, at this time.

58. See, for example, Khinshtein, *Berezovskii i Abramovich*, 89; and the unsigned article "Godfather of the Kremlin?" *Forbes*, December 30, 1996, https://www.forbes.com/forbes/1996/1230/5815090a.html?sh=33c65a5f7562. The *Forbes* article, discussed further in chapter 3, says: "According to Moscow police reports, Berezovsky started his auto dealership in close collaboration with the powerful Chechen criminal gangs. Presumably they

provided him with physical protection—a 'roof,' as it's called in Russian slang."

59. Dmitrii Gordon, *Berezovskii i Korzhakov: Kremlevskie tainy* (Moscow: Algoritm, 2013), 45.

60. See Gorbunova's account in Aven, *Vremia Berezovskogo*, 133.

61. Klebnikov, *Godfather of the Kremlin*, 38–39.

62. "Spravka FSB 'V otnoshenii ChOP 'Atoll-1,'" *Kompromat.ru*, June 9, 2000, http://www.compromat.ru/page_9782.htm?c40973262dabf77e303a0 bf66332df1fb26801=00c67cf150353ecc8434fd9b30306eb4.

63. Alex Goldfarb, *Death of a Dissident: The Poisoning of Alexander Litvinenko and the Return of the KGB*, with Marina Litvinenko (New York: Free Press, 2007), 54–55.

64. Aven, *Vremia Berezovskogo*, 149; Klebnikov, *Godfather of the Kremlin*, 116–17.

65. Aven, *Vremia Berezovskogo*, 133.

66. Mikhail Zygar, *Vse svobodny: Istoriia o tom, kak v 1996 godu v Rossii zakonchilis' vybory* (Moscow: Al'pina, 2020), Kindle ed., 41–42.

67. Timothy J. Colton, *Yeltsin: A Life* (New York: Basic Books, 2008), 340–41. A copy of the membership rules, signed by Yeltsin and the ten other founders of the club, is in the Yeltsin archives: https://yeltsin.ru/archive/ paperwork/48914/. Members were allowed to bring wives and children as guests on Sundays.

68. Aleksandr Korzhakov, *Boris El'tsin: ot rassveta do zakata. Posleslovie* (Moscow, Detektivpress, 2004). This is the second, revised edition of the original, published in 1997. Korzhakov provided extensive details about Berezovsky in interviews with Klebnikov for the latter's book but, given Korzhakov's deep hatred of Berezovsky after the two fell out in 1996, his accounts cannot be taken as reliable.

69. Boris Yeltsin, *Midnight Diaries*, trans. Catherine A. Fitzpatrick (New York: Public Affairs, 2000), 215.

70. Yeltsin, *Midnight Diaries*, 39–40.

71. Unpublished interview with Berezovsky, in Boris Berezovsky, *The Art of the Impossible* (Falmouth, MA: Terra-USA, 2006), 1:332–64 (357).

72. Hoffman, *Oligarchs*, 281–84; Gordon, *Berezovskii i Korzhakov*, 52–55.

73. Hoffman, *Oligarchs*, 527–28 (note 26).

74. Klebnikov, *Godfather of the Kremlin*, 159–69.

75. See "Kollegi Vladislava List'eva napisali imia predpolagaemogo ubiitsy," *Lenta.ru*, February 16, 2020. https://lenta.ru/news/2020/02/26/listyev/.

76. *Chestnyi Detektiv*, interview with Al'bina Nazimova, https://www.you tube.com/watch?v=NWvQNxQtXLA.

3. Elections and Beyond

1. Korzhakov, *Boris El'tsin*, 325–26.

2. Colton, *Yeltsin*, 291.

3. Yeltsin, *Midnight Diaries*, 16.

4. Berezovsky interview with Nataliya Gevorkyan, *Kommersant*, June 17, 1997, in Berezovsky, *Art of the Impossible*, 1:131–45; Berezovsky, *Avtoportret*,

41–42. Soros, who would later come to despise Berezovsky, recalled the meeting differently: "I wanted him [Berezovsky] to support Grigory Yavlinsky, whom I considered the only honest reformer among the candidates, but I was naïve. I did not realize to what extent Berezovsky was involved in dirty dealings with Yeltsin's family" (George Soros, "Who Lost Russia," *New York Review of Books*, April 13, 2000.)

5. Hoffman, *Oligarchs*, 285–93. Gusinsky was even forced to flee with his family to London for a few months.

6. Goldfarb, *Death of a Dissident*, 64–65.

7. Interview with Gevorkyan, 132.

8. Interview with Gevorkyan, 134; Colton, *Yeltsin*, 355; Hoffman, *Oligarchs*, 332–33. Hoffman writes that Gusinsky also spoke.

9. Hoffman, *Oligarchs*, 333.

10. Yeltsin, *Midnight Diaries*, 25; Colton, *Yeltsin*, 356–57; Hoffman, *Oligarchs*, 336–40.

11. Hoffman, *Oligarchs*, 348–50; Zygar, *Vse svobodny*, 204–6.

12. Klebnikov, *Godfather of the Kremlin*, 222–23. Yeltsin later said: "All the big shots of business were drawn into the election headquarters. They 'made investments'—some in logistic support, some in conceptual thinking, and some financially" (*Midnight Diaries*, 26).

13. Aven, *Vremia Berezovskogo*, 156–57; Klebnikov, *Godfather of the Kremlin*, 236–37; Colton, *Yeltsin*, 360; Goldfarb, *Death of a Dissident*, 77–78; Hoffman, *Oligarchs*, 348.

14. Goldfarb, *Death of a Dissident*, 80.

15. Berezovsky, *Art of the Impossible*, 1:138.

16. Khinshtein, *Berezovskii i Abramovich*, 209–29.

17. "Aleksei Venediktov o Borise Berezovskom," *Ekho Moskvy*, March 24, 2013, https://echo.msk.ru/programs/svoi-glaza/1038068-echo/.

18. Aven, *Vremia Berezovskogo*, 156.

19. Zygar, *Vse svobodny*, 429.

20. Zygar, *Vse svobodny*, 329–30.

21. Film *Delo Sobchaka*. Interviewed for the film, Putin says: "It was absolutely obvious to me that Western leaders treated him [Sobchak] like a potential successor to Yeltsin."

22. Film *Delo Sobchaka*.

23. See Yeltsin, *Midnight Diaries*, 323–26. Yeltsin feigned disapproval of the attack against Sobchak by Korzhakov and Skuratov, but he did nothing to stop them. Sobchak himself suggests in his book about the campaign that Yeltsin gave Korzhakov and his men orders to move against him (*Diuzhina nozhei v spinu: Pouchitel'naia istoriia o politicheskikh nravakh* [Moscow: Vagrius-Petro-News, 1999], 78–81).

24. Mikhail Vil'kobrisskii, *Kak delili Rossiiu: Istoriia privatizatsii* (St. Petersburg: Piter, 2014), 185. Vil'kobrisskii later emigrated to Israel.

25. Interview with Aleksei Shustov, *Radio Svoboda*, February 5, 2016, https://www.svoboda.org/a/27534956.html.

26. Film *Delo Sobchaka*.

27. Putin, *First Person*, 112–13.

28. Zygar, *Vse svobodny*, 330.

29. Putin, *First Person*, 113.

30. The letter is reproduced in Sobchak, *Diuzhina nozhei v spinu*, 92–93.

31. Zapol'skii, *Putinburg*, 112.

32. Zapol'skii, *Putinburg*, 433–45.

33. Belton, *Putin's People*, 113.

34. Sobchak, *Diuzhina nozhei v spinu*, 92.

35. Putin, *First Person*, 113.

36. Zapol'skii interview with *Radio Svoboda*, June 5, 2016, https://www.svoboda.org/a/27777165.html.

37. This was noted by Myers, *New Tsar*, 108.

38. Putin, *First Person*, 125–28; Blotskii, *Doroga k vlasti*, 385–94.

39. Blotskii, *Doroga k vlasti*, 361. Later in the book (386–87), Putin is quoted as saying that Iakovlev may have wanted him to leave St. Petersburg because his "especially warm relations" with the power organs made Iakovlev uncomfortable.

40. Putin, *First Person*, 122.

41. "Kudrin rasskazal o druzhbe s Putinym," *Lenta.ru*, October 12, 2020, https://lenta.ru/news/2020/10/12/kunrin_putin/.

42. See Navalny, "Dvorets dlia Putina"; David Crawford and Marcus Bensmann, "Putin's Early Years," *Correctiv*, July 30, 2015, https://web.archive.org/web/20190509203842/https://correctiv.org/en/latest-stories/the-system-of-putin/2015/07/30/putins-early-years.

43. Felshtinsky and Pribylovsky, *Corporation*, 112.

44. Blotskii, *Doroga k vlasti*, 398–99.

45. Colton, *Yeltsin*, 327.

46. Zygar, *Vse svobodny*, 114.

47. Zygar, *Vse svobodny*, 114.

48. As cited in Dawisha, *Putin's Kleptocracy*, 172.

49. Berezovsky interview with *Zavtra*, October 29, 2002, in Berezovsky, *Art of the Impossible*, 1:573–77 (576).

50. "Venediktov o Borise Berezovskom." Akhmad Kadyrov's son Ramzan would later become Chechnya's notoriously ruthless president.

51. Anatolii Kulikov, *Tiazhelye zvezdy* (Moscow: Voina i mir buks, 2002). Electronic version at https://royallib.com/book/kulikov_anatoliy/tyagelie_zvezdi.html, 105–7.

52. Kulikov, *Tiazhelye zvezdy*, 105–7; Michael Spector, "The Wars of Aleksandr Ivanovich Lebed," *New York Times*, October 13, 1996, https://www.nytimes.com/1996/10/13/magazine/the-wars-of-aleksandr-ivanovich-lebed.html; Zygar, *Vse svobodny*, 458–59.

53. *Kommersant*, October 31, 1996, English translation in Berezovsky, *Art of the Impossible*, 1:468–69.

54. Blog of Aleksei [Leonid] D'iachenko *Ekho Moskvy*, July 2, 2021, http://www.relga.ru/Environ/WebObjects/tgu-www.woa/wa/Main?textid=6680&level1=main&level2=articles.

55. Chrystia Freeland, John Thornhill, and Andrew Gowers, "Moscow's Group of Seven," *Financial Times*, November 1, 1996, https://archive.

org/details/FinancialTimes1996UKEnglish/Nov%2001%201996%2C%20
Financial%20Times%2C%20%231%2C%20UK%20%28en%29/page/n13/
mode/2up.

56. Sergei Lukianov, "The Berezovsky 7: Russia Inc.," *St. Petersburg Times*, no. 215–16, November 25–December 25, 1996, https://web.archive.org/web/20000818172446/http://www.sptimes.ru/archive/times/215-216/bc.html.

57. "Godfather of the Kremlin?," *Forbes*. A subcaption reads: "Boris Berezovsky could teach the guys in Sicily a thing or two." *Forbes* repeated the article's allegations about Berezovsky after the latter's death in 2013, adding, wrongly, that the oligarch was the key suspect in the 2004 killing of Klebnikov. See Richard Behar, "Did Boris Berezovsky Kill Himself?," *Forbes*, March 24, 2013, https://www.forbes.com/sites/richardbehar/2013/03/24/did-boris-berezovsky-kill-himself-more-compelling-did-he-kill-forbes-editor-paul-klebnikov/?sh=5a02f3567295.

58. Christian Caryl, "The Tycoon and the World He Has Made, *Wall Street Journal*, September 18, 2000, https://www.wsj.com/articles/SB96881047497103152.

59. Mrs. Justice Gloster, "Approved Judgment, Berezovsky v. Abramovich," August 31, 2012, https://www.judiciary.uk/wp-content/uploads/JCO/Documents/Judgments/berezovsky-judgment.pdf; Vladislav Dorofeev and Tat'iana Kostyleva, *Printsip Abramovicha: Talant delat' den'gi*, (Moscow: Kommersant', 2009), chap. 2, https://www.kommersant.ru/doc/1180652.

60. Gloster, "Approved Judgment, Berezovsky v. Abramovich." Also see "Bitva za 'Sibneft'," *FreeLance Bureau*, February 18, 2000, http://www.compromat.ru/page_9457.htm.

61. "AvtoVAZbank rasshiriaet svoiu deiatel'nost' v Moskve," *Kommersant*, May 23, 1995, https://www.kommersant.ru/doc/109377; Interview with Berezovsky, *Kommersant*, November 16, 1995, https://www.kommersant.ru/doc/121790; Klebnikov, *Godfather of the Kremlin*, 170–72.

62. Goldfarb, *Death of a Dissident*, 142–43; Berezovsky interview in *Kommersant*, April 13, 1999, in Berezovsky, *Art of the Impossible*, 1:186–96; Mrs. Justice Rose, "Approved Judgment, PJSC Aeroflot-Russians Airlines v Leeds & Anor (Trustees of the Estate of Boris Berezovsky) & Ors," July 6, 2018, https://www.casemine.com/judgement/uk/5b443b1f2c94e02f3f9261ce.

63. Glushkov interview in *Kommersant*, November 23, 2000, in Berezovsky, *Art of the Impossible*, 2:537–46 (542); Hoffman, *Oligarchs*, 401.

64. Alan Cullison, "A Trio of Wealthy Russians Made an Enemy of Putin: Now They're All Dead," *Wall Street Journal*, October 10, 2018, citing Glushkov's witness statement in Aeroflot v. Leeds & Anor, https://www.wsj.com/articles/a-trio-of-wealthy-russians-made-an-enemy-of-putin-now-theyre-all-dead-1539181416.

65. Rose, "Approved Judgment, Aeroflot v. Leeds & Anor"; Iurii Skuratov, *Kremlevskie podriady: Poslednee delo Genprokurora* (Moscow: Litres, 2017), https://play.google.com/books/reader?id=bUthAAAAQBAJ&pg=GBS.PT1, 159–171.

66. Lilia Shevtsova, "Dilemmas of Post-Communist Russia," *Security Dialogue* 28, no. 1 (1997): 83–96.

4. Behind Kremlin Walls

1. Zygar, *Vse svobodny*, chap. 9, 462.
2. Colton, *Yeltsin*, 381.
3. Yeltsin, *Midnight Diaries*, 73.
4. Boris Nemtsov, *Ispoved' buntaria* (Moscow: Partizan, 2007), 27.
5. Boris Nemtsov, personal site, "Umer Boris Berezovskii," http://nemtsov.ru/old/indexc212.html?id=718739.
6. Blotskii, *Doroga k vlasti*, 399.
7. Elena Tregubova, *Baiki kremlevskogo diggera* (Moscow: Ad Marginem, 2003), http://www.belousenko.com/books/kgb/tregubova_bayki.htm, chap. 8.
8. Myers, *New Tsar*, 112.
9. Nemtsov, *Ispoved' buntaria*, 55.
10. Putin, *First Person*, 87.
11. Published in disserCat, an electronic library of Russian dissertations, https://www.dissercat.com/content/strategicheskoe-planirovanie-vosproizvodstva-mineralno-syrevoi-bazy-regiona-v-usloviyakh-for.
12. Dmitrii Volchek, "Kseroks na dache: Taina fal'shivoi dissertatsii Vladimira Putina," Radio Svoboda, March 4, 2018, https://www.svoboda.org/a/29076908.html; Anastasiia Kirilenko, "Gorniaki-razboiniki: Kak 'literaturnyi negr' Putina i Sechina stal rektorom-milliarderom," *The Insider*, August 7, 2017, https://theins.ru/korrupciya/66920.
13. Kirilenko, "Gorniaki-razboiniki."
14. Fiona Hill and Clifford G. Gaddy, *Mr. Putin: Operative in the Kremlin* (Washington, DC: Brookings Institution Press, 2013), Kindle ed., chap. 9, loc. 3685–728.
15. Kirilenko, "Gorniaki-razboiniki."
16. "Putin's Doctoral Thesis Director Makes Forbes' Billionaires List," RFE/RL, April 7, 2021, https://www.rferl.org/a/litvinenko-billionaire-forbes-putin-thesis/31191104.html.
17. Liza Vel'iaminova, "Rektor-milliarder," MBX Media, March 29, 2021, https://mbk-news.appspot.com/suzhet/rektor-milliarder/.
18. Goldfarb, *Death of a Dissident*, 109.
19. Matthew Evangelista, *The Chechen Wars: Will Russia Go the Way of the Soviet Union?* (Washington, DC: Brookings Institution Press, 2002), Kindle ed., chap. 3, loc. 732–36.
20. Berezovsky news conference, May 13, 1997, reported by the Federal News Service, cited in Berezovsky, *Art of the Impossible*, 1:504.
21. Reuters, June 13, 1997, https://reliefweb.int/report/russian-federation/russia-chechen-sign-oil-deal-chechnya.
22. Goldfarb, *Death of a Dissident*, 114–15.
23. Evangelista, *Chechen Wars*, chap. 3, loc. 746–51.
24. Nemtsov, "Umer Boris Berezovskii."
25. Hoffman, *Oligarchs*, 380.
26. Hoffman, *Oligarchs*, 380–82; "Bor'ba oligarkhov za 'Sviaz'invest': Spravka," RIA Novosti, July 25, 2011, https://ria.ru/20110725/406846261.html.
27. Valentin Iumashev, "Sviaz'invest," https://nemtsovdoc.ru/life/video-text/26.

28. Hoffman, *Oligarchs*, 384–86.

29. "Zapis' telefonnogo razgovora Borisa Berezovskogo s docher'iu El'tsina—Tat'ianoi D'iachenko," Kompromat.ru, August 1, 1997, http://www.compromat.ru/page_25022.htm.

30. Nemtsov, *Ispoved' buntaria*, 24–25.

31. Nemtsov, *Ispoved' buntaria*, 24.

32. Hoffman, *Oligarchs*, 388–89.

33. Goldfarb, *Death of a Dissident*, 116.

34. Yeltsin, *Midnight Diaries*, 98.

35. Hoffman, *Oligarchs*, 393. Also see Nataliia Rostova, "Vtoraia infor-matsionnaia," Radio Svoboda, December 2, 2017, https://www.svoboda.org/a/28890678.html.

36. Nemtsov testifying during the London court trial of a defamation lawsuit brought by Berezovsky against Mikhail Fridman, May 22, 2006. See Yuri Felshtinsky's compilation of the trial transcripts (*Verdikt: Boris Berezovskii protiv oligarkhov* [Falmouth, MA: Terra-USA, 2008], 356).

37. Sergei Pluzhnikov, "'Kvartirnoe delo' Sobchaka," *Sovershenno sekretno*, February 4, 1997, http://www.compromat.ru/page_10202.htm; Felshtinsky and Pribylovsky, *Corporation*, 228–31; Dawisha, *Putin's Kleptocracy*, 152–53, 174–76.

38. Pavel Voshchanov, "Ten' Sobchaka-2," *Novaia gazeta*, June 23, 1997, http://www.compromat.ru/page_26663.htm.

39. Sergei Pluzhnikov and Sergei Sokolov, "Ten' prezidenta," Freelance Bureau, January 15, 2000, www.compromat.ru/page_9319.htm.

40. Andrei Illarionov, LiveJournal post, June 7, 2019, https://aillarionov.livejournal.com/1128924.html, citing interviews for the film *Delo Sobchaka*.

41. Yeltsin, *Midnight Diaries*, 233.

42. Skuratov, *Kremlevskie podriady*, 322.

43. A leaked transcript of the conversation was published by *Novaia gazeta* on September 29, 1998, at http://www.compromat.ru/page_26662.htm.

44. Yeltsin, *Midnight Diaries*, 234.

45. Skuratov, *Kremlevskie podriady*, 321.

46. Felshtinsky and Pribylovsky, *Corporation*, 231–32; Myers, *New Tsar*, 117–18; Skuratov, *Kremlevskie podriady*, 323.

47. Skuratov, *Kremlevskie podriady*, 323. Philip Short, apparently to show that Putin's motives were innocent, says that the idea that Sobchak was corrupt is implausible, because he didn't pay for the charter flight to Paris, which was financed by Putin's friend Gennadii Timchenko (Short, *Putin*, 752n62). But in Russia at that time, it was not necessary to have money to charter a private plane in order to be corrupt.

48. Illarionov, LiveJournal, June 7, 2019.

49. Yeltsin, *Midnight Diaries*, 234.

50. Putin, *First Person*, 117–18.

51. Illarionov, LiveJournal, June 7, 2019.

52. Hoffman, *Oligarchs*, 402.

53. Hoffman, *Oligarchs,* 407–9. On September 2, 1998, Berezovsky told Venediktov on *Ekho Moskvy*: "I designated Kiriyenko's appointment from the

start as an entirely nonsensical move . . . a person with weight, with authority [was] needed" (*Art of the Impossible*, 3:272).

54. Andrei Bagrov, "El'tsin ugrozhaet Berezovskomu emigratsiei," *Kommersant*, April 15, 1998, https://on-demand.eastview.com/browse/doc/3748132.

55. Yeltsin, *Midnight Diaries*, 246–47; Aven, *Vremia Berezovskogo*, 642–44. Yeltsin recalled that when he told Iumashev about the proposal to appoint Berezovsky, "I have never seen Yumashev so mad." Iumashev said that Berezovsky never consulted with him about his ambition to become CIS secretary. But Khinshtein claimed that Iumashev engineered Berezovsky's appointment (*Berezovskii i Abramovich*, 347).

56. Interview with NTV, June 8, 1998, in Berezovsky, *Art of the Impossible*, 2:30–36.

57. Berezovsky statement on CIS, *Nezavisimaia gazeta*, November 13, 1998, in Berezovsky, *Art of the Impossible*, 2:39–68.

58. "Aleksei Venediktov o Borise Berezovskom."

59. Berezovsky interview with Aleksei Venediktov, *Ekho Moskvy*, September 2, 1998, in Berezovsky, *Art of the Impossible*, 3:268–80.

60. Myers, *New Tsar*, 121; Dawisha, *Putin's Kleptocracy*, 181–82.

61. Putin, *First Person*, 129.

62. Putin, *First Person*, 130–32.

63. See Amy Knight, *Spies without Cloaks: The KGB's Successors* (Princeton, NJ: Princeton University Press, 1996); and Andrei Soldatov and Irina Borogan, *The New Nobility: The Restoration of Russia's Security State and the Enduring Legacy of the KGB* (New York: Public Affairs, 2010) on the evolution of the Russian security services after 1991.

64. Tregubova, *Baiki kremlevskogo diggera*, chap. 8.

65. Yeltsin, *Midnight Diaries*, 327.

66. Igor Chernyak: "Once More Kovalev Has Gotten Burnt; Why Did President Give FSB Leader a Dressing Down?," *Komsomol'skaia pravda*, July 28, 1998, Johnson's Russia List, http://www.russialist.org/archives/2289.html##5.

67. Felshtinsky and Pribylovsky, *Corporation*, 118.

68. Putin, *First Person*, 133.

69. Goldfarb, *Death of a Dissident*, 134–35. Berezovsky told Masha Gessen a slightly different version, claiming that he had actually suggested Putin as a candidate for the FSB spot to Iumashev (Gessen, *Man without a Face*, 18).

70. "Vladimir Putin: U menia bol'shoi opyt raboty v KGB SSSR," *Kommersant*, July 30, 1998, https://on-demand.eastview.com/browse/doc/3754781.

71. Yeltsin, *Midnight Diaries*, 328.

72. Tregubova, *Baiki kremlevskogo diggera*, chap. 8.

5. Turmoil

1. For an overview of the crisis, see a report from the US Congressional Research Service, "The Russian Financial Crisis of 1998: An Analysis of Trends, Causes, and Implications," February 18, 1999, https://www.everycr sreport.com/files/19990218_98-578_353c595b8980dfeaab66aa782deab289 8c3b6889.pdf.

2. Myers, *New Tsar*, 129.

3. Berezovsky interview with Venediktov, September 1998.

4. Yeltsin, *Midnight Diaries*, 183–84.

5. Shevtsova, *Putin's Russia*, 17.

6. See a report on a meeting of the CIS in late November 1998 at http://www.aparchive.com/metadata/youtube/546f5fed71383d537b613592c1397e67.

7. Goldfarb, *Death of a Dissident*, 144.

8. Putin, *First Person*, 133.

9. Tatiana Iumasheva, "Kak Primakov pytalsia uvolut' Putina," LiveJournal, March 15, 2010, https://t-yumasheva.livejournal.com/19015.html. As cited in Dawisha, *Putin's Kleptocracy*, 186.

10. Iumashev interview with Vladmir Pozner, *Vedomosti*, November 22, 2019, https://www.vedomosti.ru/politics/articles/2019/11/22/816979-on-videl-cheloveka-prodolzhit. Iumashev told Catherine Belton a similar story (Belton, *Putin's People*, 140–41).

11. Nemtsov, *Ispoved' buntaria*, 53.

12. For an English translation and analysis of the article, see Andrei Soshnikov and Carl Schreck, "The Brutal Killing of a Reporter Who Probed Putin's Past," RFE/RL, June 22, 2022, https://www.rferl.org/a/putin-journalist-killing/31910359.html.

13. *Segodnia*, August 26, 1998; *Moscow Times*, August 28, 1998. Domnin held a press conference about the murder, in which he mentioned another *Iuridicheskii Peterburg segodnia* article, about Kredit Bank and illegal campaign financing, which suggested that Berezovsky owned the bank and thus provided Berezovsky with a motive for going after his paper. But *Kommersant* reported that Kredit Bank called the newspaper and dismissed the idea of Berezovsky's ownership as ridiculous (*Kommersant*, August 26, 1998, https://www.kommersant.ru/doc/203983).

14. Apparently because Starovoitova spoke out against antisemitism, Philip Short writes, incorrectly, that she was Jewish (*Putin*, 265). In fact, she had no Jewish heritage and was a devout believer in the Russian Orthodox faith.

15. Myers, *New Tsar*, 134; Yeltsin, *Midnight Diaries*, 211.

16. "Kto ubil Galinu Starovoitovu? 20 let spustia zakazchika vse eshche ishchut," *The Insider*, November 20, 2018, https://theins.ru/obshestvo/128361.

17. Yeltsin, *Midnight Diaries*, 211.

18. Dawisha, *Putin's Kleptocracy*, 252–56. A full copy is available on the website of Dawisha, which is maintained by the Havighurst Center at Miami University of Ohio: https://www.miamioh.edu/cas/academics/centers/havighurst/additional-resources/putins-russia/index.html.

19. Knight, *Orders to Kill*, 65–71. Vladimir Zhirinovsky, head of the rightwing LDRP party, was another enemy of Starovoitova whom prosecutors later tried to incriminate.

20. Matthew Evangelista, "An Interview with Galina Starovoitova," Moscow, November 3, 1998, https://matthewevangelistacom.files.wordpress.com/2018/09/interview-with-galina-starovoytova1.pdf.

21. *Komsomol'skaia pravda*, November 27–December 4, 1998, Johnson's Russia List, http://www.russialist.org/archives/2497.html##13.

22. Knight, *Orders to Kill*, 64–67.

23. Daniel Williams, "Russian Aide's Scars Run Deep," *Washington Post*, January 30, 1999, https://www.washingtonpost.com/archive/politics/1999/01/30/russian-aides-scars-run-deep/2c14e969-9413-4a53-b696-56ce99aafe36/.

24. Knight, *Orders to Kill*, 68–69.

25. "Kto ubil Galinu Starovoitovu?"

26. "FSB prediavila Barsukovu-Kumarinu ubiistvo Starovoitovoi," Fontanka.ru, April 7, 2019, https://www.fontanka.ru/2019/04/07/026/.

27. Vitalii Portnikov, "Tak kto zhe ubil Starovoitovu?" Krym.Realii, April 10, 2019, https://ru.krymr.com/a/vitaliy-portnikov-tak-kto-zhe-ubil-starovoytovu/29872089.html.

28. Knight, *Orders to Kill*, 149–50.

29. Berezovsky witness statement for Britain's High Court, January 22, 2009, https://webarchive.nationalarchives.gov.uk/ukgwa/20160613090305/https:/www.litvinenkoinquiry.org/files/2015/04/BER000011wb.pdf.

30. Alexander Litvinenko, *LPG: Lubianskaia prestupnaia gruppirovka* (New York: Grani, 2002), chap. 6, http://www.compromat.ru/page_12267.htm.

31. Goldfarb, *Death of a Dissident*, 39–40.

32. Litvinenko, *LPG*, chap. 6; Goldfarb, *Death of a Dissident*, 129–33.

33. Aleksandr Khinshtein, "Boris Abramovich, mne porucheno vas ubit'," *Moskovskii komsomolets*, May 22, 1998, https://on-demand.eastview.com/browse/doc/97473.

34. Berezovsky, *Art of the Impossible*, 2:402–5.

35. Berezovsky, *Art of the Impossible*, 2:408–9.

36. Myers, *New Tsar*, 132.

37. "Nas peredushat, kak shchenkov," *Kommersant*, November 18, 1998, https://on-demand.eastview.com/browse/doc/3760297.

38. Myers, *New Tsar*, 133.

39. "Ofitser po vyzovu," *Moskovskii komsomolets*, November 20, 1998, https://on-demand.eastview.com/browse/doc/101370. The article was unsigned, but it was clear Khinshtein was the author.

40. Sir Robert Owen, *The Litvinenko Inquiry: Report into the Death of Alexander Litvinenko*, London, January 2016, https://webarchive.nationalarchives.gov.uk/ukgwa/20160613090324/https://www.litvinenkoinquiry.org/report, 21–25.

41. "Vladimir Putin: Vernite 'zhelzhogo Feliksa' na ploshchad'—tol'ko potom ne pishchite!," *Izvestiia*, December 19, 1998, https://on-demand.eastview.com/browse/doc/3170935.

42. Skuratov, *Kremlevskie podriady*, 167–68.

43. Khinshtein, "Kolpak dlia prezidenta," *Moskovskii komsomolets*, January 20, 1999, http://www.compromat.ru/page_25070.htm.

44. Khinshtein, "Sekretar' dlinnoe ukho," *Moskovskii komsomolets*, February 12, 1999, https://on-demand.eastview.com/browse/doc/103260.

45. See Berezovsky's interview in *Kommersant*, April 13, 1999, in Berezovsky, *Art of the Impossible*, 1:186–96 (188).

46. Skuratov, *Kremlevskie podriady*, 179; *Kommersant*, January 29, 1999, https://on-demand.eastview.com/browse/doc/3762994.

47. Hoffman, *Oligarchs*, 459–60.

48. Skuratov, *Kremlevskie podriady*, 296.

49. Skuratov, *Kremlevskie podriady*, 298.

50. Iurii Skuratov, *Variant drakona* (Moscow: Detektiv-Press, 2002), 24–26.

51. Skuratov, *Variant drakona*, 30.

52. Yeltsin, *Midnight Diaries*, 212. Iumashev assured Yeltsin that he would stay by his side.

53. Skuratov, *Kremlevskie podriady*, 180–86.

54. In a 2019 interview, Iumashev acknowledged that he was the one who passed on the tape to Bordiuzha. See Andrei Mal'gin, "Operatsiia 'preemnik,' chast' 3," LiveJournal, August 9, 2019, https://avmalgin.livejournal.com/8156562.html. Sergei Pugachev, a wealthy Russian banker who fled Russia in 2008 after falling out with Putin, told author Catherine Belton that he had obtained the tape and given it to Iumashev (Belton, *Putin's People*, 127–28). But Pugachev was not mentioned by any of those involved, and he seems to have exaggerated his role in Kremlin affairs during his interviews with Belton.

55. This communication was published in *Novaia gazeta*, July 9, 1999, http://www.compromat.ru/page_26939.htm. Chaika also reported details on the Aeroflot case.

56. "Privet iz 90-ykh: Siuzhet pro cheloveka, ochen' pokhozhego na general'nogo prokurora," https://www.youtube.com/watch?v=jqGbV6F5fAw.

57. Skuratov, *Kremlevskie podriady*, 14–16.

58. Skuratov, *Kremlevskie podriady*, 17.

59. Skuratov, *Kremlevskie podriady*, 214–16.

60. Skuratov, *Kremlevskie podriady*, 375–77.

61. Aleksandr Khinshtein, "Karla del' Ponte: My so Skuratovym khotim vernut' v Rossiiu prestupnye kapitaly," *Moskovskii komsomolets*, March 25, 1999, https://on-demand.eastview.com/browse/doc/104269; Jamestown Foundation, *Monitor* 5, no. 58 (March 24, 1999), https://jamestown.org/program/borodin-mabetex-chief-deny-charges/.

62. As reported in *The Guardian*, March 23, 1999, https://www.theguardian.com/world/1999/mar/24/7.

63. NTV, April 1, 1999, http://www.russialist.org/archives/3224.html##3.

64. Nikolai Ul'ianov, "Skuratov otstranen ot dolzhnosti," *Nezavisimaia gazeta*, April 3, 1999, https://on-demand.eastview.com/browse/doc/322674; *Kommersant*, April 3, 1999, https://www.kommersant.ru/doc/216188.

65. Skuratov, *Kremlevskie podriady*, 665.

66. Malgin, "Operatsiia 'Preemnik.'"

67. *Kommersant*, March 5, 1999, https://on-demand.eastview.com/browse/doc/3764809.

68. Yeltsin, *Midnight Diaries*, 246–47.

69. Berezovsky, *Art of the Impossible*, 2:448–51.

70. As quoted in Berezovsky, *Art of the Impossible*, 2:455.

71. ITAR-TASS, April 12, 1999, Johnson's Russia List, http://www.rus
sialist.org/archives/3238.html##9.

72. As quoted in John Dunlop, *The Moscow Bombings of September 1999: Examinations of Russian Terrorist Attacks at the Onset of Vladimir Putin's Rule* (Stuttgart: ibidem, 2014), 26.

73. Voloshin biography, *Lenta.ru*, https://lenta.ru/lib/14160884/full.htm. Also see Voloshin's interview with Aven, *Vremia Berezovskogo*, 255–64.

74. Voloshin biography.

75. Berezovsky interview with *Vedomosti*, March 24, 2000, in Berezovsky, *Art of the Impossible*, 2:277–83 (279).

76. Vladimir Volkov and Patrick Richter, "What Is behind the Dismissal of Russian Prime Minister Yevgeny Primakov," World Socialist Web Site, May 25, 1999, https://www.wsws.org/en/articles/1999/05/prim-m25.html.

77. Gessen, *Man without a Face*, 18–19.

78. Goldfarb, *Death of a Dissident*, 164–65.

79. Khinshtein, *Berezovskii i Abramovich*, 365.

80. Iren Pitch (Irene Pietsch), *Pikantnaia druzhba: Moia podruga Liudmila Putina, ee sem'ia i drugie tovarishchi* (Moscow: Zakharov, 2002), 188, 263. Finnish Ambassador Markus Lyra told Philip Short that, during a conversation he had with Putin in late 1998, Putin said of Berezovsky: "He is the worst criminal you can think of. He's going to damage Russia and will damage your country too" (Short, *Putin*, 262).

6. An Heir to the Throne

1. Irina Bobrova, "Tainaia zhizn' suprugi oligarkha," *Moskovskii komsomolets*, February 17, 2005, https://www.mk.ru/editions/daily/article/2005/02/17/199725-taynaya-zhizn-suprugi-oligarha.html.

2. Crawford and Bensmann, "Putin's Early Years"; Myers, *New Tsar*, 152.

3. Khinshtein, *Berezovskii i Abramovich*, 350–51.

4. Shevtsova, *Putin's Russia*, 28.

5. Hassan Abbas, "Who Exactly Is Sergei Stepashin?" The Jamestown Foundation, *Prism* 5, no. 10 (May 21, 1999), https://jamestown.org/program/who-exactly-is-sergei-stepashin/.

6. Colton, *Yeltsin*, 430. Stepashin said this in a 2001 interview with Colton.

7. Elena Dikun, "Primakov Is Shown the Door; Duma Threatened with Dissolution," The Jamestown Foundation, *Prism* 5, no. 10 (May 21, 1999), https://jamestown.org/program/primakov-is-shown-the-door-duma-threatened-with-dissolution/.

8. Colton, *Yeltsin*, 428–29; Vitalii Tsepliaev and Tat'iana Netreba, "Prezident gotov k pokhoronam kommunizma," *Argumenty i Fakty*, May 19, 1999, https://on-demand.eastview.com/browse/doc/2555262.

9. Carnegie Endowment for International Peace, Meeting Report, May 19, 1999, "Chubais on Stepashin and the Irreversibility of Russian Reform," https://carnegieendowment.org/1999/05/19/chubais-on-stepashin-and-irreversibility-of-russian-reform-event-118.

10. Colton, *Yeltsin*, 430.

11. See excerpts from a book by journalist Ilia Zhegulev in *Meduza*, October 20, 2021, https://meduza.io/feature/2021/10/20/pravda-li-chto-v-1999-godu-u-eltsina-ne-bylo-drugih-realnyh-variantov-preemnika-krome-putina. Also see Iumashev's comments in Aven, *Vremia Berezovskogo*, 249–50.

12. Yeltsin, *Midnight Diaries*, 284–85.

13. Associated Press Newsroom, "Germany: Stepashin Attends G8 Summit Meeting," June 19, 1999, http://www.aparchive.com/metadata/youtube/8634dabe12b4322106a018d0819fd809.

14. Stepashin interview with CBS, July 23, 1999, https://www.cbsnews.com/news/stepashin-intrreview-in-full/.

15. "Stepashin Falls Victim to Success of His Economic Policies," Bloomberg, Moscow, August 9, 1999, Johnson's Russia List, http://www.russialist.org/archives/3428.html##10.

16. Vasif Guseinov, *Ot El'tsina k . . . ? Voina kompromata* (Moscow: Olma-Press, 2000), 59–60.

17. RFE/RL *Newsline* 4, no. 20, pt. 1, January 28, 2000, https://www.rferl.org/a/1142082.html; Evangelista, *Chechen Wars*, chap. 3, loc. 838–47.

18. Dunlop, *Moscow Bombings*, 35.

19. David Hoffman, "Miscalculations Paved Path to Chechen War," *Washington Post*, March 20, 2000, https://www.washingtonpost.com/archive/politics/2000/03/20/miscalculations-paved-path-to-chechen-war/e675f17a-d286-4b5e-b33a-708d819d43f0/.

20. Emil Souleimanov, "Chechnya, Wahhabism and the Invasion of Dagestan," *Middle East Review of International Affairs* 9, no. 4 (December 2005), 48–71, https://ciaotest.cc.columbia.edu/olj/meria/meria_dec05/Souleimanov.pdf.

21. Floriana Fossato, "Caucasus: Kidnapping of Russian General Presents Complications for Chechen President," RFE/RL, March 17, 1999, https://www.rferl.org/a/1090815.html.

22. Goldfarb, *Death of a Dissident*, 186–88; Also see Andrei Illarionov, "Dagestanskaia voina—operatsiia 'preemnik,'" *The Chechen Press*, March 13, 2019, https://thechechenpress.com/news/14962-andrej-illarionov-dagestanskaya-vojna-operatsiya-preemnik.html; and a lengthy discussion of Berezovsky's ties with Chechen extremists in Dunlop, *Moscow Bombings*, 53–65. Dunlop takes a skeptical view of Berezovsky's version.

23. Goldfarb, *Death of a Dissident*, 188–89.

24. Putin, *First Person*, 188.

25. Dunlop, *Moscow Bombings*, 66–70; Andrei Piontkovskii, "Rassledovanie: Priznanie oligarkha prokuroru respubliki," *Novaia gazeta*, January 21, 2002, https://novayagazeta.ru/articles/2002/01/21/15962-priznanie-oligarha-prokuroru-respubliki.

26. Henry E. Hale, "The Origins of United Russia and the Putin Presidency: The Role of Contingency in Party-System Development, *Demokratizatsiya: The Journal of Post-Soviet Demokratization* 12, no. 2 (2004):169–94, https://demokratizatsiya.pub/archives/12_2_P0LVW06724GL62M9.pdf.

27. Mikhail Zygar, *All the Kremlin's Men: Inside the Court of Vladimir Putin* (New York: Public Affairs, 2016), 8–9.

28. Yeltsin, *Midnight Diaries*, 294–95.

29. Yeltsin, *Midnight Diaries*, 295.

30. Melissa Akin and Natalya Shulyakovskaya, "Swiss Tie Kremlin to Money-Laundering," *Moscow Times*, July 15, 1999, Johnson's Russia List, http://www.russialist.org/archives/3394.html##1.

31. As quoted in Dunlop, *Moscow Bombings*, 41.

32. Interview with Nataliya Gevorkyan, *Vremia MN*, July 13, 1999, in Berezovsky, *Art of the Impossible*, 1:197–213.

33. Timothy Heritage, "Russian Premier Demands End to Media War," Reuters, July 19, 1999, http://www.russialist.org/archives/3398.html##1.

34. Khinshtein, *Berezovskii i Abramovich*, 362. Also see Celestine Bohlen, "In Russia, a Power Play Acted out on Television," *New York Times*, September 5, 1999, https://www.nytimes.com/1999/09/05/world/in-russia-a-power-play-acted-out-on-television.html.

35. Leonid Berres and Dmitrii Dmitriev, "Ishchut chekisty v biznese zheny moskovskogo mera," *Kommersant*, July 20, 1999, https://on-demand.eastview.com/browse/doc/3771389.

36. Luzhkov interview by Evgenii Kiselev, July 18, 1999, Johnson's Russia List, http://www.russialist.org/archives/3399.html##11; Dunlop, *Moscow Bombings*, 45–46. In September, the new FSB chief, Patrushev, would even call Baturina to his office to assure her that the investigation had not been politically motivated.

37. Heritage, "Russian Premier Demands End to Media War."

38. Nemtsov, *Ispoved' buntaria*, 53. For an in-depth analysis of Stepashin's prime ministership and his relationship with the Family, see Guseinov, *Ot El'tsina k . . . ?*.

39. Aleksandr Khinshtein, "Berezovskii—krupnyi khinshchik?" *Moskovskii komsomolets*, July 16, 1999, https://on-demand.eastview.com/browse/doc/107093.

40. *Kommersant*, November 25, 1995, as cited in a biography of Chaika on the website Antikompromat, http://anticompromat.panchul.com/chaika/chaikabio.html.

41. Skuratov, *Kremlevskie podriady*, 412–13, 593–95 (595). Skuratov learned later that Chaika's official car had been parked outside the Kremlin during the night of April 1–2, when the criminal case against him was drawn up.

42. Biography of Chaika, *Meduza*, December 25, 2015, https://meduza.io/en/feature/2015/12/25/investigating-russia-s-top-prosecutor.

43. Jo Becker, Adam Goldman, and Matt Apuzzo, "Dirt on Clinton? 'I Love It,' Donald Trump Jr. Said," *New York Times*, July 11, 2017, https://www.nytimes.com/2017/07/11/us/politics/trump-russia-email-clinton.html.

44. Skuratov, *Kremlevskie podriady*, 479–83.

45. Goldfarb, *Death of a Dissident*, 174.

46. Interview with *Vedomosti*, March 24, 2000; in Berezovsky, *Art of the Impossible*, 2:277–81 (279).

47. Aven, *Vremia Berezovskogo*, 252.

48. Aven, *Vremia Berezovskogo*, 251.

49. Yeltsin, *Midnight Diaries*, 334; Putin, *First Person*, 136.

50. "Yeltsin's Speech Sacking Stepashin, Naming PM," Reuters, August 9, 1999, Johnson's Russia List, http://www.russialist.org/archives/3428. html##2. In fact the presidential elections were scheduled for June 2000, not July.

51. As quoted in Dunlop, *Moscow Bombings*, 75.

52. Interview with *Ekho Moskvy*, June 22, 2001, in Berezovsky, *Art of the Impossible*, 2:299.

53. ITAR-TASS, "Glavnoe seichas—deistvovat' v konstitutsionno-pravovom pole," *Rossiiskaia gazeta*, August 10, 1999, https://on-demand.eastview.com/browse/doc/1870181.

54. Stepashin speech to the National Press Club, Washington, DC, March 13, 2000, https://www.belfercenter.org/sites/default/files/legacy/files/russiavotes.pdf.

55. "President's Games Are Dangerous," *Moscow Times*, August 10, 1999, Johnson's Russia List, http://www.russialist.org/archives/3429.html##13.

56. "'Who Is Putin?' How Russia Reacted to Leader's Rise to Power, 20 Years Ago," *Moscow Times*, August 9, 2019, https://www.themoscowtimes.com/2019/08/09/who-is-putin-how-russia-reacted-to-leaders-rise-power-20-years-ago-a66767.

57. Andrei Shukshin, "Stepashin Warns Russia May Lose Dagestan," Reuters, August 9, 1999, Johnson's Russia List, http://www.russialist.org/archives/3428.html##10.

58. Stepashin speech to the National Press Club.

59. Myers, *New Tsar*, 156; Yeltsin, *Midnight Diaries*, 336–37; Evangelista, *Chechen Wars*, chap. 4, loc. 879–82.

60. "FOM: Presidentskii reiting Putina vysshe, chem u Primakova," *Lenta.ru*, October 20, 1999, https://lenta.ru/news/1999/10/20/putin/.

61. Malgin, "Operatsiia 'Preemnik.'"

62. Associated Press Newsroom, "Russia: The Fatherland-All Russia Alliance," August 28, 1999, http://www.aparchive.com/metadata/youtube/87278aa3eacb32d5d8c17907c95845b4.

63. Guseinov, *Ot El'tsina k . . . ?*, 93; Hale, "Origins of United Russia," 171. In October 1999, Luzhkov announced that he would not be a contender for the Russian presidency.

64. Raymond Bonner with Timothy L. O'Brien, "Activity at Bank Raises Suspicions of Russia Mob Tie," *New York Times*, August 19, 1999, https://www.nytimes.com/1999/08/19/world/activity-at-bank-raises-suspicions-of-russia-mob-tie.html.

65. Associated Press Newsroom, "Russia: Borodin Answers Swiss Bank Corruption Charges (2)," September 4, 1999, http://www.aparchive.com/metadata/youtube/1f246ba83d78263a98d2406b0cf369cb; John Tagliabue, "Swiss Investigate Possible Laundering of Russian Money," *New York Times*, September 4, 1999, https://archive.nytimes.com/www.nytimes.com/library/world/global/090499russia-launder-swiss.html.

66. "El'tsin—V panike!," *Moskovskii komsomolets*, no. 169, September 4, 1999, https://on-demand.eastview.com/browse/doc/108355.

67. Novosti, *Izvestiia*, no. 165, September 4, 1999, https://on-demand. eastview.com/browse/doc/3176994.

68. Elena Trebugova, "Obidno za Rossiiu bol'she ne budet," *Kommersant*, September 4, 1999, https://on-demand.eastview.com/browse/doc/3773696.

69. Dunlop, *Moscow Bombings*, 218–19; Knight, *Orders to Kill*, 179–99.

70. Knight, *Orders to Kill*, 81; Nikita Ermakov, "K nam po-nastoiashchemu prishel terrorizm," *Moskovskaia pravda*, September 6, 1999, https://on-demand.eastview.com/browse/doc/6691686.

71. Dunlop, *Moscow Bombings*, 217–36 (235).

72. After serving in the Leningrad KGB during the 1970s and 1980s, Patrushev was transferred in 1990 to the Karelia region, where he ran the security services there. But a scandal involving smuggling of birch timber got him into hot water, so in 1994 he was moved to Moscow to work under Stepashin, then head of the FSB's predecessor agency, the FSK. When Putin left his position as head of the GKU in May 1998, Patrushev replaced him and in October moved to the FSB, where he soon became Putin's first deputy. See https://dossier.center/patrushev/.

73. Rushailo dossier, *Kompromat: Arkhivnaia biblioteka*, https://kompromat.wiki/Рушайло_Владимир_Борисович; biography of Rushailo, *Lenta.ru*, https://m.lenta.ru/lib/14159616/full.htm.

74. Dunlop, *Moscow Bombings*, 217–36. Dunlop cites direct reports from several Russian journalists.

7. Putin's Path to Victory

1. Myers, *New Tsar*, 158; "Oni uzhe zdes'," *Kommersant*, September 14, 1999, https://on-demand.eastview.com/browse/doc/3774121.

2. The speech was published in *Kommersant*, September 15, 1999, https://on-demand.eastview.com/browse/doc/3774212.

3. Dunlop, *Moscow Bombings*, 80–85, 248–51.

4. Hale, "Origins of United Russia," 177.

5. Aleksandr Khinshtein, "Berezovskii slushaet," *Moskovskii komsomolets*, September 14, 1999, https://on-demand.eastview.com/browse/doc/108572. Khinshtein followed up the next week with further excerpts from Berezovsky's talks with Udugov: Aleksandr Khinshtein, "Berezovaia kasha," *Moskovskii komsomolets*, September 22, 1999, https://on-demand.eastview.com/browse/doc/108812.

6. Goldfarb, *Death of a Dissident*, 189–90.

7. *Novye izvestiia*, September 17, 1999, in Berezovsky, *Art of the Impossible*, 1:531–32, 3:48–51.

8. Mark Deich, "Portret bez intrigi," *Moskovskii komsomolets*, September 18, 1999, https://on-demand.eastview.com/browse/doc/108730.

9. In his March 2000 speech to the National Press Club, mentioned earlier, Stepashin would reveal publicly that the Kremlin began planning a limited military operation in Chechnya, extending only to the Terek River, as far back as March 1999, in order to eliminate terrorist strongholds.

10. Stepashin interview with Svetlana Sorokina, NTV, October 5, 1999, http://tvoygolos.narod.ru/elita/elitatext/1999.10.05.htm.

11. "Russia Sends Ground Troops into Chechnya, Raising Fears," *New York Times*, October 1, 1999, https://archive.nytimes.com/www.nytimes.com/library/world/europe/100199russia-chechnya.html.

12. Vitalii Tret'iakov, "Goniteli sem'i i annibaly 'otechestva,'" *Nezavisimaia gazeta*, October 12, 1999, https://on-demand.eastview.com/browse/doc/327784.

13. Aleksandr Lebed interview with *Le Figaro*, September 29, 1999, http://www.russianseattle.com/news_092899_exo_lebed.htm. Lebed died from injuries sustained in a helicopter crash in April 2002.

14. Dunlop, *Moscow Bombings*, 85–90. Dunlop (21–22) also describes earlier warnings, including one from Russian journalist Aleksandr Zhilin, who reported on July 22, 1999, in the newspaper *Moskovskaia pravda*, that he had received a document from trustworthy Kremlin sources outlining a plan to discredit Moscow Mayor Luzhkov by causing terrorist attacks on government buildings.

15. Dunlop, *Moscow Bombings*, 102–5.

16. See, for example, Iurii Kochergin and Leonid Krutakov, "Operatsiia 'vzorvannyi mir,'" *Moskovskii komsomolets*, September 24, 1999, https://on-demand.eastview.com/browse/doc/108893.

17. See David Satter, *Darkness at Dawn: The Rise of the Russian Criminal State* (New Haven: Yale University Press, 2003), 24–33; Dunlop, *Moscow Bombings*, 167–216; Alexander Litvinenko and Yuri Felshtinsky, *Blowing Up Russia: The Secret Plot to Bring Back KGB Terror*, trans. Geoffrey Andrews (New York: Encounter Books, 2007), 54–99.

18. *Lenta.ru*, September 24, 1999, https://lenta.ru/news/1999/09/24/patrushev/.

19. Andrei Piontkovskii, "Preredovitsa: Tak ne planiruiut voinu. Tak planiruiut krovavuiu boiniu," *Novaia gazeta*, September 27, 1999, https://on-demand.eastview.com/browse/doc/3473354.

20. As cited in Dunlop, *Moscow Bombings*, 80.

21. Satter, *Darkness at Dawn*, 29–32.

22. Amy Knight, "Finally, We Know about the Moscow Bombings," *New York Review of Books*, November 22, 2012.

23. Berezovsky interview with Nataliya Gevorkyan, *Kommersant*, November 27, 1999, in Berezovsky, *Art of the Impossible*, 2:263–73 (264).

24. Iulia Latynina, "Spustia desiat' let, ili o vzryvakh domov v Moskve," *Ezhednevnyi zhurnal*, September 28, 2009, http://www.ej.ru/?a=note&id=9486.

25. *La Repubblica*, September 15, 1999, Johnson's Russia List, http://www.russialist.org/archives/3505.html##5.

26. Tony Wesolowsky, "Russia: Financial Scandal Spreading," RFE/RL, October 15, 1999, https://www.rferl.org/a/1092408.html.

27. "Kompromat po garantii," *Kommersant*, October 15, 1999, https://on-demand.eastview.com/browse/doc/3776073.

28. Robert O'Harrow Jr. and Sharon LaFraniere, "Yeltsin's Son-in-law Kept Offshore Accounts, Hill Told," *Washington Post*, September 23, 1999,

https://www.washingtonpost.com/archive/politics/1999/09/23/yeltsins-son-in-law-kept-offshore-accounts-hill-told/69a361aa-57ce-4cac-99ab-319c5c068763/.

29. Michael Wines, "Yeltsin Son-in-law at Center of Rich Network of Influence," *New York Times*, October 7, 1999, https://www.nytimes.com/1999/10/07/world/yeltsin-son-in-law-at-center-of-rich-network-of-influence.html; Melor Sturua, "U testia za pazukhoi," *Moskovskii komsomolets*, October 9, 1999, https://on-demand.eastview.com/browse/doc/109337.

30. Iu. P. Shchekochikhin, "U dochki-dachka? Ne nuzhen nam bereg turetskii," *Novaia gazeta*, October 11, 1999, https://on-demand.eastview.com/browse/doc/3473431.

31. Leonid Krutakov, "Krakh banditskogo kapitalizma," *Moskovskii komsomolets*, October 6, 1999, https://on-demand.eastview.com/browse/doc/109224.

32. Tatiana Iumasheva, LiveJournal, February 6, 2010, https://t-yumasheva.livejournal.com/13320.html.

33. Aven, *Vremia Berezovskogo*, 252.

34. Iumasheva, LiveJournal.

35. Goldfarb, *Death of a Dissident*, 192. Also see Zygar, *All the Kremlin's Men*, 10.

36. NUPI Center for Russian Studies, https://web.archive.org/web/20010702200941/http://www.nupi.no/cgi-win/Russland/polgrupp.exe?Unity. Shoigu's career would continue to thrive after Putin became president. He became Russian minister of defense in 2012.

37. Hale, "Origins of United Russia," 169.

38. Zygar, *All the Kremlin's Men*, 11.

39. Khinshtein, *Berezovskii i Abramovich*, 398–99; Aleksandr Cherniak, *Kreml' 90-kh: Favority i zhertvy Borisa El'tsina* (Moscow: Algoritm, 2011), 59–62.

40. Myers, *New Tsar*, 165.

41. Laura Belin, "Russian Media Policy in the First and Second Chechen Campaigns," paper for the 52nd Conference of the Political Studies Association, Aberdeen, Scotland, April 2002, https://bleedingheartland.com/static/media/2018/12/Belin2002conferencepaper.pdf.

42. Hale, "Origins of United Russia," 174.

43. Hale, "Origins of United Russia," 175, 186.

44. Aleksandr Mel'man, "Kto ostanovit Dorenko?" *Moskovskii komsomolets*, October 7, 1999, https://on-demand.eastview.com/browse/doc/109285.

45. Aven, *Vremia Berezovskogo*, 239.

46. "Obychnyi den' informatsionnoi bitvy: Planerka po telefonu B. Berezovskii—S. Dorenko," *Novaia gazeta*, December 16, 1999, http://www.compromat.ru/page_25483.htm. Also see Hoffman, *Oligarchs*, 467–48.

47. Interfax, April 4, 2000, as cited in Peter Rutland, "Putin's Path to Power," *Post-Soviet Affairs* 16, no. 4 (2000): 313–54 (326).

48. Nikolai Popov, "Kak nachinalas' epokha Putina: Obshchestvennoe mnenie 1999–2000 gg.," *Kapital strany*, Moscow, 2008, https://kapital-rus.ru/articles/article/kak_nachinalas_epoha_putina_obschestvennoe_mnenie_1999-2000_gg/.

49. Hale, "Origins of United Russia," 180, citing a November 1999 poll conducted by the All-Russian Center for the Study of Public Opinion (VTsIOM).

50. *Kommersant*, November 25, 1999, https://on-demand.eastview.com/browse/doc/3779026.

51. Yeltsin, *Midnight Diaries*, 356.

52. *Nalchik*, January 18, 2000, in Berezovskii, *Art of the Impossible*, 1:538.

53. Yeltsin, *Midnight Diaries*, 6–7.

54. Putin, *First Person*, 204–5.

55. Masha Gessen, "Putin Himself First," *New Republic*, January 17, 2000, Johnson's Russia List, http://www.russialist.org/archives/4019.html.

56. Oleg Lur'e, "Turover's List: File on Corrupt Russians Revealed," *Novaia gazeta*, December 27, 1999, Johnson's Russia List, http://www.russialist.org/archives/4023.html#8; John Tagliabue and Celestine Bohlen, "Accusations of Bribery in the Kremlin Mount Up," *New York Times*, September 9, 1999. Turover, interviewed years later by Catherine Belton, said he had been at one point a top KGB foreign intelligence officer, but he offered no proof for his dubious claim. See Belton, *Putin's People*, 91–93.

57. Celestine Bohlen, "Yeltsin Resigns: The Overview," *New York Times*, January 1, 2000, https://www.nytimes.com/2000/01/01/world/yeltsin-resigns-overview-yeltsin-resigns-naming-putin-acting-president-run-march.html.

58. David Hoffman, "Russia Vote Returns Tycoon to Spotlight," *Washington Post*, December 23, 1999, https://www.washingtonpost.com/wp-srv/WPcap/1999-12/23/076r-122399-idx.html.

59. Aven, *Vremia Berezovskogo*, 341.

60. Zygar, *All the Kremlin's Men*, 24.

61. Goldfarb, *Death of a Dissident*, 195.

8. A Clash of Titans

1. Blotskii, *Doroga k vlasti*, 417.

2. Putin, *First Person*, 205–6.

3. Blotskii, *Doroga k vlasti*, 418–20.

4. Celestine Bohlen, "Yeltsin Resigns: The Overview," *New York Times*, January 1, 2000, https://www.nytimes.com/2000/01/01/world/yeltsin-resigns-overview-yeltsin-resigns-naming-putin-acting-president-run-march.html.

5. Putin, *First Person*, 144.

6. Alice Lagnado, "Russia's First Lady in Waiting," *The Times* (UK), January 8, 2000, Johnson's Russia List, http://www.russialist.org/archives/4019.html#5.

7. According to a January 25, 2000, statement from the Russian Ministries of Defense and Internal Affairs, 1,173 Russian troops had been killed in fighting in the North Caucasus since August 1999, and 7,500 Chechen and foreign militants had been killed since the Russian military began its incursion in late September (*RFE/RL Newsline*, January 26, 2000, https://www.rferl.org/a/1142080.html).

8. See, for example, Editorial, "Ending the Brutality in Chechnya," *New York Times*, December 9, 1999, citing US President Clinton, Johnson's Russia List, http://www.russialist.org/archives/3672.html##8.

9. As reproduced in Anna Politkovskaya, *A Dirty War: A Russian Reporter in Chechnya*, intro. Thomas de Waal (London: Harvill Press, 2001), 113–18.

10. Babitsky responding to interviewer Aleksandr Batchan on the program "Liberty Live," *Radio Svoboda*, December 24, 1999, https://www.svoboda.org/a/24218403.html.

11. Gessen, *Man without a Face*, 32–36. Gessen concludes that an exchange of prisoners involving Babitsky and Chechen warlords probably never took place.

12. Putin, *First Person*, 171.

13. Gessen, *Man without a Face*, 36.

14. "Dizzy with Success," *Moscow Times*, January 18, 2000, Johnson's Russia List, http://www.russialist.org/archives/4044.html#1.

15. Chubais interview with Nataliya Gevorkyan, *Kommersant*, November 24, 1999, https://on-demand.eastview.com/browse/doc/3778900.

16. Nemtsov, *Ispoved' buntaria*, 62.

17. Roi Medvedev, *Vremia Putina* (Moscow: Vremia, 2014), 41.

18. Medvedev, *Vremia Putina*, 41–42.

19. Medvedev, *Vremia Putina*, 42; Myers, *New Tsar*, 188.

20. Elena Masiuk, "Liudmila Narusova: Eto moe politicheskoe zaveshchenie," *Novaia gazeta*, November 9, 2012, https://on-demand.eastview.com/browse/doc/28007606. Narusova walked back her statements in a 2019 interview with Philip Short. She still insisted that her husband had not died of a heart attack but said cryptically that his death was "not sensational and not criminal" (Short, *Putin*, 762–63).

21. Dmitrii Volchek, "'Delo Sobchaka': Zagadki biografii pokrovitelia Putina," *Radio Svoboda*, June 9, 2018, https://www.svoboda.org/a/29278219.html.

22. Interview with *Novyi kompanion*, December 21, 1999, in Berezovsky, *Art of the Impossible*, 2:207–9 (208).

23. ORT, January 22, 2000, Johnson's Russia List, http://www.russialist.org/archives/4073.html#3.

24. Interview with *Vedomosti*, March 24, 2000, in Berezovsky, *Art of the Impossible*, 1:543–44.

25. Interview with *Kommersant*, April 7, 2000, in Berezovsky, *Art of the Impossible*, 1:545–46.

26. "Boris Berezovsky: Puppeteer or Future Victim?" *The Economist*, March 25–31, 2000, https://www.economist.com/europe/2000/03/23/boris-berezovsky-puppeteer-or-future-victim.

27. Jonathan Steele, "The Ryazan Incident: If the Russian People Can Be Bothered to Vote, They Will Vote for the Man Who Is Being Foisted on Them," *Guardian*, March 24, 2000, Johnson's Russia List, http://www.russialist.org/archives/4196.html##7.

28. Jamestown Foundation Monitor, March 20, 2000, Johnson's Russia List, http://www.russialist.org/archives/4185.html##1.

29. Bloomberg, April 4, 2000, citing Interfax, Johnson's Russia List, http://www.russialist.org/archives/4226.html##8.

30. Goldfarb, *Death of a Dissident*, 198.

31. Arkady Ostrovsky, *The Invention of Russia* (New York: Penguin, 2017), Kindle ed., chap. 9, loc. 4805.

32. *Novaia gazeta*, May 15, 2000, https://on-demand.eastview.com/browse/doc/3464309.

33. Ostrovsky, *Invention of Russia*, chap. 9, loc. 4826, citing his interview with Dorenko in June 2014.

34. Hoffman, *Oligarchs*, 483.

35. Hoffman, *Oligarchs*, 482–85.

36. Nemtsov, *Ispoved' buntaria*, 59–60.

37. Irina Nagornykh, "V Rossii nachalas' perekroika," *Kommersant*, May 16, 2000, https://on-demand.eastview.com/browse/doc/3696769.

38. For a detailed study of the reforms, see Matthew Hyde, "Putin's Federal Reforms and Their Implications for Presidential Power in Russia," *Europe-Asia Studies* 53, no. 5 (2001): 719–43.

39. *Kommersant*, May 31, 2000, in Berezovsky, *Art of the Impossible*, 3:293–301.

40. Goldfarb, *Death of a Dissident*, 204–6. David Hoffman recalled speaking with Berezovsky on May 31 at the LogoVAZ Club and observed that "he seemed frazzled. The serenity I had noticed in March was gone" (*Oligarchs*, 487).

41. Irina Rinaeva and Marina Ozerova, "Senatorskie poddavki," *Moskovskii komsomolets*, June 1, 2000, https://on-demand.eastview.com/browse/doc/71047.

42. Goldfarb, *Death of a Dissident*, 207–8.

43. "Ocherednaia bor'ba s avtoritarnoi vlast'iu," *Kommersant*, July 8, 2000, https://on-demand.eastview.com/browse/doc/3700879.

44. *Time Europe*, July 17, 2000, in Berezovsky, *Art of the Impossible*, 3:319–23.

45. Marcel Michelson, "Swiss Court Turns Down Request by Russian Tycoon," Reuters, July 24, 2000, Johnson's Russia List, http://www.russialist.org/archives/4420.html##9.

46. Siuzanna Farizova, "Berezovskii ushel iz bol'shoi politiki," *Kommersant*, July 17, 2000, https://on-demand.eastview.com/browse/doc/3701374.

47. Khinshtein, *Berezovskii i Abramovich*, 410.

48. Amelia Gentleman, "Putin Picks Off Opponents Who Matter Most, Wages Partial War on Corruption," *Guardian*, July 13, 2000, https://www.theguardian.com/world/2000/jul/14/russia.ameliagentleman?CMP=gu_com.

49. Natal'ia Shipitsyna and Aleksei Borisov, "Putin vozvrashchaet stanu v 1929 godu?," *Moskovskii komsomolets*, July 13, 2000, https://on-demand.eastview.com/browse/doc/72526.

50. Sabrina Tavernise, "Putin, Exerting His Authority, Meets with Russia's Tycoons," *New York Times*, July 29, 2000, https://www.nytimes.com/2000/07/29/world/putin-exerting-his-authority-meets-with-russia-s-tycoons.html.

51. *Izvestiia*, July 29, 2000, in Berezovsky, *Art of the Impossible*, 1:225–31 (228).

52. Gregory Feifer, "Berezovsky Starts Opposition Movement," *Moscow Times*, August 10, 2000, Johnson's Russia List, http://www.russialist.org/archives/4449.html##12.

53. For an account of the accident and its aftermath, see Zoltan Barany, "The Tragedy of the *Kursk*: Crisis Management in Putin's Russia," *Government and Opposition* 39, no. 3 (2004): 476–503.

54. Goldfarb, *Death of a Dissident*, 209.

55. Goldfarb, *Death of a Dissident*, 210–11; Hoffman, *Oligarchs*, 487–88; Berezovsky's witness statement, Berezovsky v. Abramovich, May 31, 2011, published by *The Guardian*, November 2, 2011, https://www.theguardian.com/world/interactive/2011/nov/02/boris-berezovsky-witness-statement-full 71–72. In *Avtoportret*, Berezovsky wrote: "After the tragedy with the *Kursk*, my position caused the president to become furious. It was a turning point in my relationship with him" (85).

56. See the discussion of the trial in chapter 11.

57. Hoffman, *Oligarchs*, 488–89.

58. *Vechernyi Tomsk*, August 22, 2000, in Berezovsky, *Art of the Impossible*, 1:232.

59. "Vstrecha s rodnymi," *Kommersant*, August 29, 2000, https://on-demand.eastview.com/browse/doc/3201939.

60. "Ot pervogo litsa," *Rossiiskaia gazeta*, August 23, 2000, https://on-demand.eastview.com/browse/doc/1816946.

61. "39 Percent of Russians Consider *Kursk* Sinking Tragic Coincidence—Poll," *Moscow Times*, August 24, 2000, Johnson's Russia List, http://www.russialist.org/archives/4472.html#7.

62. Gloster, "Approved Judgment, Berezovsky v. Abramovich," 274.

63. *Kommersant*, September 5, 2000, in Berezovsky, *Art of the Impossible*, 3:61–64.

64. Viktoriia Artiunova and Elena Tregubova, "Negosudarstvennykh aktsii ORT," *Kommersant*, September 5, 2000, https://www.kommersant.ru/doc/17574.

65. Robert Kaiser, "Vladimir Putin Dishes with the Media," *Washington Post*, September 8, 2000, Johnson's Russia List, http://www.russialist.org/archives/4500.html.

66. Ron Popeski, "Putin Ends U.N. Summit with Frank Interview," Reuters, September 8, 2000, Johnson's Russia List, http://www.russialist.org/archives/4500.html.

67. Andrei Piontkovsky, "Season of Discontent," *Russia Journal*, September 16, 2000, https://on-demand.eastview.com/browse/doc/1904903.

68. Yevgenia Albats, "Power Play: Berezovsky the Victim of His Own Designs," *Moscow Times*, September 7, 2000, https://www.themoscowtimes.com/archive/berezovsky-the-victim-of-his-own-designs.

69. Shevtsova, *Putin's Russia*, 113.

70. Sophie Lambroschini, "Journalists Defend Joining Berezovsky's ORT Trust," RFE/RL, September 12, 2000, Johnson's Russia List, http://www.russialist.org/archives/4511.html##4.

71. *Novye izvestiia*, September 20, 2000, Johnson's Russia List, http://www.russialist.org/archives/4537.html##11.

72. Interfax, October 16, 2000, Johnson's Russia List, http://www.russialist.org/archives/4583.html##6.

73. RFE/RL Security Watch, October 23, 2000, https://www.rferl.org/a/1344751.html.

74. The interview was published in English on the president's website, http://en.kremlin.ru/events/president/transcripts/by-date/26.10.2000.

75. Berezovsky, *Art of the Impossible*, 2:530–32.

76. Goldfarb, *Death of a Dissident*, 232–33.

77. "Zaiavlenie dlia pechati Borisa Berezovskogo," *Kommersant*, November 15, 2000, https://on-demand.eastview.com/browse/doc/3709892.

9. The Outcast versus the Tyrant

1. Andrei Gamalov, "Boris Berezovskii: 'Ia eshche nikogo ne liubil,'" *Kar'era*, February 5, 2001, http://www.compromat.ru/page_10604.htm; Irina Bobrova, "Tainaia zhizn' suprugi oligarkha," *Moskovskii komsomolets*, February 17, 2005, https://www.compromat.ru/page_16256.htm.

2. Boris Berezovsky witness statement, *Guardian*, 76–79.

3. Berezovsky witness statement, *Guardian*, 83.

4. Roman Abramovich witness statement, Berezovsky v. Abramovich, May 30, 2011, *Guardian*, November 2, 2011, https://www.theguardian.com/world/interactive/2011/nov/02/roman-abramovich-witness-statement-full. 59–60

5. Owen, *Litvinenko Inquiry*, 24–25.

6. "Does Litvinenko Know Who Is Responsible for Apartment Bombings?," Jamestown Foundation, November 2, 2000, Johnson's Russia List, http://www.russialist.org/archives/4617.html##2; Goldfarb, *Death of a Dissident*, 3–19.

7. Knight, *Orders to Kill*, 151–54; Owen, *Litvinenko Inquiry*, 26–30.

8. "Silencing Critics of the Kremlin," *New York Times*, January 23, 2002, https://www.nytimes.com/2002/01/23/opinion/silencing-critics-of-the-kremlin.html.

9. Shevtsova, *Putin's Russia*, 123.

10. Putin's List, Ustinov, database of the Free Russia Forum, https://www.spisok-putina.org/en/personas/ustinov-2/.

11. Putin's list, Murov, database of the Free Russia Forum, https://www.spisok-putina.org/en/personas/murov-3/; Knight, *Orders to Kill*, 47–49.

12. As quoted in Giacomo Tognini, "How Rich Is Putin's Right-hand Man? Inside the Murky Fortune of Igor Sechin, the Darth Vader of the Kremlin," *Fortune*, May 2, 2022, https://www.forbes.com/sites/giacomotognini/2022/05/02/how-rich-is-putins-right-hand-man-inside-the-murky-fortune-of-igor-sechin-the-darth-vader-of-the-kremlin/?sh=25fcd8195ddc.

13. Yuri Shvets, "Report on Igor Sechin, The Litvinenko Inquiry," INQ015691, https://webarchive.nationalarchives.gov.uk/ukgwa/201606130 90333/https://www.litvinenkoinquiry.org/evidence.

14. Zygar, *All the President's Men*, 305.

15. Richard Sakwa, *The Putin Paradox* (London: I. B. Tauris, 2020), 35.

16. C-Span, June 17, 2001, https://www.c-span.org/video/?c4718091/user-clip-bush-putins-soul.

17. National Public Radio, April 16, 2022, https://www.npr.org/2022/04/16/1092811802/russia-putin-bush-texas-summit-crawford.

18. Yuri Zarakhovich, "Russians Happy to Follow the Leader," *Time Europe*, December 6, 2001, Johnson's Russia List, http://www.russialist.org/archives/5593-14.php.

19. David Hoffman, "Putin Says 'Why Not?' to Russia Joining NATO," *Washington Post*, March 6, 2000, https://www.washingtonpost.com/archive/politics/2000/03/06/putin-says-why-not-to-russia-joining-nato/c1973032-c10f-4bff-9174-8cae673790cd/.

20. Sakwa, *Putin Paradox*, 1.

21. Alan Cowell, "Exiled Russian Oligarch Plots His Comeback," *New York Times*, February 18, 2003, https://www.nytimes.com/2003/02/18/world/exiled-russian-oligarch-plots-his-comeback.html.

22. George Soros, "Who Lost Russia?" *New York Review of Books*, April 13, 2000.

23. Goldfarb, *Death of a Dissident*, 248.

24. Cowell, "Exiled Russian Oligarch Plots His Comeback."

25. Author interview with Gleb Berezovsky, London, October 6, 2022.

26. Goldfarb, *Death of a Dissident*, 240–41; "Berezovskii potratil na 'liberal'nuiu' Rossiiu—ne odin, a piat' millionov dollarov," *Lenta.ru*, October 9, 2002, https://lenta.ru/news/2002/10/09/berezovsky2/.

27. "Otdel'nyi razgovor. FSB vzryvaet Rossiiu," *Novaia gazeta*, August 27, 2001, https://on-demand.eastview.com/browse/doc/3467508.

28. Lev Roitman, "O knige 'FSB vzryvet Rossiiu': Fakty ili versii?" *Radio Svoboda*, June 11, 2002, https://www.svoboda.org/a/24202391.html.

29. News on NTV/RU, December 14, 2001, in Berezovsky, *Art of the Impossible*, 2:606–8.

30. Guy Chazan, "Berezovsky, His Influence on the Wane, Alleges Putin's Involvement in Bombings," *Wall Street Journal*, December 17, 2001, Johnson's Russia List, http://www.russialist.org/archives/5604-3.php.

31. Patrick E. Tyler, "Russian Says Kremlin Faked Terror Attacks," *New York Times*, February 1, 2002, https://www.nytimes.com/2002/02/01/world/russian-says-kremlin-faked-terror-attacks.html.

32. *Assassination of Russia* (Blowing Up Russia), https://www.youtube.com/watch?v=9sx2YmSXDy8.

33. Aleksandr Vasil'ev, "Shou Berezovskogo i ego 'gadenyshei,'" *Moskovskii komsomolets*, March 7, 2002, https://on-demand.eastview.com/browse/doc/114039.

34. Nataliya Gevorkyan and Vladimir Kara-Murza, "Boris Berezovskii organizoval 'Pokushenie na Rossiiu,'" *Kommersant*, March 6, 2002, https://on-demand.eastview.com/browse/doc/4172971.

35. Goldfarb, *Death of a Dissident*, 250–51.

36. Goldfarb, *Death of a Dissident*, 258.

37. John Dunlop, *Moscow Bombings*, 161–62.

38. Knight, *Orders to Kill*, 106–11.

39. Catherine Belton, "Killing Raises Awkward Questions," *Moscow Times*, April 21, 2003, Johnson's Russia List, http://www.russialist.org/archives/7149.htm.

40. "Berezovsky Ally Held over Killing," *BBC News*, June 26, 2003, http://news.bbc.co.uk/2/hi/europe/3022446.stm.

41. Knight, *Orders to Kill*, 106–11; *BNK Informatsionnoe Agenstvo*, May 13, 2018, https://www.bnkomi.ru/data/news/78720/.

42. Nick Paton Walsh, "Russian MP Shot Dead in Contract Killing," *Guardian*, August 21, 2002, https://www.theguardian.com/world/2002/aug/22/russia.nickpatonwalsh.

43. Knight, *Orders to Kill*, 113–14.

44. Dunlop, *Moscow Bombings*, 139; Knight, "Finally, We Know about the Moscow Bombings."

45. Berezovsky, *Art of the Impossible*, 2:697–762; Zygar, *All the President's Men*, 40–41.

46. Berezovsky v. Russian Television and Radio, Royal Courts of Justice, March 10, 2010, https://www.5rb.com/wp-content/uploads/2013/10/Berezovsky-v-Russian-Television-and-Radio-No-2-2010-EWHC-476-QB.pdf.

47. David Hearst, "Judge Refuses to Extradite Chechen," *Guardian*, November 13, 2003, https://www.theguardian.com/uk/2003/nov/14/chechnya.russia.

48. Zygar, *All the President's Men*, 299.

49. John Dunlop, *The 2002 Dubrovka and 2004 Beslan Hostage Crises: A Critique of Russian Counter-Terrorism* (Stuttgart: ibidem Verlag, 2006), 103–57.

50. Zygar, *All the President's Men*, 41–42.

51. "Levada Center Polling Data," Levada.ru, https://www.levada.ru/2022/04/27/odobrenie-institutov-rejtingi-partij-i-politikov-2/.

52. Andrei A. Kovalev, *Russia's Dead End: An Insider's Testimony from Gorbachev to Putin*, trans. Steven I. Levine (Lincoln, NE: Potomac Books, 2017), Kindle ed., 269.

53. Committee to Protect Journalists, "Attacks on the Press in 2004—Russia," https://www.refworld.org/docid/47c566edc.html.

54. "Russian Federation Presidential Election," March 14, 2004, *OSCE/ODIHR Election Observation Mission Report*, https://www.osce.org/files/f/documents/7/b/33100.pdf.

55. Richard Sakwa, *Putin and the Oligarch: The Khodorkovsky-Yukos Affair* (London: I. B. Tauris, 2014), 38–41 (39).

56. Sakwa, *Putin and the Oligarch*, 41.

57. Zygar, *All the President's Men*, 50.

58. Mikhail Khodorkovsky and Nataliya Gevorkyan, *Tiur'ma i volia* (Moscow: Howard Roark, 2012), Kindle ed., 524–25. See also Sakwa, *Putin and the Oligarch*, 54–56; and Zygar, *All the President's Men*, 51–56. It should be noted that Kondaurov said elsewhere that he had no idea Khodorkovsky was going to give the presentation.

59. Khodorkovsky and Gevorkyan, *Tiur'ma i volia*, 523–24; Sakwa, *Putin and Oligarch*, 72–76.

60. Zygar, *All the President's Men*, 57–60; Belton, *Putin's People*, 232–38.

61. Sakwa, *Putin and the Oligarch*, 78–81; Khodorkovsky and Gevorkyan, *Tiur'ma i volia*, 537–39.

62. Khodorkovsky and Gevorkyan, *Tiur'ma i volia*, 73–76; Sakwa, *Putin and the Oligarch*, 72–75, 82–84; Belton, *Putin's People*, 278–303. Also see Myers, *New Tsar*, 281–90.

63. Boris Berezovsky, "The West Must Realize That Putin is Becoming a Dictator," *Daily Telegraph*, November 6, 2003, in Berezovsky, *Art of the Impossible*, 2:365–67.

64. Boris Berezovsky, "We Russians Must Remove Putin from Power," *Le Monde*, November 17, 2003, in Berezovsky, *Art of the Impossible*, 2:368–70.

65. See McCain's speech to the US Congress on November 4, 2003: https://www.aei.org/research-products/speech/senator-mccain-decries-new-authoritarianism-in-russia/.

10. The Kremlin on the Offensive

1. As quoted in Dawisha, *Putin's Kleptocracy*, 335.

2. "Putin's Way," *PBS Frontline* documentary, January 13, 2015, transcript at https://www.pbs.org/video/frontline-putins-way/.

3. Nicholas Gordon, "How Rich Is Putin? Mystery of Russian President's Net Worth Complicates Biden's Decision to Sanction Him," *Fortune*, February 25, 2022, https://fortune.com/2022/02/25/putin-net-worth-wealth-russia-ukraine-invasion-sanctions-biden-us/.

4. Myers, *New Tsar*, 270–71.

5. Goldfarb, *Death of a Dissident*, 316.

6. Al-Jazeera, March 15, 2005, https://www.aljazeera.com/news/2005/3/15/berezovsky-puts-ukraine-in-quandary; "Russia's Citizen K," *Meduza*, December 15, 2015, https://meduza.io/en/feature/2015/12/16/russia-s-citizen-k.

7. "Transcript of Berezovsky's Meeting with the Verhovna Rada Commission, October 11, 2005, in Berezovsky, *Art of the Impossible*, 2:121–29.

8. Letter to Yulia Timoshenko, May 29, 2005, in Berezovsky, *Art of the Impossible*, 2:107–10.

9. "The Gongadze Inquiry: An Investigation into the Failure of Legal and Judicial Processes in the Case of Georgy Gongadze," Report No. 3, September 2007, https://piraniarchive.files.wordpress.com/2011/05/gongadze3.pdf.

10. "Gongadze Inquiry"; "Transcript of Berezovsky's Meeting with the Verhovna Rada."

11. See statements by Felshtinsky and Goldfarb on the website fraza.iua, December 6, 2005, https://fraza.com/news/16365-felshtinskiy-mel nichenko-vsegda-vel-razgovory-o-bolshih-dengah; https://fraza.com/news/16358-goldfarb-kole-melnichenko-mesto-v-tyurme; and Dmitrii Simakin, Ekaterina Blinova, and Tat'iana Ivzhenko, "Konspirativnyi oblet: Skandal'nyi okhrannik Mel'nichenko vernulsia v Kiev cherez Moskvu, vstretivshis'

neizvestno s kem," *Nezavisimaia gazeta*, December 1, 2005, https://on-demand.eastview.com/browse/doc/8667684.

12. Myers, *New Tsar*, 277.

13. Claire Bigg, "Was Soviet Collapse Last Century's Worst Geopolitical Catastrophe?," RFE/RL, April 29, 2005, https://www.rferl.org/a/1058688.html.

14. Belton, *Putin's People*, 256.

15. Marina Volkova, "Liudmila Putina: S trudovym kodeksom u Vladimira Vladimirovicha slozhnosti," *RGRU*, June 1, 2005, https://rg.ru/2005/06/01/putina.html.

16. "Key Kremlin Figure 'Quits,'" *BBC News*, October 29, 2003, http://news.bbc.co.uk/2/hi/europe/3223847.stm.

17. See my review of Kasyanov's tell-all book, *Bez Putina*: Amy Knight, "Forever Putin?," *New York Review of Books*, February 11, 2010.

18. Aleksandr Khinshtein, "Sensatsiia: Den vyrozhdeniia Berezovskogo," *Moskovskii komsomolets*, January 23, 2006, https://on-demand.eastview.com/browse/doc/8894102.

19. Berezovsky v. Russian Television, https://www.5rb.com/wp-content/uploads/2013/10/Berezovsky-v-Russian-Television-and-Radio-No-2-2010-EWHC-476-QB.pdf. This was not the first time Berezovsky had used the British legal system to defend his name. In 2000, he filed a libel case against *Forbes Magazine* over an article by Paul Klebnikov that linked him to the Chechen mafia and to the murder of Vladislav Listev. In March 2003, *Forbes* issued a retraction. Two years later, Berezovsky sued Alfa Bank Chairman Mikhail Fridman for defamation in a London court. After a jury trial in May 2006, the court ruled in Berezovsky's favor, and Fridman was ordered to pay him 50,000 pounds, along with legal fees. See an archived *Forbes* editor's note, March 6, 2003, https://web.archive.org/web/20050112221325/http://www.forbes.com/forbes/1996/1230/5815090a_7.html; and Al'vina Kharchenko, "Prigovor v chest' Borisa Berezovskogo," *Kommersant*, May 27, 2006, https://on-demand.eastview.com/browse/doc/9537455.

20. The two interviews are reproduced on the website Kompromat.ru: http://www.compromat.ru/page_18101.htm.

21. As quoted in Martin Sixsmith, *The Litvinenko File: The Life and Death of a Russian Spy* (New York: St. Martin's, 2007), 191.

22. *BBC News*, February 27, 2006, http://news.bbc.co.uk/2/hi/uk_news/politics/4756880.stm.

23. *Gazeta.ru*, March 3, 2022, http://www.compromat.ru/page_18320.htm#1.

24. *Vremia*, March 3, 2006, http://www.vremya.ru/2006/37/51/146770.html.

25. Kompromat.ru, https://www.compromat.ru/page_18282.htm.

26. Andrew E. Kramer, "Russia Forces Tycoon to Sell His Holdings," *New York Times*, February 16, 2006, https://www.nytimes.com/2006/02/17/business/worldbusiness/russia-forces-tycoon-to-sell-his-holdings.html.

27. "Russia: 'Kommersant' Purchase Changes Media Landscape," RFE/RL, September 1, 2006, https://www.rferl.org/a/1071011.html.

28. The decision was published on the website of the law firm Carter-Ruck, which represented Berezovsky: https://www.carter-ruck.com/news/berezovsky-wins-again-on-extradition/.

29. Owen, *Litvinenko Inquiry*, 86–91.

30. Owen, *Litvinenko Inquiry*, 88.

31. Owen, *Litvinenko Inquiry*, 88.

32. Owen, *Litvinenko Inquiry*, 54.

33. Owen, *Litvinenko Inquiry*, 54–60; Knight, *Orders to Kill*, 158.

34. Alexander Litvinenko at the Frontline Club, October 19, 2006, https://www.youtube.com/watch?v=m-feiiuj2I4.

35. Lugovoi witness statement for court case Berezovsky v. Terluk, March 4, 2011, Litvinenko Inquiry Evidence, https://www.litvinenkoin quiry.org/evidence lextranet rerference INQ001788; Knight, *Orders to Kill*, 158–61.

36. Lugovoi witness statement for Berezovsky v. Terluk, October 26, 2011, Litvinenko Inquiry evidence, https://www.litvinenkoinquiry.org/evidence lextranet reference INQ001842.

37. Glushkov testimony for the Litvinenko Inquiry, February 27, 2015, https://www.litvinenkoinquiry.org/hearings; Shvets testimony for the Litvinenko Inquiry, March 12, 2015, https://www.litvinenkoinquiry.org/hearings.

38. Knight, *Orders to Kill*, 175–87.

39. Knight, *Orders to Kill*, 177.

40. Goldfarb, *Death of a Dissident*, 320–27, 335–38; *Knight, Orders to Kill*, 172–74; Berezovsky interview with British police, March 30, 2007, Litvinenko Inquiry evidence, https://www.litvinenkoinquiry.org/evidence lextranet reference INQ017595.

41. Knight, *Orders to Kill*, 182–84; transcript of press conference of Lugovoi and Kovtun, May 31, 2007, Litvinenko Inquiry evidence, https://www.litvinenkoinquiry.org/evidence lextranet reference INQ001907.

42. Myers, *New Tsar*, 314.

43. Interview with Berezovsky, November 24, 2006, Litvinenko Inquiry evidence, https://www.litvinenkoinquiry.org/evidence lextranet reference INQ002209; Litvinenko Inquiry hearings, testimony of Alex Goldfarb, February 4, 2015, https://www.litvinenkoinquiry.org/hearings.

44. Dmitrii Bykov, "Boris Berezovskii: U Putina bylo tri varianta. On vybral khudshii," *Sobesednik*, May 7, 2008, http://www.compromat.ru/page_22683.htm.

45. "Chubais uveren, chto Gaidara khoteli ubit'," *Vesti.ru*, November 29, 2006, https://www.vesti.ru/article/2307961.

46. Grani.ru, February 2, 2007, http://www.compromat.ru/page_20146.htm.

47. Yegor Gaidar, "I Was Poisoned and Russia's Political Enemies Were Surely Behind It," *Financial Times*, December 6, 2006, https://www.ft.com/content/aacc818a-855b-11db-b12c-0000779e2340.

48. Andrei Illarionov, "Spetsoperatsiia 'Otravlenie Gaidara Borisom Berezovskim,'" LiveJournal, April 9, 2019, https://aillarionov.livejournal.

com/1114866.html; Gaidar interview with Albats, *Ekho Moskvy*, June 17, 2007, https://soundstream.media/clip/17-06-2007-19-09-polnyy-al-bats-liberal-nyye-ekonomisty-i-vlast-protivorechiye-ili-neobkhodimost. In 2020, Goldfarb and Marina Litvinenko filed a defamation lawsuit against RT television.

49. Illarionov, LiveJournal.

50. Vladimir Shlapentokh, "How Putin's Russia Embraces Authoritarianism: The Case of Yegor Gaidar," *Communist and Post-Communist Studies* 40, no. 4 (2007): 493–99 (497).

51. Boris Nemtsov, "Zhit' stalo luchshe, no protivnee," *Vedomosti*, July 18, 2007, https://on-demand.eastview.com/browse/doc/12308262.

52. Knight, *Orders to Kill*, 257–81.

53. Ian Cobain, Matthew Taylor, and Luke Harding, "I Am Plotting a New Russian Revolution," *Guardian*, April 13, 2007, https://www.theguardian.com/world/2007/apr/13/topstories3.russia.

54. "Protiv Berezovskogo vozbuzhdeno delo o zakhvate vlasti," *Gazeta.ru*, April 13, 2007, https://www.gazeta.ru/news/lenta/2007/04/13/n_1057186.shtml.

55. "Boris Berezovsky—Putting One over Putin," Frontline Club, June 6, 2007, https://www.youtube.com/watch?v=lMB2o_rwW3E.

56. *BBC News*, July 18, 2007, http://news.bbc.co.uk/2/hi/uk_news/6905271.stm; Alexander Goldfarb witness statement, Litvinenko Inquiry, May 20, 2013, https://www.litvinenkoinquiry.org/evidence lextranet reference INQ017548.

57. Report by UK Select Parliamentary Commission on Foreign Affairs, November 2007, https://publications.parliament.uk/pa/cm200708/cmselect/cmfaff/51/5107.htm.

58. Thom Shanker and Mark Landler, "Putin Says U.S. Is Undermining Global Stability," *New York Times*, February 11, 2007, https://www.nytimes.com/2007/02/11/world/europe/11munich.html.

59. See Peter Reddaway, *Russia's Domestic Security Wars: Putin's Use of Divide and Rule against His Hardline Allies* (Cham, Switzerland: Palgrave Macmillan, 2018).

60. Myers, *New Tsar*, 351.

61. On Medvedev as the Russian president, see the memoirs of former US Ambassador to Russia Michael McFaul: *From Cold War to Hot Peace: The Inside Story of Russia and America* (Boston: Mariner Books, 2018).

62. Bykov, "Boris Berezovskii."

63. Sergei Sokolov, "Agenty spetssluzhb—sredi organizatorov ubiistva Anny Politkovskoi," *Novaia gazeta*, April 6, 2008, http://www.compromat.ru/page_22494.htm.

64. Knight, *Orders to Kill*, 132–43 (140). The five killers of Politkovskaya were Chechens, and there is strong reason to believe that Chechen President Ramzan Kadyrov, whom Politkovskaya had accused of being a "Chechen dragon," organized the killings. But Kadyrov never would have done this on his own initiative, as Philip Short would have us believe (see Short, *Putin*, 56–57, 70). Kadyrov always took his orders from Putin.

11. A Life Falling Apart

1. Suzanna Andrews, "The Widow and the Oligarchs," *Vanity Fair*, September 9, 2009, https://www.vanityfair.com/style/2009/10/oligarchs200910.

2. Vladimir Socor, "Badri Patarkatsishvili: From Russian Businessman to Georgian Presidential Claimant," Parts 1 and 2, Jamestown Foundation, *Eurasian Daily Monitor* 4, no. 237, December 21, 2007; Jim Nichol, "Georgia's January 2008 Presidential Election: Outcome and Implications," *CRS Report for Congress*, January 25, 2008, https://sgp.fas.org/crs/row/RS22794.pdf.

3. Andrews, "Widow and the Oligarchs."

4. Albats, "Berezovskii byl chast'iu nashei zhizni."

5. Andrews, "Widow and the Oligarchs"; Irina Khalip, "Voina za nasledstvo oligarkha Patarkatsishvili," *Novaia gazeta*, December 9, 2009, http://www.compromat.ru/page_28642.htm.

6. "Berezovskii khochet zabrat' u vdovy Patarkatsishvili 3 milliard funtov," Rosbalt.ru, February 8, 2009, https://www.rosbalt.ru/main/2009/02/08/616481.html.

7. Pavel Bandakov, "Berezovskii schitaet, chto Patarkatsishvili mog ego predat'," BBC News, January 24, 2012, https://www.bbc.com/russian/business/2012/01/120124_berezovsky_badri_court_case.

8. "How British Spin-doctors and Boris Berezovsky Tried to Help Alexander Lukashenko Win over the West," *Meduza*, September 10, 2020, https://meduza.io/en/feature/2020/09/10/guys-get-out?fbclid=IwAR2FV7cv3zwju--tWGbpkdcjiyYkcFwSPF6sunu5lZYqlOYIErbMejmb5cs.

9. Tat'iana Egorova and Mariia Rozhkova, "Berezovskii sobiraetsia v sud," *Vedomosti*, July 5, 2005, https://www.vedomosti.ru/newspaper/articles/2005/07/05/berezovskij-sobiraetsya-v-sud.

10. Sarah Lyall, "A Clash of Titans Exposes Russia's Seamy Underside," *New York Times*, November 9, 2011, https://www.nytimes.com/2011/11/10/world/europe/berezovsky-v-abramovich-offers-peek-into-post-soviet-russia.html.

11. Masha Gessen, "Comrades-in-Arms," *Vanity Fair*, November 13, 2012, https://www.vanityfair.com/news/politics/2012/11/roman-abramovich-boris-berezovsky-feud-russia.

12. Berezovsky witness statement, Berezovsky v. Abramovich.

13. Berezovsky v. Abramovich, Executive Summary of Full Judgment, https://www.bailii.org/ew/cases/EWHC/Comm/2012/2463(image1).pdf, 14.

14. Lyall, "Clash of Titans."

15. Pomerantsev, "Berezovsky's Last Days."

16. Abramovich witness statement, Berezovsky v. Abramovich, 9–18.

17. Berezovsky witness statement, Berezovsky v. Abramovich, 28.

18. Abramovich witness statement, Berezovsky v. Abramovich, 59.

19. Abramovich witness statement, Berezovsky v. Abramovich, 95–96.

20. Opus 2 International, Berezovsky v. Abramovich, Day 4, October 6, 2011, transcript, 13–14, https://pravo.ru/store/interdoc/doc/298/Day_4.pdf.

21. Opus 2 International, Berezovsky v. Abramovich, Day 4, 131–32.

22. Abramovich witness statement, Berezovsky v. Abramovich, 132–33.

23. Gloster, Approved Judgment, 147.

24. Gloster, Approved Judgment, 147.

25. Berezovsky witness statement, Berezovsky v. Abramovich, 28.

26. Gloster, Approved Judgment, 244.

27. Transcript of Deripaska testimony, November 18, 2011, https://pravo.ru/store/interdoc/doc/317/Day_29.pdf.

28. Abramovich witness statement, Berezovsky v. Abramovich, 51.

29. Gloster, Approved Judgment, 438.

30. Gloster, Approved Judgment, 448.

31. Luke Harding, "WikiLeaks cables: Dmitry Medvedev 'Plays Robin to Putin's Batman,'" *Guardian*, December 1, 2010, https://www.theguardian.com/world/2010/dec/01/wikileaks-cables-medvedev-putin-russia.

32. "Putin Announces Presidential Bid, With Medvedev Backing," RFE/RL, September 24, 2011, https://www.rferl.org/a/medvedev_says_putin_should_be_next_russian_president/24338593.html.

33. As quoted in Andrei Kolesnikov, "Fal'sh-intriga," *Novaia gazeta*, September 26, 2011, https://on-demand.eastview.com/browse/doc/26021183.

34. Stephen Blank and Carol Saivetz, "Russia Watches the Arab Spring," RFE/RL, June 24, 2011, https://www.rferl.org/a/commentary_russia_watches_arab_spring/24245990.html.

35. Levada Center, https://www.levada.ru/en/ratings/.

36. James Brooke, "Protests over Russian Elections Spread to More Cities," Voice of America, December 5, 2011, https://www.voanews.com/a/troops-patrol-moscow-to-prevent-election-protests-135109338/149195.html.

37. Ellen Barry and Michael Schwirtz, "Vast Rally in Moscow Is a Challenge to Putin's Power," *New York Times*, December 24, 2011, https://www.nytimes.com/2011/12/25/world/europe/tens-of-thousands-of-protesters-gather-in-moscow-russia.html.

38. *PBS Frontline*, "The Putin Files: Julia Ioffe," interview, June 2017, https://www.pbs.org/wgbh/frontline/interview/julia-ioffe/#highlight-2289-2302.

39. Richard Sakwa, "Whatever Happened to the Russian Opposition?" Research Paper, Russia and Eurasia Programme, Chatham House, May 2014, https://www.chathamhouse.org/sites/default/files/field/field_document/20140523SakwaFinal.pdf, 5.

40. Sakwa, "Whatever Happened to the Russian Opposition?"

41. Sakwa, "Whatever Happened to the Russian Opposition?", 12

42. "Otkrytoe pis'mo Berezovskogo Putinu," Grani.ru, January 17, 2012, https://graniru.org/Politics/Russia/President/m.194904.html#letter.

43. "Genprokuratura nashla ekstremizm v pis'me Berezovskogo," Grani.ru, May 18, 2012, https://graniru.org/Society/Media/Freepress/m.197815.html.

44. See his LiveJournal blog, April 23, 2012, https://bberezovsky.livejournal.com/2356.html and May 17, 2012, https://bberezovsky.livejournal.com/3012.html.

45. "Protiv Berezovskogo vozbuzhdeny dva ugolovnykh dela," *Grani.ru*, May 29, 2012. https://graniru.org/Politics/Russia/m.198037.html#bab.

46. Gloster, Approved Judgment, 334–35.

47. Gloster, Approved Judgment, 490.

48. Gloster, Approved Judgment, 44–45.

49. Gloster, Approved Judgment, 53–54.

50. Gessen, "Comrades-in-Arms."

51. Author interview with Luke Harding, June 29, 2022.

52. Author interview with Elena Gorbunova, London, October 6, 2022.

53. Author interview with Harding. For an in-depth study of the Russian informal economy, see Alena Ledeneva, *How Russia Really Works: The Informal Practices That Shaped Post-Soviet Politics and Business* (Ithaca, NY: Cornell University Press, 2006).

54. Luke Harding, "Humiliation for Boris Berezovsky in Battle of the Oligarchs," *Guardian*, August 31, 2012, https://www.theguardian.com/world/2012/aug/31/humiliation-boris-berezovsky-battle-oligarchs.

55. Zygar, *All the President's Men*, 237.

56. Interview with Gorbunova.

57. Harding, "Humiliation for Boris Berezovsky"; John F. Burns and Ravi Somalya, "Russian Tycoon Loses Multibillion-Dollar Case over Oil Fortune to Kremlin Favorite," *New York Times*, August 31, 2012, https://www.nytimes.com/2012/09/01/world/europe/russian-tycoon-loses-5-8-billion-case-against-ex-partner.html.

58. David Leppard, "Berezovsky Cries Foul over £3.5bn Abramovich Trial Judge," *Sunday Times*, September 22, 2012, https://www.thetimes.co.uk/article/berezovsky-cries-foul-over-pound35bn-abramovich-trial-judge-wrgwrp9dbq7.

59. "Aleksei Venediktov o Borise Berezovskom," *Ekho Moskvy*, March 24, 2013, https://echo.msk.ru/programs/svoi-glaza/1038068-echo/.

60. Amy Knight, "Putin's Downhill Race," *New York Review of Books*, September 26, 2013.

61. "Russy-2014: Boikott Olimpiada v Sochi!," https://bberezovsky.livejournal.com/4081.html.

62. Joint Stock Company (Aeroflot-Russian Airlines) v. Berezovsky & Anzor, Judgement, October 30, 2012, https://www.casemine.com/judgment/uk/5a8ff75260d03e7f57eab42c.

63. "Sroki s rodiny," *Vremia*, June 29, 2009, http://www.vremya.ru/2009/112/46/232127.html.

64. Elena Belova, "Babe—morozhennoe," *Gazeta.ru*, January 24, 2013, https://www.gazeta.ru/social/2013/01/24/4938977.shtml; Lewis Smith, "Boris Berezovsky's Former Girlfriend Claims He Owes Her Millions," *Independent*, January 23, 2013, https://www.independent.co.uk/news/uk/home-news/boris-berezovsky-s-former-girlfriend-claims-he-owes-her-millions-8464108.html.

65. As part of the deal, Berezovsky withdrew his claim against the aluminum tycoon Vasilii Anisimov, relating to a stake Berezovsky and Patarkatsishvili had in Anisimov's company Metalloinvest.

66. "Byvshei zhene Berezovskogo ne khvataet deneg, chtoby platit' sadovniku," RAPSI News, April 25, 2016, https://rapsinews.ru/international_news/20160425/275954399.html; "Berezovsky to Sell Warhol

Painting to Pay Court Fees," *Moscow Times*, March 19, 2013, https://www.themoscowtimes.com/2013/03/19/berezovsky-to-sell-warhol-painting-to-pay-court-fees-a22476; Neil Buckley, "Boris Berezovsky: A Death in Exile," *Financial Times*, March 29, 2013, https://www.ft.com/content/e472f0d4-985c-11e2-867f-00144feabdc0.

67. Myers, *New Tsar*, 432.

68. Luke Harding and Alexander Winning, "Vladimir Putin and His Wife Announce Their Separation in TV Interview," *Guardian*, June 6, 2013, https://www.theguardian.com/world/2013/jun/06/vladimir-putin-wife-lyudmila-separation.

12. Berezovsky's End

1. Aven, *Vremia Berezovskogo*, 391.

2. Quoted in Luke Harding and Robert Booth, "Berezovsky's Death Leaves Friends Suspecting Foul Play," *Guardian*, March 24, 2013, https://www.theguardian.com/world/2013/mar/24/boris-berezovsky-death-foul-play.

3. Aven, *Vremia Berezovskogo*, 391–92.

4. Mariia Mishina, "On govoril: 'Mne ochen' plokho,'" *Novoe vremia*, April 1, 2013, https://newtimes.ru/articles/detail/64627. Also see Mark Franchetti, "My Tycoon's Slide into Despair," *Sunday Times*, April 21, 2013, https://www.thetimes.co.uk/article/my-tycoons-slide-into-despair-6m83hv78b7v.

5. Aven, *Vremia Berezovskogo*, 392.

6. Aven, *Vremia Berezovskogo*, 421.

7. Mariia Timokhova, "Smert' za zakrytoi dver'iu," *Novoe vremia*, March 28, 2014, https://newtimes.ru/articles/detail/80941; recording of the public inquest into Berezovsky's death, March 26–27, 2014, Cotlick testimony. (Note: there is no written transcript of the inquest, and the recording obtained by the author from Elizaveta Berezovskaya was at times unclear, so I also rely on media accounts of the inquest.)

8. Ivan Nechepurenko, "Uncertainty Hangs over Berezovsky's Estate as New Assets Found," *Moscow Times*, August 20, 2013, https://www.themoscowtimes.com/2013/08/20/uncertainty-hangs-over-berezovsky-estate-as-new-assets-found-a26931. It does appear that by 2016, with creditors demanding payments, Berezovsky's estate became, as a British judge put it, "hopelessly insolvent." See Gorbunova v. Estate of Boris Berezovsky, Judgment, July 22, 2016, https://www.bailii.org/ew/cases/EWHC/Ch/2016/1829.html#para3.

9. Aven, *Vremia Berezovskogo*, 421.

10. Aven, *Vremia Berezovskogo*, 393.

11. Aven, *Vremia Berezovskogo*, 376.

12. Dmitrii Bykov, "Iulii Dubov: Borisa Berezovskogo ubivali trinadtsat' let," *Sobesednik*, May 7, 2013, https://sobesednik.ru/dmitriy-bykov/20130507-yulii-dubov-borisa-berezovskogo-ubivali-trinadtsat-let.

13. Luke Harding, "Boris Berezovsky and the Dangers of Being a Russian Exile in the UK," *Guardian*, March 25, 2013, https://www.theguardian.com/world/2013/mar/25/boris-berezovsky-russian-exile-uk.

14. Aven, *Vremia Berezovskogo*, 376; author interview with Gorbunova.

15. Mishina, "On govoril: 'Mne ochen' plokho.'"

16. Author interview with Iulii Dubov, London, October 7, 2022.

17. Yevgenia Albats, "Zhertvoprinoshenie," *Novoe vremia*, April 1, 2013, https://newtimes.ru/articles/detail/64622.

18. Howard Amos, "Boris Berezovsky Was 'in Talks over Return to Russia,'" *Guardian*, March 24, 2013, https://www.theguardian.com/world/2013/mar/24/boris-berezovsky-talks-return-russia.

19. Avi Navama, witness statement to police, March 25, 2013, provided, along with his witness statement on March 28, 2013, to the author by a Berezovsky family member; recording of Berezovsky inquest, Navama testimony.

20. Albats, "Zhertvoprinoshenie."

21. Navama witness statement, March 28, 2013; Albats, "Zhertvoprinoshenie"; Mark Franchetti, "The Last Days of an Oligarch," *Sunday Times*, August 8, 2015, https://www.thetimes.co.uk/article/the-last-days-of-an-oligarch-p3jbqgr6crt.

22. Navama witness statement, March 28, 2013.

23. Navama witness statement, March 25, 2013.

24. Ilia Zhegulev, "Poslednee interv'iu Borisa Berezovskogo: 'Ia ne vizhu smysla zhizni,'" *Forbes*, March 23, 2013, https://www.forbes.ru/sobytiya/obshchestvo/236176-poslednee-intervyu-borisa-berezovskogo-ya-ne-vizhu-smysla-zhizni.

25. Author interview with Gleb Berezovsky.

26. Mishina, "On govoril: 'Mne ochen' plokho.'"

27. Franchetti, "Last Days of an Oligarch."

28. Brinkmann was well known in Britain. His analysis showing that Italian banker Roberto Calvi was murdered in London in 1982 had caused an initial verdict of suicide to be overturned.

29. Mariia Timokhova, "Smert' za zakrytoi dver'iu"; Alexis Flynn, "Berezovsky Death Remains Unexplained," *Wall Street Journal*, March 27, 2014, https://www.wsj.com/articles/expert-says-berezovsky-likely-strangled-1395939091; recording of Berezovsky inquest, Brinkman testimony.

30. Timokhova, "Smert' za zakrytoi dver'iu"; Alex Spence, "'Broken' Boris Berezovsky Talked of Killing Himself after Losing Abramovich Lawsuit," *Times*, March 26, 2014, https://www.thetimes.co.uk/article/broken-boris-berezovsky-talked-of-killing-himself-after-losing-abramovich-lawsuit-hgzvvd58gc7.

31. Navama, witness statement, March 25, 2013.

32. Claire Duffin, "Oligarch Boris Berezovsky's Death: The Unanswered Questions," *Sydney Morning Herald*, March 27, 2014, https://www.smh.com.au/world/oligarch-boris-berezovskys-death-the-unanswered-questions-20140327-zqng2.html.

33. Berezovskaya interview with Dmitrii Gordon.

34. Author interview with Elizaveta Berezovskaya, London, October 7, 2022.

35. Author interview with Gleb Berezovsky.

36. Author interview with Akhmed Zakaev, London, October 8, 2022.

37. Author interview with Iulii Dubov; author's FaceTime interview with Michael Cotlick, November 22, 2022.

38. Mishina, "On govoril: 'Mne ochen' plokho.'"

39. "Oligarch Berezovsky 'a Broken Man,'" *Belfast Telegraph*, March 26, 2014, https://www.belfasttelegraph.co.uk/news/uk/oligarch-berezovsky-a-broken-man-30125952.html. Cotlick confirmed his conviction that Berezovsky's death was a suicide in his interview with this author. Cotlick claimed that the members of the Berezovsky family refused to accept that Berezovsky died from suicide because they felt guilt that they did not take care of him when he was depressed. Cotlick cut off all ties with the family after Berezovsky died.

40. Timokhova, "Smert' za zakrytoi dver'iu"; recording of Berezovsky inquest, testimony of Saeed Islam.

41. Ian Cobain, "Boris Berezovsky Inquest Returns Open Verdict on Death," *Guardian*, March 27, 2014, https://www.theguardian.com/world/2014/mar/27/boris-berezovsky-inquest-open-verdict-death.

42. Flynn, "Berezovsky Death Remains Unexplained."

43. Ian Cobain et al., "Berezovsky Found Dead at His Berkshire Home," *Guardian*, March 23, 2013, https://www.theguardian.com/world/2013/mar/23/boris-berezovsky-found-dead-berkshire-home.

44. Viktor Telegin, LiveJournal, March 24, 2013, https://dr-ionych.livejournal.com/23130.html.

45. Wikinews, https://ru.wikinews.org/wiki/Виктор_Телегин_(dr-ionych):_Письмо_Бориса_Березовского_к_Владимиру_Путину.

46. *Bezformata*, St. Petersburg, April 3, 2013, https://sanktpeterburg.bezformata.com/listnews/pismo-berezovskogo-putinu-opublikovannoe/10638681/.

47. Irina Reznik and Timofei Dziadko, "Pis'mo Berezovskogo Putinu peredal Abramovich," *Vedomosti*, April 3, 2013, https://www.vedomosti.ru/politics/articles/2013/04/03/pismo_berezovskogo_putinu_peredal_abramovich.

48. Harding, "Berezovsky and the Dangers of Being a Russian Exile."

49. Pomerantsev, "Berezovsky's Last Days."

50. *Direct Line* with Vladimir Putin, April 25, 2013, http://en.kremlin.ru/events/president/news/17976.

51. Vladimir Pastukhov, "Pis'mo nedrugu," *Polit.ru*, March 25, 2013, https://polit.ru/articles/strana/pismo-nedrugu-2013-03-25/.

52. Knight, *Orders to Kill*, 213.

53. Jane Croft, "Open Verdict Fails to Dispel Mystery over Death of Berezovsky," *Financial Times*, March 27, 2014, https://www.ft.com/content/061639fe-b5de-11e3-b40e-00144feabdc0.

54. Bykov, "Iulii Dubov: Borisa Berezovskogo ubivali trinadtsat' let."

55. Knight, *Orders to Kill*, 245.

56. *Direct Line* with Vladimir Putin, April 25, 2013.

57. Alexandra Ma, "'Traitors Will Kick the Bucket'—Watch Vladimir Putin's Chilling Warning to Spies Who Betray Russia," *Business Insider*,

March 7, 2018, https://www.businessinsider.com/putin-threatened-russian-traitors-the-year-sergei-skripal-went-to-uk-2018-3.

58. Amy Knight, *Putin's Killers: The Kremlin and the Art of Political Assassination* (London: Biteback Publishing, 2019), 320. This book, published in the UK, is an updated paperback edition of *Orders to Kill.*

59. Luke Harding, "Murder of Kremlin Critic in London 'Was Made to Look Like Suicide,'" *Guardian*, April 9, 2021, https://www.theguardian.com/uk-news/2021/apr/09/murder-kremlin-critic-london-made-look-like-suicide-nikolai-glushkov.

60. Harding, "Boris Berezovsky and the Dangers of Being a Russian Exile."

61. Luke Harding, "Murdered Russian Exile Survived Earlier Poison Attempt, Police Believe," *Guardian*, September 7, 2018, https://www.theguardian.com/uk-news/2018/sep/07/murdered-russian-exile-nikolai-glushkov-poisoning-attempt-bristol.

62. Rose, "Approved Judgment, Aeroflot v. Leeds & Anor & Ors."

63. *Life and Death of Once Most Powerful Russian Boris Berezovsky*, https://documentary.net/video/life-death-of-once-most-powerful-russian-boris-berezovsky/.

64. According to Iulii Dubov, Aven had a personal reason for writing the book: "He was jealous of Boris, because Boris had always been in the limelight, overshadowing Aven with his outsized presence, huge energy, and magnetic personality. This was an opportunity for Aven to get back at him" (author interview with Dubov).

65. See my review of the book: "Friends and Enemies," *Times Literary Supplement*, March 23, 2018, https://www.the-tls.co.uk/articles/friends-enemies-boris-berezovsky/.

66. Aven, *Vremia Berezovskogo*, 19–23.

67. Aven, *Vremia Berezovskogo*, 57, 192.

68. Aven, *Vremia Berezovskogo*, 121.

69. Aven, *Vremia Berezovskogo*, 91.

70. Aven, *Vremia Berezovskogo*, 274.

71. Aven, *Vremia Berezovskogo*, 359, 408, 422.

72. "Iz nepravdy kazhdogo mozhno slozhil pravdivuiu kartinu," *Kommersant*, February 3, 2018, https://www.kommersant.ru/doc/3539844.

73. Lozhak's commentary and the trailer for the series, "Berezovskii—eto kto," appeared on the Russian media site *Meduza*, February 22, 2018, https://meduza.io/feature/2018/02/22/berezovskiy-eto-kto-veb-serial-andreya-loshaka.

74. Anna Politkovskaya, *Putin's Russia*, trans. Arch Tait (London: Harvill Press, 2004), 270–73.

Index

Abramovich, Roman
  Berezovsky collaboration, *56*
  Berezovsky rapprochement letters, 217
  Berezovsky's London lawsuit, 3,
    190–91, 193–96, 199–205, 207,
    209, 212
  the Family and Berezovsky, 130
  ORT sale to government, 152, 201
  photograph, 56
  Sibneft and, 57, 92, 122, 150–51,
    166, 207
  United party and, 124
  wealth and financial transactions, 191
  Yeltsin successor battle, 98
Aeroflot
  Andava and Forus, 57, 93, 106, 142,
    148, 204
  AvtoVAZ Bank and, 43, 57
  Berezovsky and, 57–58, 88–89,
    93–94, 106, 142, 148–49, 157, 204,
    220, 222
  financial problems, 57
  Glushkov and, 148, 222
  London court decision, 58, 204
  Primakov and, 79
Agence France-Presse (APF), 175
Aksenenko, Nikolai, 95, 98, 108
Albats, Yevgenia, 143, 147, 183
Albright, Madeline, 135
Alekperov, Vagit, 143
Alfa Group, 27–28
Aliev, Gaidar, 64
Alkhanov, Alu, 176
All-Russian Automobile Alliance, 35
Andrews, Suzanna, 188–89
Andropov, Iurii, 15, 20, 137
Anisimov, Vasilii, 267n65
Arendt, Hannah, 5
The Assassination of Russia (documentary),
  159–60, 174
assassination plots and murders

Berezovsky, 2, 36, 85–88, 163, 175, 178,
  180, 184–85, 210, 213–15
Chechen war and, 118
FSB and, 80–81, 161
Gaidar, Egor, 182
Glushkov, Nikolai, 3, 220–22
Golovlev, Vladimir, 161
Iushenkov, Sergei, 161
Klebnikov, Paul, 239n57
Listev, Vladislav, 39, 55, 85
Litvinenko, Alexander, 3, 85–88, 163,
  169, 175, 178, 180–85, 217–18, 220
Magnitsky, Sergei, 204
Navalny, Aleksei, 3
Nemtsov, Boris, 184
Novichok, 3
Politkovskaya, Anna, 40, 164, 180,
  183, 186
Polonium-210, 3, 85, 181
Putin in Dresden and, 19
Ryazan bomb incident, 120
Shchekochikhin, Iurii, 161
Shevardnadze, Eduard, 126
Skripal, Sergei and Iulia, 3, 10, 219–20
Sobchak, Anatoly, 136, 254n20
Starovoitova, Galina, 81–85, 87,
  234n38, 243n14, 243n19
Tatum, Paul, 125, 127
Trotsky, Leon, 2
Atlangeriev, Movladi, 185
Atoll (security company), 36, 88
Aven, Oleg, 10
Aven, Petr
  Berezovsky and Abramovich case
    interview, 207
  Berezovsky and import duties, 34
  Berezovsky and yacht cruise, 56
  Berezovsky and Yeltsin introduction, 37
  Berezovsky brags about, 55
  Berezovsky friendship, 10–*11*
  on Berezovsky's depression, 209

Avan, Petr (*continued*)
  on Berezovsky's dissertation, 223
  LogoVAZ and, 27
  Putin introduction to Berezovsky, 28
  on Putin's prime minister offer, 108
  Russia under Yeltsin, 29
  St. Petersburg raw materials scam,
    30–31
  The Time of Berezovsky (Aven), 222, 224,
    270n64
  Yeltsin economic advisor, 11
AvtoVAZ, 9–10, 21–22, 27, 34–35, 38, 58,
  142, 162, 205
AvtoVAZ Bank, 43, 57

Babitsky, Andrei, 134–35, 254n11
Barsukov, Mikhail, 38, 41, 44, 46, 48, 69,
  76, 84
Basaev, Shamil, 64, 101–3, 110, 116,
  118, 164
Bastrykin, Aleksandr, 15
Baturin, Vladimir, 105
Baturina, Elena, 105, 248n36
Bedford, Peter, 214–15
Belin, Laura, 125
Belkovsky, Stanislav, 137, 166
Bell, Timothy, 188, 190
Belovezha Accords (1991), 45
Belton, Catherine, 19, 32, 49, 243n10,
  245n54, 253n56
Berezovsky, Abraham (father), 6–7
Berezovsky, Anastasia (daughter), 10
Berezovsky, Arina (daughter), 97, 150,
  211, 213
Berezovsky, Artem (son), 10
Berezovsky, Boris Abramovich
  "godfather of the Kremlin," 1, 239n57
  health issues, 72–73, 116, 207–8
  image as corrupt oligarch, 156
  last days and death of, 210–17
  photographs, xvi, *8, 11, 37, 43, 56,
    140, 202*
  The Time of Berezovsky (Aven), 222
  See also under assassination plots and
    murders
Berezovsky, Boris Abramovich, business
    career
  Abramovich lawsuit, 190–96,
    199–201, 203
  attempted coup opportunity, 26
  Channel One and ORT, 39
  Chechen gang and, 235n58

finances of, 1, 208–9, 267n8
  Kommersant Publishing House sale,
    176–77
  privatization and vouchers, 35
  raw material exporting, 27
  See also Aeroflot; Alfa Group; LogoVAZ
    and AvtoVAS; Patarkatsishvili, Badri;
    Sibneft; Sviazinvest
Berezovsky, Boris Abramovich,
    embezzlement charges
  letter to the Russian press, 149
  Sibnet sale, 151
  See also Aeroflot
Berezovsky, Boris Abramovich in Great
    Britain
  British asylum, 2, 162, 177
  court cases in, 261n19
  criminal charges and extradition
    requests, 162, 176, 200
  Forbes libel case, 55, 261n19
  Listev's murder and, 40
  Lugovoi and, 181–82
  Metalloinvest claim, 267n65
  Platon Elenin alias, 163
  sixtieth birthday at Blenheim
    Palace, 175
Berezovsky, Boris Abramovich, personal
    life
  childhood and education, 7–9
  death and death threats, 3
  family of, *8–9*
  friendships, 10, 22, 27
  Israeli citizenship, 35, 235n57
  Listev's murder and, 39–40
  Russian Orthodox conversion, 36
  Russian passport nationality, 6–7
  security for, 36
  womanizer and personality, 5, 10, 132
Berezovsky, Boris Abramovich, politics
  Belarus and, 190
  Davos pact, 44, 47
  Kirienko and, 73
  Korzhakov and, 38–39
  lack of caution, 61
  political influence, 1
  Yeltsin and, 37–38, 41–43, 45–47,
    237n4
Berezovsky, Boris Abramovich, Yeltsin
    years
  Caspian pipeline, 65
  Chechen war and, 53–54, 64, 90, 103
  economic crisis and, 80

executive secretary of the CIS, 73–74, 93
Russian Security Council deputy chief
    posting, 54–55, 68
Skuratov and, 107
smear campaign against NTV, 105
Yeltsin resignation suggestion, 79
Yeltsin successor battle, 105
Berezovskaya, Ekaterina (daughter),
    8, 213
Berezovskaya, Elizaveta (daughter), 6, 8,
    214–15, 267n7
Berezovsky, Gleb (son), 97, 150, 157,
    213, 215
Beria, Lavrenty, 6, 54
Besharova, Galina (Berezovsky's wife), 10,
    150, 205, 207–8, 215
Beyrle, John, 196
Blair, Tony, 163
Blotskii, Oleg M., 50
Blowing Up Russia (Litvinenko,
    Felshtinsky), 157
Bobkov, Filipp, 233n5
Boguslavskii, Leonid, 10, 223
Bolshakov, Aleksei, 50
Bonner, Elena, 149, 159
Bordiuzha, Nikolai, 90–91, 93–94,
    245n54
Borisenko, Viktor, 13
Borodin, Pavel, 50–51, 52–53, 60, 90, 92,
    104, 112
Borovoi, Konstantin, 119
Bortnikov, Aleksandr, 16
Borzenko, Vladimir, 223
Brezhnev, Leonid, 15, 137, 197
Brinkmann, Bernd, 214, 268n28
Brokaw, Tom, 147
Bukovsky, Vladimir, 15, 28–29, 177
Bush, George W., 155, 157, 167–68, 173
Bush, Laura, 155, 173

Calvi, Roberto, 268n28
CBS News, 100
Chaika, Artem, 107
Chaika, Iurii, 91, 94, 106–7, 174, 186,
    248n41
Channel One, 39–40, 65
Chechen gang, 35–36
Chechen Press, 178
Chechnya and Chechen war
    Berezovsky and, 116–17, 137, 176,
        247n22
    Berezovsky negotiations, 1, 101–3

Beslan middle school incident, 164
Boston Marathon bombings, 218
Caspian pipeline, 64–65
Dagestan invasion, 110–11, 113–14,
    117–18, 159
Dubrovka Theater incident, 163
exchange of prisoners, 254n11
horrors of war, 134–35, 253n7
independence for, 102
Khasavyurt Accords, 53, 116, 119
kidnapping of Shpigun, 101
Putin and, 3, 117, 125, 127, *133*–35, 137
Putin and terrorists, 115–16, 163–64
Russian failure, 41–42
Skuratov retreat opposition, 90
Stepashin and, 100, 250n9
terrorism and bombings, 114–16,
    119–20, 219
Wahhabis, 101, 113, 117
Yeltsin clan and, 119
Yeltsin presidency and, 44, 53
Chekulin, Nikita, 174–75
Chemezov, Sergei, 53
Cherkesov, Viktor, 15, 40, 77, 83, 185–86
Chernenko, Konstantin, 20
Chernomyrdin, Viktor, 39, 42, 46, 49, 54,
    56, 65, 69, 73, 78
Cherny, Mikhail, 212
Chubais, Anatoly Borisovich
    appointed first deputy premier, 60
    auction rules and, 66–67, *68*
    "bandit capitalism," 122
    Berezovsky and, 47, 55, 69, 72, 93–94,
        223–24
    Berezovsky murder implication,
        182–83
    book revenue scandal, 69
    corruption of, 61
    Gazprom and, 65
    Lebed and, 54
    market capitalism and, 35, 42
    Presidential Administration head,
        46, 50
    prime minister offer to Putin, 108
    Putin and, 72, 111, 135, 139
    Sobchak and, 25, 70–71
    Stepashin and, 98–99, 106, 109
    Yeltsin presidency and, 44–47
CIS (Commonwealth of Independent
    States), 73–74, 79, 93, 242n55
Clinton, Bill, 115
Colton, Timothy, 42, 52, 59, 99

Communist Party of the Russian Federation (CPRF), 42, 45, 83, 105, 127–28
Communist Party of the Soviet Union (CPSU), 7, 14, 20, 25, 29, 129
Corriere della Sera, 112
Cotlick, Michael, 208, 210, 212, 214–15, 218, 269n39

The Daily Telegraph, 167–68
Dawisha, Karen, 27, 234n34
del Ponte, Carla, 90–92
Deripaska, Oleg, 150, 191, 195–96
D'iachenko, Leonid, 54, 92, 122
D'iachenko, Tatiana (Yeltsin's daughter)
  Atoll secret recordings, 88
  Berezovsky and, 59–60, 89, 96, 123
  help for Yeltsin, 59
  Mabetex investigation, 92, 104
  Nemtsov and, 67
  Ogonek and, 37
  political role, 45–47, 49
  Putin and, 80
  Sibneft and, 56
Doctors' Plot, 6
Domnin, Aleksei, 81, 243n13
Dorenko, Sergei, 67, 88, 105, 123, 125–26, 127, 137, 139
Dubov, Iulii, 5, 162, 205, 208–11, 215, 218, 223, 270n64
Dunlop, John, 113–14, 119, 162, 247n22, 251n14

The Economist, 137
Ekho Moskvy, 47, 67, 69, 74, 79, 110, 175, 200, 210, 220, 224

the Family
  Berezovsky and, 79, 89, 95, 130, 137
  Chaika and, 107
  definition of, 46
  embezzlement documentary proof, 130
  Korzhakov fired, 76
  Mabetex investigation, 91–92, 104
  media and, 125
  Putin and, 51
  Ryazan bomb incident, 121
  Stepashin and, 109
  Yeltsin's inner circle, 4
  Yeltsin successor, 98, 123
Fatherland-All Russia Alliance, 111, 123–24, 127
Federal Guard Service (FSO), 38, 153

Felshtinsky, Yuri, 13, 152, 157, 159, 162, 172
The Financial Times, 55, 183
First Person (Putin), 15, 17, 30, 72, 75, 80, 129, 132, 137
Fonda, Jane, 33
Forbes, 55, 165, 200, 211, 233n69, 235n58, 239n57, 261n19
Forbes Billionaires List, 63–64, 80
Fradkov, Mikhail, 174
Fridman, Mikhail, 7, 28, 55, 67, 189, 261n19
FSB (Federal Security Service)
  Alpha antiterrorist unit, 167
  antiterrorism and extremism laws, 177
  Baturina investigation, 105
  Berezovsky and, 36
  Blowing Up Russia (Litvinenko, Felshtinsky), 157
  Cherkesov and, 15, 40
  Putin and, 4, 16, 75
  Ryazan bomb incident, 120–21, 138, 158–60, 162, 251n14
  URPO (Organized Crime Directorate), 85–88
  Yeltsin and, 76
  See also assassination plots and murders

Gaidar, Egor, 11, 30, 135, 179, 182–84
Galeotti, Mark, 19
The Gang from Lubianka (Litvinenko), 178
Gazprom, 65–66, 108, 139, 152, 166, 191
Gelman, Anna (Berezovsky's mother), 6–8
Gessen, Masha, 5, 19, 25, 28, 95, 129, 135, 201, 242n69, 254n11
Gevorkyan, Nataliya, 14, 121, 135, 194
GKU (Main Control Directorate), 50, 60–61, 75, 250n72
Gloster, Elizabeth, 191, 194–96, 200–201, 203, 209
Glushkov, Natalia, 221
Glushkov, Nikolai
  Aeroflot and, 57–58, 79, 93, 148, 204
  arrested and imprisoned, 151
  AvtoVAZ and, 22
  Berezovsky and, 105, 192, 209
  libelous theft claim, 55
  Lugovoi and, 180
  strangled, 3
  See also assassination plots and murders

Gochiiaev, Achemez, 120, 162
Godfather of the Kremlin (Klebnikov), 39–40, 55
Goldfarb, Alex
  Berezovsky and, 4, 37, 117, 123, 149, 156, 170
  Berezovsky and Putin, 95
  Berezovsky assassination plot, 163
  Berezovsky's last days and death, 223
  on Chechen war, 102
  Chubais and, 68
  Gazprom and, 65
  Litvinenko and, 152, 181, 183
  Lugovoi and, 180
  photograph, *202*
  Putin and, 76, 79, 108, 131, 141, 144, 148, 157, 160
Golovlev, Vladimir, 157, 161
Gongadze, Georgiy, 172
Gorbachev, Mikhail, 20–21, 23, 29, 41, 156
Gorbunova, Elena (Berezovsky's wife)
  about, 10
  Abramovich, Irina and, 56
  Abramovich lawsuit and, 201–2
  Berezovsky's last days, 209, 211, 213
  on Berezovsky's violent attack, 38
  common law wife, 97
  death and death threats, 36
  the Family and Berezovsky, 130
  in Israel, 235n57
  move to mansion in Mayfair district, 157
  separation and, 150, 205
  travel with, 26
Gordievsky, Oleg, 177
Grachev, Pavel, 61
Grigor'ev, Aleksandr, 71
Grinda, Jose, 33
Gruzd, Boris, 84
The Guardian, 138, 184, 202, 221
Gudavadze, Inna, 188, 190
Gurevich, Vera, 12–13
Gusak, Aleksandr, 85
Gusinsky, Vladimir
  Berezovsky and, *43*, 117, 141, 147
  Berezovsky's last days, 211
  Chubais and, 69
  Gazprom and NTV, 152–53
  in Israel, 139
  Luzhkov and, 104–5
  ORT buyout, 146, 195
  Putin and arrest, 138–39, 141, 143–44

  Sviazinvest and, 66–68
  Yeltsin presidency and, 43–44, 46
  Yeltsin's reelection and, 55
Gustafson, Thane, 154

Hale, Henry, 116, 124–26
Harding, Luke, 201–2
Hefner, Robert, 28
History of the CPSU, 123
Hoffman, David, 9, 22, 34–35, 66, 72, 89, 130, 139, 255n40
Hutchins, Chris, 26

Iakovlev, Vladimir, 48–50, 81, 235n39, 238n39
Iakovleva, Irina, 235n39
Iliukhin, Viktor, 110
Iliushin, Viktor, 44
Illarionov, Andrei, 93, 183
The Insider, 30, 62
Institute of Control Sciences, 9–10
International Civil Liberties Foundation, 156, 159, 162, 170
Islam, Saeed, 215
Iumashev, Valentin
  appointed chief of staff, 60
  Berezovsky and, 37–38, 73, 89, 108, 224
  D'iachenko, Tatiana and, 46–47, 59–60, 123
  the Family and, 130
  Nemtsov and, 67
  Presidential Administration head, 90
  Putin and, 71–72, 76, 80, 111
  Ryazan bomb incident, 138
  sex video, 245n54
  Skuratov scandal, 91
  Sobchak and, 70–71
  Stepashin and, 98–99
  Sviazinvest and, 66
  Voloshin and, 94
  Yeltsin advisor, 59
  Yeltsin election, 46–47
  Yeltsin ghostwriter, 37
Iumasheva, Tatiana. *See* D'iachenko, Tatiana
Iuridicheskii Peterburg segodnia (Legal St. Petersburg today), 81
Iushenkov, Sergei, 157, 160–61
Ivanov, Igor, 135
Ivanov, Sergei, 77, 154, 216
Ivanov, Viktor, 77
Izvestiia, 144, 176

Jewish people and antisemitism, 5–7, 9, 28, 74, 79–80, 93, 95–96, 216, 243n14
journalism and journalists
    Committee to Protect Journalists, 164
    freedom of the press, 147–48
    ORT sale to government, 147
    Putin's control, 152–53, 164–65
    Radio Liberty and, 135

Kabaeva, Alina, 206
Kadannikov, Vladimir, 21, 35, 38
Kadyrov, Akhmad, 53, 238n50
Kadyrov, Ramzan, 264n64
Kalugin, Oleg, 16, 23–24
Kasparov, Garry, 184
Kasyanov, Mikhail, 139, 167, 174
Kay, Joseph, 190
KGB (Komitet Gosudarstvenoi Bezopasnosti), 14–16, 18–20, 231n44, 232n55
al-Khattab, Ibn, 103, 110, 113, 116, 118, 160
Khinshtein, Aleksandr, 35, 86–88, 95, 98, 105–6, 116, 142, 174–75
Khodorkovsky, Mikhail
    arrest of, 168–69, 174
    Berezovsky and, 189, 207
    Berezovsky and Sibneft, 202
    oligarch meeting, 44, 55
    Putin and, 166, 184, 259n58
    reformist, 165
    safe from arrest (not), 167
Khokholkov, Evgenii, 86
Khrushchev, Nikita, 5–6
King, Larry, 147
Kirienko, Sergei, 65, 73, 75, 78, 241n53
Kirill (Russian Orthodox patriarch), 199
Kiselev, Evgenii, 104–5, 125, 165
Klebnikov, Paul, 1, 21–23, 27, 38–39, 55, 233n69, 239n57
Kodanev, Mikhail, 161
Kokh, Alfred, 66–67
Kolesnikov, Sergei, 169
Kommersant
    The Assassination of Russia (documentary) review, 160
    Berezovsky acquisition, 28
    Berezovsky letters, 86, 141, 146–47
    Berezovsky on Aeroflot, 57
    Cherkesov letter, 186
    Kredit Bank and, 243n13
    Putin and, 87, 140, 145

Putin autobiography, 137
    Starovoitova murder and, 83
    Vasiliev comment on Berezovsky, 22
    Yeltsin support, 95
Kommersant Publishing House, 105, 176–77
Komsomol (Communist Youth League), 7–8, 13
Komsomol'skaia pravda, 76, 87
Kondaurov, Aleksei, 166, 259n58
Koppel, Ted, 132
Korotkova, Nina, 8
Korzhakov, Aleksandr, 37–46, 48, 54–56, 58, 76, 85, 89, 92, 236n68, 237n23
Kovalev, Andrei, 164
Kovalev, Nikolai, 76–77, 85–86, 115, 117, 158, 164, 217
Kovalev, Sergei, 121, 158, 162
Kovalev Commission, 161–62
Kovtun, Dmitrii, 180–82
Kozyrev, Andrei, 42
Kravchenko, Iurii, 172
Kredit Bank, 243n13
Kuchma, Leonid, 74, 170, 172
Kudriavtsev, Demian, 223
Kudrin, Aleksei, 25, 49–51, 60, 69–70, 198
Kulikov, Anatolii, 45, 53–54, 69–70, 117
Kumarin (Barsukov), Vladimir, 31–32, 84, 234n38, 235n39
Kvashnin, Anatolii, 110

La Repubblica, 122
Latynina, Iulia, 110, 121
Lebed, Aleksandr, 45–46, 53–54, 119, 160, 251n13
Lebedev, Platon, 167
Le Figaro, 119, 148
Le Monde, 168
Lenin, Vladimir, 173
Lenta.ru, 120
Lesin, Mikhail, 139, 146
Levin-Utkin, Anatolii, 81
Levkin, Sergei, 34
Liberal Russia (political party), 157, 160–61, 218
Linkov, Ruslan, 81, 84
Lisovskii, Sergei, 39, 69
Listev, Vladislav, 39–40, 55, 85, 261n19
Litvinenko, Alexander
    asylum in Great Britain, 152, 162
    Berezovsky and, 152, 157, 181
    Blowing Up Russia (Litvinenko, Felshtinsky), 159

Lugovoi and, 178–79
photograph of, *158*
Putin and, 151–52
Ukraine and, 172
See also assassination plots and
  murders
Litvinenko, Anatoly, 152, *158*, 182
Litvinenko, Marina, 3, 152, 263n48
Litvinenko, Olga, 62
Litvinenko, Sonia, *158*
Litvinenko, Vladimir, 62–64
LogoVAZ and AvtoVAS, 21–22, 27–28,
  34–36, 39, 57, 97
LogoVAZ club, 37, 46–47, 65, 79,
  85, 143
Lugovoi, Andrei, 178–*79*, 180–82, 218,
  220
Lukashenko, Alexander, 190
Lukoil, 143
Lur'e, Oleg, 31, 94, 129–30
Luzhkov, Iurii, 43, 103–5, 109, 111–*12*,
  117, 122, 125, 127, 131, 142, 251n14
Lyra, Markus, 246n80

Mabetex investigation, 52–53, 90–93,
  104, 106, 112, 122, 129, 153
Mafia and mob organizations, 31–33,
  35–36, 50, 75, 136, 153, 178, 180,
  239n57
Magnitsky, Sergei, 204
Magnitsky Act, 204
Makhashev, Kazbek, 116–17
Malashenko, Igor, 46, 138
Mangold, Klaus, 209
Martynyuk, Leonid, 204
Maskhadov, Aslan, 53, 64–65, 101–*2*,
  116, 118, 120, 137
Matveev, Lazar, 23
MBX media, 64
McCain, John, 150, 168, 198, 256n55
Media-Most company, 104–5, 138–39
Medvedev, Dmitry, 25, 166, 174, 186,
  196–98, 203
Medvedev, Roy, 136
Medvedev, Sergei, 59
Meier, Andrew, 84
Melnychenko, Mykola, 172
Menatep Group, 44, 167
Metalloinvest, 267n65
Midnight Diaries (Yeltsin), 45, 70, 79, 82
Mlechin, Leonid, 20
Moscow News, 165
The Moscow Times, 109, 135, 147

Moskovskii komsomolets, 92, 119, 122–23,
  126, 141, 143, 160, 176
Murov, Evgenii, 153
MVD (Ministry of Internal Affairs)
  Atoll report, 36
  Chechen kidnapping, 61, 64, 101
  Chechnya and Chechen war, 53
  Nurgaliev, Rashid, 174
  Rushailo and, 114
  Skuratov videotape, 92
  Sobchak investigation, 69, 81
  Starovoitova murder, 82
  Stepashin and, 98
  terrorist bombing, 119
Myers, Steven Lee, 12–13, 15, 29, 61, 111,
  124, 186

Narusova, Liudmila (Sobchak's wife), 32,
  47–49, 70, 136
NATO (North Atlantic Treaty
  Organization), 100, 156, 170, 173,
  185, 203, 219
Navalny, Aleksei, 3, 19, 32, 198–99, 219
Navama, Avi, 210–15
Nemtsov, Boris
  auction rules and, 66
  Berezovsky and, 60, 69, 139–40
  Chubais and, 65, *68*
  Gazprom and, 65
  Kirienko and, 73
  murder of, 184
  Putin and, 61, 80
  Putin critic, 184, 197
  Sobchak and, 70–71
  Sochi Olympics and, 204
  SPS and, 135
  Stepashin and, 106
  Sviazinvest and, 67
  Yeltsin successor battle, 110
New York Times, 112, 122, 130, 156–57,
  159, 177, 192
Nezavisimaia gazeta, 65, 67, 95, 118
Noril'sk Nikel' mining company, 143
Notes of a President (Iumashev
  ghostwriter), 37–38
Novaia gazeta, 31, 53, 70, 119, 121–22,
  127, 129, 134, 158, 164
NTV (Russian Nationwide Television
  Channel)
  Berezovsky on the CIS, 74
  Chechen kidnapping, 64
  Chechen war and, 44, 54
  Dagestan invasion, 117–18

NTV (*continued*)
    Gasprom management, 152
    Gusinsky and, 138
    Itogi, 104–5, 125–26, 139
    nuclear submarine *Kursk*, 144
    ORT competitor, 43
    Putin and, 139
    Ryazan bomb incident program, 139
    See Big Ben and Die, 217
    Skuratov and Mabetex, 92
    Ustinov and, 153
    Yeltsin election support, 46–47
nuclear submarine *Kursk*, 144–46, 149,
    152–53
Nurgaliev, Rashid, 174

Obama, Barack, 196, 203–4, 219
Obshschaia gazeta, 119
Ogonek, 37
Open Russia Foundation, 165
Orban, Viktor, 5
Orders to Kill (Knight), 3
ORT (Public Russian Television)
    Abramovich and Sibneft case, 193
    Abromovich cedes to government,
        152, 201
    Atoll secret recordings, 88
    Berezovsky and, 39, 127, 130, 137
    Chechen war and, 54
    Dorenko, anchor, 67
    Media-Most and, 105
    NTV competitor, 43
    nuclear submarine *Kursk*, 144
    Patarkatsishvili and, 179
    sale of shares, 145–49, 151, 195
    The Sergei Dorenko Show, 125
    Sibneft funding, 56
    Yeltsin support, 46–47, 95
Our Home Is Russia (political party),
    42, 49
Owen, Robert, 178

Pastukhov, Vladimir, 218
Patarkatsishvili, Badri
    AvtoVAZ and, 21
    Berezovsky and, 36, 150, 188–89, 205, 209
    death of, 188
    fraud charges, 162
    Kommersant Publishing House
        sale, 177
    Lugovoi and, 179
    Metalloinvest claim, 267n65
    ORT and, 179

photograph, *189*
Putin threats, 146
Sibneft London trial, 57, 190–96, 200
Sibneft sale, 151
Yeltsin successor battle, 105
Patriots (P. Morgan play), 4
Patrushev, Nikolai
    Berezovsky and, 159
    deputy FSB chief, 77
    FSB under Putin, 153, 174
    Mabetex investigation, 113
    Obama terrorism meeting, 219
    Putin and, 114, 133, 248n36, 250n72
    Putin friendship, 16
    siloviki dispute, 185
    terrorism and bombings, 114, 120
Pavlovsky, Gleb, 72
People's Freedom Party, 197
Peskov, Dmitry, 216
Pichugin, Aleksei, 166
Pietsch, Irene, 95, 97
Piontkovsky, Andrei, 2, 55, 120, 147, 169
Politkovskaya, Anna, 1, 134, 178, 182,
    187, 224, 264n64
    See also assassination plots and
        murders
Politkovskaya, Vera, 187
Politkovskii, Aleksandr, 40
Politkovskii, Ilya, 187
Pomerantsev, Peter, 8, 192
Poole, Simon, 214
Potanin, Vladimir, 44, 55, 66–68, 143
President's Club, 38
Primakov, Evgeny Maksimovich
    Aeroflot investigation, 58, 148
    Berezovsky and, 79
    Berezovsky embezzlement
        investigation, 89, 93, 95
    compromise candidate, 79
    Foreign Intelligence Service head, 117
    Mabetex, 90, 92
    media and, 125
    photograph of, *112*
    Putin and, 80
    resignation of, 99, 101
    Shevardnadze assassination attempt
        and, 126
    Skuratov scandal, 91
    Voloshin and, 94
    Yeltsin and, 42, 98
    Yeltsin successor battle, 103–5, 109,
        111, 122–23, 127, 131
Prokhorenko, Aleksandr, 48

Pugachev, Sergei, 173, 245n54
Putin, Spiridon Ivanovich
    (grandfather), 11
Putin, Vladimir Spiridonovich (father),
    11–12, 98
Putin, Vladimir Vladimirovich
    legacy of, 224
    "man without a face," 5
    photographs, *xvi*, *155*, *217*
    revenge motive, 2
    shoe lifts, 232n56
    See also FIrst Person
Putin, Vladimir Vladimirovich, after KGB
    export contracts, 30–32
    FSB connections, 40
    leaving St. Petersburg, 238n39
    security and law enforcement
        power, 58
    Sobchak and, 26–27, 233n7, 237n21
    Sobchak and scandals, 29–31, 234n34
    St. Petersburg management, 40
Putin, Vladimir Vladimirovich, KGB and
    admission and training, 15
    Andropov Red Banner KGB Institute,
        18, 232n54
    becoming a spy, 13–14
    and City Committee for Foreign
        Economic Relations, 25
    in Dresden, East Germany, 18–21,
        233n5
    at Felix Dzerzhinsky Higher School, 17
    at the First Department (foreign
        intelligence), 17
    focus on enemies within, 15
    Iakovlev and, 49–50
    Leningrad post and foreign students, 23
    resignation after coup attempt, 25
    and Sobchak, 24–25
    tenure in counterintelligence, 17
Putin, Vladimir Vladimirovich, personal
    life
    dacha burned, 51
    dissertation on mining, 61–63
    education and early life, 13
    family of, 11–12, 16–*17*
    friendships, 14–16, 153
    Kudrin and, 51
    law faculty, Leningrad State University
        (LSU), 14–15
    in Leningrad with parents, 24
    Liudmila's car accident, 33
    pedophile claim, 178
    Traber, Ilya and, 32

Putin, Vladimir Vladimirovich,
    presidency of
    Abramovich and, 3
    Berezovsky and, 1
    Berezovsky resigns from Duma, 142
    Bush, George W. and, 155
    Crimean annexation, 219
    feudalism comparison, 169
    FSB and oligarchs, 4
    Great Britain and the West, 185
    leadership cult, 4
    Medvedev and, 196–98
    Munich Security Conference speech, 185
    nuclear submarine *Kursk*, 144–46, 152
    oligarchs threatened, 143–44, 146
    personal wealth of, 170
    public anger at Putin-Medvedev swap,
        197–99
    rapprochement with the West, 156
    reorganization and power, 140–42
    "Reset" with the West, 203–4
    siloviki, 153–54, 165–66, 185–86, 199
    Sochi Olympics and, 204, 219
Putin, Vladimir Vladimirovich, Yeltsin
    transition
    Chechen war and, 102–3
    prime minister offer, 107
    Yeltsin successor battle, 108–10
Putin, Vladimir Vladimirovich, Yeltsin
    years
    Borodin and, 51
    D'iachenko, Tatiana and, 60
    first deputy director of Presidential
        Administration, 74–75
    foreign property oversight position,
        50–51, 53
    FSB director, 75–78, 81
    GKU head, 60–61
    Luzhkov and, 105
    Mabetex, 92
    military force considered, 79
    Nemtsov and, 61
    Skuratov and, 91, 94
    Sobchak and, 70–72, 81
    Starovoitova murder and
        Communists, 82
    Yeltsin and, 88
Putina, Liudmila (ex-wife)
    automobile accident, 33–34
    Berezovsky and, 95–96
    divorce, 206
    in Dresden, East Germany, 18
    in Leningrad, 23–24

Putina, Liudmila (ex-wife) (*continued*)
  Liudmila's reaction to presidency, 133
  marriage of, 16–17
  Putin and, 97
  Putin's FSB job, 75
  Putin's parents, 12
  travel with Putin, 154–55, 173
  vacationing, 108
  Yeltsin's resignation, 132
Putin and Berezovsky
  Aven introduction, 28
  Berezovsky a criminal, 246n80
  Berezovsky and Putin's downfall, 156,
    159, 168, 175
  Berezovsky assassination plot, 86–88
  Berezovsky criminal prosecutions, 2–3
  Berezovsky letter on violent overthrow
    of Putin, 176
  Berezovsky rapprochement letters,
    209–11, 216–18
  on Berezovsky's death, 215
  Berezovsky's downfall attempts, 3–4,
    175–76, 184, 199
  Berezovsky's opinion of Putin, 76
  birthday party appearance, 94–95
  nuclear submarine *Kursk*, 144–45, 256n55
  Putin and FSB, 242n69
  Putin autocracy charge, 145
  Putin on Berezovsky suicide, 222
  Putin revenge, 141, 143, 147–48
  relationship questioned, 137
  Ryazan bomb incident, 121–22
  traitor or indebtedness, 2
  Yeltsin's prime minister offer, 108
  Yeltsin successor battle, 130–31
Putinburg (Zapol'skii), 24, 33
Putin's Kleptocracy (Dawisha), 27
Putin's Palace (Navalny), 19
Putin's People (Belton), 32

Radio Liberty, 134–35
Raduev, Salman, 64
Rahr, Alexander, 24, 232n55
Red Army Faction (RAF), 19
Red Lenin (Wharhol), 206
Rice, Condoleezza, 173
Right Cause (Pravoe delo) bloc, 136
Rosinvest, 170
Rosneft, 34, 154, 166–67
Rotenberg, Boris and Arkady, 204
RTR (Russia-1 tv), 91, 125, 175
Rusal, aluminum company, 34, 150,
    191–92, 195–96, 200

Rushailo, Vladimir, "Berezovsky's
    falcon," 114
Russian Investigative Committee, 15
Rybakov, Iulii, 160
Rybkin, Ivan, 54, 73

Saakashvili, Mikheil, 188–89
Sabirova, Katerina, 205, 208–10,
    212–13, 215
Sakharov, Andrei, 231n44
Sakwa, Richard, 154, 156, 165, 199
Sal'e, Marina, 30–31
Savost'ianov, Evgenii, 86
Scaramella, Mario, 180
Sechin, Igor, 25, 33, 40, 49, 51, 154,
    166–67, 185–86
Segodnia, 67, 104, 139
Seleznev, Gennadii, 83, 116
Severnaia Neft oil company, 166
Shamalov, Nikolai, 32, 51
Shaposhnikov, Evgenii, 57
Shchekochikhin, Iurii, 122, 161
Sheitelman, Mikhail, 211
Shelomova, Maria Ivanovna (Putin's
    mother), 11–12
Shevardnadze, Eduard, 126
Shevchenko, Iurii, 34, 71, 84, 136
Shevtsova, Lilia, 58–59, 79, 98, 148,
    153, 197
Shoigu, Sergei, 123, 127, 230n24,
    252n36
Short, Philip, 231n44, 233n5, 233n7,
    234n34, 241n47, 243n14, 246n80,
    254n20, 264n64
Shpigun, Gennadii, 101
Shuppe, Egor (Berezovsky son-in-law),
    179, 181, 211, 213
Shvets, Yuri, 154, 180
Sibneft
  Berezovsky and, 80
  Berezovsky and Abramovich, 55–56,
    92, 199
  Berezovsky and partners, 150
  Berezovsky criminal prosecutions,
    57–58
  Berezovsky embezzlement
    investigation, 88
  Berezovsky lawsuit, 192–95, 200, 202
  loans-for-shares auction, 56
  Patarkatsishvili and, 56
  proposed merger with Yukos, 166
  sale of, 151, 191
Skripal, Sergei and Iulia, 3, 219–20

Skuratov, Iurii, 48–49, 69–71, 81, 84, 88–94, 98, 106–7, 122, 153, 237n23
Smirnov, Vladimir, 31
Smolensky, Aleksandr, 44, 55, 189
Sobchak, Anatoly Aleksandrovich
  corruption investigation, 69–71, 90, 241n47
  death and murder theory, 136
  election loss, 40, 47–50, 81
  gambling scandal and, 30
  hospital treatment, 84
  Kumarin and, 32
  photograph of, 26
  Putin and, 24–25, 29, 31, 33, 48–50, 62, 72, 77, 93, 136
  Sechin and, 154
  St. Petersburg financial capital goal, 26–28
  Western leaders and, 237n21
  Yeltsin and, 47–48, 237n23
  Zolotov and, 153
Sobchak, Ksenia Anatolyevna (daughter), 32, 48, 136
Sokolov, Sergei, 36
Soldatov, Andrei, 18
Solidarity, 184
Solntsevo gang, 35
Solzhenitsyn, Alexander, 15
Soros, George, 42–43, 65–66, 156, 182–83, 237n4
Soskovets, Oleg, 44–46, 48, 112
Stalin, Joseph, 2–3, 6, 16, 168, 224
Stanovaya, Tatiana, 16
Starovoitova, Olga, 83–84
Steele, Jonathan, 138
Stepashin, Sergei
  Berezovsky and, 93, 109, 114
  Chechen war and, 101–2, 250n9
  Dagestan invasion, 110, 117–18
  favored for Yeltsin successor, 95, 98–99, 104
  mudslinging against opponents, 106
  prime minister, 100
  prime minister offer to Putin, 108–9
  Skuratov sex videotape statement, 92
  Starovoitova murder, 82
St. Petersburg Fuel Company, 31
St. Petersburg Real Estate Holding Co. (SPAG), 31
St. Petersburg Times, 55
Strategic Planning and Policy, 63
Straw, Jack, 176
Stroev, Egor, 73

Sumption, Jonathan, 193–94
Surkov, Vladislav, 198
Svanidze, Nikolai, 183
Sviazinvest, 66
SVR (Foreign Intelligence Service), 79
Sword and Shield (tv series), 14
Systems Research Institute, 11

Tambov crime group, 31, 33, 82, 84
Tatum, Paul, 125, 127
Telegin, Viktor, 216
Terluk, Vladimir, 163, 175
Tikhonova, Katerina Vladimirovna (Putin's daughter), 16, 33, 51
Timchenko, Gennadii, 32
Time Magazine, 142, 155
The Time of Berezovsky (Aven), 222–24
The Times, 177
Traber, Ilya "the Antiquarian," 32–33
Tregubova, Elena, 61, 76–77, 88, 113
Trepashkin, Mikhail, 162
Tretiakov, Vitalii, 118–19
Trotsky, Leon, 2–3, 149
Trump, Donald, 10, 219
Tsar Alexander II, 12
Tsarnaev, Tamerlan and Dzhokhar, 218–19
Turner, Ted, 33
Turover, Felipe, 53, 129–30, 253n56
TV6 and Berezovsky, 152–53
Tymoshenko, Yulia, 171–72

Udugov, Movladi, 64, 101–3, 116–17
Ukraine
  Berezovsky and, 170–72
  Orange Revolution, 170, 172–73
Union of Right Forces (SPS), 135, 165, 183–84
United Russia party, 123, 165, 197, 200
Unity party, 123–25, 127–28, 130–31, 149
Usmanov, Alisher, 177
Usol'tsev, Vladimir, 16, 19
Ustinov, Vladimir, 153, 166, 174

Vaksberg, Arkady, 136–37
Vasiliev, Andrei, 22, 188–89, 223
Vedomosti, 137, 184, 190, 216
Venediktov, Aleksei, 47, 74, 203, 224
Viakhirev, Rem, 65
Vil'kobrisskii, Mikhail, 48, 237n24
Vinogradov, Vladimir, 44
Vneshekonombank, 104

Voloshin, Aleksandr
    Berezovsky and, 94, 145, 167, 224
    Berezovsky lawsuit testimony, 195
    the Family and, 130
    Mabetex investigation, 113
    new political party, 123
    nuclear submarine *Kursk*, 144
    prime minister offer to Putin, 108
    Putin and, 139, 166, 174
    smear campaign against NTV, 105
Voloshin, Pavel, 121
Voronov, Vladimir, 223
Vorontsova, Maria Vladimirovna (Putin's
    daughter), 18, 51
Voshchanov, Pavel, 70

The Wall Street Journal, 159
Walters, David, 28
Warnig, Matthias, 34
Workman, Timothy, 163, 177

Yabloko political party, 138, 165, 199
Yakunin, Vladimir, 204
Yanukovich, Viktor, 170
Yavlinsky, Grigory, 45, 80, 138, 237n4
Yeltsin, Boris Nikolaevich
    anti-Communism of, 98
    Atoll spying, 36
    autumn crisis of 1998, 79
    Berezovsky and, 26–27, 37–38, 55, 68,
        148, 222, 242n55
    Berezovsky and CIS, 73–75, 93
    Berezovsky and re-election, 224
    on Berezovsky assassination plot, 87
    Berezovsky contributions, 169
    Borodin and, 52
    businessmen and, 237n12
    Chechen war and, 42, 53, 64, 118
    Chernomyrdin and, 73
    Chubais and, 25, 35, 69
    corruption cases, 90
    coup attempt, 25–26, 28, 38, 46–47, 75
    democracy under, 1–2, 41, 58, 156
    Dorenko and, 126
    early retirement, 130
    economic reform team of, 11
    FSB and Kovalev, 76
    Gaidar and, 182–83
    health issues, 41, 46, 59, 79, 82, 124
    impeachment proceedings, 78, 99
    Iumashev and, 242n55
    Kasyanov fired, 174
    Kirienko, Sergei, 78
    Korzhakov and, 38
    Kremlin corruption, 112
    Lebed and, 54
    legacy of, 224
    low popularity, 75–76
    Lugovoi and, 179
    Nemtsov and, 60, 67
    Nuremberg-style reckoning
        considered, 29
    presidency of, 40, 42–46, 88
    presidential campaign, 56
    Primakov and, 80
    prime minister offer to Putin, 109–10
    Putin and, 4, 49–50, 61, 72, 99–100,
        111, *128*, 131, 139, 144
    Putin and democracy, 170
    Putin and FSB, 77
    Putin and political enemies, 167
    resignation, 132
    Sechin and, 153–54
    Sibneft dispute, 192–94
    Skuratov scandal and resignation,
        91–92, 107, 122
    Sobchak and, 47–48, 70–72, 237n23
    Stepashin and, 100
    successor issue, 95, 103–4, 106, 108, 128
    Sviazinvest and, 66
    terrorism and bombings, 120
    Unity party, 123
    Voloshin and, 94
    See also the Family; Mabetex
        investigation; *Midnight Diaries*
Yeltsina, Naina, 42, 44, 47
Yeltsin successor battle
    Berezovsky role, 124, 126–27
    election win for Putin, 138
    Primakov and, 111, 122, 127
    Putin and, 121, 123, 125, 128–29, 132–33
Yukos oil company, 165–67, 202
Yushchenko, Viktor, 170–71, 172

Zakaev, Akhmed, 162–63, 178, 180,
    185, 215
Zapol'skii, Dmitrii, 19, 24–25, 32–33,
    49–50, 235n39
Zedelmeier, Franz, 30
Zhegulev, Ilia, 211–13
Zhilin, Aleksandr, 251n14
Zhirinovsky, Vladimir, 210, 243n19
Zolotov, Viktor, 48, 153, 185
Zubkov, Viktor, 62
Zygar, Mikhail, 103, 124, 130, 154, 163, 165
Zyuganov, Gennady, 42–43, 45–46, 127, 138